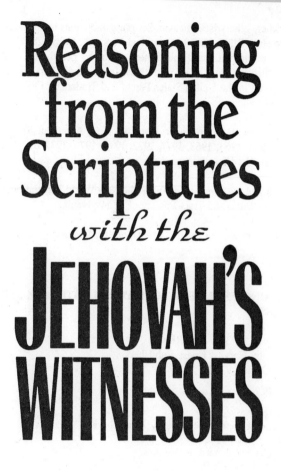

Reasoning from the Scriptures

with the

JEHOVAH'S WITNESSES

Ron Rhodes

HARVEST HOUSE PUBLISHERS
Eugene, Oregon 97402

Cover by Terry Dugan Design, Minneapolis, Minnesota

REASONING FROM THE SCRIPTURES WITH THE JEHOVAH'S WITNESSES

Copyright © 1993 by Ron Rhodes
Published by Harvest House Publishers
Eugene, Oregon 97402

Library of Congress Cataloging-in-Publication Data

Rhodes, Ron.
    Reasoning from the Scriptures with the Jehovah's Witnesses / Ron Rhodes.
        p.   cm.
    Includes bibliographical references.
    ISBN 1-56507-106-9
        1. Watch Tower Bible and Tract Society—Controversial literature.
    2. Bible—Versions, Jehovah's Witnesses.   I. Title.
    BX8526.5.R56   1993
    230'.992—dc20   93-3488
                                                                                      CIP

Printed in the United States of America.

01   02   03   /   BC   /   13   12   11   10   9   8

With much affection,
this book is dedicated to my children—
David and Kylie

Acknowledgments

Many deserve thanks for their assistance on this project. I want to first single out Marian Bodine at the Christian Research Institute (CRI) for carefully reading key portions of the manuscript prior to publication. Her suggestions were very helpful. (The manual she and her husband Jerry authored—*Witnessing to the Witnesses*—was also of great help.)

I am indebted to numerous other individuals whose books have been of great benefit in the researching and writing of the present volume. These include Robert M. Bowman, David Reed, Walter Martin, and Duane Magnani. I am very appreciative of the work these individuals have done in this field—and I highly recommend their books.

I am especially thankful to Bob Hawkins, Jr. and Eileen Mason at Harvest House Publishers for their faith in this project. A special thanks also goes to Steve Miller, my editor.

Additionally, I want to recognize Hank Hanegraaff, CRI's president, for the way he has continued Walter Martin's vision for defending the faith. God has used Hank in many ways in CRI's ministry, and I look forward to continuing serving with him in this vital ministry.

My wife, Kerri, deserves special mention—not only for her strong support and encouragement, but for reading through the manuscript for readability purposes prior to publication. Her suggestions were gladly incorporated into the book.

Finally, I want to thank my children, David and Kylie. The psalmist said, "Behold, children are a *gift* of the LORD" (Psalm 127:3a NASB). How true!

Contents

Foreword

You've probably encountered them at your door. And you may have seen their *Watchtower* and *Awake!* magazines neatly displayed upon the counters of your local laundromat. I'm speaking of the Jehovah's Witnesses—unquestionably one of the most aggressive and fastest-growing cults not just in the United States but indeed in the world.

From a personal standpoint, nothing has impacted me with regard to the Jehovah's Witnesses as much as walking the streets of São Paulo, Brazil—the world's second-largest city. There I saw firsthand virtually *hundreds* of Watchtower evangelists who were willing to do for "the skin of the truth stuffed with a lie" what Christians *should* be willing to do for the truth.

From my vantage point—as the president of the world's largest evangelical countercult ministry—I can say with great certainty that most Christians do not reach out to Jehovah's Witnesses *not* because they don't *want* to but rather because they have never been effectively trained *how* to. This is precisely why I am so excited about Ron Rhodes's new book *Reasoning from the Scriptures with the Jehovah's Witnesses.* Just as the apostle Paul effectively "reasoned... from the Scriptures" in his evangelistic encounters (Acts 17:2), so also can you learn to reason from the Scriptures with the Jehovah's Witnesses by using this book.

In this book, Ron addresses every major verse used by the Watchtower organization to lure people into their cultic web of deceit. In nontechnical and easy-to-understand language, he shows you how to be an effective witness to a mission field on your very own doorstep.

As well, Ron uncovers the deceptive tactics of Watchtower adherents in using Christian vocabulary while pouring cultic meanings into the words. With pinpoint accuracy, he teaches you how to scale this language barrier.

By the time you get to the last page of this book, you will indeed be able to communicate with Jehovah's Witnesses both *what* you believe and *why* you believe it. And remember, as you read, your labor of love may not only be used by our heavenly Father to rescue Jehovah's Witnesses *spiritually*, but you may also be used to rescue them from cultic doctrines (like their forbiddance of blood transfusions) that could lead to *physical* death as well.

You are to be commended for reading *Reasoning from the Scriptures with the Jehovah's Witnesses*. For, truly, this is a demonstration that *you* are willing to do for the truth what *they* continue to do so effectively for a lie.

—Hank Hanegraaff, President
Christian Research Institute

Introduction

Seek the truth—Listen to the truth—Teach the truth—Love the truth—Abide by the truth—And defend the truth—Unto death.

—John Huss
(A.D. 1370-1415)[1]

In 1985 the Watchtower Society published a 445-page book entitled *Reasoning from the Scriptures* (first edition: two million copies). This book, like most other Watchtower books, was designed to equip Jehovah's Witnesses to argue their peculiar doctrines from Scripture. The book set out to demonstrate how to disprove the full deity of Christ, prove that He is a created being, that the Holy Spirit is neither a person nor God but is rather God's "active force," that the doctrine of the Trinity is unbiblical and is rooted in paganism, and much more.

When one realizes that almost 4.5 million Jehovah's Witnesses are presently devoting more than one billion man-hours each year spreading these doctrines around the world,[2] it is obvious that the Christian must become equipped to answer these cultists on the doorstep. Indeed, Christians must learn to *reason from the Scriptures* with Jehovah's Witnesses.

The Jehovah's Witnesses are growing at a geometric pace in the United States. In 1940, there were 58,009 "peak" (active, baptized) Jehovah's Witnesses in the United States. This figure jumped to 108,144 by 1950; 205,900 by 1960; 416,789 by 1970; 565,309 by 1980; 850,120 by 1990; 892,551 by 1991; and is now approaching one million. The statistics for the growth of this cult around the world are even more alarming. By the end of 1992, there were almost 4.5 million active, baptized Jehovah's Witnesses in the world. (By comparison, in 1940 there were only 95,327 Jehovah's Witnesses in the world.)[3]

In keeping with these statistics, Watchtower Bible studies seem more popular than ever. The January 1, 1993, issue of *The Watchtower* magazine reports that 4,278,127 such Bible studies are presently conducted *each month*. This represents an 8.4 percent increase in Bible studies over the previous year.[4]

Distribution of the Watchtower's *New World Translation* also continues to expand on a worldwide basis. This distorted version of the Bible is already printed in whole or in part in 14 languages, and is now being translated into 16 other languages of Europe, Africa, and the Orient.[5] In view of the above facts, it is clear that the Jehovah's Witnesses are growing geometrically throughout the world.

Witnessing Encounters

Typically, in their door-to-door witnessing, the Jehovah's Witnesses point to isolated passages in the New Testament that "prove beyond any doubt" that Jesus is lesser than the Father and hence is not Almighty God. For example, they point to John 14:28, where Jesus says, "The Father is greater than I." They cite Jesus' words to Mary in John 20:17: "I am returning to my Father and your Father, to my God and your God." They quote 1 Corinthians 11:3, which says that "the head of Christ is God." They point to 1 Corinthians 15:28, where the apostle Paul says that Jesus "will be made subject to him who put everything under him, so that God may be all in all." They cite John 3:16, where Jesus is called God's "only begotten Son" (KJV). They quote Colossians 1:15, which says that Jesus is "the firstborn over all creation." They point to Revelation 3:14, which says that Jesus is the *beginning* of God's creation.

The average Christian finds great difficulty in answering Jehovah's Witnesses who cite such verses. I think Dr. Walter Martin was right when he said that the average Jehovah's

Witness can make a "doctrinal pretzel" out of the average Christian in about 30 seconds.

All this reminds me of the testimony of Don Nelson. For years Don was a committed Jehovah's Witness. But he eventually came to know the true Christ of Scripture. His story of liberation from this cult was published in the *Christian Research Newsletter*.[6]

During his early months as a Jehovah's Witness, Don recounts how the Watchtower Society trained him to defend the peculiar doctrines of the cult. "Everything the Jehovah's Witnesses told me could be 'verified' in the Word of God, they said. They spouted endless lists of 'proof texts' on every conceivable subject. Of course, when the Witnesses taught me, they were 'writing on a blank slate,' so to speak. I knew nothing of the Scriptures before I met them, and suddenly in a few short weeks, I knew everything about the Bible (so I thought)."[7]

What is of special concern is that many evangelical Christians were unable to answer the arguments Don presented on the doorstep—even though he had only been trained for a *few short weeks* by the Jehovah's Witnesses. "The first day I went witnessing door to door, I 'defeated' two Baptists, a Lutheran, and three Presbyterians in dialectic combat! I was genuinely shocked by the biblical illiteracy of most Christians."[8]

Fortunately, however, over time Don began to see the overwhelming weaknesses of the Jehovah's Witnesses' version of the Bible—the *New World Translation*. First and foremost, he discovered that none of the translators of this version knew Greek or Hebrew! "These 'scholars' of the Watchtower knew no more Greek than I did. This made me a bit uneasy."[9]

And though the *New World Translation* purported to be the finest, truest, most scholarly translation ever made, Don found that it was in reality crude, wooden, and unreadable. "The beautiful 23rd Psalm was rendered in part: 'You arrange before me a table in front of those showing hostility to me. With oil you have greased my head.' Now, while I knew nothing of the Bible before I met the Witnesses, I did know some English and I cringed at the mangling of this Hebrew poetry."[10]

Don accordingly began reading standard versions of the Bible instead of the *New World Translation* and the Lord "turned on the light" in his life. "What I found, or rather, what I was shown by the Holy Spirit, was that the New Testament is a Jesus book. I was flabbergasted. Everywhere I looked I saw Jesus."[11] Such exaltation of Jesus is nowhere to be found in the *New World Translation.*

One purpose of this book is to equip you to help the Jehovah's Witness on your doorstep see that the New Testament is indeed "a Jesus book." To do this, however, we must examine the Bible verses that make up the primary arsenal of Watchtower theology. The verses contained in this book are the ones that come up most often in witnessing encounters with Jehovah's Witnesses. By learning the contents of this book, you not only will *not* be made a "doctrinal pretzel," but instead you will also be equipped to lead a lost Jehovah's Witness to the true Christ of Scripture.

Of course, this presumes that you *want* to share the gospel with the Jehovah's Witnesses. The very fact that you are reading this book shows that you have this desire. It is truly unfortunate, however, that many Christians not only *do not* share the gospel with Jehovah's Witnesses but also show a hostile, uncaring attitude toward them.

This attitude is illustrated in the testimony of Chuck Love, who for years was a dedicated Jehovah's Witness disseminating Watchtower teachings door to door with his wife, but eventually found liberation in the true gospel of Christ. Chuck recalls what it was like during his years of witnessing activity:

> My wife and I have probably called on thousands of homes between the two of us. Not once did we encounter anyone who shared their testimony or their faith in Christ with us. Lots of people would say something like, "Oh, you're that group that doesn't believe in hell" or, "You don't believe in the

Trinity." Most people spoke to us in negative terms, telling us our beliefs were wrong but never bothering to tell us what was right. Nobody ever said anything about the love of Jesus Christ. No one ever tried to witness to us at the door.[12]

It is *imperative* that Christians not have a hostile attitude when Jehovah's Witnesses show up on the doorstep. After all, we are called to share the good news of the gospel with them so that they might be saved from sure destruction.

Look at it this way: If you came to find out that some pills in a local store had been laced with cyanide, you would do everything you could to warn individuals about the danger so they wouldn't be poisoned and killed. That would be the most loving thing you could do. What we must realize is that there is also *spiritual* cyanide being disseminated on a massive level by the Watchtower Society. Hence, the most loving thing we can do when Jehovah's Witnesses show up on our doorstep is to warn them of this poison and share the truth with them. To be hostile and turn them away is to withhold the only possible hope they have of coming to the truth and being saved.

Getting to Know
Jehovah's Witnesses

Though the specific doctrinal beliefs of the Jehovah's Witnesses will be discussed in each chapter of this book, it might be helpful at the outset to focus on a few foundational characteristics of Jehovah's Witnesses. To begin, it is critical to recognize that each member is thoroughly indoctrinated with Watchtower theology. It is sad but true that the Jehovah's Witnesses equip their members for witnessing much more thoroughly than many evangelical churches do. The average Jehovah's Witness is able to explain *and* defend what he believes, *and back it up by citing specific proof texts.*

Trained to Answer Common Objections

During their time of training, Jehovah's Witnesses are taught how to anticipate common questions and objections to what they say. Not only are they taught how to respond to *doctrinal* issues with Bible proof texts, they are also trained how to respond to common comebacks. For example, in *Reasoning from the Scriptures*, Jehovah's Witnesses are taught how to respond to people if they say: "I'm not interested," "I'm not interested in Jehovah's Witnesses," "I have my own religion," "We are already Christians here," "I'm busy," "Why do you people call so often?," "I am already well acquainted with your work," or, "We have no money."[13]

Hence, when someone raises a doctrinal objection or offers a common comeback, this automatically triggers a Watchtower response in the mind of the Jehovah's Witness.[14] Keeping this fact in mind will help you to remain patient with the Jehovah's Witness when it seems you're not getting anywhere with him or her.

You must also keep in mind that when you point out a particular verse to a Jehovah's Witness, he automatically "reads" it through the "lens" of the Watchtower Society.[15] His conditioned, preprogrammed mind replaces what the verse actually *says* with what the Watchtower Society says it *means*.[16] Granted, it can be immensely frustrating to try to get through to a Jehovah's Witness, but remember—persistence and patience really do pay off. I am personally acquainted with devout Christians who were formerly committed Jehovah's Witnesses.

One helpful technique for dealing with the triggered responses of the Jehovah's Witness is to request that he or she read a particular verse aloud, and then ask: "What is being said here?"[17] If he spouts off the typical Watchtower interpretation, ask him to read it aloud again, slowly and carefully—and follow it with another question. If you are persistent, you'll help the Jehovah's Witness see for himself that there are contradictions and problems with his view. (More on the importance of asking strategic questions shortly.)

Warned About Influence from Friends and Relatives

The Watchtower Society warns new followers that friends and relatives may very well be used by Satan to try to dissuade them from remaining with the Jehovah's Witnesses.[18] Hence, as former Jehovah's Witness David Reed notes, when a friend or relative *actually does* try to dissuade a new member in this way, it makes the Watchtower Society appear to be a true prophet.[19] This, in turn, encourages the new convert to be *even more loyal* to the Watchtower Society. As well, the friend or relative is so identified with Satan that the new convert will scarcely listen to *anything* he or she says. The Watchtower's warning hence serves as an effective way of keeping new converts so they can be thoroughly indoctrinated into the cult.[20]

Warned Against Reading "Apostate" Literature

Sometimes Christians who have read books by former Jehovah's Witnesses are tempted to pull those books out when Jehovah's Witnesses show up on the doorstep. In their zeal, they want to show how one individual was delivered from the cult. However, Jehovah's Witnesses are warned to stay away from literature written by such "apostates."

In fact, Jehovah's Witnesses are taught that reading apostate literature is as bad as reading pornographic literature.[21] If the Jehovah's Witness even suspects that you are using such material, he or she may assume that you are under bondage to the devil, just as the apostates are.[22] They will then avoid you.

The Fear of "Disfellowshipping"

Jehovah's Witnesses are instructed that unquestioned obedience to Watchtower doctrines is expected of them. If someone questions or rejects a particular Watchtower doctrine, he can be "disfellowshipped"—or kicked out of the organization.

The reason unquestioned obedience is expected is that the Watchtower Society is considered God's prophet and voice of truth for today. To question the authority of the Watchtower Society essentially amounts to questioning God's authority. Hence, challenging the Watchtower is considered an intolerable offense.

The Fear of Shunning

Jehovah's Witnesses are also warned that if they leave the Watchtower organization or are disfellowshipped, they will be shunned by family members and friends who remain in the organization.[23] Fear of such shunning makes it very difficult for anyone to leave the cult, for the sacrifice is a heavy one.

Earlier I mentioned the testimony of Chuck Love and his wife, who found liberation in the true gospel. After they turned from the Watchtower organization and became Christians, Chuck recalls that there were definite negative repercussions. "My family disowned me. My wife—who also became a Christian—received similar treatment from her family. Her parents won't even talk to her. Our brothers and sisters cut us off. And all of my close friends—those whom I thought were close friends—shut us out of their lives. When we trusted in Christ, it wasn't just a matter of changing *churches*; it was a matter of changing *lives*."[24]

Don Nelson, also mentioned earlier, had a similar experience when he became a Christian. "It is true that my wife and I have lost family and those we thought were our friends. But we say with the beloved apostle Paul: 'Whatever was to my profit I now consider loss for the sake of Christ. What is more, I consider everything a loss compared to the surpassing greatness of knowing Christ Jesus my Lord' (Philippians 3:7)."[25]

When witnessing to a Jehovah's Witness, one must ever keep in mind that he or she is strongly motivated to *remain* a Jehovah's Witness because of the possibility of shunning should he or she decide to leave. This points to the need for fervent and continuous prayer for those to whom you witness.

The Witnessing Encounter

Witnessing to Jehovah's Witnesses can be a trying experience. But your chances of success in reaching one for Christ can be greatly enhanced by *deciding in advance* how you will handle your witnessing encounters. Below are some tips I've picked up over the years.

Encourage an Examination of Beliefs

When a Jehovah's Witness shows up on your doorstep, one of the first things you should do is to encourage him or her to thoroughly examine his or her beliefs. After all, Watchtower literature itself says that one should examine one's religious beliefs to make sure those beliefs are correct.

A 1950 issue of *The Watchtower* magazine "invites careful and critical examination of its contents in the light of the Scriptures."[26] In keeping with this, a 1973 issue of *Awake!* magazine (another Watchtower publication) says that people should examine *all* the evidence, and that one arrives at the truth by examining *both sides* of a matter.[27] Second Corinthians 13:5 in the *New World Translation* says, "Keep testing whether you are in the faith, keep proving what you yourselves are."

After pointing out the above to the Jehovah's Witness, tell him or her that you would like to examine the Scriptures and test both of your religious beliefs by those Scriptures. This will lay a foundation for all that follows.

Find Common Ground

Scripture tells us that the apostle Paul was quite angry when he entered Athens and discovered that the city was full of idols (Acts 17:16). If he had acted upon his emotions, he probably would have vented his anger by dealing with the Athenians in a hostile way. But he didn't do this. Instead, Paul sought a *common ground* from which he could communicate the good news of the gospel.[28]

Paul began his message, "Men of Athens! I see that in every way you are very religious. For as I walked around and observed your objects of worship, I even found an altar with this inscription: TO AN UNKNOWN GOD. Now what you worship as something unknown I am going to proclaim to you" (Acts 17:22,23).

Applying what we learn from Paul's encounter with the Athenians to present-day encounters with Jehovah's Witnesses, the *wrong* approach would be to vent our anger by dealing with them in a hostile way. The *right* approach is to speak *kindly* and *respectfully* (like Paul did to the Athenians), and begin on the common ground of their zealous commitment to God (though, obviously, their view of God is heretical).[29] Starting off in this way, you can then discuss the specifics of Watchtower theology.

Take Your Time

When Jehovah's Witnesses show up on the doorstep, the tendency of many Christians is to lambaste them about all the heresies in their belief system. This is what I call the flame-thrower approach to cult evangelism. The problem is, this approach rarely yields positive results in terms of leading a cultist to Christ.

A much better approach is to take your time and not force the Jehovah's Witness to digest more than he or she can take during one sitting. Many cult experts have noted that it is better to focus on *one or two issues* during each meeting and deal with them thoroughly rather than to "get it all out on the table" in a single sitting. (Remember, even Jesus told the disciples: "I have many more things to say to you, but you cannot bear them now" [John 16:12 NASB]. Jesus was sensitive to how much His listeners could digest in a single sitting.[30])

If you engage in a thoughtful discussion of just one or two issues during your initial encounter with a Jehovah's Witness—and you remain *kind and respectful* in the process—he or she will not only be impressed with your manner but will likely make another appointment to come back to discuss other issues. *This is what you want to happen!*

Now, here's a warning: Jehovah's Witnesses will often try to set forth what seems to be an endless chain of proof texts in support of their theology. *Slow them down!* Suggest to them, "Instead of jumping around from verse to verse, let's make sure that we thoroughly discuss each passage before we go on to the next one."[31]

Ask Leading Questions

While talking to a Jehovah's Witness, you will not be able to force your opinion of what a verse means. But if you can help him to discover problems in Watchtower theology *for himself*, then you've really accomplished a good thing.

One great way to help a Jehovah's Witness discover problems in Watchtower theology is to ask strategic questions based on key verses, all the while remaining tactful and kind. Remember, Jesus often asked questions to make a point. David Reed notes that "rather than shower his listeners with information, [Jesus] used questions to draw answers out of them. A person can close his ears to facts he doesn't want to hear, but if a pointed question causes him to form the answer in his own mind, he cannot escape the conclusion—because it's a conclusion that he reached himself."[32] We must use this same type of methodology with Jehovah's Witnesses.

The right question asked in a nondefensive, nonchallenging, unemotional way may cause the Jehovah's Witness to find himself face-to-face with a doctrine (such as the deity of Christ) that is completely contrary to what the Watchtower Society teaches. By considering such a question, the Jehovah's Witness is forced to come to a conclusion *in his own mind*.

So, for example, you might begin by asking the Jehovah's Witness how many true Gods there are, according to John 17:3. Allow him to open his *New World Translation* and ask him to read it aloud: "This means everlasting life, their taking in knowledge of you, *the only true God*, and of the one whom you sent forth, Jesus Christ" (NWT, emphasis added). Based on this verse, the Jehovah's Witness will say that Jehovah (the Father) is the one true God.

Next, point out that according to John 1:1 in the *New World Translation*, Jesus is "a god." Ask the Jehovah's Witness if he or she agrees that Jesus is "a god." The answer will be *yes*. Then ask whether Jesus is a true God or a false God. This will cause a dilemma for the Jehovah's Witness. If he or she says Jesus is a *false* god, he is contradicting the *New World Translation* of Scripture (since John 1:1 in this version says Jesus *is a god*). If he says Jesus *is* a true God, he is also contradicting the Watchtower understanding of Scripture (John 17:3 says there is only *one true God*—Jehovah).[33]

I will examine this verse in greater detail later in the book. But I think you can see what I mean when I say that a well-placed question can be a lot more effective than assaulting a Jehovah's Witness with your proof of the deity of Christ (or any other doctrine). If you and the Jehovah's Witness mutually agree to meet *every week or two* to discuss different issues, you can rest assured that the cumulative effect of such questions on a weekly basis will slowly but surely erode his belief system so that he is more open to the true gospel. (In each chapter in this book, I will suggest sample questions you might ask the Jehovah's Witness.)

Undermine the Watchtower Society's Authority

As noted earlier, Jehovah's Witnesses read the Scriptures and interpret doctrines through the lens of the Watchtower Society. Therefore, in every encounter you have with a Jehovah's Witness, you will want to undermine the authority of the Watchtower Society by demonstrating that it is a false prophet. By so doing, you help to remove this distorted "pair of glasses" so the Jehovah's Witness can see more clearly.[34]

If you can lovingly demonstrate that the Watchtower Society has been wrong *time and time again* in terms of its many predictions—as well as changed its position on key doctrines back and forth over the years—this will serve to call into question everything else the Society teaches. As you continue to chip away at the Witness's confidence in the Watchtower Society, you will find it easier to make doctrinal points with him or her (via the leading questions I mentioned earlier).

Throughout this book many of the Watchtower's false prophecies will be exposed. You will also find prophetic issues dealt with in detail in chapter 13. You will want to thoroughly familiarize yourself with some of the major false prophecies so they will be at your fingertips during the witnessing encounter.

One more thing: Don't forget to pray consistently. Only God in His mighty power can lift the veil of cultic darkness from the human heart (2 Corinthians 4:4; cf. 3:16,17; John 8:32). Pray fervently for those you witness to and *pray often* (Matthew 7:7-12; Luke 18:1-8; James 5:16).

How to Use This Book

As you peruse the table of contents of this book, you will notice that each of the chapters deals with a specific doctrinal issue. You will also notice that there are more chapters on Jesus Christ than any other subject. This is because many of the Bible passages cited by Jehovah's Witnesses deal in some way with Christ.

Each chapter in this book begins with a short summary of what the Jehovah's Witnesses believe about a particular subject. Following this you will find individual discussions of the major passages the Jehovah's Witnesses cite in supporting their interpretation. Quotations from Watchtower books and magazines will be liberally sprinkled throughout. You will also find suggested "leading questions" that you can use in your witnessing encounters. *For your convenience, these questions are highlighted.* This makes it easy for you to quickly find the questions you need to make your point.

The book may be read straight through, in which case you will have a good grasp of Watchtower theology and how to refute it. Or, you may consult individual chapters as needed— each one is self-contained. And since each chapter deals with a distinct doctrinal teaching along with the major passages cited by the Jehovah's Witnesses, you will find that this is an easy-to-use reference tool that you can use to "bone up" in a matter of minutes on how to refute Watchtower doctrine.

1

The Watchtower Society: God's Organization or Cultic Tyrant?

Truth consists of having the same idea about something that God has.

—Joseph Joubert
(1754-1824)[1]

Truth exists; only falsehood has to be invented.

—Georges Braque
(1882-1963)[2]

The Jehovah's Witnesses are described in Watchtower literature as the "worldwide Christian society of people who actively bear witness regarding Jehovah God and his purposes affecting mankind."[3] No other group of people may lay claim to being the witnesses of Jehovah, we are told.

The Jehovah's Witnesses believe that God personally set up the Watchtower Society as His *visible* representative on earth. According to them it is through this organization and no other that God teaches the Bible to humankind today. Without the Society and its vast literature, people are said to be utterly unable to ascertain the true meaning of Scripture. Jehovah's Witnesses are reminded of this over and over again in Watchtower publications. For example, in various past issues of *The Watchtower* magazine, we read:

23

- "The Watch Tower Bible and Tract Society is the greatest corporation in the world, because from the time of its organization until now the Lord has used it as His channel through which to make known the glad tidings."[4]
- "Is not the Watch Tower Bible and Tract Society the one and only channel which the Lord has used in dispensing his truth continually since the beginning of the harvest period?"[5]
- "Jehovah's organization has a visible part on earth which represents the Lord and is under his direct supervision."[6]
- "We must not lose sight of the fact that God is directing his organization."[7]
- "Jehovah's organization alone, in all the earth, is directed by God's holy spirit or active force."[8]

Of course, if the above statements are true, then this means all other Christian organizations are *not* directed by God and hence are deceptive and are of the devil. The Jehovah's Witnesses are extremely exclusive. They view the Watchtower Society as the sole possessor and propagator of God's truth.

The Authority of the Watchtower Society

Jehovah's Witnesses believe that the Watchtower Society— as God's visible representative on earth—exercises authority over all true believers. And Jehovah's Witnesses are expected to obey the Society as the voice of God.[9]

If there is a conflict between what the Society says and what the government says, Jehovah's Witnesses are instructed to unquestioningly obey the former. So, for example, if a young man is drafted for military service, he must obey the Watchtower Society and refuse to serve in the military.

Jehovah's Witnesses believe that the teachings of the Watchtower Society are all-encompassing and should affect every area of life. One issue of *The Watchtower* magazine refers to the

Society as "an organization to direct the minds of God's people."[10] Another issue says that "Jehovah's organization...should influence our every decision."[11] In fact, *The Watchtower* goes so far as to say that "we must recognize not only Jehovah God as our Father but his organization as our Mother."[12]

Even reading the Bible is considered insufficient in and of itself in learning the things of God. *The Watchtower* tells us, "Unless we are in touch with this channel of communication [The Watchtower Society] that God is using, we will not progress along the road to life, no matter how much Bible reading we do."[13] As we shall soon see, Jehovah's Witnesses believe that specific Bible verses point to the need for the Watchtower Society for understanding the things of God.

God's "Faithful and Discreet Slave"

It is argued that Christ's "anointed" followers—viewed *as a group* or an *organization*—are the fulfillment of Jesus' words about the "faithful and discreet slave" in Matthew 24:45-47. In the *New World Translation*, this passage reads: "Who really is the faithful and discreet slave whom his master appointed over his domestics, to give them their food at the proper time? Happy is that slave if his master on arriving finds him doing so. Truly I say to you, He will appoint him over all his belongings."

I shall discuss the true meaning of this verse later in this chapter. First, let's take a brief look at Watchtower history.

Charles Taze Russell

A survey of Watchtower history reveals that Pastor Charles Taze Russell—the founder of the Jehovah's Witnesses—was once considered the "faithful and discreet slave." Jehovah's Witnesses today deny this, but Watchtower literature *proves* it.[14] The Watchtower book *The Harp of God* (published in the early 1920s) states: "Without a doubt Pastor Russell filled the office...and was therefore that wise and faithful servant, ministering to the household of faith meat in due season."[15]

The Watchtower magazine (1920) likewise said: "No one in present truth for a moment doubts that brother Russell filled the office of the 'Faithful and Wise Servant.'"[16] Indeed, "The Society by overwhelming majority vote expressed its will in substance thus: Brother Russell filled the office of 'that Servant.'"[17]

The Watchtower Society Changes Its Story

By 1927 (slightly over a decade after Russell's death), *The Watchtower* magazine was singing to a different tune. No longer was Pastor Russell considered the faithful and discreet slave. Following his death in 1916, there was a split in the organization that involved the new president, Joseph F. Rutherford. Rutherford took control of the Watchtower Society while members loyal to Russell broke away. Those who broke away— the "Russellites"—have continued to the present day to view Russell as God's special servant.[18] But the Watchtower organization under Rutherford alleged that Russell never made this claim for himself. Rather, Rutherford said, Christ's anointed followers in the Society—viewed *as a group* or an *organization*—are God's collective chosen instrument.[19]

Along these lines, the February 15, 1927, issue of *The Watchtower* magazine proclaimed that the phrase "faithful and discreet slave" does not apply to a single individual and certainly not to Pastor Russell. Indeed, the article notes, Russell never claimed to be the faithful and discreet slave.[20]

Today, one will find multiple affirmations in Watchtower literature that Christ's anointed followers viewed *as a group* are God's collective "faithful and discreet slave." For example, the book *"Let God Be True"* says that Matthew 24:45-47 "clearly shows that the Master would use one *organization*, and not a multitude of diverse and conflicting sects, to distribute his message. The 'faithful and discreet slave' is a *company* following the example of their Leader."[21] This "company" of anointed believers is led by the governing body of the Watchtower Society in Brooklyn, New York, which may be considered the administrative head of the "faithful and discreet slave."[22]

In keeping with all this, a 1969 issue of *The Watchtower* magazine informs us that God's faithful and discreet slave is God's sole "channel of communication" to His people.[23] We are told that "we all need help to understand the Bible, and we cannot find the Scriptural guidance we need outside the 'faithful and discreet slave' organization."[24]

In view of the Watchtower's change of position as to the identity of the "faithful and discreet slave":

_____ *Ask...* _____

- Did you know that in early Watchtower literature it was claimed that Charles Taze Russell was God's "faithful and discreet slave"?

- How do you explain the Watchtower Society's change of position on this very important issue?

Submission to the Faithful and Discreet Slave

Jehovah's Witnesses tell us that "it is through the columns of *The Watchtower* that Jehovah provides direction and constant Scriptural counsel to his people."[25] As well, "Through the columns of *The Watchtower* comes increased light on God's Word as Jehovah makes it known."[26]

Submission to this faithful and discreet slave (including all *Watchtower* publications) is expected of every Jehovah's Witness. This is because the anointed believers in the Watchtower Society represent God's "sole visible channel, through whom alone spiritual instruction [is] to come."[27] Hence, Jehovah's Witnesses are to "recognize and accept this appointment of the 'faithful and discreet slave' and be submissive to it."[28]

One issue of *The Watchtower* magazine asks, "What is your attitude toward directives from 'the faithful and discreet slave'? Loyalty should move you to be 'ready to obey.'"[29]

No "Private Interpretations"

Watchtower literature is replete with admonitions to "dependent" Bible interpretation—that is, *dependent on the Watchtower Society*. Jehovah's Witnesses are not to think for themselves in terms of interpreting the Bible. They are to submit their minds to the Watchtower Society. For example, we read:

- "God has not arranged for [His] Word to speak independently or to shine forth life-giving truths by itself. It is through his organization God provides this light."[30]
- "Avoid independent thinking...questioning the counsel that is provided by God's visible organization."[31]
- "Fight against independent thinking."[32]
- "Rather we should seek for dependent Bible study, rather than for independent Bible study."[33]
- "The Bible cannot be properly understood without Jehovah's visible organization in mind."[34]
- "If we have love for Jehovah and for the organization of his people we shall not be suspicious, but shall, as the Bible says, 'believe all things,' all the things that *The Watchtower* brings out."[35]
- "He does not impart his holy spirit and an understanding and appreciation of his Word apart from his visible organization."[36]

Clearly, the Watchtower Society expects unquestioning obedience of all Jehovah's Witnesses. As we shall see shortly, the Society feebly attempts to find biblical support for such dependency from passages like Acts 8:30,31 and 2 Peter 1:20,21.

Threat of Disfellowshipping

If a Jehovah's Witness disobeys the instructions of the Watchtower Society—even on a relatively minor matter—the assumption is that this individual is "apostate," and the punishment is "disfellowshipping." Those who are in good standing with the Watchtower Society are forbidden to interact or talk with one who has been disfellowshipped. The only exception is if the disfellowshipped person is in one's immediate family—such as a husband or wife, in which case it is permissible to conduct "necessary business" with him or her.[37] This fear of disfellowshipping is one of the Watchtower's most effective means of keeping members obedient to its teachings.

Let us now examine the passages that the Witnesses cite most often in support of their exalted view of the Watchtower Society.

REASONING FROM THE SCRIPTURES

Isaiah 43:10—*"Witnesses" of Jehovah?*

The Watchtower Teaching. The *New World Translation* renders Isaiah 43:10, "'You are my witnesses,' is the utterance of Jehovah, 'even my servant whom I have chosen.'" Appropriating this verse for themselves, the Jehovah's Witnesses believe that out of all the religious groups on planet earth, *they alone* are chosen by God and have been deemed His "witnesses."[38]

The Biblical Teaching. In context, Isaiah 43:10 is referring *strictly to Israel* as a collective witness to God's majesty, authority, faithfulness, and truth. This is in marked contrast to pagans who cannot witness to such attributes in their false gods. Israel as a witness was to testify that Yahweh is the only *true* God.

Now, here is the point to emphasize: It is a wild, wild leap to take a verse referring to Israel as God's witness to the pagan nations in Old Testament times (over seven centuries *before* the time of Christ) and claim its fulfillment in a modern-day religious group some nineteen centuries *after* the time of Christ. This is a classic example of what James W. Sire calls "Scripture twisting."[39]

To help a Jehovah's Witness understand the folly of the Watchtower interpretation of Isaiah 43:10:

_____ *Ask*... _____

- If the Jehovah's Witnesses are the *only* true witnesses for God, and if the Jehovah's Witnesses as an organization came into being in the late nineteenth century (which is a historical fact), does this mean God was *without a witness* for over eighteen centuries of church history?

_____

Help the Jehovah's Witness to understand the implications of that question. If there was not a witness for God for over eighteen centuries, this implies that God *did not care* for people to come to know Him during those many centuries.[40]

After driving this point home, switch gears and direct the Witness to the New Testament, where the clear focus is not on being witnesses of *Jehovah* but on being witnesses of *Jesus Christ*.[41] Indeed, before ascending into heaven, Jesus told the disciples, "You shall receive power when the Holy Spirit has come upon you; and *you shall be My witnesses* both in Jerusalem, and in all Judea and Samaria, and even to the remotest part of the earth" (Acts 1:8 NASB, emphasis added).

As we examine the rest of the New Testament, it becomes clear that the disciples did indeed become *Christ's* (not *Jehovah's*) witnesses. And the consistent central feature of their witness was Christ's *bodily, physical* resurrection from the dead. This doctrine is the heart of the gospel (1 Corinthians 15:1-4) and is made a matter of salvation by the apostle Paul (Romans 10:9,10). Yet the Jehovah's Witnesses deny this doctrine (believing instead in a "spiritual" resurrection).

Point out the following verses to the Jehovah's Witness, showing that the disciples were witnesses of *Christ* and His resurrection, not of Jehovah:

- "This Jesus God raised up again, to which *we are all witnesses*" (Acts 2:32 NASB, emphasis added).
- Jesus was the one "whom God raised from the dead, a fact to which *we are witnesses*" (Acts 3:15 NASB, emphasis added).
- "And with great power *the apostles were giving witness* to the resurrection of the Lord Jesus, and abundant grace was upon them all" (Acts 4:33, emphasis added).
- "But God raised Him from the dead; and for many days He appeared to those who came up with Him from Galilee to Jerusalem, *the very ones who are now His witnesses* to the people" (Acts 13:30,31 NASB, emphasis added).

You might want to request the Jehovah's Witness to read aloud from the above passages and then:

_____ *Ask...* _____

- According to these passages, were the early Christians witnesses of Jehovah or of Jesus Christ?

_____

Matthew 24:45-47—God's *"Faithful and Discreet Slave"*

The Watchtower Teaching. As noted earlier, the Jehovah's Witnesses argue that Christ's words about the "faithful and discreet slave" do not refer to the Christian in general but to Christ's anointed followers viewed as a group or as an organization (made up of 144,000 individuals), headed by the governing body of the Watchtower Society in Brooklyn, New York. This organization *alone* has been appointed by God to watch over His affairs on earth. It is alleged that no one can understand the Bible apart from the insights of the people in this organization as set forth in various Watchtower publications.

In contrast to the "faithful and discreet slave" (Matthew 24:45-47), the "evil slave" mentioned in verses 48-51 is said to refer to apostate Christendom—that is, all Christian denominations apart from the Jehovah's Witnesses. But is this what the Scriptures really teach?

The Biblical Teaching. In answering the Jehovah's Witness on this passage, you will want to ask the same essential questions that are listed in the discussion of Isaiah 43:10:

_____ *Ask...* _____

- Since the anointed believers *as an organization* are claimed to be God's collective "faithful and discreet slave" that *alone* guides people in their understanding of Scripture, *and* since this organization did not come into existence until the late-nineteenth century, does this mean God had *no true representatives* on earth for many, many centuries?

- What does this imply about God? Does it mean He didn't care for people to understand the Bible for all those centuries?

After asking these questions, emphasize that the idea of God having no true representatives on earth for so many centuries clearly goes against what we learn elsewhere in Scripture regarding the continued survival, growth, and health of the church throughout history. For example, in Matthew 28:20 Jesus said to His followers: "I am with you *always*, even to the end of the age" (emphasis added). This implies that there would *always* be followers of Jesus on the earth. (How else could Jesus be "with" them "always" if they weren't there?) There is no hint in this passage that there would be an eighteen-century period during which Christ would have no true representatives on earth (cf. Ephesians 4:11-16).

Now, having made this point, we must address the question: What does the parable in Matthew 24:45-47 actually mean? In this parable, Jesus likens a follower or disciple to a servant who has been put in charge of his master's household. In the parable, Jesus contrasts *two possible ways* that each professed disciple could carry out the task—*faithfully* or *unfaithfully*. Each respective servant has the potential to be faithful *or* unfaithful in regard to his duties.

The servant who chooses to be faithful conscientiously fulfills his responsibilities and obligations while his master is away. He honors the stewardship entrusted to him. He pays careful attention to the details of his assigned task, and seeks to avoid living carelessly and becoming lax in service. He so governs his life that he will be prepared whenever his master returns.

By contrast, the servant who chooses to be unfaithful calculates that his master will be away for a long time and hence decides to mistreat his fellow servants and "live it up" himself. He lives carelessly, callously, and self-indulgently, and does not fulfill his responsibilities to his master. It is clear that this servant is a servant *in name only*—a hypocrite. He is not a *true* servant.

Hence, this parable indicates that those who profess to serve Christ must make a pivotal choice: be faithful servants, doing the Lord's will at all times, or be unfaithful servants, neglecting God's will and living self-indulgently. Those who are faithful will be rewarded at the Lord's return, entering His kingdom; those who are unfaithful will be punished at the Lord's return, being excluded from His kingdom.

To sum up, then, this passage is not referring to an organization (the Watchtower Society) that is permanently distinct from a separate group (apostate Christendom). Rather it is referring generally to all who profess to follow Christ and is exhorting them to be faithful as opposed to unfaithful servants of Christ.

Acts 8:30,31—*The Need for the Watchtower Society*

The Watchtower Teaching. According to Acts 8:30,31, Philip encountered a man reading the Book of Isaiah and asked him: "Do you actually know what you are reading?" (NWT). The man said: "Really, how could I ever do so, unless someone guided me?" Philip then sat down with the man to instruct him.

The Jehovah's Witnesses cite this verse to support their view that the Watchtower Society is God's Bible-interpreting organization on earth. They say that humankind *needs* the Watchtower Society in order to understand Scripture, just as the man reading Isaiah needed Philip. Indeed, the Watchtower book *"Your Will Be Done on Earth"* says that "in order to understand God's Word and discern his will we . . . need the help of his dedicated, organized people [anointed believers in the Watchtower Society]. The Ethiopian Bible reader acknowledged that fact."[42]

The Biblical Teaching. The Jehovah's Witnesses are reading something into this passage that simply is not there. Yes, this passage does indicate that guidance is sometimes needed to help people understand Scripture. The meaning of certain Scripture passages is not always self-evident, even to those who are earnest seekers. (Peter even acknowledged that some of the apostle Paul's writings were hard to understand—2 Peter 3:16.) This is one reason God gives teachers to the church (Ephesians 4:11). As well, this is the reason for the illuminating ministry of the Holy Spirit (John 16:12-15; 1 Corinthians 2:9-12).

But *no*—there is no evidence in this passage of an organization whose infallible views must be accepted by all true followers of God. In our text, *one man* (Philip) preached to an Ethiopian man *directly from Scripture* (not from literature designed by an organization), after which time the Ethiopian confessed his faith in Christ and became baptized (Acts 8:34-38).[43]

Significantly, the Bible tells us that "when they came up out of the water, the Spirit of the Lord suddenly took Philip away, and *the eunuch did not see him again*, but went on his way rejoicing" (Acts 8:39, emphasis added). The eunuch did not have to join and submit to an organization.[44] Indeed, the eunuch never saw Philip again! As well, he had no sense of loss when his teacher left, but rather went on his way rejoicing in the Savior.

To drive these points home to a Jehovah's Witness:

_____ *Ask...* _____

- Where in the biblical text do you see any support for the idea that people must *join* an organization and *submit* to the interpretations of such an organization? (Only one man—Philip—is mentioned in the text. And after this single encounter, the eunuch never saw him again.)

- Did Philip use *Scripture alone* in talking to the eunuch, or did he have to use additional literature?

- If *Scripture alone* was sufficient for Philip and the eunuch, is not Scripture alone sufficient for us as well?

---

2 Timothy 3:16,17—*Is the Bible Sufficient?*

The Watchtower Teaching. The *New World Translation* renders 2 Timothy 3:16,17: "All Scripture is inspired of God and beneficial for teaching, for reproving, for setting things straight, for disciplining in righteousness, that the man of God may be fully competent, completely equipped for every good work."

Though the Jehovah's Witnesses give lip service to believing this verse,[45] in their actions they deny it. A person cannot become equipped by reading the Bible alone, they say, but must read Watchtower literature. Without this literature, it is alleged, a person cannot truly understand the Bible. One former Jehovah's Witness said that to gain eternal life, he was told that certain things were necessary: "[I was told] I should study the Bible diligently, and only through Watchtower publications."[46]

We see this same mentality illustrated in the Watchtower publication *Studies in the Scriptures*:

> Not only do we find that people cannot see the divine plan in studying the Bible by itself, but we see, also, that

if anyone lays the *Scripture Studies* aside, even after he has used them, after he has become familiar with them, after he has read them for ten years—if he then lays them aside and ignores them and goes to the Bible alone, though he has understood his Bible for ten years, our experience shows that within two years he goes into darkness. On the other hand, if he had merely read the *Scripture Studies* with their references, and had not read a page of the Bible, as such, he would be in the light at the end of the two years, because he would have the light of the Scriptures.[47]

The Biblical Teaching. There are two key questions that must be asked of the Jehovah's Witness in regard to this issue. (These questions are similar to some of the ones asked earlier, but they are critically important.)

_____ *Ask...* _____

- How did people understand the Bible for the nineteen centuries *prior* to the existence of the Watchtower Society? (If one cannot understand the Bible without Watchtower literature, as claimed, then apparently people could not understand the Bible for nineteen centuries.)

- What kind of a God would give His people a Bible with no means of understanding it?

_____

After helping the Jehovah's Witness to understand the implications of these questions, you can then turn your attention to 2 Timothy 3:16,17. To lay the groundwork for these two verses, first point the Jehovah's Witness to verse 15, where Paul tells Timothy that "from childhood you have known the sacred writings *which are able to give you the wisdom* that leads to salvation through faith which is in Christ Jesus" (NASB, italics added).

In Timothy's era, Jewish boys formally began studying the Old Testament Scriptures when they were five years of age. Timothy had been taught the Scriptures by his mother and grandmother beginning from childhood. Clearly, verse 15 indicates that the *Scriptures alone* were sufficient to provide Timothy with the necessary wisdom that leads to salvation through faith in Christ. And for us today, the *Scriptures alone* are still the sole source of spiritual knowledge.

_____ *Ask...* _____

- According to 2 Timothy 3:15, were the *Scriptures alone* sufficient to provide Timothy what he needed to know to be saved?

- If the Scriptures alone were sufficient for Timothy, then aren't the Scriptures alone sufficient for us?

Then, verses 16 and 17 tell us that *all Scripture* is "profitable for teaching, for reproof, for correction, for training in righteousness; that the man of God may be adequate, equipped for every good work" (NASB). This verse does not say that Scripture *as seen through the lens of the Watchtower Society* is "profitable for teaching, for reproof," and so forth. It is *Scripture alone* that does these things. And the reason Scripture can do these things is that "all Scripture is inspired by God" (verse 16a). The word "inspired" means "God-breathed." Scripture is sufficient because it finds its source in God. Watchtower literature, by contrast, finds its source in sinful humanity.

It is noteworthy that the word "adequate" (in the phrase "that the man of God may be adequate") means "complete, capable, fully furnished, proficient in the sense of being able to meet all demands."[48] Scripture alone makes a person complete, capable, and proficient. Scripture furnishes all that one must know to be saved and to grow in grace.

2 Peter 1:20,21—No "Private Interpretations"

The Watchtower Teaching. Second Peter 1:20 says, "For you know this first, that no prophecy of Scripture springs from any private interpretation" (NWT). The Jehovah's Witnesses sometimes cite this verse to support their contention that people are not to come up with their own private interpretations of Scripture but rather are to give heed to what is set forth by the Watchtower Society.[49] But is that the true meaning of this passage?

The Biblical Teaching. The word "interpretation" in 2 Peter 1:20 literally means "unloosing" in Greek.[50] The verse could be paraphrased: "No prophecy of Scripture is a matter of one's own *unloosing*." In other words, the prophecies did not stem merely from the prophets themselves or by human imaginings, but ultimately came *from God* (as verse 21 goes on to emphatically state). Hence, this passage is not dealing with how to interpret Scripture but rather how Scripture *came to be written*.[51]

With this in mind, let us consider verses 20 and 21 together: "But know this first of all, that no prophecy of Scripture is a matter of one's own [unloosing], *for* no prophecy was ever made by an act of human will, but men moved by the Holy Spirit spoke from God" (NASB, emphasis added). Now the word "for" at the beginning of verse 21 carries an *explanatory* function—indicating that verse 21 explains verse 20 by restating its contents and then pointing to God as the author of Scripture. Hence, the context of verse 21 indicates that the *collective focus* of verses 20 and 21 is Scripture's *origin*, not its *interpretation*.

In keeping with this, we must emphasize that the word "moved" (in the phrase "men moved by the Holy Spirit spoke from God") literally means "borne along" or "carried along." Luke uses this same word in the Book of Acts to refer to a ship being borne along or carried along by the wind (Acts 27:15, 17). The experienced sailors on the ship could not navigate it because the wind was so strong. The ship was being driven, directed, and carried about by the wind.

This is similar to the Spirit's driving, directing, and carrying the human authors of the Bible as they wrote (2 Peter 1:20,21). The word "moved" is a strong one, indicating the Spirit's complete superintendence of the human authors. Of course, just as sailors are individually active and consciously involved while on a ship, in the same way, the authors of God's Word were individually active and consciously involved in writing Scripture. But it was the Spirit who ultimately directed them or carried them along.

In view of the above facts, 2 Peter 1:20,21 cannot be used to support the Watchtower Society's view that people are not to come up with their own private interpretations of what Scripture means. As we have seen, the passage has to do with Scripture's *origin*, not its *interpretation*.

Besides, contrary to the Watchtower position, the apostle Paul said that Christians are to test everything (whether the teaching of an individual *or* an organization—1 Thessalonians 5:21). The Berean Christians were commended for testing Paul's teachings to make sure that what he said was in accord with the Scriptures (Acts 17:11). We are called upon by God to test our beliefs! Instead of unquestioningly swallowing the interpretations of an organization like the Watchtower Society, we are to measure such interpretations against what all of Scripture teaches.

In support of that, you will want to point the Jehovah's Witness to 2 Corinthians 13:5 in the *New World Translation*: "Keep testing whether you are in the faith, keep proving what you yourselves are." Along these same lines, *The Watchtower* magazine "invites careful and critical examination of its contents in the light of the Scriptures."[52]

After making the above points:

_____ *Ask...* _____

- Were the Bereans right to test the apostle Paul's teachings by Scripture (Acts 17:11)? (He will have to say yes.)

- Do you believe followers of God should obey the instruction in 1 Thessalonians 5:21 to test all things? (He will have to say yes.)

- Do you believe followers of God should obey 2 Corinthians 13:5 and test whether they are "in the faith"? (He will have to say yes.)

- Since God commands us to test all things by Scripture—and since *The Watchtower* magazine itself invites a critical examination of its contents in the light of Scripture—are you willing to examine the teachings of the Watchtower Society in the light of *Scripture alone*?

- If you find that certain teachings of the Watchtower Society go against what Scripture says, what will you do?

These questions can help you point out that the focus of your discussion should be the Scriptures alone, and not what the Watchtower Society says those Scriptures mean.

1 Corinthians 1:10—*Absolute Unity of Thought?*

The Watchtower Teaching. The *New World Translation* renders 1 Corinthians 1:10: "Now I exhort you, brothers, through the name of our Lord Jesus Christ that you should all speak in agreement, and that there should not be divisions among you, but that you may be fitly united in the same mind and in the same line of thought."

The Watchtower Society sees two applications for 1 Corinthians 1:10. First, the verse is used to impose conformity on the doctrinal beliefs of Jehovah's Witnesses.[53] The book *Reasoning from the Scriptures* tells us that "such unity would never be achieved if the individuals did not meet together, benefit from the *same spiritual feeding program*, and respect the agency [the Watchtower Society] through which such instruction was provided."[54] We also read that God "wants his earthly servants united, and so he has made understanding the Bible today dependent upon associating with his organization [the Watchtower Society]."[55]

And second, the Watchtower Society says this verse proves that the Jehovah's Witnesses are the only true Christians because they are in "complete agreement" with the Watchtower Society and are "united in the same mind and in the same line of thought." The Society boasts that Witnesses all over the world are of "one heart and soul."[56] Such unity, it is said, does not exist among the denominations of Christendom.[57]

The Biblical Teaching. In your discussions with Jehovah's Witnesses, you must dispel the myth that absolute unity in a group is a proof that they are the only true Christians and that those who do not have unity are false believers. Point out that the very reason the apostle Paul wrote this verse to the Corinthians was because *they were already lacking in unity* (*see* 1 Corinthians 6:13; 8:10; 10:25; 11:2-16; 14; 15). Some of them were saying, "I follow Paul" and, "I follow Apollos" and, "I follow Cephas" and, "I follow Christ" (1 Corinthians 1:12).

___ Ask... ___

- Does the divisiveness of the Corinthians mean that they were not Christians? (Paul clearly believed they were Christians—1 Corinthians 1:2.)

After making this simple point, you must then gently but firmly explain that 1 Corinthians 1:10 *does not* teach that we are to attain unity by submitting to an organization or agency through which doctrinal teaching is disseminated. The apostle Paul never (here or elsewhere) even remotely suggests that Christians are to render unquestioning obedience to any such group. Indeed, as noted earlier, Paul said that we are to test everything and not unquestioningly accept what a particular teacher says (1 Thessalonians 5:21). The Berean Christians were commended for testing all that Paul said to make sure that what he said was in accord with the Scriptures (Acts 17:11). We are to do likewise.

To emphasize your point:

_____ *Ask . . .* _____

- Where in 1 Corinthians 1:10 is there *any* reference or allusion to an organization?

- Where in 1 Corinthians 1:10 does it say unity is to be achieved by *submission* to such an organization?

_____

Another point you will want to make here is that in arguing *from the Bible* for the need for the Watchtower Society (from verses like 1 Corinthians 1:10), the Jehovah's Witnesses are guilty of committing a logical fallacy known as arguing in a circle. How so, you ask? Well, consider the "circularity" of the following logic: *The Watchtower Society says* people need to understand Scripture because *Scripture itself says* that people need to understand Scripture—and we know that *Scripture says* that people need to understand Scripture because the *Watchtower Society says* that *Scripture says* this.[58] Such circular reasoning obviously does not lend genuine support to the Watchtower position.

The Watchtower Society is also self-contradictory. As apologist Robert Bowman notes, the appeal, "Read these verses in the Bible and you will see that you need God's organization to understand the Bible," implies *both*, "You *can* understand the Bible" *and*, "You *cannot* understand the Bible."[59] Both of these statements cannot be true at the same time. They are contradictory.

After pointing out the above facts, you will want to return to 1 Corinthians 1:10 and focus fully on the historical situation with which Paul was dealing in Corinth. Begin by explaining to the Jehovah's Witness that the church in Corinth was divided into four basic factions, each having its own leader and particular emphasis—Paul (the Corinthians' father in Christ), Apollos (who had great rhetorical skills as a preacher), Cephas (who personally walked with Christ and was leader of the twelve), and Christ Himself (1 Corinthians 1:12). Apparently, each respective faction was acting in an antagonistic way toward the other three.

Seeking to do away with such divisiveness, the apostle Paul emphasized that we are all one in Christ. He taught that pivotal idea by asking, "Is Christ divided?" (or, more literally, "Is Christ *parceled out* among you?" [1 Corinthians 1:13]).

Paul's desire for the Corinthian Christians was that they "all . . . agree" (1 Corinthians 1:10). In New Testament Greek, this phrase carries the idea of "speak the same thing." It is an expression adapted from Greek political life that might be paraphrased, "Drop party cries."[60]

Paul wanted the Corinthian Christians to be "made complete in the same mind and in the same judgment" (1 Corinthians 1:10 NASB). The words "made complete" come from a Greek word that refers to the setting of bones by a physician and the mending of broken nets by a fisherman.[61] The idea is that Paul wanted the church to be without hurtful divisions and strife—the kind of strife that causes individual believers to separate from one another.

Now, it is important to note that Paul *was not* asking the Christians in Corinth to do away with *all* diversity and individuality. This is clear in 1 Corinthians 3:6-9, where diversity in doing the work of ministry is not opposed. Perhaps the best example of acceptable diversity among Christian brethren is found in the Book of Romans,[62] where Paul writes:

> One man has faith that he may eat all things, but he who is weak eats vegetables only. Let not him who eats regard with contempt him who does not eat, and let not him who does not eat judge him who

eats, for God has accepted him. Who are you to judge the servant of another? To his own master he stands or falls; and stand he will, for the Lord is able to make him stand. One man regards one day above another, another regards every day alike. Let each man be fully convinced in his own mind (Romans 14:2-5 NASB).

You might want to request the Jehovah's Witness to read aloud from Romans 14:2-5 and then:

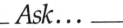

_____ *Ask...* _____

- Doesn't this passage indicate that it is acceptable for Christians to differ on certain religious issues?

_____

To sum up, then, in 1 Corinthians 1:10 Paul was not asking the Christians to do away with all diversity but rather to get rid of their unbrotherly, divisive attitude. Paul desired a unity of the parts—like a quilt made up of patches of many colors and designs.

John 17:3—*"Taking in Knowledge"*

The Watchtower Teaching. The *New World Translation* renders John 17:3: "This means everlasting life, their taking in knowledge of you, the only true God, and of the one whom you sent forth, Jesus Christ."

This verse allegedly points to the need for the Watchtower Society's Bible study—something they say helps people "take in" knowledge of God.[63] And since this taking in of knowledge leads to eternal life, the Watchtower Bible study is exceedingly important. One issue of *The Watchtower* magazine boldly invites people: "Come to Jehovah's organization for salvation."[64]

The Biblical Teaching. You must first point out to the Jehovah's Witness that the *New World Translation* mistranslates this verse. Indeed, the verse is more literally translated from the Greek text, "Now this is eternal life: that *they may know you*" (emphasis added). Jesus is thus talking about *personal* knowledge of God, not *general* knowledge of the Bible.[65] The Greek word for "know" in this context is one that specifically indicates great intimacy with *another person*.[66]

This is in harmony with what we learn elsewhere in Scripture. For example, Jesus indicates that general knowledge of the Bible is insufficient in itself to save someone. Jesus told a group of Jews: "You diligently study the Scriptures, because you think that by them you possess eternal life. These are the Scriptures that testify about me, yet you refuse to come to me to have life" (John 5:39,40). These lost Jews "knew" the *shell* of the Bible but they neglected the *kernel* within it—Jesus Christ. Such knowledge did them no good at all.

After reading aloud from John 5:39,40:

_____ *Ask...* _____

- According to John 5:39,40, is knowledge of Scripture sufficient for salvation? (The answer will be no.)

- What *is* required for salvation, according to this passage?

In keeping with the above, the apostle Paul referred to those who were "always learning but never able to acknowledge the truth" (2 Timothy 3:7). As former Jehovah's Witness David Reed says, "The 'facts' that keep filling Witnesses' heads never make up for the lack of actually *knowing* Jesus, the living truth."[67]

Scripture consistently emphasizes that salvation is rooted in a personal relationship with Jesus Christ—and Him alone. Jesus said, "I am the way and the truth and the life. No one comes to the Father except through me" (John 14:6). Peter said of Jesus, "There is salvation in no one else; for there is no other name under heaven that has been given among men, by which we must be saved" (Acts 4:12 NASB). Scripture is clear that Christ's divine mission was to be a Savior to the world (John 3:16; 4:42; 6:33; 1 John 4:14; 5:20).

Salvation, then, is found in knowing Christ personally. It is not found in taking in knowledge of God from Watchtower literature.

Acts 20:20—House-to-House Witnessing

The Watchtower Teaching. In Acts 20:20, the apostle Paul is quoted as saying: "I did not hold back from telling you any of the things that were profitable nor from teaching you publicly and from house to house" (NWT). The Jehovah's Witnesses use this verse as a proof text for witnessing house to house.

The Watchtower book *"Let God Be True"* affirms that "[Jesus] and his apostles preached publicly and from house to house (Acts 20:20). Every true Christian minister of the gospel is commanded to follow in their footsteps and must do as they did (1 Peter 2:21; Luke 24:48; Acts 1:8; 10:39-40). Since Jehovah's Witnesses take the message to the people, their preaching is distinguishable from that of the religious clergy, who require people to come to them and sit at their feet to be preached to."[68] In other words, because other so-called Christian groups *do not* go preaching door to door, the Jehovah's Witnesses are clearly the only *true* people of God.

The Biblical Teaching. First, we must point out that there is good reason to believe that the word "house" in Acts 20:20 most likely refers to house-churches.[69] In the early days of Christianity, there was no centralized church building where believers could congregate. Rather, there were many small house-churches scattered throughout the city.

As we examine the New Testament, the early Christians are seen "breaking bread from house to house" (Acts 2:46; cf. 5:42) and gathering to pray in the house of Mary, the mother of Mark (Acts 12:12). In his book *The Church in God's Program,* theologian Robert L. Saucy notes that "the practice of meeting in homes evidently became the established pattern, for we hear of the church in a house (Col. 4:15; Rom. 16:5; 1 Cor. 16:19; Phil. 2). The use of specific church buildings did not appear before the end of the second century."[70]

In light of the above, it may be that the apostle Paul's ministry was actually from house-church to house-church. This interpretation seems especially likely in view of the fact that when Paul said, "I did not shrink from declaring *to you* anything that was profitable, and teaching *you* publicly and from house to house" (Acts 20:20, emphasis added), he was speaking not to people in general but to "elders of the church" (see verse 17). If this interpretation is correct, then Acts 20:20 does not support the Watchtower contention that the Jehovah's Witnesses are the only true believers because they are the only followers of Jehovah who go house to house.

Even if a house and not a house-church is meant in Acts 20:20, it still would not support the Watchtower interpretation. That something took place in the first century of church history is not grounds for saying that the same thing should be done throughout every century in church history.

For example, we read of individual members of the early church that "no one claimed that any of his possessions were his own, but they shared everything they had" (Acts 4:32).

_____ *Ask...* _____

- Does the fact that a redistribution of wealth happened historically in the early church mean that *you* must give up all *your* personal property so it can be equally distributed among the poorer Jehovah's Witnesses at the Kingdom Hall?

Drive this point home to the Jehovah's Witness! Then, restate your main point: That something took place in the first century of church history is not grounds for saying that the same thing should be done throughout every century in church history.

A Consistent Pattern

We have seen in this chapter that the Watchtower Society is *not* God's visible representative on earth today; is *not* God's channel of truth for believers today; is *not* the sole authoritative interpreter of the Bible; is *not* God's "faithful and discreet slave"; and *cannot* justify its existence from the pages of Scripture (like it claims to be able to).

Instead, we have seen that the Watchtower Society consistently twists the true meaning of Scripture to suit its own ends. We shall see this pattern repeated in every chapter of this book as we deal with specific doctrinal issues.

2

Jehovah's Witnesses
and the Divine Name

*Many will say to me on that day, "Lord, Lord, did
we not prophesy in your name, and in your name
drive out demons and perform many miracles?"
Then I will tell them plainly, "I never knew you.
Away from me, you evildoers!" (Matthew 7:22,23).*

—Jesus Christ

Jehovah's Witnesses are told through Watchtower publications that God's true name is Jehovah. They are taught that
superstitious Jewish scribes long ago removed this sacred
name from the Bible. But there is no need to worry, the
Watchtower Society says! The Society's *New World Translation*
of the Holy Scriptures has "faithfully" restored the divine
name in the Old Testament where the Hebrew consonants
YHWH appear.[1]

Moreover, the name "Jehovah" has been inserted in the
New Testament by the Watchtower New World Bible Translation Committee in verses where the text is believed to refer to
the Father.[2] They have taken the liberty to do this *despite* the
fact that it blatantly goes against the thousands of Greek
manuscripts of the New Testament that we have—some of
which date from the second century. (The New Testament
always uses the words "Lord" [Greek: *kurios*] and "God"
[Greek: *theos*], *never* "Jehovah"—even in quotations from the
Old Testament.[3])

49

When a Jehovah's Witness shows up on your doorstep, he or she will often point to the importance of using God's correct name, Jehovah. He or she will typically open up the *New World Translation* and cite such passages as Romans 10:13: "Everyone who calls on the name of Jehovah will be saved," and Ezekiel 39:6: "People will have to know that I am Jehovah." In citing such passages the Witness often convinces the unwary and biblically illiterate person that the proper use of God's "correct" name (Jehovah) is absolutely essential to one's salvation. More than a few converts have been won to the Watchtower Society by utilizing such an approach.

The Jehovah's Witnesses believe that because they are the only group that refers to God by His "true" name, Jehovah, they are the only true followers of God. Indeed, all other so-called Christian denominations are part of a false, satanically inspired Christendom.

The Origin of the "Divine Name"

When I teach on the cults, I am sometimes asked where the name Jehovah came from. Many Bible students realize this name is not found in the Hebrew and Greek manuscripts from which English translations of the Bible are derived.[4] (The Old Testament contains the name "Yahweh"—or, more literally, *YHWH* [the original Hebrew had only consonants].) This being so, then, where did the name Jehovah come from?

To answer this question, we must recognize that the ancient Jews had a superstitious dread of pronouncing the name YHWH. They felt that if they uttered this name, they might violate the Third Commandment, which deals with taking God's name in vain (Exodus 20:7). So, to avoid the possibility of breaking this commandment, the Jews for centuries substituted the name "Adonai" (Lord) or some other name in its place whenever they came across it in public readings of Scripture.

Eventually, the fearful Hebrew scribes decided to insert the vowels from Adonai (a-o-a) within the consonants YHWH.[5]

The result was Yahowah, or Jehovah. Hence, the word Jehovah is derived from a consonant-vowel combination from the words *YHWH* and Adonai. Watchtower literature acknowledges this fact.[6]

The point I want to make here is that the term Jehovah is not actually a biblical term. It is a man-made term.

What About "Jehovah" in Legitimate Translations?

There are other Bible translations besides the *New World Translation* (that is, *legitimate* translations) that have used the name Jehovah—either consistently, as in the *American Standard Version* (1901), or in isolated instances. An example of a version that uses Jehovah only in isolated instances (just four times) is the *King James Version* (*see* Exodus 6:3; Psalm 83:18; Isaiah 12:2; 26:4).[7] The *New English Bible* also uses Jehovah in Exodus 3:15 and 6:3. Jehovah's Witnesses often impress people by pointing to such verses where the name Jehovah is used in these translations. It gives the appearance that the Jehovah's Witnesses are right in saying that God's only true name is Jehovah.

Now, before proceeding further, I must pause to make an important point. Though there is no biblical justification for the term Jehovah, it is important to recognize that scholars are not precisely clear as to the correct way to pronounce the Hebrew word *YHWH*.[8] Though most modern scholars believe Yahweh is the correct rendering (as I do), we really cannot criticize the Jehovah's Witnesses for using the term Jehovah where the Hebrew consonants YHWH appear in the Old Testament (though they *can* be criticized and proven wrong regarding the insertion of this name in the New Testament). After all, some evangelical Christians and some legitimate Bible translations (in the Old Testament) use the term Jehovah as well.

Because many people have accepted the term Jehovah as the conventional way of referring to God, our primary point of contention with the Jehovah's Witnesses must not be the term itself, but rather in how they use this term in their biblical interpretation and theology. As we shall see, the way they use this term is truly heretical.

Is Jesus Jehovah?

A central feature of Watchtower theology is that Jesus is *not* Jehovah. They say Jesus was a created angel—Michael the Archangel, to be more specific. *The Watchtower* magazine suggests, "There is Scriptural evidence for concluding that Michael was the name of Jesus Christ before he left heaven and after his return."[9] Indeed, " 'Michael the great prince' is none other than Jesus Christ himself."[10]

The Jehovah's Witnesses concede that Jesus is a "mighty god," but they deny that He is *God Almighty* like Jehovah is.[11] *The Watchtower* magazine asks, "If Jesus of the 'New Testament' is Jehovah of the 'Old Testament,' as many claim, should there not at least be one Biblical reference saying that Jesus is Jehovah? Yet there is not one."[12]

Jehovah's Witnesses often quote Jesus' own words from Luke 4:8 as found in the *New World Translation*: "It is Jehovah your God you must worship, and it is to him alone you must render sacred service" (note the unjustified insertion of *Jehovah* in this New Testament verse). Verses such as this, Jehovah's Witnesses say, show that Jesus is not Jehovah. Only the Father is Jehovah, they say.

_____ REASONING FROM THE SCRIPTURES_____

Two of the more common passages cited by Jehovah's Witnesses to support their view of the divine name are Exodus 3:15 and Matthew 6:9. But there are many other lesser passages they may bring up when they are on your doorstep.

As I examine these two passages in detail below, keep in mind that they are representative of a larger group. The scriptural arguments I will suggest in refuting the Watchtower interpretation of these passages can be adapted for use with the other passages as well.

Exodus 3:15—*Jehovah: God's Name Forever?*

The Watchtower Teaching. Exodus 3:15 tells us that after Moses asked God what His name was, God said: "This is what you are to say to the sons of Israel, 'Jehovah the God of your forefathers, the God of Abraham, the God of Isaac and the God of Jacob, has sent me to you.' This is my name to time indefinite, and this is the memorial of me to generation after generation" (NWT).

The Jehovah's Witnesses teach that this verse constitutes a command to refer to God as Jehovah forever and ever. One Watchtower publication tells us:

> To this very generation in the twentieth century, to our own generation since A.D. 1914, the name of the eternal God is JEHOVAH. To all eternity this is his holy name, and, as the memorial of him, it is the name by which we are to remember him to all eternity. It is his unchangeable name. From the beginning of man's existence to Moses' day it had not changed; and from Moses back there in 1514 B.C.E. till today that name has not changed. So after all these thousands of years of time it is fitting for us to use that name in a worthy way. [13]

As noted earlier, the Watchtower Society teaches that since the Jehovah's Witnesses are the *only* ones who consistently call God by this name, they alone are true followers of God. All others are outside of Jehovah's kingdom.

The Biblical Teaching. In responding to the Watchtower interpretation of Exodus 3:15, one must challenge the claim that only the name Jehovah applies uniquely to the true God of Scripture. God is identified in other ways in Scripture besides the name Jehovah. One example of this is the expression "the

God of Abraham, the God of Isaac, and the God of Jacob"—an expression that occurs many times in Scripture.[14] This shows that though God *is* known by the name Jehovah (or, more properly, Yahweh), He is not known *only* by the name Jehovah (or Yahweh). He is known by other names as well. Hence, Exodus 3:15 cannot be taken to mean that Jehovah is the *only* name by which God can be addressed.

_____ *Ask . . .* _____

- Since God is often identified as "the God of Abraham, the God of Isaac, and the God of Jacob"—without any mention of the name Jehovah—doesn't this mean that the name Jehovah is not the only way that God can be addressed?

In keeping with this, it is noteworthy that in New Testament times, Jesus never addressed the Father as Jehovah.[15] If the Jehovah's Witnesses are correct that God must always be called by the name Jehovah, then Jesus was way out of line. (Note that the *New World Translation* sometimes puts "Jehovah" in Jesus' mouth in the New Testament, but the translators do so in direct violation of the thousands of Greek manuscripts that we have.)

Consider the Lord's Prayer. Jesus did not begin this prayer with the words, "*Jehovah God*, who art in heaven." Rather, He said, "*Our Father*, who art in heaven" (Matthew 6:9 NASB, emphasis added).[16] Jesus began other prayers this way as well (Matthew 11:25; 26:39-42; Mark 14:36; Luke 10:21; 22:42; 23:34).[17] It is not surprising that Jesus taught His followers to pray this way. Indeed, in view of the fact that we are God's children, we are uniquely privileged to come before the Father and call out to Him, "Abba! Father!" (Romans 8:15; Galatians 4:6). The fact that we can address God as Father proves that we are not to woodenly interpret Exodus 3:15 as meaning that Jehovah is the only expression by which God can be addressed.[18]

In view of this:

___ Ask... ___

• Since Jesus never addressed the Father as Jehovah, and since He taught that we can address God as Father, doesn't this mean that the name *Jehovah* is not the only expression by which God can be addressed?

Along these same lines, we must reiterate that according to the Greek manuscripts of the New Testament, the word Jehovah does not occur a single time in the New Testament. This is highly significant, for if Jehovah was to be the sole name for God in all generations, then the word would certainly occur in the New Testament. But it does not occur there anywhere, despite the fact that the Watchtower's *New World Translation* deceitfully inserts the term throughout the New Testament in verses thought to refer exclusively to the Father.

Now, having said all this, let us briefly look at Exodus 3:15 to find out what this verse really means. The name Yahweh (remember, Jehovah is not really the correct form here) is connected with the Hebrew verb "to be." We first learn of this name in Exodus 3, where Moses asked God by what name He should be called. God replied to him, "I AM WHO I AM.... Thus you shall say to the sons of Israel, 'I AM has sent me to you'" (verse 14 NASB).

The phrase "I AM" is not the word Yahweh. However, "I AM" (in verse 14) and Yahweh (in verse 15) are both derivatives of the *same* verb, "to be." The name "I AM WHO I AM" that God revealed to Moses in verse 14 is intended as a full expression of His eternal nature, and is then shortened to Yahweh in verse 15. The names have the same root meaning and can be considered essentially interchangeable.

Before proceeding further, it is critical to keep in mind that in the ancient world a name was not a mere label as it is today.

A name was considered as equivalent to whomever or whatever bore it. Knowing a person's name amounted to knowing his essence and being.

A survey of Scripture shows that the *name* and *being* of God often occur together in the form of a *parallelism* (a literary form indicating a close parallel relationship). The Psalms illustrate this for us (emphasis added): "Therefore I will praise *you* among the nations, O LORD; I will sing praises to *your name*" (Psalm 18:49); "Sing to *God*, sing praise to *his name*, extol *him* who rides on the clouds—*his name* is the LORD—and rejoice before him" (Psalm 68:4); "Remember how the enemy has mocked *you, O LORD*, how foolish people have reviled *your name*" (Psalm 74:18); "I will praise *you, O LORD my God*, with all my heart; I will glorify *your name* forever" (Psalm 86:12). Clearly, Scripture portrays God and His name as being inseparable. To know one is to know the other.

Now, most scholars today agree that the name Yahweh conveys the idea of eternal self-existence. As I point out in my book *Christ Before the Manger: The Life and Times of the Preincarnate Christ*, Yahweh never came into being at a point in time, for He has always existed. He was never born. He will never die. He does not grow older, for He is beyond the realm of time. To know Yahweh is to know the eternal one.[19] Scholars have also noted that the name communicates that God is absolutely supreme and is in control of everything. Hence, the name Yahweh reveals God as eternal Lord and supreme Ruler of the universe.

So, when God told Moses that "this is My name forever, and this is My memorial-name to all generations" (Exodus 3:15), He was telling Moses not only His name but that He would manifest Himself (through all generations) in *the nature expressed* by that name (that is, His eternal self-existence and sovereign Lordship). And He would do this so that all generations would both know Him and revere Him as He really is.

In Exodus 3:15, then, the focus is not limited to a mere external name of God, but—more importantly—deals with the fact that people of all generations would come to understand who God is in His true nature and being. God would testify to all generations that in His nature He is eternally self-existent and the sovereign Lord of the universe. This is in contrast to false gods who are not self-existent (they don't really exist at all) and are not sovereign over anything (1 Kings 18:36). God is completely unique as the self-existent and sovereign Ruler of the universe, and this uniqueness was to be made known to all generations by the term Yahweh.

To recap: 1) God *is* known by the name Jehovah (Yahweh), but He is not known *only* by the name Jehovah (Yahweh); 2) God is identified in other ways in Scripture *besides* by the name Jehovah; 3) Jesus never referred to God as Jehovah, but rather called Him "Father"; 4) believers are uniquely privileged to call God "Father"; 5) the word Jehovah never occurs in the New Testament (according to *all* the Greek manuscripts); and 6) in Exodus 3:15 the focus is not limited to a mere name of God, but—more importantly—deals with the fact that people of all generations would come to understand who God is in His true nature and being.

In view of the above, the claim that God must always be referred to by the name Jehovah (or Yahweh) does not coincide with the scriptural evidence. Though it is most certainly right to call God "Yahweh," it is also right to address Him in other ways, as both the Old and New Testaments testify.

Matthew 6:9—*"Sanctifying God's Name"*

The Watchtower Teaching. In Matthew 6:9 we are told: "You must pray, then, this way: 'Our Father in the heavens, let your name be sanctified' " (NWT). The only way God's name can be sanctified, Jehovah's Witnesses tell us, is by calling Him by His *true* name, "Jehovah," and by treating that name as holy.[20] Indeed, in order for our prayers to be heard, we must address God by this name. To call God by any other name is to dishonor Him.[21]

We noted earlier the Watchtower view that superstitious Jewish scribes removed the sacred name Jehovah from the Bible. In keeping with this, Jehovah's Witnesses also tell us that most Bible translations today deceive people because they omit Jehovah as God's name. In 1961 the Watchtower Bible and Tract Society published a book entitled after Matthew 6:9—*"Let Your Name Be Sanctified"*—in which we read:

> The translating of the Book [the Bible] into more languages or dialects continues on, that the Book may reach more and more people whose eternal life is in danger. But from many of these translations we cannot learn the name of our Creator, because another word or a title has been used instead of his name. By such translations the name has not been respected, honored, or held sacred; it has, in fact, been hidden from readers who need to know the name for their own salvation.[22]

How can we come to know this "name" that will yield our salvation? This same Watchtower book tells us:

> If we have our own eternal interests at heart, we will be anxious to acquaint ourselves with God, to know him as he is and not as Christendom has misrepresented him. This acquaintance we can attain by reading and studying the Book of his name, the Holy Bible, and by intimately associating ourselves with his approved visible organization, the "people for his name," the remnant of his anointed witnesses, the "faithful and discreet slave" class.[23]

The Biblical Teaching. Is it true, as the Watchtower Society claims, that superstitious Jewish scribes removed the sacred name Jehovah from the Bible? This is preposterous! There is not a shred of evidence to support this claim. (You might even ask the Jehovah's Witness to produce hard evidence for this assertion.)

Indeed, the claim is especially absurd in view of the fact that the Watchtower Society elsewhere argues for the profound accuracy of both the Old and New Testament manuscripts.[24] For example, in the Watchtower book *Reasoning from the Scriptures*, Sir Frederic Kenyon's book *The Chester Beatty Biblical Papyri* is quoted approvingly. This book shows the textual reliability of both the Old and New Testaments.[25]

Let us be clear on this: The Watchtower's position that the divine name was stripped from the Bible by superstitious scribes is a fabrication—an out-and-out lie! Not only is there not a shred of evidence to support this contention, but there is also a great volume of evidence to the contrary. In fact, the more manuscript evidence we examine, the clearer it becomes that the ancient scribes were amazingly accurate in their transmission of the biblical text.

_____ *Ask...* _____

- How can the Watchtower Society argue for the profound accuracy of the Old and New Testament manuscripts and at the same time say that the name *Jehovah* was stripped from these manuscripts by superstitious Jewish scribes?

One of my co-workers at the Christian Research Institute—Marian Bodine, an expert in Watchtower theology—says that the Watchtower's insertion of the name Jehovah in the New Testament (against all manuscript evidence) "is just another attempt on the part of the Jehovah's Witnesses to cloud the truth—that is, that the name the New Testament consistently uplifts is Jesus, not Jehovah."[26] Marian suggests that there are a number of questions you can ask an interested Witness in order to demonstrate that the New Testament consistently uplifts Jesus, not Jehovah (be sure to look up the accompanying verses when talking to the Jehovah's Witness):

Ask...

- In whose name should we meet together (Matthew 18:20; 1 Corinthians 5:4)?

- Demons are subject to whose name (Luke 10:17; Acts 16:18)?

- Repentance and forgiveness should be preached in whose name (Luke 24:47)?

- In whose name are you to believe and receive the forgiveness of sins (John 1:12; 3:16; Acts 10:43; 1 John 3:23; 5:13)?

- By whose name, and _no other_, do we obtain salvation (Acts 4:12)?

- Whose name should be invoked as we bring our petitions to God in prayer (John 14:13,14; 15:16; 16:23,24)?

- In whose name is the Holy Spirit sent (John 14:26)?

- Whose name and authority was invoked by the disciples in healing the sick and lame (Acts 3:16; 4:7-10,30)?

- Whose name did Paul tell us to call upon (1 Corinthians 1:2)?

- Whose name is above every name (Ephesians 1:21; Philippians 2:9-11)?[27]

The answer to each of the above questions is obviously _Jesus Christ_—and should serve to get the attention of the fair-minded Jehovah's Witness. The above Scripture references should be more than adequate to demonstrate the name by which true followers of God should be identified.

You might also point out that the above reference to Philippians 2:9-11—where we are told that Christ was given a name above every name "that at the name of Jesus every knee should bow . . . in heaven and on earth and under the earth, and every tongue confess that Jesus Christ is Lord"—is taken from an Old Testament passage about Yahweh. Indeed, Paul—an Old Testament scholar *par excellence*—is alluding to Isaiah 45:22-24: "I am God, and there is no other. By myself I have sworn, my mouth has uttered in all integrity a word that will not be revoked: Before me every knee will bow; by me every tongue will swear." Paul was drawing on his vast knowledge of the Old Testament to make the point that what is true of Yahweh is also true of Christ, the Lord of all humankind.

After you have made the above points, you are then ready to add the doctrinal "clincher." In Acts 1:8, Jesus affirmed to the disciples: "You will receive power when the Holy Spirit comes on you; and *you will be my witnesses* in Jerusalem, and in all Judea and Samaria, and to the ends of the earth" (emphasis added). We are called to be witnesses of *Jesus Christ*, not of Jehovah!

____ *Ask...* _____

- According to Acts 1:8 of whom are we to be witnesses?

- With your exclusive emphasis on Jehovah, can you honestly say that you are being obedient to Acts 1:8?

_____

Now, if Jesus is the name by which true followers of God are to be identified (as we have argued), then what is meant in Matthew 6:9, where Jesus said: "You must pray, then, this way: 'Our Father in the heavens, *let your name be sanctified*' " (NWT, emphasis added)? Well, first, notice that Jesus never calls God "Jehovah" in this verse (or anywhere else, for that matter). He calls God "Father." This in itself refutes the Watchtower position.

Matthew 6:9 is better translated, "Pray, then, in this way: 'Our Father who art in heaven, hallowed be Thy name." Now, keep in mind what was said earlier about how the ancients viewed one's *name*. A name among the ancients was considered as equivalent to whomever or whatever bore it. Knowing a person's name amounted to knowing his essence and being. Thus God's name refers to God as He has revealed Himself to humankind. God's name is a reflection of *who He is*. Hence, Matthew 6:9 involves not just honoring God's name, but especially honoring the *Person* that the name represents.

Against this backdrop, it is significant that the word "hallowed" in the Greek text means "to hold in reverence," "to treat as holy," "to esteem, prize, honor, and adore." Now, of course, God is already holy. This is not a prayer for God or His name to become holy, but rather that He and His name be treated as holy and revered by His people (cf. Exodus 20:8; Leviticus 19:2,32; Ezekiel 36:23; 1 Peter 1:15). We hallow God's name not by outwardly calling Him "Jehovah" (a word that is nowhere—I repeat *nowhere!*—in the context) but by ordering our thoughts and conduct so that we do not dishonor Him in any way.

The contrast to "hallow" is "to profane"—which means "to treat indifferently," "to neglect," "to treat lightly." This is the way many pagans have treated God throughout history. Unlike such pagans, God's children—by their thoughts and conduct—are to treat Him with great reverence.

Jesus *Is* Yahweh

As noted earlier, the Jehovah's Witnesses argue that if Jesus really was Jehovah or Yahweh, then there would be at least one biblical reference saying that He is Yahweh. I shall argue that Jesus definitely is Yahweh, but first I need to make a point.

Let us recall that the name Yahweh does not appear in the New Testament (in most Bibles). Hence, it seems rather obvious that there can be no verse in the New Testament that comes right out and declares, "Jesus is Yahweh."[28] On the other hand, as Watchtower expert Robert M. Bowman notes, "The Bible also never says in just so many words that the

Father is Jehovah."[29] In other words, the Father is never *explicitly* called "Jehovah" or "Yahweh."

However, we are told in Scripture that Yahweh is the only true God (Genesis 2:4; Deuteronomy 6:4; Isaiah 45:5,21). Hence, because we also know that the Father is the only true God (John 6:27; 17:3), we logically conclude that the Father is Yahweh. By the same token, we know from specific passages of Scripture that Jesus is truly God (John 1:1; 8:58; 20:28; Titus 2:13; Hebrews 1:8). Hence, *He too is Yahweh.*[30] Besides, as I shall argue later in the book, Jesus clearly indicated His identity as Yahweh in John 8:58 when He said to some Jews, "Before Abraham was born, I am" (cf. Exodus 3:14).

A comparison of the Old and New Testaments provides powerful testimony to Jesus' identity as Yahweh. Support for this is found, for example, in Christ's crucifixion. In Zechariah 12:10 Yahweh is speaking prophetically: "They will look on me, the one they have pierced." Though Yahweh is speaking, this is obviously a reference to Christ's future crucifixion.[31] We know that "the one they have pierced" is Jesus, for He is described this same way by the apostle John in Revelation 1:7. (As one might expect, however, the *New World Translation* mistranslates Zechariah 12:10 to avoid any connection with Christ. I'll discuss this deception in detail in the next chapter.)

The Septuagint provides us with additional insights on Christ's identity as Yahweh. The Septuagint is a Greek translation of the Hebrew Old Testament that dates prior to the birth of Christ. It renders the Hebrew phrase for "I AM" (God's name) in Exodus 3:14 as *ego eimi*.[32] On a number of occasions in the Greek New Testament, Jesus used this term as a way of identifying Himself as God.[33] For example, in John 8:24 (NASB) Jesus declared, "Unless you believe that I am [I AM or *ego eimi*] He, you shall die in your sins." The original Greek text for this verse does not have the word *he*. The verse is literally, "If you do not believe that I AM, you shall die in your sins."

Then, according to verse 28, Jesus told the Jews, "When you lift up the Son of Man, then you will know that I am [I AM, or *ego eimi*] He." Again, the original Greek text reads, "When you lift up the Son of Man, then you will know that I AM" (there is no *he*). Jesus purposely used the phrase as a means of pointing to His identity as Yahweh.[34]

It is also highly revealing that Old Testament passages about Yahweh were directly applied to Jesus in the New Testament. For instance, Isaiah 40:3 says: "In the desert prepare the way for the LORD [*Yahweh*]; make straight in the wilderness a highway for our God [*Elohim*]." Mark's Gospel tells us that Isaiah's words were fulfilled in the ministry of John the Baptist preparing the way for Jesus Christ (Mark 1:2-4).

Still another illustration is Isaiah 6:1-5, where the prophet recounts his vision of Yahweh "seated on a throne, high and exalted" (verse 1). He said, "Holy, holy, holy is the LORD [*Yahweh*] Almighty; the whole earth is full of his glory" (verse 3). Isaiah also quotes Yahweh as saying: "I am the LORD; that is my name! I will not give my glory to another" (42:8). Later, the apostle John—under the inspiration of the Holy Spirit— wrote that Isaiah "saw Jesus' glory" (John 12:41). Yahweh's glory and Jesus' glory are equated.

Christ's deity is further confirmed for us in that many of the actions of Yahweh in the Old Testament are performed by Christ in the New Testament. For example, in Psalm 119 we are told about a dozen times that it is Yahweh who gives and preserves life. But in the New Testament, Jesus claims this power for Himself: "For just as the Father raises the dead and gives them life, even so the Son gives life to whom he is pleased to give it" (John 5:21). Later in John's Gospel, when speaking to Lazarus's sister Martha, Jesus said: "I am the resurrection and the life. He who believes in me will live, even though he dies; and whoever lives and believes in me will never die" (John 11:25).

In the Old Testament the voice of Yahweh was said to be "like the roar of rushing waters" (Ezekiel 43:2). Likewise, we read of the glorified Jesus in heaven: "His feet were like bronze glowing in a furnace, and his voice was like the sound of rushing waters" (Revelation 1:15). What is true of Yahweh is just as true of Jesus.

It is also significant that in the Old Testament, Yahweh is described as an "everlasting light," one that would make the sun, moon, and stars obsolete: "The sun will no more be your light by day, nor will the brightness of the moon shine on you, for the LORD will be your everlasting light, and your God will be your glory. Your sun will never set again, and your moon will wane no more; the LORD will be your everlasting light, and your days of sorrow will end" (Isaiah 60:19,20). Jesus will also be an everlasting light for the future eternal city in which the saints will dwell forever: "The city does not need the sun or the moon to shine on it, for the glory of God gives it light, and the Lamb is its lamp" (Revelation 21:23).

David F. Wells, in his book *The Person of Christ*, points us to even further parallels between Christ and Yahweh:

> If Yahweh is our sanctifier (Exod. 31:13), is omnipresent (Ps. 139:7-10), is our peace (Judg. 6:24), is our righteousness (Jer. 23:6), is our victory (Exod. 17:8-16), and is our healer (Exod. 15:26), then so is Christ all of these things (1 Cor. 1:30; Col. 1:27; Eph. 2:14). If the gospel is God's (1 Thess. 2:2, 6-9; Gal. 3:8), then that same gospel is also Christ's (1 Thess. 3:2; Gal. 1:7). If the church is God's (Gal. 1:13; 1 Cor. 15:9), then that same church is also Christ's (Rom. 16:16). God's Kingdom (1 Thess. 2:12) is Christ's (Eph. 5:5); God's love (Eph. 1:3-5) is Christ's (Rom. 8:35); God's Word (Col. 1:25; 1 Thess. 2:13) is Christ's (1 Thess. 1:8; 4:15); God's Spirit (1 Thess. 4:8) is Christ's (Phil. 1:19); God's peace (Gal. 5:22; Phil. 4:9) is Christ's (Col. 3:15; cf. Col. 1:2; Phil. 1:2; 4:7); God's "Day" of judgment (Isa. 13:6) is Christ's "Day" of judgment (Phil. 1:6, 10; 2:16; 1 Cor. 1:8); God's grace (Eph. 2:8, 9; Col. 1:6; Gal. 1:15) is Christ's grace (1 Thess. 5:28; Gal. 1:6; 6:18); God's salvation (Col. 1:13) is Christ's salvation (1 Thess. 1:10); and God's will (Eph. 1:11; 1 Thess. 4:3; Gal. 1:4) is Christ's will (Eph. 5:17; cf. 1 Thess. 5:18). So it is no surprise to hear Paul say that he is both God's slave (Rom. 1:9) and Christ's (Rom. 1:1;

Gal. 1:10), that he lives for that glory which is both God's (Rom. 5:2; Gal. 1:24) and Christ's (2 Cor. 8:19, 23; cf. 2 Cor. 4:6), that his faith is in God (1 Thess. 1:8, 9; Rom. 4:1-5) and in Christ Jesus (Gal. 3:22), and that to know God, which is salvation (Gal. 4:8; 1 Thess. 4:5), is to know Christ (2 Cor. 4:6).[35]

Clearly, then, Jesus is Yahweh (or Jehovah) and is eternally self-existent—co-equal and co-eternal with God the Father and God the Holy Spirit. Before time began, Christ was "I AM." He was before all things. Like the Father and the Holy Spirit, He is everlastingly the living one.

After pointing out the above proofs of Jesus' identity as Yahweh:

_____ *Ask...* _____

• In view of the fact that numerous Old Testament passages about Yahweh are directly applied to Jesus in the New Testament, what does this tell you about Jesus' true identity?

You might also want to utilize the information in the following chart when sharing with a Jehovah's Witness. This chart lists the names, titles, and attributes of Yahweh and Jesus, showing their common identity. What is true of Yahweh is also true of Jesus. This is the single most important point you can make to the Jehovah's Witness regarding the issue of the divine name.

A Comparison of Yahweh and Jesus

Description	As Used of Yahweh	As Used of Jesus
Yahweh ("I AM")	Exodus 3:14 Deuteronomy 32:39 Isaiah 43:10	John 8:24 John 8:58 John 18:4-6
God	Genesis 1:1 Deuteronomy 6:4 Psalm 45:6,7	Isaiah 7:14; 9:6 John 1:1,14 John 20:28 Titus 2:13 Hebrews 1:8 2 Peter 1:1
Alpha and Omega (First and Last)	Isaiah 41:4 Isaiah 48:12 Revelation 1:8	Revelation 1:17,18 Revelation 2:8 Revelation 22:12-16
Lord	Isaiah 45:23	Matthew 12:8 Acts 7:59,60 Acts 10:36 Romans 10:12 1 Corinthians 2:8 1 Corinthians 12:3 Philippians 2:10,11
Savior	Isaiah 43:3 Isaiah 43:11 Isaiah 63:8 Luke 1:47 1 Timothy 4:10	Matthew 1:21 Luke 2:11 John 1:29 John 4:42 Titus 2:13 Hebrews 5:9
King	Psalm 95:3 Isaiah 43:15 1 Timothy 6:14-16	Revelation 17:14 Revelation 19:16
Judge	Genesis 18:25 Psalm 50:4,6 Psalm 96:13 Romans 14:10	John 5:22 2 Corinthians 5:10 2 Timothy 4:1

Light	2 Samuel 22:29 Psalm 27:1 Isaiah 42:6	John 1:4,9 John 3:19 John 8:12 John 9:5
Rock	Deuteronomy 32:3,4 2 Samuel 22:32 Psalm 89:26	Romans 9:33 1 Corinthians 10:3,4 1 Peter 2:4-8
Redeemer	Psalm 130:7,8 Isaiah 48:17 Isaiah 54:5 Isaiah 63:9	Acts 20:28 Ephesians 1:7 Hebrews 9:12
Our Righteousness	Isaiah 45:24	Jeremiah 23:6 Romans 3:21,22
Husband	Isaiah 54:5 Hosea 2:16	Matthew 25:1 Mark 2:18,19 2 Corinthians 11:2 Ephesians 5:25-32 Revelation 21:2,9
Shepherd	Genesis 49:24 Psalm 23:1 Psalm 80:1	John 10:11,16 Hebrews 13:20 1 Peter 2:25 1 Peter 5:4
Creator	Genesis 1:1 Job 33:4 Psalm 95:5,6 Psalm 102:25,26 Isaiah 40:28	John 1:2,3,10 Colossians 1:15-18 Hebrews 1:1-3,10
Giver of Life	Genesis 2:7 Deuteronomy 32:39 1 Samuel 2:6 Psalm 36:9	John 5:21 John 10:28 John 11:25
Forgiver of Sin	Exodus 34:6,7 Nehemiah 9:17 Daniel 9:9 Jonah 4:2	Mark 2:1-12 Acts 26:18 Colossians 2:13 Colossians 3:13

Lord Our Healer	Exodus 15:26	Acts 9:34
Omnipresent	Psalm 139:7-12 Proverbs 15:3	Matthew 18:20 Matthew 28:20 Ephesians 3:17; 4:10
Omniscient	1 Kings 8:39 Jeremiah 17:9,10,16	Matthew 11:27 Luke 5:4-6 John 2:25 John 16:30 John 21:17 Acts 1:24
Omnipotent	Isaiah 40:10-31 Isaiah 45:5-13	Matthew 28:18 Mark 1:29-34 John 10:18 Jude 24
Preexistent	Genesis 1:1	John 1:15,30 John 3:13,31,32 John 6:62 John 16:28 John 17:5
Eternal	Psalm 102:26,27 Habakkuk 3:6	Isaiah 9:6 Micah 5:2 John 8:58
Immutable	Isaiah 46:9,16 Malachi 3:6 James 1:17	Hebrews 13:8
Receiver of Worship	Matthew 4:10 John 4:24 Revelation 5:14 Revelation 7:11 Revelation 11:16	Matthew 14:33 Matthew 28:9 John 9:38 Philippians 2:10,11 Hebrews 1:6
Speaker with Divine Authority	"Thus saith the Lord," used hundreds of times	Matthew 23:34-37 John 7:46 "Truly, truly, I say . . ."[36]

3

The Christ of the New World Translation

The New World Translation *is "a frightful mistranslation... erroneous... pernicious... reprehensible."*

—Bruce M. Metzger[1]

The Watchtower Society teaches that Jesus Christ is a mere angel—the first being God created in the universe. As *The Watchtower* magazine puts it, "there is Scriptural evidence for concluding that Michael was the name of Jesus Christ before he left heaven and after his return."[2] Indeed, "'Michael the great prince' is none other than Jesus Christ Himself."[3]

The Watchtower Society says that it was through this created angel that God brought all other things into being. Michael the Archangel was created first, and then he was used by God to create all other things in the universe (*see* Colossians 1:16). The Watchtower book *Aid to Bible Understanding* explains: "Jehovah's first creation was his 'only-begotten Son' (John 3:16), 'the beginning of the creation by God' (Rev. 3:14). This one, 'the first-born of all creation,' was used by Jehovah in creating all other things, those in the heavens and those upon the earth, 'the things visible and the things invisible' (Col. 1:15-17)."[4]

Now, the Jehovah's Witnesses concede that Jesus is a "mighty god," but they deny that He is God Almighty like

Jehovah is.[5] *The Watchtower* magazine asks, "If Jesus of the 'New Testament' is Jehovah of the 'Old Testament,' as many claim, should there not at least be one Biblical reference saying that Jesus is Jehovah? Yet there is not one."[6]

The Jehovah's Witnesses often appeal to a set of so-called proof texts to demonstrate that Jesus is lesser than the Father (Jehovah). For example, Jesus Himself said "the Father is greater than I" (John 14:28). Jesus referred to the Father as "my God" (John 20:17). First Corinthians 11:3 tells us that "the head of Christ is God," and 1 Corinthians 15:28 tells us that Jesus "will be made subject to him who put everything under him, so that God may be all in all." Jesus is called God's "only begotten son" in John 3:16 (NASB), and "the firstborn over all creation" in Colossians 1:15. He is also said to be the "Beginning" of God's creation in Revelation 3:14 (NASB). Clearly, the Jehovah's Witnesses say, Jesus is not God in the same sense Jehovah is.

In keeping with this, the Watchtower Society teaches that Jesus was not worshiped in the same sense that the Father (Jehovah) was. *The Watchtower* magazine says "it is unscriptural for worshipers of the living and true God to render worship to the Son of God, Jesus Christ."[7] Even though the same Greek word used for worshiping Jehovah *(proskuneo)* is used of Jesus Christ, the Watchtower Society says that the word is to be translated "obeisance" and not "worship" when used of Christ. Hence, for example, the *New World Translation* (1971) renders Hebrews 1:6: "But when he again brings his Firstborn into the inhabited earth, he says: 'And let all God's angels do obeisance to him.' "

Besides denying Christ's deity and that He was worshiped as deity, the Watchtower Society also takes a controversial stand on Christ's crucifixion. Jehovah's Witnesses teach that Jesus was not crucified on a cross but rather on a stake. *Awake!* magazine states that "no biblical evidence even intimates that Jesus died on a cross."[8] The cross, Jehovah's Witnesses say, is a pagan religious symbol the church adopted when Satan took control of ecclesiastical authority in the early centuries of

Christianity. *The Watchtower* magazine tells us that "Jesus most likely was executed on an upright stake without any crossbeam. No man today can know with certainty even how many nails were used in Jesus' case."[9]

When Jesus died, He became nonexistent and was raised (or, more accurately, was *re-created*) three days later as a spirit creature (that is, as Michael the Archangel). A *physical* resurrection did not occur. In *Studies in the Scriptures*, we find this statement: "We deny that He was raised in the flesh, and challenge any statement to that effect as being unscriptural."[10]

One reason Jesus didn't rise from the dead in a body of human flesh is related to His work of atonement, the Watchtower Society teaches. The Watchtower publication *You Can Live Forever in Paradise on Earth* says that "having given up his flesh for the life of the world, Christ could never take it again and become a man once more."[11] Christ *forever* sacrificed His human flesh at the cross. Hence, at the "resurrection" He became not a glorified human being but rather was re-created as the archangel Michael.

In keeping with this, the Watchtower Society teaches that Jesus did not appear to His disciples in the same body in which He died. In the Watchtower publication *"The Kingdom Is at Hand,"* we read: "Therefore the bodies in which Jesus manifested himself to his disciples after his return to life were not the body in which he was nailed to the tree."[12] In order to convince Thomas of who He was, "He used a body with wound holes."[13]

What, then, happened to the human body of Jesus that was laid in the tomb? *The Watchtower* magazine reports that His body "was disposed of by Jehovah God, dissolved into its constituent elements or atoms."[14] Indeed, the Watchtower publication *"Things in Which It Is Impossible for God to Lie"* tells us that "the human body of flesh, which Jesus Christ laid down forever as a ransom sacrifice, was disposed of by God's power."[15]

Consistent with Jesus' alleged spiritual resurrection is the teaching that a spiritual "second coming" of Christ occurred in 1914. Words normally translated "coming" in the New Testament (in references to the Second Coming) are translated by the Jehovah's Witnesses as "presence." Hence, the "second coming" refers to Christ's spiritual presence with man since the year 1914. Since Christ returned spiritually, He has been ruling as King on earth through the Watchtower Society.

A key aspect of Watchtower theology is that all the prophecies in Scripture, including those dealing with Armageddon, will take place before "this generation" (Matthew 24:34) passes away. According to the Jehovah's Witnesses, the generation being referred to here is the generation of Witnesses living in 1914 when Christ came again spiritually. And supposedly, all prophecies will be fulfilled before this group of people dies out.

To lend support to its deviant teachings, the Watchtower Society has published a theologically biased translation of the Bible known as the *New World Translation*. Our purpose in the present chapter is to examine how the *New World Translation* *mis*translates key verses that have been traditionally understood to strongly support the deity of Christ. Since Jehovah's Witnesses who show up on your doorstep will likely cite some of these verses when "witnessing" to you, it is critical that you be aware of the distortions in their translation of the Bible.

REASONING FROM THE SCRIPTURES

Colossians 1:16,17—*Christ the Created Creator?*

The Watchtower Teaching. The *New World Translation* renders Colossians 1:16,17, "By means of him *all [other] things* were created in the heavens and upon the earth, the things visible and the things invisible, no matter whether they are thrones or lordships or governments or authorities. *All [other] things* have been created through him and for him. Also, he is before *all [other] things* and by means of him *all [other] things* were made to exist" (emphasis added).

Notice the insertion of the word "other" four times in this passage. The Jehovah's Witnesses' motive for doing this is clear. They do not want it to appear that Christ is *un*created and that He existed before all things. The *New World Translation* makes it appear that Jesus was created *first*, and then He was used by Jehovah to create *all other* things in the universe. The Watchtower publication *"Let God Be True"* comments: "He is not the author of the creation of God; but, after God had created him as his firstborn Son, then God used him as his working Partner in the creating of all the rest of creation."[16] It is also suggested that this created firstborn Son was the "close associate" to whom Jehovah was speaking in Genesis 1:26: "Let *us* make man in *our* image, according to *our* likeness"[17] (emphasis added).

In support of its position, the Watchtower Society points to 1 Corinthians 8:6, which indicates that God created the world "through" (Greek: *dia*) Jesus Christ. The Greek preposition in this verse (*dia*) points to Christ's secondary, lesser role in the creation of the universe.

The Watchtower publication *Aid to Bible Understanding* suggests that Jesus existed for quite a long time prior to man's creation. Citing scientific evidence regarding the estimated age of the universe, it is suggested that Jesus' existence as a spirit creature (that is, as the archangel Michael) began billions of years prior to the creation of the first human being. After this extended time, Jehovah used Jesus to create "all other" things in the universe.[18]

The Watchtower Society tries to justify its insertion of "other" in Colossians 1:16,17 by pointing out that the Greek word for "all" (*panta*) can be translated in some New Testament contexts as "all other" in order to make the English rendition more smooth. As an example, they point to Jesus' words in Luke 13:2: "Do you suppose that these Galileans were greater sinners than *all other* [*panta*] Galileans, because they suffered this fate?" (emphasis added). Because such a translation is acceptable in Luke 13:2, it is also acceptable in Colossians 1:16,17.[19]

The Biblical Teaching. In answering the Jehovah's Witnesses on this issue, it is important to first note that the word "other" appears in brackets in the *New World Translation*'s rendering of Colossians 1:16,17. According to the Foreword in the *New World Translation*, "brackets enclose words inserted to complete the sense in the English text."[20] In other words, they claim that the bracketed word contributes to smoother English *without changing the meaning of the text*.

As noted earlier, the Jehovah's Witnesses often appeal to passages such as Luke 13:2, where the word "other" is added. And, indeed, in Luke 13:2 the addition of the word "other" does not change the meaning of the text and *does* help the English text to read more smoothly. However, the insertion of the word "other" four times in Colossians 1:16,17 *does not* contribute to smoother reading but rather *changes entirely the meaning of the text*.[21] The intent of the Watchtower Society is clear: to enforce the idea that Jesus Christ is a created being and is therefore not God Almighty.

Greek scholar and theologian Robert Reymond concludes that "sheer theological perversity leads the Jehovah's Witnesses in their *New World Translation* to insert the bracketed word 'other' ('all [other] things') throughout the passage in order to justify their Arian view of the son as being properly part of the created order."[22] (Arius was a heretic in the early centuries of Christianity whose view of Christ is a forerunner to the Watchtower position.)

It is highly revealing of the Watchtower Society's dishonesty that the 1950 version of the *New World Translation* did not put brackets around the four insertions of "other" in the text of Colossians 1:16,17.[23] This made it appear that the word was actually translated from the original Greek text. The Watchtower Society was pressured into putting brackets around these words in all editions of the *New World Translation* since 1961 as a result of evangelical scholars openly exposing this perversion of the text of Scripture.[24]

One such scholar is Bruce M. Metzger, who, in an article entitled "The Jehovah's Witnesses and Jesus Christ," said that the word "other" is "not present in the original Greek and was obviously inserted to make the passage refer to Jesus as being on a par with other created things."[25] Metzger points out that Paul originally wrote Colossians in part to combat a notion of Christ similar in some ways to that held by the Jehovah's Witnesses: "Some of the Colossians advocated the Gnostic notion that Jesus was the first of many other created intermediaries between God and men."[26]

When speaking with a Jehovah's Witness about Colossians 1:16,17, you might want to point out that the Watchtower's own Greek interlinear version of the Bible shows that the Greek word *panta* means "all" things and not "all other" things. Despite this, the Watchtower Society continues today to deceive people by inserting the word "other" into the text of Colossians 1:16,17 in the *New World Translation*.

What about the Watchtower claim that Christ played a "junior partner" role in the creation since the New Testament says that God made the world *through* (Greek: *dia*) Christ? This is unacceptable for several reasons. First, while it is true that the Greek word *dia* is used several times of Christ's role as Creator of the universe (John 1:3; 1 Corinthians 8:6; Colossians 1:16; Hebrews 1:2), the New Testament also states that the world came into being through (*dia*) God (Romans 11:36), specifically through (*dia*) the Father (Hebrews 2:10).[27] Hence, as I point out in my book *Christ Before the Manger: The Life and Times of the Preincarnate Christ*, the Greek word *dia* cannot be taken to indicate a secondary, lesser role.[28] Though the New Testament teaches that the world was created "through" Christ, it also teaches that the world was created "through" the Father. Hence, Christ did not act as a junior partner in the creation of the universe.

In view of the above:

_____ *Ask* . . . _____

• Since you conclude that Jesus played a secondary role in making the universe because creation is said to be "through" (*dia*) Christ (John 1:3), then what are we to conclude about Jehovah when Romans

11:36 and Hebrews 2:10 say the universe was created "through" (*dia*) Jehovah?

- If the same word used to describe Jehovah's work in creation is used to describe Christ's work in creation, then doesn't this militate against the Watchtower view that Christ played a secondary role?

It is important to point out to the Jehovah's Witness the scriptural teaching that *only God* is the Creator. God says in Isaiah 44:24: "I, the LORD [Yahweh], am the *maker of all things*, stretching out the heavens *by Myself*, and spreading out the earth *all alone*" (NASB, emphasis added). Clearly, this verse makes it impossible to argue that Christ was created first by Jehovah and then Jehovah created all other things through Christ. The fact that Jehovah is the "maker of all things" who stretched out the heavens "by Myself" and spread out the earth "all alone" (Isaiah 44:24)—and the accompanying fact that Christ Himself is the Creator of "all things" (John 1:3)—proves that Christ is God Almighty, just as the Father is.

_____ Ask... _____

- Jehovah says in Isaiah 44:24, "I, the LORD, am the *maker of all things*, stretching out the heavens *by Myself*, and spreading out the earth *all alone*." How do you reconcile this with the Watchtower teaching that Jehovah first created Christ and then Christ created everything else?

Now, having made these points, let us look briefly at what the apostle Paul is really teaching in Colossians 1:16,17. In this passage Paul affirms that by Christ "all things were created: things in heaven and on earth, visible and invisible, whether thrones or powers or rulers or authorities; all things were created by him and for him. He is before all things, and in him all things hold together" (Colossians 1:16,17).

The little phrase "all things" means that Christ created *the whole universe of things*. Notice that in the space of five verses (verses 16-20), the apostle Paul mentions "all creation," "all things," and "everything"—thereby indicating that Christ is supreme over all. "Every form of matter and life owes its origin to the Son of God, no matter in what sphere it may be found, or with what qualities it may be invested. . . . Christ's creative work was no local or limited operation; it was not bounded by this little orb [earth]."[29] Everything—whether simple or complex, visible or invisible, heavenly or earthly, immanent or transcendent—is the product of Christ.

Paul also states of Christ that "all things were created . . . *for* him" (emphasis added). Creation is "for" Christ in the sense that He is the end for which all things exist. They are meant to serve His will and to contribute to His glory.[30] Christ is truly pre-eminent.

Other passages that speak of Christ as the Creator include John 1:3, Hebrews 1:2,10, and Revelation 3:14. The Son's role as Creator is at the very heart of New Testament revelation. And the significance of the work of creation as ascribed to Christ is that it reveals His divine nature: "There is no doubt that the Old Testament presents God alone as Creator of the universe (Gen. 1, Isa. 40, Ps. 8). And when the disciples of Christ declare Jesus to be the one through whom all things were created, the conclusion that they were thereby attributing deity to him is unavoidable."[31]

Besides being the Creator of the universe, we are told in verse 17 that Christ is the Preserver of the universe: "He is before all things, and *in him all things hold together* (emphasis added)." Verses 16 and 17, taken together, clearly show that the Creator Himself sustains that which He sovereignly brought into being.

In the phrase "before all things," the word "before" indicates that Christ existed before all things in point of time.

"Priority of existence belongs to the great FIRST Cause. He who made all necessarily existed before all. Prior to His creative work, He had filled the unmeasured periods of an unbeginning eternity. Matter is not eternal. . . . He pre-existed it, and called it into being."[32]

Some scholars find significance in the fact that a present tense is used in the phrase "he *is* before all things." Were Christ merely preexistent, one might say that Christ "*was* before all things." The present tense seems to indicate eternal, unending existence. The sense of the phrase is that "he eternally existed before all things."[33]

Paul then makes an astounding statement: "In him all things hold together." Athanasius, early church father and champion of orthodoxy (A.D. 296-373), explained the gist of this verse by suggesting that Christ

> spreads His power over all things everywhere, enlightening things seen and unseen, holding and binding all together in Himself. Nothing is left empty of His presence, but to all things and through all, severally and collectively, He is the giver and sustainer of life. . . . He holds the universe in tune together. He it is who, binding all with each, and ordering all things by His will and pleasure, produces the perfect unity of nature and the harmonious reign of law.[34]

Truly, Christ's powerful arm upholds the universe in all of its grandeur. If He were to withdraw His sustaining power for even just a moment, all things would collapse into chaos. Without denying the validity and use of "secondary causes" (such as the law of gravity,[35] which He Himself ordained), it is Christ who maintains the universe in continuous stability. "His great empire depends upon Him in all its provinces—life, mind, sensation, and matter; atoms beneath us to which geology has not descended, and stars beyond us to which astronomy has never penetrated."[36] Indeed, "the immaterial bonds which hold together the atom as well as the starry heavens are traced in this passage to the power and activity of the Son of God."[37]

Colossians 2:9—*The Fullness of the Deity in Christ*

The Watchtower Teaching. The *New World Translation* renders Colossians 2:9, "Because it is in him that all the *fullness of the divine quality* dwells bodily" (emphasis added). This is in contrast to, for example, the New American Standard Bible which renders the verse, "For in Him all the *fulness of Deity* dwells in bodily form" (emphasis added).

The Jehovah's Witnesses do not want it to appear that the "fulness of Deity" dwells in Jesus. After all, this would mean that Jesus is God Almighty. Thus, they purposely mistranslate this verse to make it appear that only the "fullness of the divine quality" dwells in Jesus. They are willing to concede that Jesus has godlike *qualities*, but that's as far as they will go. This is in keeping with their view that Jesus is "*a* god" (John 1:1, emphasis added).

In keeping with this, the Jehovah's Witnesses flatly deny that Jesus is coequal with the Father. The Watchtower book *Reasoning from the Scriptures* argues, "Being truly 'divinity,' or of 'divine nature,' does not make Jesus as the Son of God coequal and coeternal with the Father, any more than the fact that all humans share 'humanity' or 'human nature' makes them coequal or all the same age."[38]

The Biblical Teaching. Colossians 2:9 is not saying that Jesus has mere divine qualities. Rather, it is saying that the absolute "fulness of Deity" dwells in Christ in bodily form. Scholars are unanimous on this point. For example:

- New Testament scholar Joseph B. Lightfoot says the phrase "fulness of deity" means "the totality of the divine powers and attributes."[39]
- Greek scholar J.H. Thayer—whose Greek lexicon is called "comprehensive" by the Watchtower Society[40]—

says the Greek word in Colossians 2:9 refers to "deity, that is, the state of being God, Godhead."[41]

• Greek scholar Richard C. Trench says that "St. Paul is declaring that in the Son there dwells all the fullness of absolute Godhead. . . . He was, and is, absolute and perfect God."[42]

• Greek scholar John A. Bengel states that the Greek word refers "not merely [to] the *Divine attributes*, but [to] the *Divine Nature* itself."[43]

• Bible scholar H.C.G. Moule states that the Greek word "is as strong as possible; *Deity*, not only *Divinity*."[44]

• Theologian Robert Reymond says the Greek word refers to "the being of the very essence of deity."[45]

• In keeping with all this, theologian Benjamin B. Warfield concludes that "the very deity of God, that which makes God God, in all its completeness, has its permanent home in our Lord, and that in a 'bodily fashion,' that is, it is in Him clothed with a body."[46]

After pointing out the above to a Jehovah's Witness:

_____ *Ask...* _____

• Greek scholars are unanimous that Colossians 2:9 points to the absolute deity of Jesus Christ. Can you name a *single* Greek scholar on par with J.H. Thayer who agrees with the Watchtower rendering of this verse?

The incarnate Christ was just as divine as the Father, and was in no sense less than God as a result of taking on a human nature. Indeed, Paul is declaring in Colossians 2:9 that in the Son there dwells all the *fullness* (literally, "full measure," "completeness," "totality," "sum-total") of absolute divinity: "They were no mere rays of divine glory which gilded Him, lighting up His Person for a season and with splendor not His own; but He was, and is, absolute and perfect God."[47]

Share the above definition of "fullness" with the Jehovah's Witness, and then:

_____ *Ask . . .* _____

- What do you think it says about Christ's nature when it is declared that the "full measure," "complete-ness," "totality," and "sum-total" of deity dwells in Him?

It is highly revealing that even some Watchtower literature supports this correct view. *The Bible in Living English*, trans-lated by Steven T. Byington, was published by the Watchtower Society in 1972, and it renders this verse, "In him all the fullness of deity is resident in bodily form."[48] One must wonder how this slipped by the Watchtower editors!

Zechariah 12:10—*"The One Whom They Pierced"*

The Watchtower Teaching. The *New World Translation* renders Zechariah 12:10, "And I will pour out upon the house of David and upon the inhabitants of Jerusalem the spirit of favor and entreaties, and *they will certainly look to the One whom they pierced through*, and they will certainly wail over Him as in the wailing over an only [son]; and there will be a bitter lamentation over him as when there is bitter lamentation over the firstborn [son]" (emphasis added). By contrast, the New American Standard Bible renders the critical part of this verse, "They will *look on Me* whom they have pierced" (emphasis added).

Here is the critical point: In this passage it is Yahweh (or Jehovah) who is speaking. It is Jehovah God Himself who says (according to the New American Standard Bible and other legitimate translations), "They will *look on Me* whom they have pierced." Obviously, this means that Jesus is Jehovah. But this goes against Watchtower theology. In order to *avoid* Jesus appearing to be Jehovah or Almighty God, the Watchtower Society deliberately altered the text. In the *New World Translation*, it is not Jehovah that is pierced. Rather, "the One" (Jesus, as *distinct from* Jehovah) is pierced.

The Biblical Teaching. There are several points you will want to make as you discuss Zechariah 12:10 with a Jehovah's Witness. First, it is very clear that Yahweh or Jehovah is the speaker in this verse. In fact, verses 2 through 12 are a single discourse tied to the "Thus declares the LORD [Yahweh]" (NASB) in verse 1. Indeed, as Robert Reymond notes, "It is Yahweh who speaks in the first person throughout this segment of the Oracle and accordingly who specifically states that the house of David and the inhabitants of Jerusalem 'will look unto Me whom they pierced.' "[49]

Second, we know beyond any doubt that "Me whom they have pierced" (NASB) is a reference to Jesus Christ. For one thing, John's Gospel interprets this reference as a prophecy of Christ's death on the cross (John 19:37). Also, Jesus is explicitly described as the "pierced" one in Revelation 1:7.

Third, and most important, there is virtually no justification in the Hebrew text for translating the disputed portion of Zechariah 12:10 as "they will certainly look *to the One* whom they pierced through" (emphasis added), as opposed to "they will *look on Me* whom they have pierced" (emphasis added). Indeed, Reymond notes that the rendering "they will look *on Me*" has the support of "the large majority of reliable Hebrew manuscripts, the LXX [Septuagint], the Old Latin [version], the Syriac Peshitta, the Aramaic Targums, and the Greek versions of Aquilla, Symmachus, and Theodotion."[50] In other words, *the majority of the best manuscripts contradict the Watchtower rendering of Zechariah 12:10.*

Very clearly, then, Yahweh Himself positively affirms that "they will look *on Me* whom they have pierced." And since the one "whom they have pierced" is Jesus Christ (John 19:37; Revelation 1:7), it is plain that the verse points to the common identity of Yahweh and Jesus. In other words, Jesus *is* Yahweh. He is just as much God Almighty as God the Father is. No more, and no less.

After going over the above points carefully with a Jehovah's Witness:

_____ *Ask...* _____

- Do you think it is important to use the most reliable manuscripts when translating the Bible? (The answer will be yes.)

- Why does the *New World Translation* go against the majority of the best and most reliable Hebrew manuscripts in regard to the proper rendering of Zechariah 12:10?

- According to the most reliable Hebrew manuscripts available, who is Jesus in Zechariah 12:10?

Acts 20:28—*Purchased by God's Blood*

The Watchtower Teaching. Acts 20:28 in the *New World Translation* reads, "Pay attention to yourselves and to all the flock, among which the holy spirit has appointed you overseers, to shepherd the congregation of God, *which he purchased with the blood of his own [Son]*" (emphasis added). This is in contrast to, for example, the New American Standard Bible's rendering: "Be on guard for yourselves and for all the flock, among which the Holy Spirit has made you overseers, to shepherd *the church of God which He purchased with His own blood*" (emphasis added).

Notice that the *New World Translation* renders this verse to make it appear that the church was purchased not by *God's* blood but by Jesus' (thus portraying Jesus as distinct from God Almighty). The Watchtower Society tries to justify this warped translation by arguing that it agrees with 1 John 1:7, which says that "the blood of Jesus His Son cleanses us from all sin" (NASB). John 3:16 is also sometimes cited. *Reasoning from the Scriptures* comments, "As stated in John 3:16, did God send his only-begotten Son, or did he himself come as a man, so that we might have life? It was the blood, not of God, but of his Son that was poured out."[51]

The Biblical Teaching. The *New World Translation* rendering of this verse goes against all the legitimate translations of Scripture. For example, as noted above, the New American Standard Bible refers to "the church of God which He purchased with His own blood." The New International Version refers to "the church of God, which he bought with his own blood." The King James Version refers to "the church of God, which he hath purchased with his own blood."

Why do these standard translations render the text this way? One reason is that there is not a single Greek manuscript containing the word "Son."[52] Hence, the Watchtower translation—"... which he purchased with the blood *of his own [Son]*"—is unwarranted.[53]

_____ *Ask...* _____

- Why does the Watchtower Society insert the word "Son" into this verse when not a single New Testament Greek manuscript contains the word?

- Do you think it is acceptable to insert words into the Bible that are not found in the original Greek manuscripts?

Regarding the Greek text of this passage, renowned Greek scholar A.T. Robertson comments that the church was purchased "through the agency of (*dia*) his own blood. Whose blood? If *tou theou* (God) is correct, as it is, then Jesus is here called 'God' who shed his own blood for the flock. It will not do to say that Paul did not call Jesus God, for we have Rom. 9:5;

Col. 2:9; and Tit. 2:13 where he does that very thing, besides Col. 1:15-20 and Phil. 2:5-11."[54]

As you discuss the correct meaning of Acts 20:28 with a Jehovah's Witness, it is critical to point out that in the incarnation Jesus was both *fully God* and *fully man*. As God, He had all the attributes of deity. As a man, He had all the attributes of humanity. Though Christ had *two natures*—one human and one divine—He was always *one person*. In the incarnation, the person of Christ is the partaker of the attributes of both natures so that whatever may be affirmed of either nature—human or divine—may be affirmed of *one person*.

In His human nature, Christ knew hunger (Luke 4:2), weariness (John 4:6), and the need for sleep (Luke 8:23). In His divine nature, Christ was omniscient (John 2:24), omnipresent (John 1:48), and omnipotent (John 11). And all of these—the attributes of both His human nature and His divine nature—were experienced by the *one person* of Christ.

With that in mind, it is significant to note that both human and divine characteristics and deeds may be attributed to Christ's person under *any of His names*—whether they be divine or human titles.[55] Indeed, "regardless of the designation Scripture employs, the *person* of the Son, and not one of His natures, is always the subject of the statement."[56] Theologian Robert Gromacki explains:

> It is proper to say that Jesus was the Redeemer even though no human could save another. It is also correct to state that the Son of God thirsted although God doesn't have to drink to sustain Himself. *Human attributes were ascribed to Him under a divine title*: Emmanuel, the Son of God, was born (Matt. 1:23; Luke 1:35) and the Lord of glory was crucified (1 Cor. 2:8). On the opposite side, *divine attributes were ascribed to Him under a human title*: the Son of man ascended to heaven where He was before (John 6:62) and the slain Lamb was worthy

to receive power, riches, wisdom, strength, honor, glory, and blessing (Rev. 5:12).[57]

Now, here's the important point: Obviously, God *as God* does not bleed. He has no blood in His divine nature to shed. However, Christ in the incarnation is the God-man. It is from the vantage point of His manhood that Christ could shed His blood. Yet, as noted above, human attributes can be ascribed to Christ under a divine title. This is the case in Acts 20:28. We find a reference to God, who purchased the church "with His own blood." Christ is referred to with a divine name ("God"), but the action ascribed to Him is rooted in His humanity (He shed His "blood"). Clearly, then, the thought of Acts 20:28 is that "it was at the cost of the life of the *incarnate* Second Person of the Godhead that the elect people of God were redeemed."[58] Christ the God-man shed His blood.

After going over all this very carefully with the Jehovah's Witness:

___ Ask... ___

- Since Christ is both *fully God* and *fully man*—and since both human and divine characteristics and deeds may be attributed to Christ's person under *any of His names* (whether they be divine or human titles)—can you see how Christ as God can be said to shed His blood to purchase the church?

If he or she says no, then carefully go over the above facts again—looking up and reading aloud each Bible reference cited.

Titus 2:13—*Our Great God and Savior*

The Watchtower Teaching. The *New World Translation* renders Titus 2:13, "While we wait for the happy hope and glorious manifestation of *the great God and of [the] Savior of us, Christ Jesus*" (emphasis added). This is in contrast to, for example, the New American Standard Bible, which renders this verse, "Looking for the blessed hope and the appearing of the glory of *our great God and Savior, Christ Jesus*" (emphasis added).

Notice how the two translations are different. The Jehovah's Witnesses mistranslate Titus 2:13 to make it appear that two different persons are in view—God Almighty and Christ the Savior. Yet all legitimate translations have only one person in view in this verse—our great God and Savior, Jesus Christ.

The Jehovah's Witnesses attempt to justify this warped translation by asking which rendering agrees with Titus 1:4, which refers to "God the Father *and* Christ Jesus our Savior" (emphasis added). Though they acknowledge that God Himself is sometimes called "Savior," Titus 1:4 clearly distinguishes God Almighty from the One through whom He saves the world (Jesus Christ).[59] Thus they reason that this same distinction must be carried over to Titus 2:13.

The Biblical Teaching. A study of the Old Testament indicates that it is *only God* who saves. In Isaiah 43:11, God asserts: "I, even I, am the LORD [Yahweh], and apart from me *there is no savior*" (emphasis added). This is an extremely important verse, for it indicates that 1) a claim to be Savior is, in itself, a claim to deity; and 2) there is only *one* Savior—God.

Since the New Testament clearly refers to Jesus Christ as the Savior, the only conclusion that makes sense is that Christ is indeed God. Shortly after His birth, an angel appeared to a group of nearby shepherds and said, "Today in the town of David a Savior has been born to you; he is Christ the Lord" (Luke 2:11). John's Gospel records the conclusion reached by the Samaritans: Jesus "really is the Savior of the world" (John 4:42).

_____ *Ask* . . . _____

- If *only God* can save—and if there is *no other Savior* than God (Isaiah 43:11)—then doesn't this mean

that New Testament references to Jesus *as Savior*
point to His deity?

• If not, then how do you reconcile Jesus' role as
Savior with Isaiah 43:11?

In Titus 2:13 Paul encourages Titus to await the blessed
hope, the "glorious appearing of our great God and Savior,
Jesus Christ." An examination of Titus 2:10-13, 3:4, and 3:6
reveals that the phrases *God our Savior* and *Jesus Christ our
Savior* are used interchangeably four times. The parallel truths
that only God is the Savior (Isaiah 43:11) and that Jesus
Himself is the Savior constitute a powerful evidence for
Christ's deity.

One must keep in mind that the apostle Paul (who wrote
Titus) had been trained in the strictest form of Judaism (its
main tenet being *monotheism*—the belief that there is only one
true God). It is against this backdrop that Paul unabashedly
affirms that Jesus is "our great God and Savior."

Now, we must emphasize that Greek grammarians have
taken a solid stand against the Watchtower's view that there
are *two* persons—Jehovah *and* the Savior Jesus—in Titus
2:13. Indeed, these scholars are emphatic that only *one*
person—"our great God and Savior, Jesus Christ"—is found
in this verse. Greek scholar Bruce Metzger writes:

> In support of this translation ["our great God and
> Savior"] there may be quoted such eminent gram-
> marians of the Greek New Testament as P.W.
> Schmiedel, J.H. Moulton, A.T. Robertson, and
> Blass-Debrunner. All of these scholars concur in
> the judgment that only one person is referred to in
> Titus 2:13 and that therefore, it must be rendered,
> "our great God and Savior, Jesus Christ."[60]

Likewise, Dana and Mantey's authoritative *Manual Grammar of the Greek New Testament* positively affirms that Titus

2:13 "asserts that Jesus is the great God and Savior."[61]

Such Greek scholars argue their case based upon a detailed study of a number of identical sentence constructions in the Greek New Testament. Greek scholars have thus come up with a guiding principle or rule for interpreting such constructions: "When two nouns in the same case are connected by the Greek word 'and,' and the first noun is preceded by the article 'the,' and the second noun is not preceded by the article, the second noun refers to the same person or thing to which the first noun refers, and is a farther description of it."[62]

In Titus 2:13, two nouns—"God" and "Savior"—are joined together with the Greek word for "and," and a definite article ("the") is placed only in front of the first noun ("God").[63] The sentence literally reads: "*the* great God *and* Savior of us." In this particular sentence construction in the Greek New Testament, the *two nouns* in question—"God" and "Savior"—are referring to the *same* person, Jesus Christ.[64] As scholar Robert Reymond explains, "The two nouns ['God' and 'Savior'] both stand under the regimen of the single definite article preceding 'God,' indicating . . . that they are to be construed corporately, not separately, or that they have a single referent."[65] Indeed, "the presence of only one definite article has the effect of binding together the two titles ['God' and 'Savior']."[66] (For those interested in a detailed study of this type of sentence construction in the Greek, excellent materials are available.[67])

After discussing that carefully with the Jehovah's Witness:

_____ *Ask. . .* _____

- In view of what top Greek scholars say about Titus 2:13, are you willing to consider the possibility that only one person is in view in this verse and not two?

- If only one person is in view in Titus 2:13, then what does this tell you about Jesus' true identity?

Another indication that only one person (Jesus Christ) is present in Titus 2:13 is the fact that the Greek word for "appearing" ("looking for the blessed hope and the *appearing* of the glory of our great God and Savior, Christ Jesus" NASB) is used by the apostle Paul *exclusively* of Jesus Christ in the New Testament (*see* 2 Thessalonians 2:8; 1 Timothy 6:14; 2 Timothy 1:10; 4:1,8; Titus 2:13).[68] Robert Reymond notes that "inasmuch as 'appearing' is never referred to the Father but is consistently employed to refer to Christ's return in glory, the *prima facie* conclusion is that the 'appearing of the glory of our great God' refers to Christ's appearing and not to the Father's appearing."[69]

Along these same lines, the *New Treasury of Scripture Knowledge* points out that those who deny the above "are faced with the problem that if two persons are meant, then Paul is predicting the simultaneous glorious advent of both the Father and the Son at Christ's second coming."[70] Such an idea is completely foreign to the whole of Scripture.

Now, there is one further point that bears mentioning. Notice that in the New Testament, Jesus placed Himself on an equal par with the Father as the proper object of men's trust. Jesus the Savior told the disciples: "Do not let your hearts be troubled. Trust in God; *trust also in me*" (John 14:1, emphasis added). Reymond notes that "if Jesus was not in fact divine, such a saying would constitute blasphemy of the first order."[71] Truly Jesus is both God *and* Savior!

_____ *Ask...* _____

- If Jesus placed Himself on an equal par with the Father as the proper object of men's trust (as He did in John 14:1), then wouldn't this have been blasphemy unless Jesus Himself was truly God and Savior?

Hebrews 1:8—*"Thy Throne, O God..."*

The Watchtower Teaching. Hebrews 1:8 in the *New World Translation* reads, "But with reference to the Son: '*God is your throne forever and ever*, and [the] scepter of your kingdom is the scepter of uprightness'" (emphasis added). This is in contrast to, for example, the New American Standard Bible, which renders this verse, "But of the Son He [the Father] says, '*Thy throne, O God*, is forever and ever, and the righteous scepter is the scepter of His kingdom'" (emphasis added, insert mine).

The Watchtower Society mistranslates this verse so that Jesus cannot be called "God." It is made to appear that Jesus' power and authority has its source in Jehovah God ("God is your throne forever").[72] The meaning is entirely changed from one that *exalts* Jesus to one that *diminishes* Jesus.

The Watchtower Society argues that Hebrews 1:8 is a quote from Psalm 45:6, which in its context was addressed not to God but to a human king of Israel. Obviously, the writer of this verse did not think that this Israelite king was Almighty God.[73] Rather, Jehovah God is portrayed as the source of this king's authority. The same is true, then, regarding Jesus in Hebrews 1:8.

The Biblical Teaching. The *New World Translation* goes against all the standard, legitimate translations of Hebrews 1:8. Similar to the New American Standard Bible, the New International Version reads, "Your throne, O God, will last for ever and ever." Likewise, the King James Version reads, "Thy throne, O God, is for ever and ever."

We must acknowledge that the Watchtower translation "God is your throne" is grammatically possible from the Greek text.[74] But—as scholars *unanimously* agree—it is entirely foreign to the context. That is one reason legitimate translations *always* render the phrase to read, "Thy throne, O God."

Context is extremely important in Hebrews 1. The reader must keep in mind that one of the primary purposes of Hebrews, particularly in chapter 1, is to demonstrate the superiority of Jesus Christ—His superiority to the prophets (1:1-4), to the angels (1:5–2:18), and to Moses (3:1-6). How is this superiority demonstrated? Well, for example, Christ is shown to be God's ultimate revelation (verse 1); He is the Creator and Sustainer of the universe (verses 2,3); and He has the very nature of God (verse 3). None of these things could be said of the prophets (or the angels or Moses, for that matter)!

Now, in Hebrews 1:5–2:18 we read about Christ's superiority over the angels. In verse 6, for example, we are told that Christ is worshiped by the angels. In view of this, here's the problem with verse 8: If the point of Hebrews 1:8 was simply to show that Jesus derives His authority from Jehovah God, as the Watchtower Society argues, then *Jesus' superiority is not demonstrated in the least*. After all, the angels (and the prophets and Moses) *also* derived their authority from Jehovah God.[75] The Watchtower interpretation is completely foreign to the context of the passage.

___ *Ask...* ___

- If the purpose of Hebrews 1:5–2:18 is to demonstrate Jesus' superiority over the angels (as the context clearly indicates), then how does the Watchtower interpretation of Hebrews 1:8 show such superiority?

By contrast, the translation, "Thy throne, O God, is forever and ever" (NASB) fits the context perfectly. It shows that, in contrast to the angels, Christ's throne—His sovereign rule—will endure forever. This is consistent with what we learn elsewhere in Scripture regarding Christ's kingship.

For example, Genesis 49:10 prophesied that the Messiah would come from the tribe of Judah and reign as a king. The Davidic covenant in 2 Samuel 7:16 promised a Messiah who would have a dynasty, a people over whom He would rule, and an *eternal* throne. In Psalm 2:6, God the Father is portrayed announcing the installation of God the Son as King in Jerusalem. Psalm 110 affirms that the Messiah will subjugate His enemies and rule over them. Daniel 7:13,14 tells us that the Messiah-King will have an *everlasting* dominion. These and many other Old Testament passages point to Christ's role as sovereign King.

When we get to the New Testament, we find that before Jesus was born an angel appeared to Mary and told her: "You will be with child and give birth to a son. . . . The Lord God will give him the throne of his father David, and he will reign over the house of Jacob *forever*; his kingdom *will never end*" (Luke 1:31-33, emphasis added).

After Jesus was born in Bethlehem, some Magi from the east came to Jerusalem and asked, "Where is the one who has been born king of the Jews? We saw his star in the east and have come to worship him" (Matthew 2:1,2). When they found Jesus, they bowed down and worshiped Him, even though He was just a babe (verse 11).

During His three-year ministry, Jesus proclaimed the good news of the kingdom to thousands of people (Matthew 9:35). He also told many parables to help them understand more about the nature of the kingdom (Matthew 13ff.). Certainly the kingdom was the very core of His teachings.

The Book of Revelation tells us that when Christ returns to earth in physical, bodily form, He will come as KING OF KINGS AND LORD OF LORDS (Revelation 19:16). In that day, there shall be no dispute as to Christ's right to rule on the throne of God.

The point of all this is simply to illustrate that Christ's eternal kingship and right to rule on the throne is a common and consistent emphasis in Scripture. Hence, the phrase "Thy throne, O God, is forever and ever" (NASB) not only perfectly fits the context of the Book of Hebrews, it also fits the context of all of Scripture as well.

The Jehovah's Witness may try to argue that only Jehovah-God can reign on the throne of God. If this happens, point out that Jesus Himself said that "all that belongs to the Father is mine" (John 16:15). Also, Revelation 22:1 makes explicit reference to "the throne of God *and of the Lamb*" (emphasis added)—indicating that Christ rightfully sits on the throne of God, exercising the same authority as the Father.

There is one further consideration. Hebrews 1:8, as noted earlier, is actually a quotation from Psalm 45:6. It is important to note that in Psalm 45:5 *and* 6 we find a clear example of Hebrew parallelism. This means the literary structure of one verse is seen to be identical to that of another. Theologian Millard Erickson notes that "God is your throne" is "a most unlikely interpretation, because the preceding verse in the Septuagint translation of the psalm which is being quoted begins, 'Thy weapons, O Mighty One, are sharpened,' and the nature of Hebrew parallelism is such as to require the rendering, 'Thy throne, O God.'"[76] In other words, verse 5 says, "Thy weapons, *O Mighty One*" (emphasis added). And because this verse has a literary structure that is parallel to verse 6, the only translation that does justice to verse 6 is, "Thy throne, *O God*." Hence, the Watchtower rendering of Hebrews 1:8 is unacceptable.

After sharing this with the Jehovah's Witness:

_____ *Ask . . .* _____

- In view of the nature of Hebrew parallelism, can you see how the Watchtower's translation of Hebrews 1:8—"God is your throne"—is unacceptable?

The Truth About the
New World Translation

From reading all the above, it seems utterly clear that a primary goal of the *New World Translation* committee was to strip from the Bible any vestige of Jesus Christ's identification with Yahweh.[77] The fact is, the *New World Translation* is an incredibly biased translation.

Dr. Robert Countess, who wrote a doctoral dissertation on the Greek text of the *New World Translation*, concluded that the translation "has been sharply unsuccessful in keeping doctrinal considerations from influencing the actual translation.... It must be viewed as a radically biased piece of work. At some points it is actually dishonest. At others it is neither modern nor scholarly."[78] No wonder British scholar H.H. Rowley asserted, "From beginning to end this volume is a shining example of how the Bible should not be translated."[79] Indeed, Rowley said, this translation is "an insult to the Word of God."[80]

Are Drs. Countess and Rowley alone in their assessment of the *New World Translation*? By no means! Dr. Julius Mantey, author of *A Manual Grammar of the Greek New Testament*, calls the *New World Translation* "a shocking mistranslation."[81] Dr. Bruce M. Metzger, professor of New Testament at Princeton University, calls the *New World Translation* "a frightful mistranslation," "erroneous," "pernicious," and "reprehensible."[82] Dr. William Barclay concluded that "the deliberate distortion of truth by this sect is seen in their New Testament translation.... It is abundantly clear that a sect which can translate the New Testament like that is intellectually dishonest."[83]

Now, in view of this universal "thumbs down" by legitimate biblical scholars, it is highly revealing that the Watchtower Society has always resisted efforts to identify members of the *New World Translation* committee. The claim was that they preferred to remain anonymous and humble, giving God the credit and glory for this translation. However, as former Jehovah's Witness David Reed notes, "An unbiased observer will quickly note that such anonymity also shields the translators from any blame for errors or distortions in their renderings. And it prevents scholars from checking their credentials."[84]

The Watchtower Society must have been utterly embarrassed when the names of the translators of the *New World Translation* were made known to the public. The reason for that is the translation committee was completely unqualified for the task. Four of the five men in the committee had no Hebrew or Greek training whatsoever (they had only a high-school education). The fifth—Fred W. Franz—claimed to know Hebrew and Greek, but upon examination under oath in a court of law in Edinburgh, Scotland, he was found to fail a simple Hebrew test.

Note the following cross-examination, which took place November 24, 1954, in this court:

> "Have you also made yourself familiar with Hebrew?"
> *"Yes."*
> "So that you have a substantial linguistic apparatus at your command?"
> *"Yes, for use in my biblical work."*
> "I think you are able to read and follow the Bible in Hebrew, Greek, Latin, Spanish, Portuguese, German, and French?"
> *"Yes."*[85]

The following day, Franz was put on the stand again, and the following interview took place:

> "You, yourself, read and speak Hebrew, do you?"
> *"I do not speak Hebrew."*
> "You do not?"
> *"No."*
> "Can you translate that into Hebrew?"
> *"Which?"*
> "That fourth verse of the second chapter of Genesis?"
> *"You mean here?"*
> "Yes."
> *"No."*[86]

The truth of the matter is that Franz—like the others on the *New World Translation* committee—cannot translate Hebrew or Greek. In fact, Franz dropped out of the University of Cincinnati after his sophomore year—and even while there, he had not studied anything related to theological issues.

If the average Jehovah's Witness only knew the true history of the translation he holds to so dearly...

4

Jehovah's Witnesses and the Gospel of John

I can assure you that the rendering which the Jehovah's Witnesses give John 1:1 is not held by any reputable Greek scholar.

—Charles L. Feinberg[1]

Without doubt, John's Gospel is the richest book in the New Testament in regard to various evidences for Christ's deity. Unlike the Synoptic Gospel writers (Matthew, Mark, and Luke), John begins his Gospel in eternity: *"In the beginning* was the Word, and the Word was with God, and the Word was God" (John 1:1, emphasis added). It is from this eternal perspective that John understands the true significance of the work of Christ.

In John's Gospel, Jesus claims to be God (John 8:58), is recognized by others as being God (20:28), and is portrayed as being preexistent and eternal (1:15,30; 3:31), self-existent (1:4; 5:26), omnipresent (1:47-49), omniscient (2:25; 16:30; 21:17), omnipotent (1:3; 2:19; 11:1-44), and sovereign (5:21,22, 27-29; 10:18). Christ is also recognized as being the Creator of the universe (1:3), and He claims to be the theme of the entire Old Testament (5:39,40). These and many other evidences in John's Gospel point to the full deity of Jesus Christ.

Consequently, the Watchtower Society must do something to "take the wind out of the sails" of John's Gospel. They do this (surprise!) by mistranslating key verses. In this chapter, our goal will be to consider how the Jehovah's Witnesses distort John 1:1 and 8:58. In so doing, we will unearth even further evidence regarding the deviousness of the *New World Translation*.

_____ REASONING FROM THE SCRIPTURES _____

John 1:1—*Jesus Christ: "a god" or "God"?*

The *New World Translation* renders John 1:1, "In the beginning the Word was, and the Word was with *God*, and the Word was *a god*" (emphasis added). Notice the two references to God in this verse (the Greek word for "God" in both cases is *theos*). The Watchtower Society teaches that there is justification for translating the first occurrence of *theos* as "God" but the last occurrence as "a god." This is in contrast to all standard Bible translations (the King James Version, the New American Standard Bible, the New International Version, and so on), which translate both occurrences of *theos* as "God."

How does the Watchtower Society argue its position? First, the Society notes that in the Greek text there is a definite article "the" (Greek: *ho*) before the first occurrence of "God" (*ho theos*—literally, "the God"). However, there is *no* definite article ("the") before the second occurrence of "God" in the Greek text (it simply reads *theos*—literally, "God").[2]

Now, I don't want to get too technical—but I need to try to explain the Watchtower view, and frankly, it's a little complex. Please try to stay with me in what follows.

The Watchtower Society argues that in the Greek text, a noun (such as "God") joined to a definite article ("the") points to an *identity* or a *personality*. Thus, the first occurrence of "God" (*theos*) in John 1:1—since it is preceded by the definite article "the" (*ho*)—points to the person of Jehovah-God. Now, while *ho theos* is viewed as referring to the person of Jehovah-God in this verse, *The Watchtower* magazine points out by contrast that the same phrase (*ho theos*) is never used of Jesus Christ in the New Testament.[3]

In regard to the second occurrence of "God" (*theos*) in John 1:1, the Watchtower Society argues that in the Greek text, when a singular predicate noun (such as the second occurrence of "God" in John 1:1) has no definite article ("the") and it occurs *before* the verb (as is true in the Greek text of John 1:1), then this points to a *quality* about someone.

As the Watchtower publication *Reasoning from the Scriptures* puts it, the Greek text of John 1:1 "is not saying that the Word (Jesus) was the same as the God *with whom* he was but, rather, that the Word was godlike, divine, a god."[4] So, the Watchtower Society teaches, the Word (Jesus) has a *divine quality* but is not God Almighty.[5] Jehovah's Witnesses therefore say that Jesus is "a god."

What further justification is there for calling Jesus "a god"? For one thing, the Watchtower Society says, Jesus truly is a "mighty one" and is before all other creatures. Also, He holds a high official capacity. Moreover, because He is the *Son of God*—because He is in a pre-eminent position as God's "Firstborn"—because Jehovah created all other things in the universe through Him—and because He is God's "spokesman"[6]—He is rightly called "a god." But still, *He is not God Almighty like Jehovah is.*[7] Indeed, there is only one Almighty God, and that is Jehovah.[8]

According to Watchtower authorities, the proof that Jesus is not God Almighty is based on the fact that the Word was said to be "with God." If He was *with* Almighty God, then, of course, He could not *be* that Almighty God.[9] In other words, one cannot at the same time be *with* a person and be the *same as* that person.

Further justification for the Watchtower rendering of John 1:1 is found in a number of biblical authorities. For example:

> • Dr. Julius R. Mantey—a Greek scholar who is the coauthor of the authoritative text *A Manual Grammar of the Greek New Testament*—is cited as supporting the Watchtower translation, "the Word was a god."[10]

• Dr. Philip B. Harner's scholarly article entitled "Qualitative Anarthrous Predicate Nouns" in the *Journal of Biblical Literature* is cited as supporting the Watchtower translation.[11]

• Dr. John L. McKenzie's *Dictionary of the Bible* is cited as supporting the Watchtower translation.[12]

• The translation of the New Testament by Johannes Greber (1937) was cited for many years as supporting the Watchtower translation.[13]

Surely the support of such biblical authorities means that the Watchtower translation of John 1:1 must be correct. So many fine scholars could not possibly be wrong.

The Biblical View of John 1:1

Before examining the text of John 1:1, it is critical that we investigate the biblical authorities cited above. Our purpose will be to discover whether the Watchtower's translation of John 1:1 really enjoys the widespread scholarly support that is claimed.

Citing Johannes Greber As an Authority

It is true that Johannes Greber rendered the latter part of John 1:1 as "the Word was a god" (*The New Testament*, 1937).[14] However, is Greber really a biblical scholar?

By no means! In fact, Johannes Greber was a spiritist who authored a book entitled *Communication with the Spirit World of God*. In this book, Greber claims that spirits helped him in his translation of the New Testament.[15] Greber also reported seeing the translation come in "large illuminated letters and words passing before his eyes."[16]

According to the April 1, 1983, issue of *The Watchtower* magazine, the Watchtower Society claims that it didn't discover Greber was a spiritist until the 1980 edition of his New Testament was published.[17] The Society says that when it discovered this heinous fact, it immediately ceased citing Greber.

This is a blatant fabrication and misrepresentation of the facts. In reality, the Watchtower knew as far back as 1956, that Johannes Greber was a spiritist.[18] The February 15, 1956, issue of *The Watchtower* magazine contains nearly a full page on Greber and his spiritism.[19] Yet, despite the knowledge that Greber was a spiritist, the Society continued to cite him as an authority in support of its translation of John 1:1 (*see* the 1961 edition of the *New World Translation*).

_____ *Ask*... _____

- What does it say about the Watchtower Society when you know that, for over twenty years, it knowingly cited an occultic spiritist—Johannes Greber—in support of its rendering of John 1:1?

Misquoting Julius R. Mantey

Did Julius R. Mantey, author of *A Manual Grammar of the Greek New Testament*, really support the Watchtower translation of John 1:1? On the contrary, he utterly repudiated it!

Dr. Mantey was personally interviewed by Dr. Walter Martin of the Christian Research Institute. In the interview, Martin asked Mantey about the Watchtower translation of John 1:1, "The Word was *a god*." Mantey responded: "The Jehovah's Witnesses have forgotten entirely what the order of the sentence indicates—that the 'Logos' [or Word] has the same substance, nature, or essence as the Father. To indicate that Jesus was just 'a god,' the Jehovah's Witnesses would have to use a completely different construction in the Greek."[20]

Dr. Martin then responded, "You once had a little difference of opinion with the Watchtower about this and wrote them a letter. What was their response to your letter?"[21]

Dr. Mantey said, "Well...I was disturbed because they had misquoted me in support of their translation. I called their attention to the fact that the whole body of the New Testament was against their view. Throughout the New Testament, Jesus is glorified and magnified—yet here they were denigrating Him and making Him into a little god of a pagan concept."[22]

Noting that the Jehovah's Witnesses are notorious for quoting biblical scholars in support of their theology, Dr. Martin asked Dr. Mantey, "Do they quote these people in context?"[23]

Dr. Mantey responded, "No. They use this device to fool people into thinking that scholars agree with the Jehovah's Witnesses. Out of all the Greek professors, grammarians, and commentators they have quoted, only one (a Unitarian) agreed that 'the word was *a god.*'"[24]

Dr. Mantey then spoke of the deceptive nature of the *New World Translation*: "I believe it's a terrible thing for a person to be deceived and go into eternity lost, *forever lost* because somebody deliberately misled him by distorting the Scripture! . . . Ninety-nine percent of the scholars of the world who know Greek and who have helped translate the Bible are in disagreement with the Jehovah's Witnesses. People who are looking for the truth ought to know what the *majority* of the scholars really believe. They should not allow themselves to be misled by the Jehovah's Witnesses and end up in hell."[25]

Misquoting Philip B. Harner

Philip B. Harner is another scholar who has been misquoted in favor of the *New World Translation*'s rendering of John 1:1. Not only does Harner's article in the *Journal of Biblical Literature* not support the Watchtower's rendering of John 1:1, he emphatically argues against it![26]

Without going into all the technical details of Harner's article, he clearly states that had the Greek sentence of John 1:1 been constructed in a particular way (*ho logos en theos*), then it *could* be translated as "the Word was a god." But John did not use that construction. Rather, he wrote the sentence in such a way (*theos en ho logos*) that it can *only* mean that the Word is as fully God as the other person called "God" (the Father), with whom He existed "in the beginning"—"the

Word was *with God*, and the Word *was God*"[27] (emphasis added). Because of the word order used by John, the verse can only be interpreted to mean that the Word (Jesus) was God in the same sense as the Father.[28]

Misquoting John L. McKenzie

Still another scholar quoted out of context by the translators of the *New World Translation* is John L. McKenzie. By citing McKenzie out of context and by quoting only a portion of his article, he is made to *appear* to teach that the Word (Jesus) is less than Jehovah because he said "the word was a divine being."[29] The Watchtower reasoning seems to be that since Jesus was just a "divine being," He is less than Jehovah.[30] However, as apologist Robert M. Bowman correctly notes, "On the same page McKenzie calls *Yahweh* (Jehovah) 'a divine personal being'; McKenzie also states that Jesus is called 'God' in both John 20:28 and Titus 2:13 and that John 1:1-18 expresses 'an identity between God and Jesus Christ.'"[31] So McKenzie's words actually argue *against* the Watchtower position.

After sharing the above with a Jehovah's Witness:

_____ *Ask...* _____

- What conclusion can you make about the Watchtower Society when you learn that it consistently quotes scholars *out of context* to support its distorted views?

Only One True God

Having shown that the Watchtower Society consistently misrepresents what various scholars have said about John 1:1, you must then emphasize that the polytheistic teaching that there is both a "God Almighty" *and* a lesser "mighty god" goes against the clear teaching of Scripture that there is only one true God (e.g., John 17:3). Note, for example, the following key passages from the Old Testament:

- "See now that I, I am He, And *there is no god besides Me*" (Deuteronomy 32:39 NASB, emphasis added).
- "Before Me there was *no God* formed, and there will be *none* after Me" (Isaiah 43:10 NASB, emphasis added).
- "Is there *any God* besides Me, or is there any other Rock? *I know of none*" (Isaiah 44:8 NASB, emphasis added).
- "I am the LORD, and there is no other; *besides Me there is no God*" (Isaiah 45:5 NASB, emphasis added).

In view of such passages, it is patently obvious that the interpretation of John 1:1 that which argues for both a "God Almighty" and a lesser "god" cannot be reconciled with the rest of Scripture.

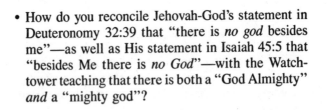

_____ *Ask...* _____

- How do you reconcile Jehovah-God's statement in Deuteronomy 32:39 that "there is *no god* besides me"—as well as His statement in Isaiah 45:5 that "besides Me there is *no God*"—with the Watchtower teaching that there is both a "God Almighty" *and* a "mighty god"?

The Truth About Definite Articles

The Watchtower Society argues that since the second occurrence of *theos* ("God") in John 1:1 has no definite article ("the"), it thus refers to a lesser deity who simply has godlike qualities. But must *theos* ("God") without *ho* ("the") refer to someone less than Jehovah?

By no means! You must emphasize to the Jehovah's Witness that the Greek word *theos* ("God") without the definite article *ho* ("the") is used of Jehovah-God in the New Testament—with the exact same Greek construction used of Jesus in John 1:1. Indeed, the *Greek-English Lexicon of the New Testament and Other Early Christian Literature* by William F. Arndt and F. Wilbur Gingrich says that the word *theos* is used "quite predominantly of the true God, sometimes *with*, sometimes *without* the article."[32] An example of this is Luke 20:38, where we read of Jehovah, "He is *a God*, not of the dead, but of the living" (NWT, emphasis added).[33] Clearly, then, a Jehovah's Witness cannot say Jesus is not God Almighty on the basis that the second *theos* in John 1:1 lacks a definite article.

____ *Ask*... ____

- If the Greek word for God (*theos*) can be used of Jehovah without a definite article in New Testament passages like Luke 20:38, doesn't this undermine the Watchtower argument that Jesus is a *lesser* god because the definite article is not used with *theos* in John 1:1?

Translating Nouns That Have No Definite Article

It is critical to recognize that it's not necessary to translate Greek nouns that have no definite article as having an *in*definite article.[34] In other words, *theos* ("God") without the definite article *ho* ("the") does not need to be translated as "*a* God" as the Jehovah's Witnesses have done. Greek grammarians—including Julius Mantey and E.C. Colwell—agree that *theos* in John 1:1 most definitely does not have an "indefinite" sense, and thus should not be translated with an indefinite article ("a").[35] (Those who are interested in the more technical aspects of translating from the Greek text should study Colwell's Rule.[36])

The Need for Consistency

In his book *Scripture Twisting*, James Sire notes that "the *New World Translation* is not consistent in the application of their rule by which they claim to translate 'a god.' "[37] In other words, if we translate other passages in the New Testament the way the Jehovah's Witnesses translate John 1:1, we come out with some very strange-reading verses indeed. Matthew 5:9 is an example: "Blessed are the peacemakers, for they will be called sons *of a god*" (instead of "sons of God"). Likewise, the rule of consistency would force us to translate John 1:6, "There came a man who was sent from *a god*" (instead of "sent from God"). We would also have to translate John 1:18, "No one has ever seen *a god*" (instead of "seen God").

Walter Martin thus rightly points out that in the Greek text the lack of an article with *theos* does not mean that a god other than the true God of Scripture is in mind. "Let one examine these passages where the article is not used with *theos* and see if the rendering 'a god' makes sense (Matt. 5:9; 6:24; Luke 1:35,78; 2:40; John 1:6,12,13,18; 3:2,21; 9:16,33; Rom. 1:7,17,18; 1 Cor. 1:30; 15:10; Phil. 2:11,13; Titus 1:1)."[38] Martin's point is that "the writers of the New Testament frequently *do not* use the article with *theos* and yet the meaning is perfectly clear in the context, namely that the one true God is intended"[39] (emphasis added).

Christ Didn't Just Have "Divine Qualities"

Any translation that renders the Greek text in John 1:1 to say that Christ just has divine qualities—but is not God Almighty—is reading a theological bias into the text. As *The New Treasury of Scripture Knowledge* points out, "translators and translations which choose to render this phrase 'a god' or 'divine' are motivated by theological, not grammatical, considerations. The phrase 'a god' is particularly objectionable, because it makes Christ a lesser god, which is polytheism, and contrary to the express declaration of Scripture elsewhere (Deut. 32:39). For clearly if Christ is 'a god,' then he must be either a 'true god' or a 'false god.' If 'true,' we assert polytheism; if 'false,' he is unworthy of our credence."[40]

Theologian Robert Reymond notes that no standard Greek lexicon offers "divine" as a possible meaning of *theos*, nor does the noun *theos* ("God") become an adjective (conveying the idea of "divine") when it appears without an article. "If John had intended an adjectival sense [i.e., 'the Word was *divine*'], he had an adjective (*theios*) ready at hand."[41] Indeed, it would have been much more logical for John to have employed the adjective *theios* if he wanted to communicate that Jesus was divine. Instead, John says the Word is God (*theos*)!

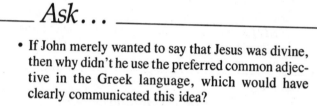

_____ *Ask...* _____

- If John merely wanted to say that Jesus was divine, then why didn't he use the preferred common adjective in the Greek language, which would have clearly communicated this idea?

- If John merely wanted to say that Jesus was divine, then why did he use one of the strongest words for absolute deity (*theos*) in the Greek language?

It is not surprising to find Leon Morris, an expert on John's Gospel, commenting thus on John 1:1: "John is not merely saying that there is something divine about Jesus. He is affirming that He is God, and doing so emphatically as we see from the word order in the Greek."[42] New Testament scholar F.F. Bruce agrees, noting that the structure of this clause in the Greek "demands the translation 'The Word was God.'"[43]

Christ Is Definitely God

As if all that weren't enough to prove the deity of Christ in John 1:1, it is also critical to note that—contrary to the claim of the Watchtower Society—*theos* ("God") with the definite article *ho* ("the") is indeed used of Jesus Christ in the New

Testament. One example of this is John 20:28, where Thomas says to Jesus, "My Lord and my God!" The verse reads literally from the Greek, "The Lord of me and the God [*ho theos*] of me." Clearly, Christ is just as much God as the Father is. Other examples of *ho theos* ("the God") being used of Christ include Matthew 1:23 and Hebrews 1:8. We see again, then, that the same words used of the Father's deity are used in reference to Jesus' deity.

_____ *Ask...* _____

- If *theos* ("God") with the definite article *ho* ("the") is used in the New Testament of Jesus Christ *just as it is used of Jehovah-God*, then doesn't this mean Jesus is just as much God as the Father is?

In the Beginning

We must make a few more points about John 1:1. First, the words "in the beginning" in John 1:1 are translated from the Greek words *en arche*. It is highly significant that these are the very words that begin the Book of Genesis in the Septuagint (the Greek translation of the Hebrew Old Testament, which predates the time of Christ). The obvious conclusion we must draw is that John's "beginning" is identical to the Genesis "beginning." (Further parallels between the two accounts are found in the fact that both refer to God, creation, light, and darkness.[44])

To properly interpret the phrase "in the beginning," we must briefly address the question, When did time begin? Scripture is not clear about the connection between time and eternity. Some prefer to think of eternity as time—a succession of moments—without beginning or ending. However, there are indications in Scripture that time itself may be a created reality, a reality that began when God created the universe.

The Book of Hebrews contains some hints regarding the relationship between time and eternity. Hebrews 1:2 tells us that the Father "has spoken to us by his Son, whom he appointed heir of all things, and *through whom he made the universe*" (emphasis added). The last part of this verse is rendered more literally from the Greek text "through whom he made *the ages*." Likewise, Hebrews 11:3 tells us that "by faith we understand that *the universe* was formed at God's command" (emphasis added). The Greek text reads more literally, "By faith we understand that *the ages* were formed at God's command."

Scholars have grappled with what may be meant here by the term "ages." Lutheran commentator R.C.H. Lenski says the term means "not merely vast periods of time as mere time, but 'eons' with all that exists as well as all that transpires in them."[45] New Testament scholar F.F. Bruce says that "the whole created universe of space and time is meant."[46]

Church father and philosopher Augustine (A.D. 354-430) held that the universe was not created *in* time, but that time itself was created along with the universe.[47] Reformed theologian Louis Berkhof agrees, and concludes, "It would not be correct to assume that time was already in existence when God created the world, and that He at some point in that existing time, called 'the beginning,' brought forth the universe. The world was created *with* time rather than *in* time. Back of the beginning mentioned in Genesis 1:1 lies a beginningless eternity."[48]

In view of the above, we may conclude that when the apostle John said, "In the beginning was the Word, and the Word was with God, and the Word was God" (John 1:1), the phrase "in the beginning" has specific reference to the beginning of time when the universe was created. When the time-space universe came into being, Christ the divine Word *was already existing*.

It is important to grasp this, because John tells us that "in the beginning [when time began] *was* the Word" (emphasis added). The verb "was" in this verse is an imperfect tense in the Greek text, indicating continued existence. When the time-space universe came into being, Christ the divine Word *was already existing* in a loving, intimate relationship with the Father and the Holy Spirit. The imperfect tense "reaches back indefinitely beyond the instant of the beginning."[49] Leon Morris notes that "the verb 'was' is most naturally understood of the eternal existence of the Word: 'the Word continually was.' "[50] Thus, the *Logos* did not come into being at a specific point in eternity past, but at that point at which all else began to be, He already was. No matter how far back we go in eternity past, we will never come to a point at which we could say of Christ, as Arius once did, that "there was a time when he was not."

Unbroken, Intimate Fellowship

When heaven and earth came into being at the Creation, there was Christ, already existing in close association with the Father. This close association is affirmed in John's Gospel: "the Word was *with* God" (1:1, emphasis added). Benjamin Warfield tells us that "it is not merely coexistence with God that is asserted, as two beings standing side by side, united in a local relation, or even in a common conception. What is suggested is an active relation of intercourse."[51] The Greek preposition for "with" is *pros*, and carries the idea of intimate, unbroken fellowship and communion. Christ the *Word* spent eternity past in company with and in intimate, unbroken fellowship with the Father in an eternal, loving relationship. "Both the Word and His relationship to the Eternal [the Father] are eternal. There was never part of His pre-existence which found Him to be separated in any sense from the Godhead."[52]

It is important to recognize that in John 1:1,2, Christ the Word is said to be distinct from and at the same time equal with God. He was *with* God (the Greek preposition *pros* implies two distinct persons), and at the same time is said to *be* God. Hence, the Father and the Word "are not the same, but they belong together. The fact that One may be said to be 'with' the Other clearly differentiates them. Yet, though they are distinct, there is no disharmony. John's expression points us to the perfect unity in which they are joined."[53]

We see, then, that John 1:1,2 suggests Trinitarian distinctions: "Now all is clear; we now see how this Word who is God 'was in the beginning,' and how this Word who is God was in eternal reciprocal relation with God. . . . The [Word] is one of the three divine persons of the eternal Godhead."[54]

——— REASONING FROM THE SCRIPTURES ———

John 8:58—*Limited Preexistence or Eternal?*

The *New World Translation* renders John 8:58, "Jesus said to them: 'Most truly I say to you, Before Abraham came into existence, *I have been*'" (emphasis added). By contrast, the New American Standard Bible renders this verse, "Jesus said to them, 'Truly, truly, I say to you, before Abraham was born, *I AM*'" (emphasis added).

The Jehovah's Witnesses are willing to concede that Jesus was *preexistent* ("I have been") but not that He was *eternally preexistent* ("I AM"). In most translations, Jesus' "I AM" statement in John 8:58 is seen to be connected with God's name in Exodus 3:14 (NASB): "I AM WHO I AM"—a name indicating eternal existence. But the *New World Translation* renders Jesus' words in John 8:58 as "I have been," not "I AM." That is one of the clearest examples of the Jehovah's Witnesses mistranslating the Bible in order to support a doctrinal bias.

The Witnesses try to argue their position by asking, "Which rendering agrees with the context?" They then suggest that the question of the Jews in verse 57—"You are not yet fifty years old, and have You seen Abraham?" (NASB)—was a question dealing with *age*, not *identity*. They claim that when Jesus responded to the question, He was speaking not of His identity (as the "I AM" of Exodus 3:14) but of His age, or length of existence.[55] Jesus said "I have been" as a way of indicating His preexistence to the Jews.

In the Watchtower publication *The Greatest Man Who Ever Lived*, we read of Jesus' preexistence: "He was a very special person because he was created by God before all other things. For countless billions of years, before even the physical universe was created, Jesus lived as a spirit person in heaven and enjoyed intimate fellowship with his Father, Jehovah God, the Grand Creator."[56]

Now, besides mistranslating John 8:58, the Jehovah's Witnesses also mistranslate Exodus 3:14: "At this God said to Moses: 'I SHALL PROVE TO BE WHAT I SHALL PROVE TO BE.' And he added: 'This is what you are to say to the sons of Israel, "I SHALL PROVE TO BE has sent me to you."'"

In the *New World Translation*, then, the connection between John 8:58 and Exodus 3:14 is completely cloaked—from both sides. The Jehovah's Witnesses say that in Exodus 3:14 God called Himself "I SHALL PROVE TO BE WHAT I SHALL PROVE TO BE," while in John 8:58 Jesus said, "Before Abraham was, I have been." The obvious goal of the Watchtower Society is to keep Jesus from being identified as God Almighty. No one reading the *New World Translation* would see the relationship between Exodus 3:14 and John 8:58.

The Biblical Teaching on John 8:58

I noted in chapter 2 that names have significance in the Bible. We learn much about God by the names used of Him in both the Old and New Testaments. The same is true in Exodus 3:14: We learn something about God by how He identifies Himself in this passage.

The name Yahweh, which occurs some 5,300 times in the Old Testament, is connected with the Hebrew verb "to be." We first learn of this name in Exodus 3:14, where Moses asked God by what name He should be called. God replied, "I AM WHO I AM. . . . Thus you shall say to the sons of Israel, 'I AM has sent me to you'" (NASB).

Remember, the phrase "I AM" is not the word Yahweh. However, I AM (in verse 14) and Yahweh (in verse 15) are both derivatives of the same verb, "to be." The name I AM WHO I AM in verse 14 is intended as a full expression of God's eternal nature, and is then shortened to Yahweh in verse 15. The names have the same root meaning and can be considered interchangeable.

"I AM" may seem like an odd name to the modern ear. But I think Moses understood what God was saying to him. The name conveys the idea of eternal self-existence. Yahweh never came into being at a specific point in time, for He has always existed. He was never born; He will never die. He does not grow older, for He is beyond the realm of time. To know Yahweh is to know the eternal one.[57]

In view of all that, it is interesting that Bible expositor James K. Hoffmeier suggests that in Exodus 3, "Moses is not demanding to know God's name per se, but the character behind that name. God's answer supports this, because he does not [first] say 'Yahweh' (v. 14) but [first] interprets the name 'I AM WHO I AM.' This may appeal to his infinite existence: 'the Lord God Almighty, *who was, and is, and is to come*' (Rev. 4:8b)."[58] The name communicates the idea, "I am the One who *is*."[59]

Bible scholars are also careful to point out that "I AM WHO I AM" expresses not just abstract existence, but rather points to God's active manifestation of existence. God's existence is not a static (inactive) one but a dynamic (active) one. God is involved with His people. He is the covenant-God of Israel who delivers His people.[60] Along these lines, Old Testament scholars Carl F. Keil and Franz Delitzsch say the name "I AM" expressed to God's people "the nature and operations of God and that God would *manifest in deeds* the nature expressed in the name."[61] Indeed, all that is implied in the name "I AM" shall be "manifested through the ages to come."[62]

Reasoning with the Jehovah's Witnesses

I suggest that in answering the Watchtower position on Christ's deity, most of our attention should focus on John 8:58.

And in addressing how Jehovah's Witnesses interpret John 8:58, the key issue is the proper translation and interpretation of the Greek words *ego eimi*. Are these words properly translated "I AM" (as most translations render the words), or is "I have been" a legitimate translation too (as in the *New World Translation*)?

Scholars agree that the Watchtower Society has no justification for translating *ego eimi* in John 8:58 as "I have been." It is highly revealing that at one time, the Jehovah's Witnesses attempted to classify the Greek word *eimi* as a perfect indefinite tense rather than a present tense. (Such a tense would allow for the translation "I have been.") However, this claim proved to be very embarrassing when Greek scholars pointed out to the Jehovah's Witnesses that there is no such thing as a perfect indefinite tense in Greek grammar.[63] *Eimi* is clearly a *present active indicative* form—as any beginner's Greek grammar will show. Nevertheless, the Watchtower's theological bias has kept it from translating the word correctly in the present tense.

Former Jehovah's Witness David Reed notes that the Witnesses' own study Bibles prove that Jesus was claiming to be the "I AM" in John 8:58. "Their 1984 large-print *New World Translation of the Holy Scriptures with References* has a footnote on Exodus 3:14, admitting that the Hebrew would be rendered into Greek as '*Ego eimi*'—'*I am*.' And their 1985 *Kingdom Interlinear Translation of the Greek Scriptures* reveals that Jesus' words at John 8:58 are the same: '*ego eimi*.'"[64] When one consults these two Watchtower publications, the connection between John 8:58 and Exodus 3:14 is clear.

Along these same lines, it is highly significant that the Septuagint—the Greek translation of the Hebrew Old Testament that dates prior to the birth of Christ—renders the Hebrew phrase for "I AM" in Exodus 3:14 as *ego eimi*.[65] Expositor Leon Morris notes that *ego eimi* is "an emphatic form of speech and one that would not normally be employed in ordinary speech. Thus to use it was recognizably to adopt the divine style."[66] John's readers, who would definitely have been familiar with the Septuagint, would have surely seen the connection between John 8:58 and Exodus 3:14.

_____ *Ask...* _____

- Since the Septuagint (the Greek translation of the Hebrew Old Testament that dates prior to the birth of Christ) renders the Hebrew phrase for "I AM" in Exodus 3:14 as *ego eimi*—and since this is the *same phrase* Jesus utters in John 8:58—is it not clear that a connection exists between the two verses?

- Don't you think that first-century Jews, who would have been very familiar with the Septuagint, would have seen this connection between the two verses?

Especially noteworthy is that the words *ego eimi* appear often in John's Gospel—not just in John 8:58. And many scholars have noted that when Jesus speaks these words, they always carry great significance.[67] Interestingly, the words are *always* translated as "I am"—even in the *New World Translation* (John 8:58 is the only exception).[68] Elsewhere—in John 4:26; 6:35,48,51; 8:12,24,28,58; 10:7,11,14; 11:25; 14:6; 15:1,5; and 18:5,6,8—the Jehovah's Witnesses correctly translate *ego eimi* as "I am."

Now, here's the important point: Even a cursory examination of John's Gospel shows that these "I am" sayings are intended to be related to each other. Thus, John 8:58 should be translated the same way as all the other occurrences of *ego eimi*—that is, as "I am."

_____ *Ask...* _____

- Since all the "I am" sayings are clearly intended to be related to each other in John's Gospel, why does the *New World Translation* correctly translate *ego eimi* as "I am" throughout the Gospel of John except in John 8:58, where it translates *ego eimi* as "I have been"? Shouldn't there be consistency in translation?

Let us look at a few other examples in the Greek New Testament where Jesus used the term *ego eimi* as a way of identifying Himself as God.[69] In John 8:24 Jesus declared, "Unless you believe that I am [*ego eimi*] He, you shall die in your sins" (NASB). The original Greek text for this verse does not have the word "he." The verse literally reads, "If you do not believe that I am, you shall die in your sins."

Then, according to verse 28, Jesus told the Jews, "When you lift up the Son of Man, then you will know that I am [*ego eimi*] He" (NASB). Again, the original Greek text reads, "When you lift up the Son of Man, then you will know that I am" (there is no *he*). It seems clear that Jesus purposely used the phrase *ego eimi* as a means of identifying Himself as Yahweh.[70]

It is patently obvious that Jesus' use of *ego eimi* in John 8:58 was a reference not to His age (as the Watchtower Society teaches) but to His identity. As a matter of fact, the key issue throughout the entire eighth chapter of John's Gospel is Christ's identity (*see* verses 12, 19, 24, 25, 28, and 53).[71] Thus, in reference to Jesus, the Jews were more concerned with the question, "Who do you think you are?" rather than, "How old are you?"[72]

In John 8:58, then, Jesus *in context* is revealing His identity when He says, "Before Abraham was born, I AM" (John 8:58). Since "I AM" echoes the words of God in Exodus 3:14—"I AM WHO I AM"—Jesus was revealing His identity as the One who is eternally self-existent. Jesus' use of *ego eimi* constituted a claim to be eternal—to exist without ever having experienced a beginning—in contrast to Abraham, who had a beginning.

Such a conclusion adds tremendous significance to Jesus' encounter with the Jews. Knowing how much they venerated Abraham, Jesus in John 8:58 deliberately contrasted the created origin of Abraham with His own eternal, uncreated nature. As Robert Bowman notes, "It was not simply that He was older than Abraham, although his statement says that much too, but that his existence is of a different kind than Abraham's—that Abraham's existence was created and finite, beginning at a point in time, while Christ's existence never began, is uncreated and infinite, and therefore eternal."[73] In Jesus, therefore, "we see the timeless God, who was the God of Abraham and of Isaac and of Jacob, who was before time and who will be after time, who always is."[74] *That* is Jesus' true identity.

Jesus' claim becomes all the more definite when one realizes that He began His assertion of deity with the words, "*I tell you the truth*... before Abraham was born, I am" (emphasis added). In the King James Version, the phrase "I tell you the truth" is rendered "verily, verily." Jesus used such language only when He was making an important and emphatic statement. His words represent the strongest possible oath and claim.[75] We might paraphrase it, "I assure you, most solemnly I tell you." Jesus did not want anyone to be confused about the fact that He was claiming to be eternal God. He was saying in the strongest possible terms that He had an independent, continuous existence from before time.

And, of course, when Jesus made this claim, the Jews immediately picked up stones to kill Him, for they recognized He was implicitly identifying Himself as Yahweh—the "I AM WHO I AM" of the Old Testament (Exodus 3:14). They were acting on the prescribed penalty for blasphemy in the Old Testament law: death by stoning (Leviticus 24:16). Certainly there can be no doubt that the Jews interpreted Jesus' words as a claim to be Yahweh.

After demonstrating to the Jehovah's Witness the utter unreliability of the *New World Translation* (based on chapters 3 and 4 in this book):

Ask . . .

- In view of what you have learned, do you really want to continue trusting the *New World Translation* to guide you and your family in your eternal destiny?

5

Is Christ Inferior to the Father?

Part 1

> Christ is *"equal to the Father as touching his Godhood and inferior to the Father as touching his manhood."*
>
> —The Athanasian Creed
> (Date unknown)

To support the claim that Jesus was a lesser deity than the Father, Jehovah's Witnesses often point to passages in the New Testament that seem to indicate that Jesus is inferior in some way to the Father. For example, Jesus said, "The Father is greater than I" (John 14:28), and referred to the Father as "my God" (John 20:17). First Corinthians 11:3 tells us that "the head of Christ is God," and 1 Corinthians 15:28 says that Jesus "will be made subject to him who put everything under him, so that God may be all in all." Jesus is called God's "only begotten Son" (John 3:16 NASB), the "firstborn over all creation" (Colossians 1:15), and the "Beginning" of God's creation (Revelation 3:14 NASB). Clearly, the Witnesses say, Jesus is not God in the same sense Jehovah is.

As we answer the Jehovah's Witnesses on such passages, it is critical that each passage be examined *in its proper context.* Every word in the Bible is a part of a sentence; every sentence is a part of a paragraph; every paragraph is a part of a book; and every book is a part of the whole of Scripture. There is thus both an immediate and a broader context for each respective verse.

The immediate context of a statement is the paragraph (or paragraphs) of the biblical book in question. No text of Scripture is independent from the statements around it. Interpreting a text apart from its immediate context is like trying to make sense of a Rembrandt painting by looking at only a single square inch of the painting, or like trying to analyze Handel's "Messiah" by listening to a few short notes. *The immediate context is absolutely critical to a proper understanding of individual Scripture texts.*

The broader context of any given text is the whole of Scripture. We must always bear in mind that on any given issue, the interpretation of a specific passage must not contradict the total teaching of Scripture. Individual texts do not exist as isolated fragments, but as parts of a whole. The exposition of these texts must therefore involve exhibiting them in right relation both to the whole and to each other. This principle is grounded in the fact that each of the biblical writers wrote within the larger context of previous biblical teaching. And they all assumed that *all of Scripture*—although communicated through many human instruments—had *one author* (God) who didn't contradict Himself (2 Peter 1:21).

In this chapter, we will see that many of the Watchtower's interpretations of Scripture tend to ignore completely the immediate and broader contexts of the verse in question. We will also see that many of the Watchtower arguments are based upon a woeful misunderstanding of the nature of the incarnation, that event in which Jesus (eternal God) took on a human nature. In the incarnation, Jesus was both *fully God* and *fully man*. And, as we shall see, many of the passages cited by the Jehovah's Witnesses to "prove" Jesus' inferiority relate to Christ *from the vantage point of His manhood*. Let us now examine some of these passages.

_____ **REASONING FROM THE SCRIPTURES** _____

Revelation 3:14—*Jesus the "Beginning" of God's Creation?*

The Watchtower Teaching. The *New World Translation* renders Revelation 3:14, "And to the angel of the congregation in Laodicea write: These are the things that the Amen says, the faithful and true witness, *the beginning of the creation by God*" (emphasis added). Jehovah's Witnesses cite this verse to prove that Jesus is a created being. Indeed, Jesus was "the first of Jehovah-God's creations."[1] The Witnesses relate this verse to passages like John 1:14, where we are told that Jesus is the "only begotten" of the Father.[2]

In support of this interpretation, the Watchtower publication *Should You Believe in the Trinity?* states: "'Beginning' [Greek: *arche*] cannot rightly be interpreted to mean that Jesus was the 'beginner' of God's creation. In his Bible writings, John uses various forms of the Greek word *arche* more than 20 times, and these always have the common meaning of 'beginning.' Yes, Jesus was created by God as the beginning of God's invisible creations."[3]

The Biblical Teaching. In responding to the Watchtower's interpretation of Revelation 3:14, it is critical to note that there is a wide range of meanings for the Greek word *arche*, which is translated "beginning" in the *New World Translation*. Though *arche* can mean "beginning," the word is truly unique and also carries the important *active* meaning of "one who begins," "origin," "source," "creator," or "first cause." Evangelical scholars agree that this is the intended meaning of the word in Revelation 3:14.[4]

The authoritative *Greek-English Lexicon of the New Testament and Other Early Christian Literature* by William Arndt and F. Wilbur Gingrich says the meaning of *arche* in Revelation 3:14 is "first cause."[5] Indeed, in Revelation 3:14, *arche* is used to refer to "the active beginning of the creation, the One who caused the creation, referring to Jesus Christ not as a created being, but the One who created all things (John 1:3)."[6]

A brief perusal of some of today's translations reflects this meaning of the word:

> • The Jerusalem Bible translates *arche* in Revelation 3:14 as "the ultimate source" (of God's creation).
> • The New English Bible translates *arche* as "the prime source" (of God's creation).
> • Barclay's translation renders *arche* as "the moving cause" (of God's creation).
> • Knox's version translates *arche* as "the source" (of God's creation).
> • Both Williams's and Goodspeed's translations render *arche* as "the beginner" (of God's creation).

It is worth noting that the English word *architect* is derived from *arche*. We might say that Jesus is the architect of all creation (John 1:3; Colossians 1:16; Hebrews 1:2). Commenting on this verse, Greek exegete Henry Alford states that in Christ "the whole creation of God is begun and conditioned; He is its source and primary fountainhead."[7]

It is also noteworthy that the only other times *arche* is used in the Book of Revelation, it is used of God as "the *beginning* and the end" (Revelation 1:8; 21:6; 22:13).[8] Certainly the use of *arche* with God Almighty does not mean that He had a created beginning. Instead, these verses communicate that God is both the *beginner* and the *consummation* of creation. He is the first cause of creation; He is its final goal.[9] The Greek word *arche* is used in the same sense in Revelation 3:14: Christ is the *beginner* of God's creation (cf. John 1:3; Colossians 1:16; Hebrews 1:2).

_____ *Ask...* _____

> • Since the use of *arche* with God Almighty does not mean that He had a created beginning (Revelation

1:8; 21:6; 22:13), why go against John's usage in
Revelation and insist that when used of Christ the
word *arche* indicates a created beginning?

Now, we should note that another possible meaning of *arche*
is "ruler" or "magistrate." In support of this interpretation is
the fact that when *arche* is used of a person in Scripture, it is
almost always used of a ruler.[10] Indeed, the plural form of this
word is typically translated "principalities" (or something
similar) in the New Testament (cf. Romans 8:38; Ephesians
3:10; Colossians 2:15).[11] David Reed notes that the Watchtower Bible translates the plural of this word as "government
officials" in Luke 12:11.[12] Elsewhere in the New Testament,
the word carries the idea of "rule" or "domain" (Luke 20:20;
Jude 6).[13]

The English word *archbishop* is related to this sense of the
Greek word *arche*. An archbishop is one who is in authority
over other bishops. He rules over other bishops.

If "ruler" is the correct meaning for *arche* in Revelation
3:14, then it means that Christ has *authority* over all creation.
This meaning is reflected in the New International Version,
where we read that Christ is the "ruler of God's creation"
(Revelation 3:14).

Based on our study of the scriptural context, I believe that
arche in Revelation 3:14 carries the primary meaning of
"beginner," "first cause," or "originator" of God's creation.
And a second possible meaning is that Christ is the "ruler"
over God's creation. It may be that in the case of Christ, *both*
senses are intended inasmuch as Christ is elsewhere portrayed
in Scripture as both the Creator (Hebrews 1:2) and Ruler
(Revelation 19:16) of all things.

The interpretation that Christ is the "beginner" of God's
creation harmonizes with other New Testament passages about
Christ as Creator—whereas the Watchtower interpretation

simply doesn't fit the whole of Scripture. For example:

- "For by him all things were created: things in heaven and on earth, visible and invisible, whether thrones or powers or rulers or authorities; all things were created by him and for him. He is before all things, and in him all things hold together" (Colossians 1:16,17).
- "But in these last days he has spoken to us by his Son, whom he appointed heir of all things, and through whom he made the universe" (Hebrews 1:2).
- "Through him all things were made; without him nothing was made that has been made" (John 1:3).

_____ Ask... _____

- Did you know that the same John who wrote Revelation 3:14 wrote John 1:3—"Through him all things were made; without him nothing was made that has been made"?

It is the consistent testimony of Scripture that Christ is not a created being but is rather the Creator of all things. It would be appropriate to remind the Jehovah's Witness at this point of the scriptural teaching that _only_ God is the Creator. God says in Isaiah 44:24, "I, the LORD [Yahweh], am the maker of _all things_, stretching out the heavens _by Myself_, and spreading out the earth _all alone_" (emphasis added). Clearly, this verse makes it impossible to argue that Christ was created first by Jehovah and then Jehovah created all other things through Christ. The fact that Jehovah is the "maker of all things" who stretched out the heavens "by Myself" and spread out the earth "all alone" (Isaiah 44:24)—and the accompanying fact that Christ is the Creator of "all things" (John 1:3; Colossians 1:16; Hebrews 1:2)—proves that Christ is God Almighty, just as the Father is.

_____ *Ask* . . . _____

> • Jehovah says in Isaiah 44:24, "I, the LORD, am the maker of *all things,* stretching out the heavens *by Myself,* and spreading out the earth *all alone.*" How do you reconcile this with the Watchtower teaching that Jehovah first created Christ and then Christ created everything else?

Proverbs 8:22,23—*Jesus the "Earliest" of Jehovah's Achievements?*

The Watchtower Teaching. The *New World Translation* renders Proverbs 8:22,23, "Jehovah himself *produced me* at the beginning of his way, *the earliest of his achievements of long ago.* From time indefinite I was installed, from the start, from times earlier than the earth" (emphasis added). Jehovah's Witnesses say this verse is a direct reference to the creation of Jesus Christ. Though Proverbs 8 actually deals with the subject of wisdom, the Jehovah's Witnesses say that "most scholars agree that it is actually a figure of speech for Jesus as a spirit creature prior to his human existence."[14]

In the Watchtower book *Aid to Bible Understanding*, we read, "Many professed Christian writers of the early centuries of the Common Era understood this section [in Proverbs 8] to refer symbolically to God's Son in his prehuman state.... There can be no denying that the Son was 'produced' by Jehovah 'at the beginning of his way, the earliest of his achievements of long ago,' nor that the Son was 'beside [Jehovah] as a master worker' during earth's creation."[15]

The Biblical Teaching. The Watchtower interpretation of Proverbs 8 not only violates the context of the Book of Proverbs, it also violates the whole of Scripture. As you respond to the Watchtower's interpretation, you will first want to emphasize that the first nine chapters of Proverbs deal with *wisdom personified.* A personification is a rhetorical figure of speech in which inanimate objects or abstract concepts are endowed with human qualities or are represented as possessing human form.[16] In Proverbs chapters 1–9, wisdom is figuratively endowed with human qualities.[17]

With that in mind, you will want to make the following important point: *There is no indication in the text that Proverbs 8 is to be taken any differently than chapters 1 through 7 and 9.* This being so, apologist Robert Bowman notes that "if we take 8:22 to speak literally about Christ, we must also assume that Christ is a woman who cries in the streets (1:20-21), and who lives with someone named 'Prudence' (8:12) in a house with seven pillars (9:1)!"[18] Proverbs 1–9 makes no sense if one tries to read Christ into the text.

_____ Ask . . . _____

- If "wisdom" in Proverbs 8 is referring to Christ, and if the "wisdom" in Proverbs 8 is the same "wisdom" as in the first nine chapters of Proverbs (as the context clearly indicates), then who is the "Prudence" that Jesus lives with (Proverbs 8:12)?

- Do you believe that Christ is a woman who cries in the streets (Proverbs 1:20,21)?

You must also raise the important issue as to whether or not God has *always* possessed wisdom. By definition, wisdom must be as old as God.[19] (The Jehovah's Witness will not be willing to concede that there was a time when God had no wisdom.)

_____ Ask . . . _____

- If "wisdom" in Proverbs 8 had a beginning, then doesn't this mean that God did not have wisdom until a certain point when He acquired it? What kind of "God" is that?

The point you want to make here, of course, is that God's wisdom is just as eternal as God Himself. There never was a time in which God was without wisdom. Indeed, in Proverbs 8:23 in the New American Standard Bible we read, "From everlasting I [wisdom] was established." This is a poetic way of stating the eternal nature of God's wisdom.[20] It is highly revealing that the same phrase—"from everlasting"—is used in Psalm 90:2 to describe the eternality of God Himself.[21]

To sum up, then, Proverbs 8:22,23 is speaking meta-phorically of God's eternal wisdom and how it was "brought forth" (verse 24) to take part in the creation of the universe. Proverbs 8 is not saying that wisdom came into being at a point in time. And it certainly is not saying that Jesus is a created being, since the passage is not dealing with Jesus but with wisdom personified.

Colossians 1:15—*Jesus the "Firstborn" Over All Creation*

The Watchtower Teaching. The *New World Translation* renders Colossians 1:15, "He is the image of the invisible God, *the firstborn of all creation*" (emphasis added). The Jehovah's Witnesses cite this verse to support their view that Jesus came into being at a point in time as a created angel. Ignoring all biblical evidence to the contrary, they argue that the word "firstborn" in this verse means "first-created."[22]

In the book *Reasoning from the Scriptures*, the Watchtower Society argues that the word "firstborn" indicates that "Jesus is the eldest in Jehovah's family of sons."[23] Indeed, the book says, the term "firstborn" occurs over 30 times in the Bible, and in every case that it is applied to living creatures, the firstborn is part of a larger group. Just as the "firstborn" of Pharaoh refers to the first one born to Pharaoh, so is Jesus the first one "born" or created by Jehovah. Indeed, Jesus is "ranked with God's creation, being first among them and also most beloved and most favored among them."[24] As we read in the Watchtower book *The Greatest Man Who Ever Lived*, Jesus was "a very special person because he was created by God before all other things."[25]

The Biblical Teaching. The Jehovah's Witnesses have wrongly understood Colossians 1:15 to mean that there was a time when Christ did not exist, and that He came into being at a point in time. "Firstborn" does not mean "first-created." Rather, as Greek scholars agree, the word (Greek: *prototokos*) means "first in rank, pre-eminent one, heir."[26] The word carries the idea of positional preeminence and supremacy. Christ is the firstborn in the sense that He is positionally pre-eminent over creation and supreme over all things. He is also the heir of all creation in the sense that all that belongs to the Father is also the Son's.

Point out to the Jehovah's Witness that the Watchtower argument regarding Colossians 1:15 is illogical. As noted earlier, the Watchtower Society argues that just as the "first-born" of Pharaoh refers to the first one born to Pharaoh, so Christ as the "firstborn" is the first one created by Jehovah. Well, notice that Colossians calls Christ "the firstborn *of all creation*" (i.e., not the firstborn of Jehovah). If we are to draw a direct parallel between the firstborn of Pharaoh and the firstborn of all creation, then we must conclude that creation "parented" Jesus. This is the reverse of what happened, for in the very next verse in Colossians we are told that *Christ "parented" creation*—that is, He created all things in the universe (Colossians 1:16). Christ was not produced by the creation; rather, Christ produced the creation.[27]

As we attempt to understand the Bible, it is critical that we interpret words according to the meaning intended by the speaker or writer of those words. We cannot and must not superimpose meanings onto words that are foreign to the author's intended meaning.

Let me give an example. Let's say an uneducated person from a foreign country learned the English language and came to America. While in America, he hears someone refer to Wall Street. From what he knows, this must refer to a literal, paved street named *Wall Street*. But that is not the intended meaning of the one who spoke those words. In actuality, he was referring to the New York Stock Exchange.

My point is that we must understand what the original speaker or writer intended by the words he or she used. Without this understanding, we will misinterpret what he or she is saying.

With that in mind, let us note that among the ancient Hebrews, the word "firstborn" referred to the son in the family who was in the *preeminent position*, regardless of whether or not he was literally the first son born to the parents. This firstborn son would not only be the preeminent one, he would also be the heir to a double portion of the family inheritance.

This meaning of firstborn is illustrated in the life of David. He was the youngest (*last*-born) son of Jesse. Nevertheless, Psalm 89:27 says of him, "I also shall make him My first-born, the highest of the kings of the earth" (NASB). Though David was the *last* one born in Jesse's family, David is called the firstborn because of the preeminent position in which God placed him.[28]

We find another example of this meaning of "firstborn" in comparing Genesis 41:50,51 with Jeremiah 31:9. Manasseh was actually the first son born to Joseph, and Ephraim was born some time later. Nevertheless, Ephraim is called the "firstborn" in Jeremiah 31:9 because of his preeminent position.[29] He was not *born* first, but he was the *firstborn* because of his preeminence.

Likewise, as expositor Ray Stedman notes, "Ishmael was thirteen years older than Isaac, but it is Isaac who is the firstborn. Though Esau was born first, Jacob becomes the firstborn."[30] Clearly, then, the term "firstborn" refers not to the first one born but to the preeminent one in the family.

_____ *Ask...* _____

- In view of the fact that David was the last-born son of Jesse, what do you think Scripture means when it calls him the firstborn (Psalm 89:27)? (David was the *preeminent* son.)

> • In view of the fact that Ephraim was born to Joseph
> after Manasseh, what do you think Scripture means
> when it calls him the *firstborn* (Jeremiah 31:9)?
> (Ephraim was the *preeminent* son.)

Addressing what the term "firstborn" came to mean to
those living in biblical times, scholar F.F. Bruce comments:
"The word first-born had long since ceased to be used exclusively in its literal sense, just as *prime* (from the Latin word
primus—'first') with us. The Prime Minister is not the first
minister we have had; he is the most preeminent. . . . Similarly,
first-born came to denote [among the ancients] not priority in
time but pre-eminence in rank."[31]

Bruce says that for Colossians 1:15 to mean what the
Jehovah's Witnesses want it to mean (God's first creation),
Paul would not have called Christ the "firstborn" (*prototokos*)
but the "first-created" (*protoktisis*)—a term that is *never* used
of Christ in the New Testament.[32] Indeed, as exegete J.B.
Lightfoot notes, "The fathers of the fourth century rightly
called attention to the fact that the Apostle writes not *protoktisis* ['first-created'], but *prototokos* ['firstborn']."[33]

In view of this distinction between "firstborn" and "first-
created":

_____ Ask... _____

> • Why didn't the apostle Paul use the term "first-
> created" (*protoktisis*) in Colossians 1:15 if he in-
> tended to communicate that Christ was the first one
> created by Jehovah?[34]

Now, since a key aspect of the word "firstborn" has to do
with being an *heir*, we must ask: In what sense is Jesus an heir?
Robert Bowman points out that "Christ, as the Son of God, is

the Father's 'heir' because *everything that is the Father's is also the Son's*. Of course, this is a figure of speech, and should not be pressed too literally (God the Father will never die and 'leave his inheritance' to the Son!). The point is simply that just as we say a man's firstborn son is usually the heir of all his property, so Colossians 1:15 calls Christ the 'firstborn [heir] of all creation.' "[35] The "estate" inherited by the "heir" (Christ) is "all creation." That Christ is the heir of all things makes sense, because Christ is also the *Maker* of all things (Colossians 1:16). By divine right, all of creation belongs to Him.

John 3:16—*Jesus the "Only Begotten" Son*

The Watchtower Teaching. The *New World Translation* renders John 3:16, "For God loved the world so much that he gave his *only-begotten Son*, in order that everyone exercising faith in him might not be destroyed but have everlasting life" (emphasis added).

In what sense is Jesus God's "only-begotten" Son? *Aid to Bible Understanding* tells us that "by virtue of his being the sole *direct* creation of his Father, the firstborn Son was unique, different from all others of God's sons, all of whom were created or begotten by Jehovah *through* that firstborn Son."[36]

The Watchtower booklet *Should You Believe in the Trinity?* points out that Isaac is called Abraham's "only-begotten" son in Hebrews 11:17. The booklet says that "there can be no question that in Isaac's case, he was only-begotten in the normal sense."[37] This is the same sense in which the word is used of Jesus Christ: "Almighty God can rightly be called his [Jesus'] Begetter, or Father, in the same sense that an earthly father, like Abraham, begets a son."[38]

The Watchtower Society concludes from this verse that "the phrase 'Son of God' refers to Jesus as a separate created being, not as part of a Trinity. As the Son of God, he could not be God himself."[39] Indeed, "God is the senior. Jesus is the junior—in time, position, power, and knowledge."[40]

The Biblical Teaching. Let us address this last Watchtower argument first. To begin, it is critical to note that Isaac *was not*

Abraham's "only-begotten" son in the sense that Isaac was the only son Abraham begat. Abraham had a number of sons, including Ishmael, whose birth preceded Isaac's. It is clear from the full scriptural context that Isaac was Abraham's "only-begotten" son in the sense that he was Abraham's *unique* son.[41]

_____ *Ask...* _____

- Since there were other sons born (or "begotten") to Abraham—thereby showing that Isaac was not literally Abraham's *only*-begotten son—what do you think Scripture means when it calls Isaac the "only-begotten" son of Abraham?

- Is it not clear from the context that since God's covenant purposes were to be carried out through Isaac and his family line, Isaac was called "only-begotten" in the sense of his uniqueness?

_____

Regarding the Watchtower argument that Jehovah begat Jesus in the same sense that Abraham begat Isaac, Robert Bowman makes an interesting observation: "If this line of reasoning were sound . . . it would suggest a conclusion rather embarrassing to JWs. For if God is Jesus' Father 'in the same sense that an earthly father . . . begets a son,' then it would seem that Jesus must have had a heavenly Mother, as well as heavenly Father."[42]

Again, the critical point you must make to the Jehovah's Witness is this: The words "only begotten" do not mean that Christ was created (as the heretic Arius taught). Rather they mean that He was "unique," "specially blessed," or "favored." Theologian John F. Walvoord, in his classic book *Jesus Christ Our Lord*, notes that "the thought is clearly that Christ is the Begotten of God in the sense that no other is."[43] Reformed scholar Benjamin Warfield likewise comments, "The adjective 'only begotten' conveys the idea, not of derivation and subordination, but of uniqueness and consubstantiality: Jesus is all that God is, and He alone is this."[44]

Jesus: The Eternal Son of God. The notion that the title *Son of God* indicates inferiority to the Father is based on a faulty conception of what the phrase "son of . . ." meant among the ancients. Though the term *can* refer to "offspring of" in some contexts, it actually carries the more important meaning "of the order of."[45] The phrase is often used that way in the Old Testament. For example, "sons of the prophets" meant "of the order of prophets" (1 Kings 20:35). "Sons of the singers" meant "of the order of singers" (Nehemiah 12:28). Likewise, the phrase "Son of God" means "of the order of God," and represents a claim to undiminished deity.

Ancient Semitics and Orientals used the phrase "son of . . ." to indicate likeness or sameness of nature and equality of being.[46] Hence, when Jesus claimed to be the Son of God, His Jewish contemporaries fully understood that He was making a claim to be God in an unqualified sense. Warfield affirms that, from the earliest days of Christianity, the phrase "Son of God" was understood to be fully equivalent to God.[47] This is why, when Jesus claimed to be the Son of God, the Jews insisted, "We have a law, and according to that law he [Christ] must die, because he claimed to be the Son of God" (John 19:7). Recognizing that Jesus was identifying Himself as God, the Jews wanted to put Him to death for committing blasphemy (*see* Leviticus 24:16).

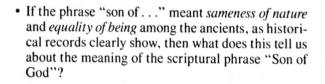

Ask . . .

- If the phrase "son of . . ." meant *sameness of nature* and *equality of being* among the ancients, as historical records clearly show, then what does this tell us about the meaning of the scriptural phrase "Son of God"?

Scripture indicates that Christ's Sonship is an *eternal* Sonship.[48] It is one thing to say that Jesus *became* the Son of God; it is another thing altogether to say that He was *always* the Son of God. We must recognize that if there was a time when the Son was not the Son, then, to be consistent, there was also a time when the Father was not the Father. If the first person's designation as "Father" is an eternal title, then the second person's designation as "Son" must be so regarded. Seen in this way, Christ's identity as the Son of God does not connote inferiority or subordination either of essence or position.

Sonship Prior to the Incarnation. Clear evidence for Christ's eternal Sonship is found in the fact that He is represented as already being the Son of God before His human birth in Bethlehem. Recall Jesus' discussion with Nicodemus in John 3, for instance, when He said, "For God so loved the world that he *gave* his one and only Son, that whoever believes in him shall not perish but have eternal life. For God did not *send* his Son *into* the world to condemn the world, but to save the world through him" (John 3:16,17, emphasis added). That Christ, as the Son of God, was *sent* into the world implies that He was the Son of God *before* the incarnation.

This is also seen in John 11, where we find Jesus comforting Martha and Mary over the death of their brother, Lazarus. Before Jesus brought Lazarus back to life, He said to Martha: "I am the resurrection and the life. He who believes in me will live, even though he dies; and whoever lives and believes in me will never die. Do you believe this?" (John 11:25,26). Martha responded: "Yes, Lord . . . I believe that you are the Christ, the Son of God, who was to come into the world" (verse 27). Lest Martha's words be misunderstood, we must emphasize that her statement reflects a sense that the Son of God has moved—*from* the realm of heaven and eternity *to* the realm of earth and time.

The Son of God in the Book of Proverbs. Proverbs chapter 30 was authored by a godly man named Agur. In the first four verses, he reflects on man's inability to comprehend the infinite God. Consequently he abases himself and humbly acknowledges his ignorance. He effectively communicates the idea that reverence of God is the beginning of true wisdom.

In verse 4, Agur's reflections are couched in a series of questions. He asks,

> Who has gone up to heaven and come down? Who has gathered up the wind in the hollow of his hands? Who has wrapped up the waters in his cloak? Who has established all the ends of the earth? What is his name, and the name of his son? Tell me if you know!

Many scholars—including renowned Old Testament scholars F. Delitzsch and A.R. Fausset—concede to the likelihood of this being an Old Testament reference to the first and second persons of the Trinity, the eternal Father and the eternal Son of God.[49] And it is highly significant that this portion of Scripture is not predictive prophecy speaking about a *future* Son of God. Rather, it speaks of God the Father and God the Son in *present-tense terms* during *Old Testament times*.

This means the answer to each of the four questions in Proverbs 30:4 must be God. And the very fact that Agur asked about the name of God's Son seems to imply a recognition, by divine inspiration, of plurality within the Godhead.[50]

Further evidence for Christ's eternal Sonship is found in Hebrews 1:2, which says God created the universe *through* His Son—implying that Christ was the Son of God *prior* to the Creation. Moreover, Christ as the Son is explicitly said to have existed "before all things" (Colossians 1:17; compare with verses 13,14). And Jesus, speaking as the Son of God (John 8:54-56), asserts His eternal preexistence before Abraham (verse 58).[51]

Clearly, then, in view of all the above, the scriptural view is that Jesus is *eternally* the Son of God. Any attempt to relegate Christ to a position less than God simply because of His title *Son of God* is to woefully misunderstand what the term really meant among the ancients.

Micah 5:2—*The "Origin" of Jesus*

The Watchtower Teaching. The *New World Translation* renders Micah 5:2, "And you, O Bethlehem Ephrathah, the one too little to get to be among the thousands of Judah, from you there will come out to me the one who is to become ruler in Israel, *whose origin is from early times, from the days of time indefinite*" (emphasis added).

The Jehovah's Witnesses often cite this verse to prove that Jesus came into being at a point in time, and thus cannot be Almighty God like the Father is. According to their translation, Jesus' origin is "from early times, from the days of time indefinite." The Witnesses conclude from this verse that though Jesus is a created being, He was created a long time ago. Indeed, "if the estimates of modern-day scientists as to the age of the physical universe are anywhere near correct, Jesus' existence as a spirit creature began thousands of millions of years prior to the creation of the first human."[52]

The Biblical Teaching. The New International Version renders Micah 5:2, "Though you are small among the clans of Judah, out of you will come for me one who will be ruler over Israel, *whose origins are from of old, from ancient times*" (emphasis added). This is clearly a prophecy of Christ and His approaching birth in Bethlehem. More important than His birthplace, however, is Micah's affirmation of Christ's eternal nature.[53]

You will want to point out to the Jehovah's Witness that the phrase "from of old," is the exact same one used by the prophet Habakkuk to refer to Jehovah-God's eternal nature (Habakkuk 1:12). Certainly this doesn't mean that Jehovah is a created being. We may conclude, then, that Micah's use of the phrase points to *Christ's* eternal nature, just as the term points to Jehovah's eternal nature in the Book of Habakkuk. Moreover, the phrase "from ancient times" is literally "days of *immeasurable* time"[54] (emphasis added). Taken together, the two terms convey "the strongest assertion of infinite duration of which the Hebrew language is capable."[55] Hence, these terms place Christ beyond time altogether. He is, along with the Father and the Holy Spirit, the eternal One—and His rule reaches back into eternity.

_____ *Ask...* _____

- Since the phrase "from of old" is used by the prophet Habakkuk to refer to *Jehovah-God's* eternal nature (Habakkuk 1:12), then, to be consistent, shouldn't we conclude that the identical phrase in Micah 5:2 refers to *Christ's* eternal nature?

Now, it is critical to understand what the Hebrew term for "origins" means in the phrase "whose *origins* are from old, from ancient times" (Micah 5:2). It does not mean that Christ had an origin in the sense that He had a beginning. Rather, the Hebrew term literally means "goings out" or "goings forth." The last part of Micah 5:2 could thus be rendered, "Whose *goings out* are from of old, from ancient times." Indeed, the Septuagint—a Greek translation of the Hebrew Old Testament that dates prior to the time of Christ—translates the phrase this way.[56]

Old Testament scholar John A. Martin suggests that these "goings out" probably refer to Christ's "victories in Creation, theophanies [preincarnate appearances], and providential dealings" in the universe.[57] Robert Reymond likewise relates Christ's "goings out" to the creation and sustenance of the universe.[58] Charles C. Ryrie says the phrase "refers primarily to Christ's preincarnate appearances as the Angel of the Lord, thus affirming the existence of Christ before His birth in Bethlehem."[59] Clearly, Micah 5:2 constitutes a powerful evidence for the eternal deity of Christ. The Jehovah's Witnesses abuse this verse by saying it proves that Jesus is a created being.

1 Corinthians 11:3—*God, the Head of Christ?*

The Watchtower Teaching. The *New World Translation* renders 1 Corinthians 11:3, "But I want you to know that the head of every man is the Christ; in turn the head of a woman is the man; in turn *the head of the Christ is God*" (emphasis added). The Jehovah's Witnesses say that because Jehovah is said to be the head of Christ, then Christ cannot be God. If Christ were God, then *He* would be the head.

The book *Reasoning from the Scriptures* argues that 1 Corinthians 11:3 shows that Jehovah is superior in rank to Jesus, thereby proving that Jesus is not God Almighty. The book also argues that since 1 Corinthians was written around A.D. 55 (22 years after Jesus had ascended into heaven), then this superior rank of Jehovah over Jesus applies to the *present* relationship between the two in heaven. If Jesus were truly God Almighty, then there would be no one in a superior rank to Him. In keeping with this, the booklet *Should You Believe in the Trinity?* comments, "Not only is Almighty God, Jehovah, a personality separate from Jesus but He is at all times his superior. Jesus is always presented as separate and lesser, a humble servant of God."[60]

The Biblical Teaching. A close examination of 1 Corinthians 11:3 shows that it has nothing to do with inferiority or superiority of one person over another; rather, it has to do with *patterns of authority*. Notice that Paul says the man is the head of the woman, even though men and women are utterly equal in their essential being. The Bible clearly teaches that men and women are equal in terms of nature. They are both human and both are created in God's image (Genesis 1:26-28). They are also said to be one in Christ (Galatians 3:28). These verses, taken with 1 Corinthians 11:3, show us that *equality of being* and *social hierarchy* are not mutually exclusive. Even though men and women are completely equal in terms of their nature, there is nevertheless a functional hierarchy that exists between them.

In the same way, Christ and the Father are utterly equal in their divine being (Jesus said, "I and the Father are one" [John 10:30]), even though Jesus is *functionally* under the Father's headship. There is no contradiction in affirming both an *equality of being* and a *functional subordination* among the Persons in the Godhead. Christ in His divine nature is fully equal to the

Father, even though *relationally* (or *functionally*) He is subordinate or submissive to the Father, especially since becoming a man. So in no way does 1 Corinthians 11:3 imply that Jesus is less than God.

_____ Ask... _____

- Are women inferior in nature to men because men exercise headship over women?

- If the man's headship over the woman does not mean that women are inferior in nature, then why does the Watchtower teach that the Father's headship over Christ means that Christ is inferior in nature?

---

1 Corinthians 15:28—*Is Christ "Subject" to the Father?*

The Watchtower Teaching. First Corinthians 15:28 in the *New World Translation* reads, "But when all things will have been subjected to him, then *the Son himself will also subject himself* to the One who subjected all things to him, that God may be all things to everyone" (emphasis added). *Reasoning from the Scriptures* cites this as a passage that proves beyond any doubt that Jesus is not equal to the Father and is not God Almighty.[61] The Watchtower book *"Let God Be True"* likewise tells us that all people—Jesus included—are in complete subjection to Jehovah-God.[62] If Christ were God Almighty, it is argued, He wouldn't be in subjection to anyone.

The Biblical Teaching. As you answer the Jehovah's Witnesses on this verse, you must emphasize that the word "subject" in 1 Corinthians 15:28 has nothing to do with Christ's essential nature or being. Rather, the word points to Christ's *functional* subjection to God the Father as the God-man and Mediator in the outworking of the plan of salvation. "As the perfect man, Christ had to be obedient to God and thus fulfill God's plan to redeem humanity. Jesus voluntarily submitted to that plan, to God the Father, in order to save humanity from eternal separation from God."[63]

Jehovah's Witnesses try to make much of the fact that even now, in the glorified state, Christ is in subjection to the Father. They thus imply that Jesus is not God in the same sense that the Father is. This position assumes, however, that Jesus did not retain His human nature. The Jehovah's Witnesses try to argue that Jesus was raised not in a human body but was raised (or *re-created*) as a spirit creature. If a Witness can be shown that Jesus *still* retains His human nature, then his position largely evaporates—for Christ as a man (today and forever) will always be in subjection to the Father.

It is critical, then, that you establish your case for Christ's continued existence as the glorified God-man, still in full retention of His human nature. Point out that Christ was raised immortal in the *very same human body* in which He died (Luke 24:37-39; Acts 2:31; 1 John 4:2; 2 John 7). Jesus Himself said that "a spirit does not have flesh and bones as you see that I have" (Luke 24:39). When Christ ascended into heaven, He ascended in the *same physical human body*, as witnessed by several of His disciples (Acts 1:11). As the Mediator between God and man, Christ is specifically said to *presently possess* a human nature (1 Timothy 2:5). When Christ returns, He will return as the "Son of Man"—a messianic title that clearly points to His humanity (Matthew 26:64).

Because Christ still possesses His human nature, then, Christ is *still* in submission to the Father.[64] But in no way does this make Jesus lesser than the Father in terms of His divine nature. Christ is the *God-man*. On the human side, Jesus is lesser than the Father. But on the divine side, Jesus is forever equal to the Father. You must drive this point home to the Jehovah's Witness.

Another point is that even apart from His humanity, Jesus has always been and forever will be in subjection to the Father because *this is the nature of the relationship of the Persons in the Trinity*. Jesus' subjection to the Father transcends His short life on earth as God-incarnate.

Again, this does not mean that Jesus is any less God than the Father; it simply reflects the hierarchical relationship in the

Trinity. As noted earlier, you must point out that there is no contradiction in affirming both an *equality of being* and a *functional subordination* among the Persons in the Godhead. Christ in His divine nature is fully equal to the Father, though relationally (or functionally) He is subordinate or submissive.

That's how it is with men and women. Though they are completely equal in their nature (Genesis 1:26-28; Galatians 3:28), there is a hierarchical relationship that exists between them (1 Corinthians 11:3). *The New Treasury of Scripture Knowledge* comments, "The subordination . . . of the Son to the Father is a voluntary though evidently permanent relationship which does not detract from or deny the equal deity of the Son, any more than the divine order of the submission of the wife to the husband (1 Corinthians 11:3) in the husband/wife relationship detracts from her essential equality and humanity, or implies her inferiority."[65]

——— *Ask . . .* ———

- Do you think that an *equality of being* and a *functional subordination* are incompatible with each other?

- Do you think that an *equality of being* and *functional subordination* are illustrated in the relationship that exists between men and women (1 Corinthians 11:3)? (You might read this verse aloud.)

- If the man's headship over the woman does not mean that the woman has an inferior nature, then why does the Watchtower say that the Father's headship over Christ means that Christ has an inferior nature?

Finally, you must explain to the Jehovah's Witness what 1 Corinthians 15:28 is really teaching. In the eternal plan of salvation, the eternal Son's role was to become the Mediator (the "go-between") between man and God the Father. But this role as Mediator is not eternal in its scope. In that future time when the task of man's redemption is complete, the Mediator (Christ) voluntarily surrenders the kingdom to the One who sent Him into the world to accomplish redemption, God the Father.

At that time, the Son's mediatorial role will be completed. "When he delivers up the administration of the earthly kingdom to the Father, then the *triune God* will reign as God and no longer through the incarnate Son."[66] Indeed, "throughout the endless ages of eternity, the triune God Jehovah will permeate the universe with His celestial love and glory. God will then be immediately known by all. What a glorious destiny awaits the redeemed of the Lord."[67]

• • •

In this chapter, we have examined a number of "proof texts" used by the Watchtower Society to argue for Christ's alleged inferiority to the Father. We shall examine further Watchtower proof texts in chapter 6.

6

Is Christ Inferior to the Father?

Part 2

In the previous chapter we saw that the Watchtower Society consistently twists and distorts Scripture passages to make it appear that Christ is inferior to the Father. In the present chapter, we will continue our examination, beginning with a *standard* Watchtower "proof text"—John 14:28, where Jesus states: "The Father is greater than I."

REASONING FROM THE SCRIPTURES

John 14:28—*"The Father Is Greater than I"*

The Watchtower Teaching. The *New World Translation* renders John 14:28, "You heard that I said to you, I am going away and I am coming back to you. If you loved me, you would rejoice that I am going my way to the Father, because *the Father is greater than I am*" (emphasis added). The book *"Let God Be True"* tells us that Jehovah is greater than Jesus not only in regard to *office* but also in regard to His *person*.[1] Jehovah is *intrinsically* greater than Jesus.

The Watchtower Society concludes from this that because Jehovah is the "greater" of the two, Jesus cannot be God Almighty. The fact that Jesus is *lesser* than Jehovah proves that He cannot be God *in the same sense* that Jehovah is.[2] Indeed, "on numerous occasions Jesus expressed his inferiority and subordination to his Father. . . . Even after Jesus' ascension into heaven his apostles continued to present the same picture."[3]

The Biblical Teaching. It is critical to recognize that in John 14:28, Jesus is not speaking about His nature or His essential being (Christ had earlier said, "I and the Father are one" in this regard [John 10:30]), but rather about His lowly position in the incarnation.[4] The Athanasian Creed affirms that Christ is "equal to the Father as touching his Godhood and inferior to the Father as touching his manhood."[5]

In his commentary *Exposition of the Gospel of John*, Arthur W. Pink relates Christ's statement that the Father was "greater" than Him to the great humiliation Christ suffered in becoming a man:

> In becoming incarnate and tabernacling among men, [Christ] had greatly humiliated Himself, by choosing to descend into shame and suffering in their acutest forms. . . . In view of this, Christ was now contrasting His situation with that of the Father in the heavenly Sanctuary. The Father was seated upon the throne of highest majesty; the brightness of His glory was uneclipsed; He was surrounded by hosts of holy beings, who worshiped Him with uninterrupted praise. Far different was it with His incarnate Son—despised and rejected of men, surrounded by implacable enemies, soon to be nailed to a criminal's cross.[6]

Now, it is important that you emphasize the distinction between the Greek words for *greater* (*meizon*) and *better* (*kreitton*).[7]

Jesus specifically said, "The Father is *greater* than I" not, "The Father is *better* than I." The word "greater" is used to point to the Father's greater position (in heaven), not a greater nature. Had the word "better" been used, however, this would indicate that the Father has a better nature than Jesus.

This distinction is made clear in Hebrews 1:4, where "better" is used in regard to Jesus' superiority over the angels. The word "better" in this verse indicates that Jesus is not just higher than the angels *positionally*; rather, He is higher than the angels *in His very nature*. Jesus is different (better) in kind and in nature from the angels.

This distinction between "greater" and "better" can be illustrated in the president of the United States.[8] The president is in a higher position than the rest of us. Therefore, the president is greater (*meizon*) than the rest of us. However, he is still just a human being—and thus he is not better (*kreitton*) than the rest of us.

Notice that Jesus never used the word "better" regarding His relationship with the Father, for He is not inferior or lower in nature than the Father. Rather, Jesus used a word ("greater") that points to the Father being higher in position only. During the time of the incarnation, Jesus functioned in the world of humanity, and this necessitated Jesus being lower than the Father positionally.

 Ask...

- Is the president of the United States intrinsically better than us *by nature*, or is it more correct to say that his *position* is greater than ours?

- In view of the distinction between the Greek words for "greater" (meaning higher *in position*) and "better" (meaning higher *in nature*), is it not clear that in John 14:28 Jesus is speaking of the Father's higher position and not higher nature?

The Lower Position of Christ: Philippians 2:6-9. As you discuss how the Father is "greater" than Christ, you will want to focus some of your attention on Philippians 2:6-9. The apostle Paul, speaking of the incarnation, said that Christ, "being in very nature God, did not consider equality with God something to be grasped, but made himself nothing, taking the very nature of a servant, being made in human likeness" (verses 6,7).

Paul's affirmation that Christ was "in very nature God" is extremely significant. Christ in His essential being *is* and *always has been* eternal God—just as much as the Father and the Holy Spirit. Theologian Charles Ryrie notes that the word "nature" in the Greek connotes "that which is intrinsic and essential to the thing. Thus here it means that our Lord in His preincarnate state possessed essential deity."[9] Reformed theologian Benjamin Warfield comments that the word "nature"— "is a term which expresses the sum of those characterizing qualities which make a thing the precise thing that it is."[10] Used of God, the word refers to "the sum of the characteristics which make the being we call 'God,' specifically God, rather than some other being—an angel, say, or a man."[11]

Now, here is something you will want to emphasize: The word "being" (in the phrase "being in very nature God") is a present tense participle and carries the idea of continued existence as God.[12] Here the thought is that "Christ always has been in the form of God with the implication that He still is."[13] Robert Reymond notes that "when we take into account the force of the present participle, which conveys the idea of 'continually [beforehand] subsisting' (which in turn excludes any intimation that this mode of subsistence came to an end when He assumed the form of servant), we have here as bold and unqualified an assertion of both the preexistence and the full and unabridged deity of Jesus Christ as one could ever hope to find in the pages of the New Testament."[14] Thus, Philippians 2:6-9 indicates that Jesus Christ, in eternity past, continually and forever existed in the form of God, outwardly manifesting His divine attributes. *This* is the One who was born from the womb of Mary as a human being, all the while retaining His full deity.

Having said all that about Christ's essential deity, a key question remains: In what way did Christ "make himself nothing" when He became incarnate (Philippians 2:7)? Paul's statement that Christ made Himself nothing in the incarnation involves three basic issues: the veiling of His preincarnate glory, a voluntary nonuse (on some occasions) of some of His divine attributes, and the condescension involved in taking on the likeness of men.

First, we can be certain that Jesus never gave up His deity when He became incarnate. Indeed, this is impossible, since God cannot cease to be God. Regarding the veiling of Christ's preincarnate glory, Scripture indicates that it was necessary for Him to give up the *outer appearance* of God in order to take upon Himself the form of man. Of course, Christ never actually surrendered His divine glory. Recall that on the Mount of Transfiguration (prior to His crucifixion), Jesus allowed His intrinsic glory to shine forth for a brief time, illuminating the whole mountainside (Matthew 17). Nevertheless, it was necessary for Jesus to veil His preincarnate glory in order to dwell among mortal men.

Had Christ not veiled His preincarnate glory, mankind would not have been able to behold Him. It would have been the same as when the apostle John, over fifty years after Christ's resurrection, beheld Christ in His glory and said, "I fell at His feet as though dead" (Revelation 1:17); or, as when Isaiah beheld the glory of Christ in his vision in the temple and said, "Woe to me, I am ruined" (Isaiah 6:5; *see* John 12:41).

Second, when Christ made Himself "nothing" in the incarnation, He submitted to a *voluntary nonuse of some of His divine attributes* (on some occasions) in order to accomplish His objectives. Christ could never have actually surrendered any of His attributes, for then He would have ceased to be God.[15] But He could (and did) voluntarily cease using some of them (on occasion) during His time on earth (approximately 4 B.C. to A.D. 29) in order to live among men and their limitations.

Though Christ sometimes chose not to use His divine attributes, at other times He *did* use them. For example, on different occasions during His three-year ministry, Jesus exercised the divine attributes of *omniscience* (that is, all-knowingness—John 2:24; 16:30), *omnipresence* (being everywhere-present—John 1:48), and *omnipotence* (being all-powerful, as evidenced by His many miracles—John 11). Hence, whatever limitations Christ may have suffered when He "made Himself nothing" (Philippians 2:7), He did not subtract a single divine attribute or in any sense make Himself less than God.

The question that arises at this point is, Why did Jesus choose on occasion *not* to use some of His divine attributes? It would seem that He did so to remain consistent with His purpose of living among human beings and their limitations. He does not seem to have used His divine attributes on His own behalf, though certainly they were gloriously displayed in the many miracles He performed for others.

To be more specific, the scriptural testimony indicates that Christ never used His omniscience to make His own life *as a human being* easier. "He suffered all the inconveniences of His day even though in His divine omniscience He had full knowledge of every human device ever conceived for human comfort."[16]

Nor did Christ use His omnipotence or omnipresence to make His life on earth easier. Though He could have, in His omnipotence, just willed himself instantly from Bethany to Jerusalem, He traveled by foot instead—like every other human—and experienced fatigue in the process. Of course, as God, Christ in His divine nature (with His attribute of omnipresence) was in both Bethany and Jerusalem at the same time. But during His three-year ministry He voluntarily chose not to use this attribute on those occasions that would have made His life easier. "In a word, He restricted the benefits of

His attributes as they pertained to His walk on earth and voluntarily chose not to use His powers to lift Himself above ordinary human limitations."[17]

Third, when Christ made Himself "nothing" in the incarnation He condescended Himself by taking on the "likeness" (literally "form" or "appearance") of men, and taking on the *form* ("essence" or "nature") of a bondservant.[18] Christ was thus truly human. This humanity was one that was subject to temptation, distress, weakness, pain, sorrow, and limitation.[19] Yet at the same time, it must be noted that the word "likeness" suggests *similarity but difference*. As theologian Robert Lightner explains, "Though His humanity was genuine, He was different from all other humans in that He was sinless."[20] Nevertheless, Christ's taking on the likeness of men represented a great condescension on the part of the second Person of the Trinity.

Theologians have been careful to point out that the incarnation involved a gaining of *human* attributes and not a giving up of *divine* attributes. The apostle Paul made this clear when he affirmed that in the incarnation Christ was "taking the very nature of a servant," "being made in human likeness," and "being found in appearance as a man" (Philippians 2:7,8). As J.I. Packer puts it, "He was no less God then [in the incarnation] than before; but He had begun to be man. He was not now God *minus* some elements of His deity, but God *plus* all that He had made His own by taking manhood to Himself. He who *made* man was now learning what it felt like to *be* man."[21] In other words, the incarnation involved not the subtraction of deity but the addition of humanity.

So, in order to dwell among human beings, Christ made Himself nothing in the sense that He veiled His preincarnate glory, He submitted to a voluntary nonuse (without a surrendering) of some of His divine attributes, and He condescended Himself by taking on a human nature. All this adds great significance to Jesus' statement that "the Father is greater than I" (John 14:28). Clearly, Jesus was making the statement from the vantage point of the incarnation.

John 20:17—*"My God and Your God"*

The Watchtower Teaching. John 20:17 in the *New World Translation* reads, "Jesus said to her: 'Stop clinging to me. For I have not yet ascended to the Father. But be on your way to my brothers and say to them, "I am ascending to *my Father and your Father and to my God and your God*" '" (emphasis added).

Because Jesus referred to "my Father" and "my God," the Jehovah's Witnesses argue, Jesus cannot possibly be Almighty God Himself. Indeed, as *Reasoning from the Scriptures* puts it, "to the resurrected Jesus, the Father was God, just as the Father was God to Mary Magdalene."[22] By contrast, "never in the Bible is the Father reported to refer to the Son as 'my God.' "[23]

The Biblical Teaching. Why did Jesus call the Father "my God"? Does this imply that Jesus Himself is *not* God? By no means! Prior to the incarnation, Christ, the second Person of the Trinity, had only a divine nature. But in the incarnation Christ took on a human nature. It is thus in His humanity that Christ acknowledged the Father as "my God." Jesus in His divine nature could never refer to the Father as "my God," for Jesus was fully equal to the Father in every way.

Bible scholar Paul G. Weathers provides some keen insights on this issue:

> Since Christ came as man, and since one of the proper duties of man is to worship, pray to, and adore [God], it was perfectly proper for Jesus to call the Father "my God" and to address him in prayer. Positionally speaking as a man, as a Jew, and as our high priest ("made like his brothers in every way," Heb. 2:17), Jesus could address the Father as "God." However, Jesus did not relate to the Father in this way until he "emptied himself" and became man, as it says in Phil. 2:6-8.[24]

There is another point we must make regarding Jesus' statement that He was ascending "to my God and your God" (John 20:17). Why didn't Jesus just say, "I am ascending to *our*

Father and *our* God"? The reason is that Jesus was always careful to distinguish His relationship with the Father from the relationship humans had to the Father. As Robert Bowman notes, Jesus was careful to distinguish the two "because he was God's Son *by nature*, whereas Christians are God's 'sons' *by adoption*. Similarly, the Father was Jesus' God because Jesus humbled himself to become a man (Phil. 2:7), whereas the Father is our God because we are by nature creatures."[25]

Regarding this important distinction, Bible scholar Robert Reymond comments:

> It is significant that nowhere in the teaching of Jesus did He ever speak of God to His disciples as "our Father" or "our God." Throughout His ministry He consistently spoke of the Father as "the Father" or "My Father," but never as "our Father." (The "Our Father" of the so-called "Lord's Prayer" is not an exception to this inasmuch as there Jesus is instructing His disciples on how *they* should corporately address God in prayer.) Here [in John 20:17], in keeping with His established pattern of speech, He avoided the obviously shorter form of expression ("our") and chose to remain with the longer form ("My" and "your"). I suggest that His concern here was to maintain the distinction between the sense in which He is God's Son by nature and by right and the sense in which His disciples are God's sons by grace and by adoption.[26]

_____ *Ask*... _____

- Why do you think Jesus was always so careful to distinguish His relationship with the Father from the relationship humans have to the Father?

- Why did Jesus always say, "My Father" or, "Your Father" but never, "Our Father"?

Regardless of what response you receive from a Witness, you can use these questions to drive home the point that Christ was God's Son *by nature*, whereas Christians are God's sons *by adoption*. Because He is God's Son by nature, Jesus is truly God. Because He is also a man by nature (in the incarnation), He can call the Father "my God."

Mark 13:32—*No One Knows the Day or the Hour*

The Watchtower Teaching. The *New World Translation* renders Mark 13:32, "Concerning that day or the hour nobody knows, neither the angels in heaven nor the Son, but the Father." Jehovah's Witnesses say that because Christ was ignorant of the time of the end, He cannot be Almighty God because God knows all things. "Had Jesus been the equal Son part of a Godhead, he would have known what the Father knows. But Jesus did not know, for he was not equal to God."[27] Only the Father is Jehovah and is all-knowing.

The Biblical Teaching. Though a bit complex, you must make the point that the eternal Son of God—who, prior to the incarnation, was *one in person and nature* (wholly divine)—became, in the incarnation, *two in nature* (divine *and* human) while remaining *one person*. The Son, who had already been a person for all eternity past, joined Himself not with a human person but with a human nature at the incarnation.

One of the most complex aspects of the relationship between Christ's two natures is that, while the attributes of one nature are never attributed to the other, the attributes of *both* natures are properly attributed to His *one* person. Thus Christ at the same moment in time had what seem to be contradictory qualities. He was finite and yet infinite, weak and yet omnipotent, increasing in knowledge and yet omniscient, limited to being in one place at one time and yet omnipresent. In the incarnation, the person of Christ is the partaker of the attributes of both natures, so that whatever may be affirmed of *either* nature—human or divine—may be affirmed of the *one* person.

Though Christ sometimes operated in the sphere of His humanity and in other cases in the sphere of His deity, in all cases what He did and what He was could be attributed to His one person. Even though Christ in His human nature knew hunger (Luke 4:2), weariness (John 4:6), and the need for sleep (Luke 8:23), in His divine nature He was also omniscient (John 2:24), omnipresent (John 1:48), and omnipotent (John 11). All of that was experienced by the one person of Jesus Christ.

The Gospel accounts clearly show that at different times, Christ operated under the *major* influence of one or the other of His two natures. Indeed, He operated in the human sphere to the extent that it was necessary for Him to accomplish His earthly purpose as determined in the eternal plan of salvation. At the same time, He operated in the divine sphere to the extent that it was possible in the period of His humiliation (Philippians 2:6-9).

Here is the key point: Both of Christ's natures come into play in many events recorded in the Gospels. For example, Christ's initial approach to the fig tree to pick and eat a fig to relieve His hunger reflected the natural ignorance of the *human* mind (Matthew 21:19a). (That is, in His humanity He did not know from a distance that there was no fruit on that tree.) But then He immediately revealed His *divine* omnipotence by causing the tree to wither (verse 19b).

On another occasion, Jesus in His *divine* omniscience knew that His friend Lazarus had died, so He set off for Bethany (John 11:11). When Jesus arrived, He asked (in his *humanness*, without exercising omniscience) where Lazarus had been laid (verse 34). Robert Reymond notes that "as the God-man, [Jesus] is simultaneously omniscient as God (in company with the other persons of the Godhead) and ignorant of some things as man (in company with the other persons of the human race)."[28]

All that helps to give a proper understanding of Jesus' comment in Mark 13:32: "But of that day or hour no one knows, not even the angels in heaven, nor the Son, but the Father alone" (NASB). *In this passage, Jesus was speaking from the vantage point of His humanity.* Thus, as a human being Jesus was not omniscient but was limited in understanding just as all human beings are. If Jesus had been speaking from the perspective of His divinity, He wouldn't have said the same thing.

Now, it is critical that you point out to the Jehovah's Witness that Scripture is abundantly clear that in His divine nature, Jesus *is* omniscient—*just as omniscient as the Father.* The apostle John said that Jesus "did not need man's testimony about man, for he knew what was in a man" (John 2:25). The disciples said, "Now we can see that *you know all things* and that you do not even need to have anyone ask you questions. This makes us believe that you came from God" (John 16:30, emphasis added). After the resurrection, when Jesus asked Peter for the third time if Peter loved Him, the disciple responded, "Lord, *you know all things*; you know that I love you" (John 21:17, emphasis added).

Bible scholar Thomas Schultz has provided an excellent summary of the massive evidence for Christ's omniscience:

> First, He knows the inward thoughts and memories of man, an ability peculiar to God (1 Kings 8:39; Jeremiah 17:9-16). He saw the evil in the hearts of the scribes (Matthew 9:4); He knew beforehand those who would reject Him (John 10:64) and those who would follow Him (John 10:14). He could read the hearts of every man and woman (Mark 2:8; John 1:48; 2:24,25; 4:16-19; Acts 1:24; 1 Corinthians 4:5; Revelation 2:18-23). A mere human can no more than make an intelligent guess as to what is in the hearts and minds of others.
>
> Second, Christ has a knowledge of other facts beyond the possible comprehension of any man. He knew just where the fish were in the water (Luke 5:4,6; John 21:6-11), and He knew just which fish contained the coin (Matthew 17:27). He knew future events (John 11:11; 18:4), details that would be encountered (Matthew 21:2-4), and He knew that Lazarus had died (John 11:14).

Third, He possessed an inner knowledge of the Godhead showing the closest possible communion with God as well as perfect knowledge. He knows the Father as the Father knows Him (Matthew 11:27; John 7:29; 8:55; 10:15; 17:25).

The fourth and consummating teaching of Scripture along this line is that Christ knows all things (John 16:30; 21:17), and that in Him are hidden all the treasures of wisdom and knowledge (Colossians 2:3).[29]

Certainly a key affirmation of Christ's omniscience is the fact that He hears and answers the prayers of His people. "When Jesus claimed for Himself the prerogative to hear and to answer the prayers of His disciples," Robert Reymond suggests, "He was claiming omniscience. One who can hear the innumerable prayers of His disciples—offered to Him night and day, day in and day out throughout the centuries—keep each request infallibly related to its petitioner, and answer each one in accordance with the divine mind and will would need Himself to be omniscient."[30]

After sharing some of the above verses regarding Christ's omniscience with the Jehovah's Witness (you might want to read them aloud):

___ *Ask . . .* _____

- Can anyone do the things Christ did in these verses without having the attribute of omniscience?

- Can anyone other than God have the attribute of omniscience?

- Since Christ in the incarnation had both a *human* nature and a *divine* nature—and since Christ in His divine nature exercised His omniscience on numerous occasions in the Gospels—can you see how Jesus was speaking *from His human nature* when He said He didn't know the day or the hour?

Mark 10:17,18—*"No One Is Good Except God Alone"*

The Watchtower Teaching. The *New World Translation* renders Mark 10:17,18, "And as he was going out on his way, a certain man ran up and fell upon his knees before him and put the question to him: 'Good Teacher, what must I do to inherit everlasting life?' Jesus said to him: *'Why do you call me good? Nobody is good, except one, God'* " (emphasis added).

The Jehovah's Witnesses claim that this verse proves Jesus is not God, for, as Jesus acknowledged, only God is truly good. Commenting on this verse, the booklet *Should You Believe in the Trinity?* tells us, "Jesus was saying that no one is as good as God is, not even Jesus himself. God is good in a way that separates him from Jesus."[31] *Aid to Bible Understanding* likewise says that "Jesus Christ, though he had this quality of moral excellence, would not accept 'Good' as a title. . . . He thus recognized Jehovah as the ultimate standard of what is good."[32]

The Biblical Teaching. Jesus was not claiming in Mark 10:17,18 that He didn't have the "goodness" characteristic of God. Nor was He denying that He was God. Rather, Jesus was asking the young ruler to examine the implications of what he was saying. In effect, Jesus said, "Do you realize what you are saying when you call Me good? Are you saying I am God?"[33] As scholar John D. Grassmick puts it, "Jesus' response did not deny His own deity but was a veiled claim to it. The man, unwittingly calling Him 'good,' needed to perceive Jesus' true identity."[34]

Regarding this, apologist Norman Geisler writes, "The young man did not realize the implications of what he was saying. Thus Jesus was forcing him to a very uncomfortable dilemma. Either Jesus was good and God, or else He was bad and man. A good God or a bad man, but not merely a good man. Those are the real alternatives with regard to Christ. For no good man would claim to be God when he was not."[35]

Thus, Jesus' statement to the young ruler may be summarized this way: "If I am not deity, don't call me good, for only

God is good."[36] Or perhaps: "You have given me a title which belongs only to God. Do you understand and mean it?"[37] Clearly, Matthew 10:17,18 does not support the Watchtower contention that Jesus is not God Almighty simply because He lacks the goodness of God.

After explaining this to the Jehovah's Witness:

_____ *Ask . . .* _____

- Where in the text does Jesus explicitly say He is not good? (Merely asking the question, "Why do you call me good?" is not a confession that Christ is not good.)

- Doesn't the context clearly show that Jesus was really saying, "You have given me a title which belongs only to God. Do you understand and mean it?"

---

1 Corinthians 8:6—*"One God, the Father . . . One Lord, Jesus Christ"*

The Watchtower Teaching. The *New World Translation* renders 1 Corinthians 8:6, "There is actually to us *one God the Father*, out of whom all things are, and we for him; and there is *one Lord, Jesus Christ*, through whom all things are, and we through him" (emphasis added).

The Jehovah's Witnesses argue that since there is "one God" (Jehovah) who is distinct from "one Lord" (Jesus), then Jesus cannot be God. This verse presents the Father as being in a "class" distinct from Jesus Christ.[38] According to *Reasoning from the Scriptures*, this verse indicates that Jehovah is utterly unique, with no one else sharing His exalted position. Jehovah stands in clear contrast to all other alleged objects of worship.[39]

The Biblical Teaching. Though the Father is called "one God" and Jesus Christ is called "one Lord" in 1 Corinthians

8:6, it is illegitimate to conclude that Jesus is not God *just as it is illegitimate to conclude that the Father is not Lord.* After all, there are many places throughout Scripture where the Father is called Lord and the Son is called God.

It is critical to force the Jehovah's Witness to carry his logic to the end. Indeed, if the reference to the Father being the "one God" proves that Jesus is not God, then by that same logic we must conclude that the reference to Jesus Christ as the "one Lord" means that the Father is not Lord.[40] And no Witness will be willing to concede that the Father is not Lord. *Don't allow him or her to sidestep this issue.* He or she cannot interpret the first part of this verse one way and the second part another way.

The faulty logic of Jehovah's Witnesses here is the assumption that the use of a title for one person in one context automatically rules out its application to another person in another context.[41] Instead of making such a faulty assumption, the proper policy would be to consult what *all of Scripture* has to say about the Father and Jesus Christ and then come to one's conclusion. From Scripture we know that the Father is called God (1 Peter 1:2) and Lord (Matthew 11:25), and we know that Jesus Christ is called God (John 20:28; Hebrews 1:8) and Lord (Romans 10:9).[42] When we let Scripture interpret Scripture, it becomes clear that the Watchtower interpretation of 1 Corinthians 8:6 is in gross error.

_____ *Ask. . .* _____

- Does the fact that Jesus is called the "one Lord" in this verse mean that the Father (Jehovah) is not Lord? (He'll say no. Share the above verses with him.)

- Why not? (His or her answer should be interesting!)

- Can you see that since Jesus as "one Lord" does not mean that the Father is not Lord, then—by the same logic—the Father as "one God" does not mean that Jesus is not God?

Psalm 110:1—*Jehovah and "My Lord"*

The Watchtower Teaching. Psalm 110:1 in the *New World Translation* reads, *"The utterance of Jehovah to my Lord* is: 'Sit at my right hand until I place your enemies as a stool for your feet'"* (emphasis added). The Jehovah's Witnesses say that since Jehovah is speaking in this verse, and since the "Lord" is a distinct person from Jehovah, then Jesus must not be God Almighty. *Reasoning from the Scriptures* explains that in Matthew 22:41-45 Jesus claims that He Himself is the "Lord" referred to by David in this psalm. They therefore conclude that Jesus is not Jehovah, but is the one to whom Jehovah's words were spoken.[43]

The Biblical Teaching. This verse makes perfect sense within the scope of trinitarian theology. In the broader context of Matthew 22:41-46, we find Christ "putting the Pharisees into a corner" by asking them a question relating to the person of the Messiah. He asked, "Whose son is he?" (Matthew 22:42).

They responded, "The Son of David." Their answer was correct since the Old Testament thoroughly established the Davidic lineage of the Messiah (2 Samuel 7:14). *But their answer was also incomplete.* Scripture not only teaches that the Messiah would be the Son of David in terms of His *humanity*, it also teaches that He is *God*—and it is the latter fact that Christ wanted the Pharisees to acknowledge.

Christ, of course, anticipated the Pharisees' half-answer. That's why in the next verse He quoted a Davidic psalm: "The LORD says to my Lord: 'Sit at my right hand until I put your enemies under your feet'" (Matthew 22:43; cf. Psalm 110:1). Now, the words "my Lord" are a reference to David's Messiah. This divine Messiah is invited to sit at the right hand of "the LORD" (God the Father). Here we have the first person of the Trinity speaking to the second person of the Trinity.[44]

In His discussion with the Pharisees, Jesus asked them that if the Messiah was the "son" or descendant of David, "how is it then that David, speaking by the Spirit, calls Him 'Lord'?" (Matthew 22:43). It seems odd that David would call his own son "my Lord." Certainly the fact that the Messiah was David's son testified to the *humanity* of the Messiah. But David's reference to "my Lord" also points to the *undiminished deity* of the Messiah, since "Lord" (Hebrew: *adonai*) was a title for deity.[45] The Messiah would be *David's son*, but He would also be *David's God*. The Messiah would be both God *and* man. To drive this point home, Christ continued to interrogate the Pharisees: "If then David calls Him 'Lord,' how can he be his son?" (verse 45).

The Pharisees were trapped, and they knew it. J. Dwight Pentecost, in his excellent volume *The Words and Works of Jesus Christ*, explains:

> If the Pharisees answered that David called Him his Lord because He is God, then they could not object to Christ, David's Son according to the flesh, claiming to be the Son of God. If they agreed that Messiah was to be truly human and truly God, they must cease their objections to Christ's claim concerning His person. The Pharisees realized the dilemma that faced them and refused to answer. None could refute the wisdom with which He spoke, and "from that day on no one dared to ask him any more questions" (v. 46).[46]

Obviously, far from showing that Christ is less than the Father, Psalm 110:1 actually points to the undiminished deity of Jesus Christ.

After explaining all this to the Jehovah's Witness:

____ *Ask . . .* _____

- Did you know that the same word used for "Lord" (*adonai*) in Psalm 110:1 of Jesus Christ is also used of the Father numerous times in Scripture (Exodus 23:17; Deuteronomy 10:17; Joshua 3:11)?

- Is it not clear from the context of Matthew 22 that Jesus' main point to the Pharisees was that the Messiah would be *David's son* as well as *David's God*?

Isaiah 9:6—*Jesus a "Mighty God"*?

The Watchtower Teaching. The *New World Translation* renders Isaiah 9:6, "For there has been a child born to us, there has been a son given to us; and the princely rule will come to be upon his shoulder. And his name will be called Wonderful Counselor, *Mighty God*, Eternal Father, Prince of Peace" (emphasis added).

The Jehovah's Witnesses concede that Jesus is a "mighty God" but they are adamant that He is not God Almighty like Jehovah is.[47] They further argue that "to call Jehovah God 'Almighty' would have little significance unless there existed others who were also called gods but who occupied a lesser or inferior position."[48]

The Biblical Teaching. As you answer the Jehovah's Witness on this passage, you will want to point out that in the very next chapter in Isaiah (10:21) Jehovah Himself is called "Mighty God" (using the same Hebrew word).[49] The very fact that Jehovah is called "Mighty God" completely obliterates the Watchtower argument that the expression must refer to a lesser deity as opposed to "Almighty God." And because Jehovah is called "Mighty God," the fact that Jesus too is called "Mighty God" points to His equality with God the Father.

In further support of this, you might want to point out that Jehovah is called "Mighty God" in Jeremiah 32:17,18: "Ah Lord GOD! Behold, Thou hast made the heavens and the earth by Thy great power and by Thine outstretched arm! Nothing is too difficult for Thee, who showest lovingkindness to thousands, but repayest the iniquity of fathers into the bosom of their children after them, O great and *mighty God*. The LORD [Jehovah] of hosts is His name" (NASB, emphasis added).[50]

Because the Bible shows that both Jehovah and Jesus are called "Mighty God":

_____ *Ask...* _____

- Since Jehovah is called "Mighty God" (Isaiah 10:21) just as Jesus is called "Mighty God" (Isaiah 9:6), doesn't this mean the Watchtower Society is wrong in saying that the designation "Mighty God" indicates a lesser deity?

- If Jesus is a Mighty God just as Jehovah is a Mighty God, what does this tell you about Jesus' divine nature?

- If Jehovah is a Mighty God and if Jesus is a Mighty God, then how can there *not* be two Mighty Gods in heaven unless the doctrine of the Trinity is true?

To emphasize that there is no more than *one* Mighty God in heaven, you will want to cite the following verses:

> • Isaiah 44:6b: "I am the first and I am the last; apart from me there is no God."
> • Isaiah 44:8b: "Is there any God besides Me? No, there is no other Rock; I know not one."
> • Isaiah 45:5a: "I am the LORD, and there is no other; apart from me there is no God."

In view of those verses:

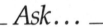

_____ *Ask...* _____

- How do you relate these verses in Isaiah 44 and 45 to Isaiah 10:21, which says that *Jehovah* is a Mighty God, and Isaiah 9:6, which says that *Jesus* is a Mighty God?

To further substantiate your case, you might want to mention that the phrase "Mighty God" is translated from the Hebrew word *Elohim*. *Elohim* is a very common name for God in the Old Testament; it is used about 2,570 times. It literally means "strong one," and its plural ending (*im* in Hebrew) indicates fullness of power.[51] *Elohim* is portrayed in the Old Testament as the powerful and sovereign Governor of the universe, ruling over the affairs of humankind. As related to God's sovereignty, the word *Elohim* is used to describe Him as the "God of all the earth" (Isaiah 54:5), the "God of all flesh" (Jeremiah 32:27 NASB), the "God of heaven" (Nehemiah 2:4), and the "God of gods and Lord of lords" (Deuteronomy 10:17).

With that in mind, you will want to show the Jehovah's Witness that in Isaiah 40:3, Jesus is called both *Yahweh* (Jehovah) and *Elohim* in the same verse: "In the desert prepare the way for the LORD [*Yahweh*]; make straight in the wilderness a highway for our God [*Elohim*]." This verse was written in reference to the future ministry of Jesus Christ (*see* John 1:23), and represents one of the strongest affirmations of Christ's deity in the Old Testament. Also, in referring to "*our* God" (as opposed to "their" God [of the New Testament]) Isaiah was affirming that Jesus Christ was the God of both the Old and New Testaments. Clearly, then, the Watchtower teaching that Jesus is a lesser god than Jehovah is emphatically wrong.

Jesus As "Everlasting Father." If you have the opportunity, you might also state the significance of the fact that Jesus is called "Everlasting Father" in Isaiah 9:6. Now this name has caused some confusion for Christians. In the Trinity, Jesus (the second person) is always distinguished from the Father (the first person). So why does Isaiah refer to Jesus the Messiah as "Everlasting Father"?

As we seek to interpret the meaning of this phrase, it is critical to keep in mind what other scriptures have to say about the distinction between the Father and the Son. For example, the New Testament calls Jesus "the Son" over 200 times. Moreover, the Father is considered by Jesus as *someone other than Himself* over 200 times in the New Testament. And over

50 times in the New Testament the Father and Son are seen to be distinct *within the same verse* (*see*, for example, Romans 15:6; 2 Corinthians 1:4; Galatians 1:2,3; Philippians 2:10,11; 1 John 2:1; 2 John 3).[52]

Now, if the Father and the Son are distinct, then in what sense can Jesus be called "Everlasting Father"? "Everlasting Father" in Isaiah 9:6 is better translated "Father of eternity." The words *Father of* in this context carry the meaning "possessor of eternity." "Father of eternity" is here used "in accordance with a custom usual in Hebrew and in Arabic, where he who possesses a thing is called the father of it. Thus, *the father of strength* means strong; *the father of knowledge*, intelligent; *the father of glory*, glorious."[53] Along these same lines, *the father of peace* means peaceful; *the father of compassion* means compassionate; and *the father of goodness* means good.[54] According to this common usage, the phrase "Father of eternity" in Isaiah 9:6 means eternal. Christ as the "Father of eternity" is an eternal being.[55] Bible scholar John A. Martin thus rightly concludes that the phrase "Everlasting Father" is simply "an idiom used to describe the Messiah's relationship to time, not His relationship to the other Members of the Trinity."[56]

Further support for this view is found in what are known as the Targums—simplified paraphrases of the Old Testament Scriptures utilized by the ancient Jews. It is highly revealing that the Targum of Isaiah renders Isaiah 9:6, "His name has been called from of old, Wonderful Counselor, Mighty God, *He who lives forever*, the Anointed One (or Messiah), in whose days peace shall increase upon us."[57] Clearly, the ancient Jews considered the phrase "Father of eternity" a reference to the eternality of the Messiah. There can be no doubt that this is the meaning Isaiah intended to communicate to his readers.

John 4:23—*Worship the Father Only?*

The Watchtower Teaching. John 4:23 in the *New World Translation* reads, "Nevertheless, the hour is coming, and it is now, when the true worshipers will *worship the Father* with spirit and truth, for, indeed, the Father is looking for suchlike ones to worship him" (emphasis added). Jehovah's Witnesses often cite this verse in support of their position that only God the Father—that is, Jehovah—is to be worshiped. Jesus, a lesser deity, is not to be worshiped.[58]

Even though the same Greek word used to speak of worshiping Jehovah (*proskuneo*) is used of Jesus Christ in the New Testament, the Watchtower Society says that the word is to be translated "obeisance" and not "worship" when used of Christ.[59] Christ may be *honored*, but not worshiped—for worship may be rendered only to Jehovah-God.

The Biblical Teaching. To begin, it is intriguing to note that at one time the Watchtower Society actually endorsed the worship of Jesus. An early issue of *The Watchtower* magazine (1880) said that "to worship Christ in any form cannot be wrong."[60] Some years later, another issue of the magazine (1892) said, "Yes, we believe our Lord Jesus while on earth was really worshipped, and properly so. While he was not *the* God, Jehovah, he was *a* God."[61]

Then, many years later, *The Watchtower* magazine dogmatically stated that "it is unscriptural for worshipers of the living and true God to render worship to the Son of God, Jesus Christ."[62] Indeed, the magazine warns: "Do not erroneously conclude that Christians are to worship Christ; that is not what he taught."[63]

In view of this change of position:

——— *Ask...* ————————

- Why did early issues of *The Watchtower* magazine say that we should worship Jesus while later issues say we should not worship Him?

- Since later issues of *The Watchtower* magazine said it is "unscriptural" to worship Christ, does that mean the earlier issues of *The Watchtower* magazine were "unscriptural"?

• What does this major reversal say about the
Watchtower Society's claim to be a true prophet
of God?

The Watchtower's theological bias comes through loud and
clear when we examine how it translates the Greek word for
worship, *proskuneo*. As noted earlier, when used in reference to
Jehovah, the *New World Translation* correctly translates the
word as "worship" (22 times). But when *proskuneo* is used of
Christ, it is translated "obeisance," "reverence," and "hom-
age." The Watchtower Society's translation completely ob-
scures the fact that Jesus is worshiped *as God* in the New
Testament.

The fact is, Christ was worshiped as God (*proskuneo*) many
times according to the Gospel accounts—and *He always
accepted such worship as appropriate*. Jesus accepted worship
from Thomas (John 20:28). All the angels are told to worship
Jesus (Hebrews 1:6). The wise men worshiped Jesus (Matthew
2:11); a leper worshiped Him (Matthew 8:2); a ruler bowed
before Him in worship (Matthew 9:18); a blind man worshiped
Him (John 9:38); a woman worshiped Him (Matthew 15:25);
Mary Magdalene worshiped Him (Matthew 28:9); and the
disciples worshiped Him (Matthew 28:17).

Furthermore, it is significant that when Paul and Barnabas
were in Lystra and they miraculously healed a man by God's
mighty power, those who were in the crowd shouted, "The
gods have come down to us in human form!" (Acts 14:11).
When Paul and Barnabas perceived that the people were
preparing to worship them, "they tore their clothes and rushed
out into the crowd, shouting: 'Men, why are you doing this?
We too are only men, human like you'" (verse 15). As soon as
they perceived what was happening, they immediately corrected the gross misconception that they were gods.

By contrast, *Jesus never sought to correct His followers*, or
"set them straight," when they bowed down and worshiped

Him. Indeed, He considered such worship as perfectly appropriate. That He accepted worship and did not correct those who worshiped Him is yet another affirmation that He truly was God in the flesh.

In your encounters with Jehovah's Witnesses, you might show that in the Book of Revelation, God the Father and Jesus Christ are clearly seen as receiving *the same worship*. Point them to Revelation 4:10, where the Father is worshiped, and Revelation 5:11-14, where we see all of heaven worshiping the Lamb of God, Jesus Christ.

Ask. . .

- What can we conclude about Jesus' true identity when we read in the Book of Revelation that He receives the *same worship* that is given to the Father?

That Jesus is worshiped says a lot about His true identity, for it is the consistent testimony of Scripture that only God can be worshiped. Exodus 34:14 tells us: "For you shall not worship any other god, for the LORD, whose name is Jealous, is a jealous God" (NASB, cf. Deuteronomy 6:13; Matthew 4:10). The fact that Jesus is worshiped on numerous occasions shows that He is in fact God.

Hebrews 1:6—"Obeisance" to Jesus?

The Watchtower Teaching. The *New World Translation* renders Hebrews 1:6, "But when he again brings his Firstborn into the inhabited earth, he says: 'And let all God's angels do obeisance to him'" (emphasis added). Though this verse uses the same Greek word (*proskuneo*) that is used elsewhere to speak of worshiping the Father, because it is used here in reference to Jesus Christ, the Watchtower Society has translated it as "obeisance."[64] This means that Jesus is to be *honored*, but not worshiped as God.

The Biblical Teaching. It is interesting to note that the 1961 edition of the *New World Translation* translated Hebrews 1:6, "But when he again brings his First-born into the inhabited earth, he says: 'And let all God's angels *worship* him'" (emphasis added). By contrast, the 1971 edition reads, "But when he again brings his Firstborn into the inhabited earth, he says: 'And let all God's angels *do obeisance* to him'" (emphasis added).

_____ *Ask . . .* _____

- Why did the 1961 edition of the *New World Translation* render Hebrews 1:6 to say that we should *worship* Jesus, while the 1971 edition says we should merely do *obeisance* to Him?

- What does this major change say about the Watchtower Society's claim to be a true prophet of God?

If the Watchtower Society is correct in saying that Jesus is a created being and is not to be worshiped, then the Father Himself is guilty of committing a horrible sin because in Hebrews 1:6 He commanded the angels to commit a sacrilegious act by worshiping (*proskuneo*) a mere creature.

Worse comes to worse when it is realized that the Jehovah's Witnesses say Jesus was an angelic being in his prehuman state (as Michael the Archangel) and returned to the angelic state after His death on the cross. This being the case, the angels mentioned in Hebrews 1:6 are actually commanded to worship a fellow angel—they are told to worship one of their own! Why would God allow this, especially since He has elsewhere said that worship is to be rendered to Him alone (Exodus 34:14; Deuteronomy 6:13; Matthew 4:10)?

Elsewhere in the New Testament, angels are clearly shown to *reject* worship. Former Jehovah's Witness David Reed therefore suggests this:

Invite the JW to turn to Revelation 22:8-9 in his own *Kingdom Interlinear Translation*, where the same word *proskuneo* is used in the original Greek. There the apostle John says, "I fell down to worship [root: *proskuneo*] before the feet of the angel.... But he tells me: 'Be careful! Do not do that!... Worship [root: *proskuneo*] God.'" Point out to the Jehovah's Witness that the worship that the *angel refused to accept*, but told John to give to God, is the same *proskuneo* that the Father commanded to be given to his Son Jesus at Hebrews 1:6. So, the Son is certainly not an angel.[65]

We must also emphasize that context is extremely important in properly interpreting Hebrews 1. It must be kept in mind that one of the primary purposes of Hebrews, particularly in chapter 1, is to demonstrate the superiority of Jesus Christ—including His superiority to the prophets (1:1-4), the angels (1:5–2:18), and Moses (3:1-6). How is this superiority demonstrated? Christ is shown to be God's ultimate revelation (verse 1); He is affirmed as the Creator and Sustainer of the universe (verses 2,3); and He is said to have the very nature of God (verse 3). None of these things could be said of the prophets, the angels, or Moses.

Again, Hebrews 1:5–2:18 states Christ's superiority over the angels. In Hebrews 1:6, we are told that Christ is worshiped (*proskuneo*) by the angels. But in the *New World Translation*, this superiority is obscured because of the way the Watchtower has butchered this verse.

Commentator Ray Stedman notes that "in the Song of Moses, the angels are called to worship Yahweh (Jehovah). New Testament writers apply such passages without hesitation to Jesus. Many places in Scripture witness the obedience of the angels, notably Job 38:7, Luke 2:13, and Revelation 5:11-12. Mark 3:11 indicates that even the demons (fallen angels) fell down before Jesus when they saw him and addressed him as the Son of God."[66]

Clearly, Christ was worshiped with the same kind of worship (*proskuneo*) rendered to the Father. There can be no getting around this fact. So, again:

_____ *Ask...* _____

- What does it say about Jesus' true identity that He receives the same worship that is given to the Father?

_____

7

Mistaken Identity:
Is Christ the Archangel Michael?

*To which of the angels did God [the Father] ever
say, "You are My Son...?"*

—Hebrews 1:5

According to the Watchtower Society, Jesus Christ is a mere
angel—the first being Jehovah-God created in the universe.
The Watchtower magazine says "there is Scriptural evidence
for concluding that Michael was the name of Jesus Christ
before he left heaven and *after* his return."[1] Indeed, " 'Michael
the great prince' is none other than Jesus Christ Himself."[2]

The Watchtower Society teaches that it was through this
created archangel that God brought all other things into being.
Michael was created first, and then he was used by God to
create the rest of the universe (*see* Colossians 1:16 NWT).[3]

Michael (Jesus) conceivably existed in his prehuman state
for billions of years, according to Watchtower literature. At
the appointed time, he was born on earth as a human being—
ceasing his existence as an angel. In order to "ransom"
humankind from sin, Michael willingly gave up his existence
as a spirit creature (angel) when his life force was transferred
into Mary's womb by Jehovah.

This was *not* an incarnation (God in the flesh). Rather, Jesus
became a perfect human being—nothing more and nothing
less. He was equal in every way to Adam prior to the Fall. He

173

lived His life as a human being, fulfilled the ministry appointed to Him by Jehovah, and died faithfully for the ransom of humankind.

At the "resurrection," Jesus was not physically raised from the dead as a glorified human being. Rather, Jesus was "put to death in the flesh and was resurrected an invisible spirit creature."[4] The Watchtower book *Let God Be True* tells us that "Jehovah God raised [Jesus] from the dead, not as a human Son, but as a mighty immortal spirit Son."[5]

The Jehovah's Witnesses "deny that He was raised in the flesh, and challenge any statement to that effect as being unscriptural."[6] Indeed, "the *man* Jesus is dead, forever dead."[7]

If this is true, then what became of Jesus? According to Watchtower literature, Jesus Christ resumed His identity as Michael the archangel at the "resurrection" (which is obviously more of a *re-creation*). The Watchtower book *Aid to Bible Understanding* explains that "by retaining the name Jesus after his resurrection (Acts 9:5), the 'Word' shows that he is identical with the Son of God on earth. His resuming his heavenly name Michael and his title (or, name) 'The Word of God' (Rev. 19:13) ties him in with his prehuman existence."[8]

Now, the Jehovah's Witnesses relate Christ's resurrection as a spirit creature to the doctrine of the atonement. They say Jesus *gave up* His human life as a ransom sacrifice for the benefit of humankind. Jesus *forever gave His body* as a ransom. In the Watchtower book *You Can Live Forever in Paradise on Earth*, we read, "Having given up his flesh for the life of the world, Christ could never take it again and become a man once more."[9] *Let God Be True* likewise tells us that "God did not purpose for Jesus to be humiliated thus forever by being a fleshly man forever. No, but after he had sacrificed his perfect manhood, God raised him to deathless life as a glorious spirit creature."[10]

In support of this, the Jehovah's Witnesses often cite Hebrews 10:5, a verse in which Jesus says to God the Father, "Sacrifice and offering you did not want, but you prepared *a body* for me" (NWT, emphasis added). Jesus also said that "the bread that I shall give is *my flesh* in behalf of the life of the world" (John 6:51 NWT, emphasis added).

In view of the above, it follows that "Christ could not take his body back again in the resurrection, thereby taking back the sacrifice offered to God for mankind. Besides, Christ was no longer to abide on earth. His 'home' is in the heavens with his Father, who is not flesh, but spirit."[11]

But if Christ was not physically raised from the dead, then what happened to His human body? There are conflicting answers to this question in Watchtower literature. In an early Watchtower publication—*Studies in the Scriptures*, by Pastor Russell—we are told, "Whether it [the body of Jesus] was dissolved into gases or whether it is still preserved somewhere as the grand memorial of God's love, of Christ's obedience, and of our redemption, *no one knows*."[12] Another early Watchtower publication said that Jesus' fleshly body "was disposed of by Jehovah God, dissolved into its constituent elements or atoms."[13] More recently (1975), *The Watchtower* magazine affirmed that "Jehovah God disposed of the sacrificed body of his Son."[14] Likewise, the Watchtower book *"Things in Which It Is Impossible for God to Lie"* says "the human body of flesh, which Jesus Christ laid down forever as a ransom sacrifice, was disposed of by God's power."[15]

A related question that must be addressed is, If Christ was not physically raised from the dead, then how did He prove His "resurrection" to the disciples and His followers? Jehovah's Witnesses say that Jesus appeared or "materialized" to His followers in different "bodies" than the one that was laid in the tomb.[16] Indeed, "the bodies in which Jesus manifested himself to his disciples after his return to life were not the body in which he was nailed to the tree."[17] *Aid to Bible Understanding* tells us, "Jesus appeared to his disciples on different occasions in various fleshly bodies, just as angels had appeared to men of ancient times. Like those angels, he had the power to construct and to disintegrate those fleshly bodies at will, for the purpose of proving visibly that he had been resurrected."[18]

Even today, Jesus exists as a spirit creature—the archangel Michael. He does not exist in a material, fleshly body. His "resurrection" was not a resurrection *of material flesh* but rather was a "re-creation" of the archangel Michael.

In summary, 1) Jesus existed for billions of years in His prehuman state as the archangel Michael; 2) He gave up His spirit existence as an angel when His life force was transferred to Mary's womb by Jehovah, and, following His birth, He lived a normal human life and was eventually crucified; and 3) at the resurrection, He was not raised from the dead in physical, bodily form but rather was re-created as the archangel Michael.

—————— REASONING FROM THE SCRIPTURES ——————

Daniel 10:13,21; 12:1—*Michael the Great Prince*

The Watchtower Teaching. Daniel 10:13 calls Michael "one of the foremost princes." He is likewise called the "prince" of God's people in verse 21. Then, in Daniel 12:1, we read that during the time of the end, "Michael will *stand up*, the great prince who is *standing* in behalf of the sons of your people" (emphasis added).

Based upon these verses, Jehovah's Witnesses argue that in His prehuman state Jesus was the archangel Michael and was a great prince of the people of God. They also say that the prophecy in Daniel 12:1 points to Michael's (Jesus') enthronement as king in heaven in 1914.[19] Indeed, "the Michael that *stands up* as the 'great prince' to fulfill Daniel 12:1 is the Lord Jesus Christ at God's right hand."[20] (The phrase "stand up" is interpreted by the Watchtower Society to mean "take control and reign as king."[21])

According to Watchtower theology, then, these verses in Daniel indicate that Jesus was Michael in both His prehuman state *and* in His posthuman state (that is, following His resurrection). Jesus' progressive existence may be summed up as *angel-human-angel*.

The Biblical Teaching. As you respond to the Watchtower interpretation of Daniel 10:13,21 and 12:1, there are several important points you will want to make. First:

_____ *Ask...* _____

• Where in the text of Daniel 10 and 12 is there any *explicit* statement that this is a reference to Jesus Christ?

The Jehovah's Witnesses will not be able to point you to such an explicit statement. But they will probably try to argue that Michael is called a "chief prince," thus appealing to his authority over the other angels. This *must* be Christ, they will tell you. However, it is vital to mention that in Daniel 10:13 Michael is specifically called "*one of* the chief princes" (emphasis added). The fact that Michael is "one of" the chief princes indicates that he is one among a group of chief princes. How large that group is, we are not told. But the fact that Michael is one among equals proves that he is not unique. By contrast, the Greek word used to describe Jesus in John 3:16 is *monogenes*—which means "unique," "one of a kind."

_____ *Ask...* _____

• If Jesus is the first and highest of all created beings, as the Watchtower teaches—and if Jesus in His prehuman state was Michael the Archangel—then why is Michael called "*one of* the chief princes" in Daniel 10:13?

• Doesn't this verse indicate that Michael is one among a group of equals?

You will also want to emphasize that Jesus is never called "Chief Prince" in the Bible. (If they argue that He is called that in Daniel 10:13, ask them again where Jesus is *explicitly* mentioned in the text.)

The fact is, Jesus is called the "King of kings and Lord of lords" in Revelation 19:16. This is a title that indicates absolute sovereignty and authority. A King of kings/Lord of lords is much higher in authority than a mere "Chief Prince" (who is one among equals). The first one has absolute sovereignty and authority; the latter has derived, limited authority.

As stated in earlier chapters, you might want to point out that the whole focus of Hebrews 1–3 is to demonstrate the superiority of Jesus Christ—including His superiority over the prophets (1:1-4), the angels (1:5–2:18), and Moses (3:1-6).[22] How is this superiority demonstrated? Christ is shown to be God's ultimate revelation (1:1); He is affirmed as the Creator and Sustainer of the universe (1:2,3); and He is said to have the very nature of God (1:3). None of these things could be said of the prophets, the angels, or Moses.

We read in Hebrews 1:5–2:18 of Christ's superiority over the angels. In Hebrews 1:5, we are told that no angel can ever be called God's son: "To which of the angels did He [God] ever say, 'Thou art My Son...'?" Since Jesus *is* the Son of God, and since no angel can ever be called God's Son, then Jesus cannot possibly be the archangel Michael.

_____ *Ask...* _____

• If no angel can ever be called God's Son (Hebrews 1:5)—and if Jesus is in fact the Son of God—then doesn't this mean that Jesus cannot be the archangel Michael?

Moving on to Hebrews 1:6, we are told that Christ is worshiped (*proskuneo*) by the angels. As noted earlier in chapter 5, this is the exact same word used in reference to worshiping Jehovah God. Christ was worshiped with the same kind of worship rendered to the Father. There can be no getting around this fact. Jesus is not an angel; He is *worshiped* by the angels.

Commentator Ray Stedman's point about this passage is worth repeating. He notes that "in the Song of Moses, the angels are called to worship Yahweh (Jehovah). New Testament writers apply such passages without hesitation to Jesus. Many places in Scripture witness the obedience of the angels, notably Job 38:7, Luke 2:13, and Revelation 5:11-12. Mark 3:11 indicates that even the demons (fallen angels) fell down before Jesus when they saw him and addressed him as the Son of God."[23]

Another argument that can be drawn from the Book of Hebrews is that we are explicitly told in Hebrews 2:5 that the world *is not* (and *will not be*) in subjection to an angel. Interestingly, the Dead Sea Scrolls (discovered at Qumran in 1947) reflect an expectation that the archangel Michael would be a supreme figure in the coming Messianic Kingdom. It may be that some of the recipients of the Book of Hebrews were tempted to assign angels a place above Christ. Whether or not this is so, Hebrews 2:5 makes it absolutely clear that no angel (the archangel included) will rule in God's kingdom. Christ the glorified God-man will reign supreme (Revelation 19:16).

Now, if no angel can rule the world (Hebrews 2:5), then *Christ cannot be the archangel Michael*, since Scripture repeatedly says Christ is to be the ruler of God's kingdom (e.g., Genesis 49:10; 2 Samuel 7:16; Psalm 2:6; Daniel 7:13,14; Luke 1:32,33; Matthew 2:1,2; 9:35; 13ff.; Revelation 19:16). Do not allow the Jehovah's Witness to sidestep this issue.

_____ *Ask...* _____

- If no angel can rule the world (Hebrews 2:5)—and if Scripture clearly says that Christ *is* ruler of the world (Luke 1:32,33; Revelation 19:16)—then doesn't this mean that Christ cannot be the archangel Michael?

There is one other argument I want to mention. It is based on the biblical doctrine of the immutability of Christ. Immutability—one of the key attributes of God in the Bible—refers to the idea that Christ (as God) is unchangeable, and thus unchanging. This does not mean that Christ is immobile or inactive, but it does mean that He never grows or develops or changes in His essential nature as God. This is in dire contrast to the Watchtower teaching that Christ was created as an angel, later became a human being, and then (at the "resurrection") became an angel again.

A key passage relating to the immutability of Christ is Hebrews 1:10-12, where the Father speaks of the Son's unchanging nature: "In the beginning, O Lord, you laid the foundations of the earth, and the heavens are the work of your hands. They will perish, but *you remain*; they will all wear out like a garment. You will roll them up like a robe; like a garment they will be changed. But *you remain the same*, and your years will never end" (emphasis added).

Hebrews 1:10-12 is actually a quotation from Psalm 102:25-27. It is highly intriguing to note that the words in this psalm are addressed to Jehovah, but are applied directly to Jesus Christ in Hebrews 1:10-12. This represents a strong argument for Christ's full deity.

Hebrews 1:10-12 teaches that even when the present creation wears out like an old garment, Jesus will remain unchanged. The reference here is to "the transformation of the heavens and earth which will occur after the Millennium [Christ's future 1000-year rule on earth] and will introduce the eternal state (2 Peter 3:10-13). Yet even after those cataclysmic events the Son's years will never end."[24]

Christ's immutability is also affirmed in Hebrews 13:8, where we are told that "Jesus Christ is the *same yesterday and today and forever*" (emphasis added). If Christ is the same yesterday, today, and forever, then He couldn't have been an *angel*, become a *human*, and then been re-created as an *angel*.

Now, it is true that in the incarnation Christ the eternal Son of God took on a human nature, but orthodox scholars have always held that it is the divine nature of Christ that remains unchanged and is therefore immutable.[25] Unlike the doctrine of the incarnation, the Watchtower Society teaches that Jesus' existence throughout history may be summed up angel-human-angel. This represents a change in nature—and it contradicts Hebrews 13:8 and other passages on Christ's immutability.

_____ Ask... _____

- Since Scripture teaches that Jesus is "the same yesterday and today and forever" (Hebrews 13:8), then how can it be said that Jesus was an angel, became a man, and then became an angel again?

1 Thessalonians 4:16—*The Voice of an Archangel*

The Watchtower Teaching. The *New World Translation* renders 1 Thessalonians 4:16, "The Lord himself will descend from heaven with a commanding call, with an archangel's voice and with God's trumpet, and those who are dead in union with Christ will rise first." The Watchtower Society argues that the *Lord Himself* issues forth a commanding call with the voice of the archangel, thereby proving that He *is* the archangel Michael.

In support of this interpretation, *Aid to Bible Understanding* comments, "Michael is the only one said to be the 'archangel,' meaning 'chief angel' or 'principal angel.' The term occurs in the Bible only in the singular. This seems to imply that there is but one whom God has designated chief or head of the angelic host. At 1 Thessalonians 4:16 the voice of the resurrected Lord Jesus Christ is described as being that of an archangel, suggesting that he is, in fact, himself the archangel."[26]

The Biblical Teaching. In your answer to the Jehovah's Witness begin by addressing the claim that because "archangel" occurs in the singular, this must mean that "there is but one whom God has designated chief or head of the angelic host." Point the Witness to Daniel 10:13, where Michael is specifically called "one of the chief princes." The fact that Michael is "one of" the chief princes indicates that he is one among a group of chief princes. How large that group is, we are not told. But the fact that Michael is *one* among equals proves that he is not totally unique.

_____ *Ask*... _____

- If Jesus is the *first and highest* of all created beings, as the Watchtower teaches—and if Jesus in His prehuman state was Michael the archangel—then why is Michael called "one of the chief princes" in Daniel 10:13? Doesn't this indicate that Michael is *one among equals*?

You might also point out that simply because the word "archangel" (in 1 Thessalonians 4:16) occurs in the singular and with a definite article (*the* archangel) does not mean there is only one archangel. In his book *Angels: Elect and Evil*, theologian Fred Dickason notes that "the definite article with archangel does not necessarily limit the class of archangel to Michael. The article may be one of identification as the *well-known* archangel instead of limitation as the *only* archangel. There may be others of the same class or rank, since he is described as 'one of the chief princes' (Dan. 10:13)."[27] Jewish tradition has always held that there are seven archangels.[28]

After sharing this, read 1 Thessalonians 4:16 aloud from a reliable translation, such as the New International Version: "For the Lord himself will come down from heaven, with a loud command, with the voice of the archangel and with the trumpet call of God, and the dead in Christ will rise first." Former Jehovah's Witness David Reed suggests mentioning to the Jehovah's Witness that "if using an archangel's voice makes the Lord an archangel, then having God's trumpet makes him God—even though Watchtower leaders would have us look at only the first part of the verse."[29] That is a legitimate point. One must be consistent in how one approaches the text. One cannot just use the portion of the verse that—stripped from its context—supports one's view.

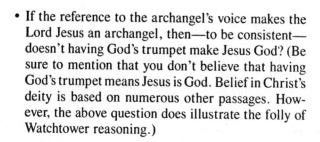

Ask...

- If the reference to the archangel's voice makes the Lord Jesus an archangel, then—to be consistent— doesn't having God's trumpet make Jesus God? (Be sure to mention that you don't believe that having God's trumpet means Jesus is God. Belief in Christ's deity is based on numerous other passages. However, the above question does illustrate the folly of Watchtower reasoning.)

A careful look at 1 Thessalonians 4:16 reveals that the text _never explicitly says_ that Jesus _Himself_ speaks with the voice of the archangel. This is an unwarranted assumption of the Watchtower Society, based on a strong theological bias. It is much more natural and logical to read the verse as saying that when Jesus comes from heaven to rapture the church from the earth, He will be _accompanied_ by the archangel since it is the archangel's voice (distinct from Jesus) that issues the shout.

This is not unlike what will happen at the Second Coming of Christ (seven years after the Rapture, following the Tribulation period). At the Second Coming, "the Lord Jesus shall be revealed from heaven _with His mighty angels_ in flaming fire" (2 Thessalonians 1:7 NASB, emphasis added). If the angels accompany Christ at the Second Coming, then surely the archangel Michael will accompany Him as well.

The Authority to Rebuke Satan. A key observation regarding Michael the archangel is that he does not have the authority to rebuke Satan. Point the Jehovah's Witness to Jude 9, which says, "But even the archangel Michael, when he was disputing with the devil about the body of Moses, did not dare to bring a slanderous accusation against him, but said, 'The Lord rebuke you!'" By contrast, Jesus rebuked the devil on a number of different occasions (*see*, for example, Matthew 4:10; 16:23; Mark 8:33).[30] Since Michael *could not* rebuke the devil in his own authority and Jesus could (and did), Michael and Jesus cannot be the same person.

_____ *Ask...* _____

- Since Michael the archangel could not rebuke the devil in his own authority and Jesus could (and did), doesn't that mean Michael and Jesus cannot be the same person?

Notice in Jude 9 that Michael the archangel said *"The Lord* rebuke you!" (emphasis added). The Greek word for "Lord" in this verse is *kurios*. It is the standard word for "Lord" in the New Testament. It is also a direct parallel to the word *Yahweh* or *Jehovah* in the Old Testament. Now, it's crucial to note that while Jesus is called *kurios* ("Lord") many times in the New Testament, Michael is never called *kurios*.

For example, we are told that Jesus is *kurios* ("Lord") in Philippians 2:9-11, and that at the name of Jesus every knee will bow in heaven and on earth, and *every tongue* will confess that Jesus is Lord. The apostle Paul, an Old Testament scholar par excellence, is here alluding to Isaiah 45:22,23: "I am God, and there is no other. By myself I have sworn, my mouth has uttered in all integrity a word that will not be revoked: Before me every knee will bow; by me every tongue will swear." Paul was drawing on his vast knowledge of the Old Testament to make the point that Jesus Christ is *kurios* and *Yahweh*—the *Lord* of all humankind.

Now, the point of my saying all this is that when Michael said *"the Lord* rebuke you," he was appealing directly to the sovereign authority of the Lord of the universe. And *Jesus is clearly the sovereign Lord of the universe.*

Christ Created the Angels. A final point you will want to make is that Christ is the *Creator*, and angels are among the *created*. Colossians 1:16,17 tells us that by Christ "all things were created: things in heaven and on earth, visible and invisible, whether thrones or powers or rulers or authorities; all things were created by him and for him. He is before all things, and in him all things hold together."

Notice that Paul says Christ created "thrones," "powers," "rulers," and "authorities." In the rabbinic (Jewish) thought of the first century, these words were used to describe the different orders of angels (*see* Romans 8:38; Ephesians 1:21; 3:10; 6:12; Colossians 2:10,15; Titus 3:1). Apparently there was a heresy flourishing in Colossae (to where Paul wrote the Book of Colossians) that involved the worship of angels. The end result of that worship was that Christ had been degraded. To correct this grave error, Paul emphasized that Christ is the one who created all things—including all the angels—and thus, He is supreme and is alone worthy to be worshiped. Since Michael is an angel, he would be one of Christ's created beings. Christ therefore cannot be the archangel Michael.

Christ's "Resurrection" As the Archangel Michael

1 Peter 3:18—*Did Jesus "Resurrect" from the Dead as a Spirit Creature?*

The Watchtower Teaching. First Peter 3:18 in the *New World Translation* reads, "Why, even Christ died once for all time concerning sins, a righteous [person] for unrighteous ones, that he might lead you to God, he being put to death in the flesh, but being *made alive in the spirit*" (emphasis added).

The Jehovah's Witnesses cite this verse to support their view that Jesus was resurrected with a spirit body, not a physical one. The Watchtower book *"Let Your Name Be Sanctified"* says that "Jesus was raised to life as an invisible spirit. He did not take up again that body in which he had been killed as a human sacrifice to God."[31] Indeed, Jesus "was not raised out of the grave a human creature, but he was raised a spirit."[32] Jesus' resurrection was "in the spirit," suitable to spirit life in heaven.[33]

In the book *Reasoning from the Scriptures*, the Watchtower Society says it is clear that Jesus was raised with a spirit body because in the Greek text the words "flesh" and "spirit" are put in contrast to each other ("he being put to death in the *flesh*, but being made alive in the *spirit*")[34] (emphasis added). Just as Jesus died in the flesh, so He was resurrected in the spirit.

The Biblical Teaching. The New International Version translates 1 Peter 3:18, "For Christ died for sins once for all, the righteous for the unrighteous, to bring you to God. He was put to death in the body but made alive *by the Spirit*" (emphasis added; *see* also the King James Version).

This verse does not refer to a spiritual resurrection of Christ; rather, as many scholars agree, it refers to Christ's physical resurrection *by the Holy Spirit*.[35] I believe 1 Peter 3:18 is saying that Jesus was raised from the dead—"quickened"— by the Holy Spirit.[36] Indeed, "God did not raise Jesus a spirit but raised Him *by* His Spirit."[37] This is consistent with Romans 1:4, which tells us that it was "through the Spirit of holiness" that Jesus was "declared with power to be the Son of God by his resurrection from the dead."

Of course, this is not to deny that the Father and Son were involved in the resurrection as well. God the Father is often said to have raised Christ from the dead (Acts 2:32; 13:30; Romans 6:4; Ephesians 1:19,20). But without diminishing the Father's key role in the resurrection, it is just as clear from Scripture that Jesus raised Himself from the dead. In John 10:17,18, Jesus said of His life, "I lay down my life—only to take it up again. No one takes it from me, but I lay it down of my own accord. I have authority to lay it down and authority to take it up again." Thus, it is clear that each of the three persons in the Trinity—the Father, Son, *and* the Holy Spirit—were involved in Christ's resurrection.

A foundational principle of Bible interpretation is that *Scripture interprets Scripture*. This principle says that if one interprets a specific verse in such a way that it is clearly contradicted by other Bible verses, then one's interpretation is proven incorrect. *Scriptural harmony is essential.*

In view of that principle, 1 Peter 3:18 cannot possibly be taken to mean that Jesus was raised from the dead in a spiritual body. During your discussion with the Jehovah's Witness, you will want to make the following point:

• The resurrected Christ Himself said, "See My hands and My feet, that it is I Myself; touch Me and see, for a spirit does not have flesh and bones as you see that I have" (Luke 24:39 NASB). Notice three things here: 1) The resurrected Christ says in this verse that He is *not a spirit*; 2) His resurrection body is made up of *flesh and bones*; and 3) Christ's physical hands and feet represent physical proof of the materiality of His resurrection from the dead. Along these same lines, we read in Acts 2:31 that "he was not abandoned to the grave, nor did his body see decay." Why didn't His flesh decay? Because Jesus was raised from the dead in a material, fleshly body.

_____ *Ask...* _____

• Jesus said in Luke 24:39 that He was *not a spirit* and that He had a *flesh-and-bones body*. How do you relate this to the Watchtower teaching that Jesus was raised as a spirit creature without a physical body?

___

Further support for a physical resurrection can be found in Christ's own words recorded in John 2:19-21, which—in the *New World Translation*—reads, "In answer Jesus said to them: 'Break down this temple, and in three days I will raise it up.'

Therefore the Jews said: 'This temple was built in forty-six years, and will you raise it up in three days?' *But he was talking about the temple of his body*" (emphasis added). Jesus said here that He would be raised from the dead *bodily*, not as a spirit creature.

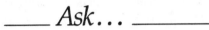

_____ *Ask...* _____

- How does Jesus define the "temple" in John 2:19-21?

- Since the "temple" is Jesus' body, and because He said He would *raise* this "temple" (body), then isn't Jesus here speaking of a *bodily* resurrection in John 2:19-21?

After asking those questions, continue by making the following points:
- Jesus' resurrection body retained the physical wounds from the cross. Indeed, the resurrected Christ revealed His crucifixion scars to the disciples (Luke 24:39), and even challenged doubting Thomas to touch His wounds (John 20:27).
- The resurrected Christ ate physical food on four different occasions. And He did this as a means of proving that He had a real, physical body (Luke 24:30; 24:42,43; John 21:12,13; Acts 1:4). Norman Geisler rightly observes that "it would have been deception on Jesus' part to have offered His ability to eat physical food as a proof of His bodily resurrection if He had not been resurrected in a physical body."[38]
- The physical body of the resurrected Christ was touched and handled by different people. For example, He was touched by Mary (John 20:17) and by some women (Matthew 28:9). He also challenged the disciples to physically touch Him so they could rest assured that His body was a material one (Luke 24:39).
- The Greek word for body (*soma*), when used of a person, always means a *physical* body in the New Testament. There are

no exceptions to this. Greek scholar Robert Gundry, in his authoritative book *Soma in Biblical Theology*, points to "Paul's exceptionless use of *soma* for a physical body."[39] Hence, all references to Jesus' resurrection "body" (*soma*) in the New Testament must be taken to mean a resurrected physical body.

• The body that is "sown" in death is the *very same body* that is raised in life (1 Corinthians 15:35-44). That which goes into the grave is raised to life (*see* verse 42).

Here's one final argument you may want to bring up: Contrary to the Watchtower position that at the resurrection Jesus was raised as a spirit creature—as the archangel Michael, leaving His humanity forever behind—the New Testament clearly teaches the continuation of Jesus' humanity in the resurrection and beyond.

To prove this, first point out (and be sure to open your Bible to specific verses) that Christ was raised immortal in the *very same human body* in which He died (Luke 24:37-39; Acts 2:31; 1 John 4:2; 2 John 7). And when Christ ascended into heaven, He did so in the same physical human body—as witnessed by several of the disciples (Acts 1:11). First Timothy 2:5, a verse that speaks of the postresurrection Jesus, tells us, "For there is one God, and one mediator between God and men, *the man* Christ Jesus" (emphasis added). When Christ returns, He will return as the "Son of Man"—a messianic title that points to His humanity (Matthew 26:64). There can be no doubt that Scripture consistently affirms that Christ forever retained His humanity in the resurrection.

1 Corinthians 15:44-50—*A Nonphysical Resurrection?*

The Watchtower Teaching. The entire chapter of 1 Corinthians 15 deals with the resurrection. The *New World Translation* renders verse 44, "It is sown a physical body, it is raised up a spiritual body. If there is a physical body, there is also a spiritual one." The Jehovah's Witnesses cite this verse to support the contention that Jesus was raised from the dead as a spirit creature. Verse 50 is often cited as well: "Flesh and blood cannot inherit God's kingdom, neither does corruption inherit incorruption." Jesus *must* have had a spiritual resurrection, we are told, since flesh-and-blood bodies cannot exist in heaven.

The Watchtower Society argues that at the moment of the resurrection, Jesus "was granted immortality and incorruption, which no creature in the flesh can have."[40] Mortality and corruption belong to the fleshly body. The resurrection body is immortal and incorruptible because it is by nature a spiritual body. Though flesh and blood cannot inherit God's kingdom, the spiritual body is ideally suited for spirit life in heaven.[41]

The Biblical Teaching. The Jehovah's Witnesses have completely misunderstood the meaning of the word "spiritual" in 1 Corinthians 15:44. The primary meaning of "spiritual body" here is not an immaterial body but a supernatural, *spirit-dominated* body. "The Greek words *soma pneumatikos* (translated 'spiritual body' here) mean a body *directed by* the spirit, as opposed to one under the dominion of the flesh."[42]

Drawing on what was said earlier, remind the Jehovah's Witness that it is an indisputable fact that the Greek word for "body" (*soma*), when used of a person, always refers to a *physical body* in the New Testament. There are no exceptions to this. Greek scholar Robert Gundry, in his authoritative book *Soma in Biblical Theology*, speaks of "Paul's exceptionless use of *soma* for a physical body."[43] Hence, all references to Jesus' resurrection body (*soma*) in the New Testament must be taken to mean a resurrected, *physical* body. This supports the view that the phrase "spiritual body [*soma*]" refers to a spirit-dominated and supernatural physical body.

It is also important to recognize that the apostle Paul often uses the word "spiritual" in 1 Corinthians to refer to something supernatural. The spiritual body is supernatural because "it is not ruled by flesh that perishes but by the spirit that endures (1 Cor. 15:50-58)."[44] That Paul intends the meaning of supernatural in 1 Corinthians 15:40-50 seems clear from the obvious contrasts he presents in the chapter. Note the following:[45]

Preresurrection Body	Postresurrection Body
Earthly (v. 40)	Heavenly
Perishable (v. 42)	Imperishable
Weak (v. 42)	Powerful
Natural (v. 44)	[*Supernatural*]
Mortal (v. 53)	Immortal

Some scholars believe that the Greek word translated "spiritual" in 1 Corinthians 15 should actually be translated "supernatural" in this context. In fact, this exact same Greek word is translated "supernatural" in 1 Corinthians 10:4, which makes reference to the "supernatural rock" that followed the Israelites in the wilderness. In view of the contrasts in verses 40-50 (earthly/heavenly, perishable/imperishable, weak/powerful, mortal/immortal), the translation "supernatural" (as a contrast to *natural*) would fit the context much better than the word "spiritual."

 *Ask...*

- In view of the obvious contrasts in 1 Corinthians 15:40-50—earthly/heavenly, perishable/imperishable, weak/powerful, mortal/immortal—can you see that Paul's intended meaning regarding the contrast to the *natural* body is a *supernatural* body?

You must emphasize to the Jehovah's Witness that the apostle Paul's usage of the word "spiritual" does not demand a reference to immateriality or nonphysicality. Note, for example, that Paul spoke of a "spiritual man" in 1 Corinthians 2:15. It is clear from the context that he did not mean an invisible, immaterial man with no corporeal body. Rather, he was speaking of a "flesh-and-blood human being whose life was lived by the supernatural power of God. He was referring to a literal person whose life had spiritual direction."[46] Likewise, the phrase "spiritual body" in 1 Corinthians 15:44-50 does not point to an immaterial body but rather a spirit-dominated and supernatural physical body (*soma*).

_____ *Ask...* _____

- Did you know that in 1 Corinthians 2:15 Paul uses the same Greek word for *spiritual* that he used in 1 Corinthians 15:44-50? (Read the verse aloud.)

- In the context of 1 Corinthians 2:15, is Paul speaking of an invisible spirit-creature that has no physical body, or a flesh-and-blood human being who is still in some sense spiritual?

- Can you see that, according to Paul's usage, being "spiritual" does not demand immateriality or non-physicality? (Emphasize that the same is true in 1 Corinthians 15.)

_____

Now, what about 1 Corinthians 15:50, which says that "flesh and blood cannot inherit the kingdom of God; nor does the perishable inherit the imperishable"? You need to begin by refuting the Watchtower claim that material, physical bodies cannot exist in heaven. Point out that the phrase "flesh and blood" is simply an idiom used in Scripture to refer to mortal humanity. This verse is saying that *mortal humanity* cannot inherit the kingdom of God. Mortal humanity must be made immortal humanity in order to survive in heaven. The resurrection body will be endowed with special qualities that will enable it to adapt perfectly to life in God's presence.

In support of this view, take the Jehovah's Witness to the latter part of verse 50, which refers to "perishable" human flesh. This helps to set the proper context for interpreting the entire verse. Clearly, Paul is not speaking of flesh as such, but of perishable flesh. Paul is "not affirming that the resurrection body will not have flesh, but that it will not have *perishable* flesh."[47]

In view of the above facts, apologist Norman Geisler summarizes the meaning of "flesh and blood" in 1 Corinthians 15:50: "'Flesh and blood' in this context apparently means mortal flesh and blood, that is, a mere human being. This is supported by parallel uses in the NT. When Jesus said to Peter, 'Flesh and blood has not revealed this to you' (Matt. 16:17), He could not have been referring to the mere substance of the body as such, which obviously could not reveal that He was the Son of God. Rather, the most natural interpretation of 1 Corinthians 15:50 seems to be that *humans, as they now are, earth-bound and perishable creatures*, cannot have a place in God's glorious, heavenly kingdom."[48]

Now turn the Jehovah's Witness to verse 53, which says that "this perishable must *put on* the imperishable, and this mortal must *put on* immortality" (NASB, emphasis added). In other words, we do not stop being human and give up our physical bodies to enter into heaven. Rather, we "put on" immortality to our mortal humanity. Nothing is taken away from us (materiality); rather, something is added or "put on" (immortality). Therefore, 1 Corinthians 15 cannot be used as a proof text to support the Watchtower doctrine that Jesus was raised a spirit creature.

_____ *Ask...* _____

- What do you think the words "put on" (1 Corinthians 15:53) mean in this context?

- Taken in their natural sense, don't the words "put on" indicate *adding* something to humanity (immortality) rather than *taking away* something from humanity (the material body)?

You might want to close your discussion regarding the whole issue of Jesus and the archangel Michael by briefly reviewing your main points on each of the key verses listed above. The accumulative weight of these arguments should serve to get the Jehovah's Witness's attention so that he or she will question the teachings of the Watchtower Society.

8

Identifying the Holy Spirit

> *The Holy Spirit is a person, not a force, and that person is God, just as fully God and in the same way as are the Father and the Son.*
>
> —Millard J. Erickson[1]

According to the Watchtower Society, the Holy Spirit is neither a person nor God. Rather, the Holy Spirit is God's impersonal "active force" for accomplishing His will in the world.[2] Indeed, as *Reasoning from the Scriptures* argues, the Holy Spirit "is not a person but is a powerful force that God causes to emanate from himself to accomplish his holy will."[3] This denial of the Holy Spirit's personality and deity is consistent with the Watchtower's denial of the doctrine of the Trinity.

The Watchtower publication *Should You Believe in the Trinity?* says that to a certain extent, the Holy Spirit can be likened to electricity, "a force that can be adapted to perform a great variety of operations."[4] Just as human beings use electricity to accomplish a variety of purposes, so God uses the impersonal force known as the Holy Spirit to accomplish His purposes.

It was this powerful force that came upon Jesus in the form of a dove at His baptism (Mark 1:10). "This active force of God enabled Jesus to heal the sick and raise the dead."[5] This same power is available to Christians, and enables them to endure trials of faith and do things they could not do otherwise.[6]

The Watchtower Society argues that proof is found in Scripture's portrayal of people being filled, baptized, and anointed by the Holy Spirit. These kinds of expressions would be appropriate, the Watchtower says, *only* if the Holy Spirit were a force and not a person.[7] After all, how can one person fill thousands of other people at one and the same time? A person cannot be split up in that way.

Besides, if the Holy Spirit were a person, it would have a name just as the Father and the Son do. We know from Scripture, the Watchtower says, that the Father's personal name is Jehovah. Likewise, the Son's personal name is Jesus. But nowhere in Scripture is a personal name applied to the Holy Spirit.[8] Therefore, the Holy Spirit must not be a person like the Father and the Son.

The Watchtower Society concedes that there are certain verses where the Holy Spirit is said to speak to people—thereby seeming to indicate personality. The Jehovah's Witnesses argue, however, that "while some Bible texts say that the spirit speaks, other texts show that this was actually done through humans or angels (Matthew 10:19,20; Acts 4:24,25; 28:25; Hebrews 2:2). The action of the spirit in such instances is like that of radio waves transmitting messages from one person to another far away."[9] Indeed, "God, by his spirit, transmits his messages and communicates his will to the minds and hearts of his servants on earth, who, in turn, may convey that message to yet others."[10]

Though the Holy Spirit is not a person, the Watchtower Society says this active force of God is often *personified* in Scripture. This is not unlike other things that are personified in Scripture—such as wisdom, sin, and death. For example, the booklet *Should You Believe in the Trinity?* cites the *New English Bible's* rendering of Genesis 4:7: "Sin is a demon crouching at the door." This personifies sin as a wicked spirit at Cain's door.[11] But, of course, "sin is not a spirit person; nor does personifying the holy spirit make it a spirit person."[12]

In view of these and other arguments, the Watchtower Society concludes, "No, the holy spirit is not a person and it is not part of a Trinity. The holy spirit is God's active force that he uses to accomplish his will. It is not equal to God but is always at his disposition and subordinate to him."[13]

———Reasoning from the Scriptures———

Genesis 1:1,2—*God's Active Force at the Creation*

The Watchtower Teaching. The *New World Translation* renders Genesis 1:1,2, "In the beginning God created the heavens and the earth. Now the earth proved to be formless and waste and there was darkness upon the surface of the watery deep; and *God's active force was moving to and fro over the surface of the waters*" (emphasis added). The Jehovah's Witnesses argue from this verse that "God's spirit was his active force working to shape the earth."[14]

The Watchtower Society says that just as a human craftsman would use his hands and fingers to exert force to build a house, so God used His *active force* (the Holy Spirit) to build the universe. Indeed, the Holy Spirit of God is even spoken of in Scripture as His "hands" and "fingers" (Psalm 8:3; 19:1; Matthew 12:28; Luke 11:20).[15]

The Watchtower Society admits that the Hebrew word *ruach* (which is the word rendered "active force" in Genesis 1:2 NWT) is translated many times as "spirit" in the Old Testament. However, it is also translated as "wind" or in "other ways to denote an invisible active force."[16] This gives justification, the Society says, for translating Genesis 1:2, "God's active force was moving to and fro over the surface of the waters."

If one were to ask what "wind" and "spirit" have in common, the answer is simple: These words "refer to that which is invisible to human sight and which gives evidence of force in motion. Such invisible force is capable of producing visible effects."[17] Thus, the Witnesses reason, the invisible force of God's Spirit brought the universe into being at the creation.

The Biblical Teaching. To begin, it is true that the Hebrew word *ruach* can have a variety of meanings—including breath, air, strength, wind, breeze, spirit, courage, temper, and Spirit (i.e., Holy Spirit).[18] But does that give license to the Watchtower Society to translate it "active force" in Genesis 1:1,2 and other passages referring to God's Spirit?

By no means! In fact, when *ruach* is used of God's Spirit, we consistently find clear evidences for the *personality* of the Holy Spirit. The presence of personal attributes in such contexts rules out the translation "active force." After all, an active force has no personal characteristics. H.C. Leupold, in his commentary *Exposition of Genesis*, says that *ruach* in Genesis 1:2 "must definitely be rendered 'the Spirit of God.'" Indeed, he reflects the universal consensus of Bible scholars that there is no warrant for any other translation in this context.[19]

Let us now examine some of the evidences for the personality of the Holy Spirit in Scripture. (Note that the following arguments apply not just to refuting the Watchtower's interpretation of Genesis 1:1,2, but all other passages they cite on the Holy Spirit as well.)

The Holy Spirit Has All the Attributes of Personality

It has long been recognized that the three primary attributes of personality are mind, emotions, and will. A "force" does not have these attributes. If it can be demonstrated that the Spirit has a mind, emotions, and a will, the Watchtower position that the Spirit is an "active force" crumbles like a house of cards.

The Holy Spirit Has a Mind. This is made clear from a number of passages. For example, the Holy Spirit's intellect is seen in 1 Corinthians 2:10, where we are told that "the Spirit searches all things" (cf. Isaiah 11:2; Ephesians 1:17). The Greek word for "searches" means to thoroughly investigate a matter. The Holy Spirit—with His mind—investigates the things of God and makes these matters known to believers. Note that Jesus once told a group of Jews, "You *search* the

Scriptures, because you think that in them you have eternal life" (John 5:39 NASB, emphasis added). The Lord used the same Greek word there that is used in 1 Corinthians 2:10. Just as the Jews used their minds to search the Scriptures, so the Holy Spirit uses His mind in searching the things of God.

We are also told in 1 Corinthians 2:11 that the Holy Spirit knows the thoughts of God. How can the Spirit "know" the things of God if the Spirit does not have a mind? A force does not know things. Thought processes require the presence of a mind.

Romans 8:27 tells us that just as the Holy Spirit knows the things of God, so God the Father knows "the *mind of the Spirit*" (emphasis added). According to Arndt and Gingrich's highly respected *Greek-English Lexicon of the New Testament and Other Early Christian Literature*, the word translated "mind" in this verse means "way of thinking, mind(-set), aim, aspiration, striving."[20] A mere force does not have a "way of thinking, mind-set, aim, aspiration," or "striving."

The Holy Spirit Has Emotions. That the Holy Spirit has emotions is clear from a number of passages. For example, in Ephesians 4:30 we are admonished, "Do not grieve the Holy Spirit of God." Grief is an emotion, and emotions cannot be experienced by a force. Grief is something one *feels*. The Holy Spirit feels the emotion of grief when believers sin. In the context of Ephesians, such sins include lying (verse 25), anger (verse 26), stealing (verse 28), laziness (verse 28), and speaking words that are unkind (verse 29).

To illustrate my point, it is noteworthy that the Corinthian believers experienced *sorrow* after the apostle Paul wrote them a stern letter (2 Corinthians 2:2,5). There we see the same Greek word that is used in Ephesians 4:30 (translated "grieve"). Just as the Corinthian believers experienced sorrow or grief, so the person of the Holy Spirit can experience sorrow or grief.

The Holy Spirit Has a Will. We are told in 1 Corinthians 12:11 that the Holy Spirit distributes spiritual gifts "to each one individually *just as He wills*" (NASB, emphasis added). The phrase "He wills" translates from the Greek word *bouletai*, which refers to "decisions of the will after previous delibera-tion."[21] The Holy Spirit makes a sovereign choice regarding what spiritual gifts each respective Christian receives. A force does not have such a will.

It is noteworthy that the same Greek word used to describe the Holy Spirit's will is used to describe Jehovah-God's will in James 1:18. Just as the person of the Father exercises His will, so the person of the Holy Spirit exercises His will.

Another key example of the Holy Spirit exercising His will is found in Acts 16:6. Here, the Spirit forbids Paul to preach in Asia and then redirects him to minister in Europe.

_____ *Ask...* _____

- How do you reconcile the Watchtower view that the Holy Spirit is a "force" with the scriptural teaching that the Holy Spirit 1) has a mind and can "know" things, 2) has emotions and can feel love and grief, and 3) has a will by which decisions are made and communicated?

The Holy Spirit's Works Confirm His Personality

The Holy Spirit is seen doing many things in Scripture that only a person can do. Indeed, many of His works are similar to the works of both the Father and the Son. For example, the Holy Spirit *teaches* believers (John 14:26), He *testifies* of Christ (John 15:26), He *guides* believers (Romans 8:14), He *commissions* people to service (Acts 13:4), He *issues commands* (Acts 8:29), He *restrains sin* (Genesis 6:3), He *intercedes* or prays (Romans 8:26), and He *speaks* to people (John 15:26; 2 Peter 1:21). Let us look at three of these in a little more detail.

The Holy Spirit Testifies. John 15:26 tells us that the Holy Spirit "will bear witness" (NASB) of Christ. The Greek word for "bear witness" is used to describe the disciples' testifying about Christ in John 15:27. John the Baptist is said to be one who has "borne witness" (NASB) to the truth in John 5:33. God the Father "bore witness" in Acts 15:8 (NASB). Just as the disciples, John the Baptist, and the Father (who are all *persons*) testified or bore witness, so the Holy Spirit as a person testifies or bears witness about Christ. A force cannot bear witness to something; only a person can do that.

The Holy Spirit Intercedes (Prays) for Believers. Romans 8:26 tells us, "In the same way, the Spirit helps us in our weakness. We do not know what we ought to pray, but the Spirit himself intercedes for us with groans that words cannot express." Elsewhere in Scripture we are told that Jesus Christ *intercedes* (same Greek word) for believers (Romans 8:34; Hebrews 7:25). Just as Christ (as a person) intercedes for believers, so the Holy Spirit (as a person) intercedes for believers. A force cannot intercede or pray on behalf of another.

The Holy Spirit Issues Commands. Acts 8:29 tells us that it was the Holy Spirit who directed Philip to speak to the Ethiopian eunuch. Acts 13:2 tells us that the Holy Spirit commanded that Paul and Barnabas were to be set apart for missionary work. We likewise see in Acts 13:4 that these two men were "sent on their way by the Holy Spirit."

Just as the Spirit sent Paul and his coworkers to certain places, so He also forbade them to go to other places. For example, Acts 16:6 tells us that the Spirit prohibited Paul and Silas from preaching in Asia. A force cannot send individuals to certain places and forbid them to go to others. Only a person with a mind and a will can do that.

_____ *Ask*... _____

- How do you reconcile the Watchtower view that the Holy Spirit is a "force" with the scriptural teaching that the Holy Spirit does things that only a person can do—such as pray for believers, speak to people, issue commands to people, bear witness, and teach people?

The Holy Spirit Is Treated As a Person

As Charles Ryrie points out in his book *The Holy Spirit*, "certain acts are performed toward the Holy Spirit which would be most incongruous if He did not possess true personality."[22] Let us briefly look at some of those acts.

The Holy Spirit Can Be Grieved. As we noted earlier, Ephesians 4:30 tells us not to grieve the Holy Spirit by sin. A force cannot experience the emotion of grief. Only a person can do so.

The Holy Spirit Can Be Blasphemed. One does not normally think of a force (electricity, for example) or a thing (such as a computer) being *blasphemed*. Normally one thinks of persons being blasphemed. We see from Scripture that God the Father can be blasphemed (Revelation 13:6; 16:9), as well as God the Son (Matthew 27:39; Luke 23:39). In like manner, we are told that the Holy Spirit can be blasphemed (Matthew 12:32; Mark 3:29,30).

Now, pay particular attention to Matthew 12:32: "Whoever shall speak a word *against the Son of Man*, it shall be forgiven him; but whoever shall speak *against the Holy Spirit*, it shall not be forgiven him, either in this age, or in the age to come" (emphasis added). Notice that the person of the Son of Man is set in clear contrast to the person of the Holy Spirit.[23] Both are portrayed as persons in this verse.

The Holy Spirit Can Be Lied To. According to Acts 5:3, Ananias and Sapphira were guilty of lying to the Holy Spirit. They lost their lives for this grievous offense. One cannot lie to a force or to a thing; only a person can be lied to. Can you imagine how people would respond to you if you confessed to lying to the electricity in your house this morning?

The Holy Spirit Can Be Obeyed. Scripture portrays believers as obeying the Holy Spirit's commands and instructions. We noted earlier how Paul and Barnabas obeyed the Spirit (Acts 13:2). Peter also obeyed the Spirit by going to the house of Cornelius to share the gospel (Acts 10). A force or a thing cannot be obeyed; only a person can be.

The Holy Spirit Is Sent. John 14:26 tells us that the Holy Spirit is sent by the Father (cf. John 16:7). One does not "send" an impersonal force.[24] Rather, a person is sent to accomplish some specific task. Just as Jesus was sent by the Father (John 6:38), so too was the Holy Spirit sent by the Father.

___ *Ask...* _____

• How do you reconcile the Watchtower view that the Holy Spirit is a "force" with the scriptural teaching that the Holy Spirit can be lied to, grieved, obeyed, and blasphemed?

The Holy Spirit Is Contrasted with Unclean Spirits

Mark 3:29,30 portrays the Holy Spirit in a clear contrast with an unclean spirit. Jesus was accused by some hostile Jewish leaders of having an unclean spirit. He responded by saying that He had the Holy Spirit. Here's the key point: Just as an unclean spirit is a personal being (and you'll want to emphasize that the Watchtower Society teaches that unclean spirits *are* personal beings), so too is the *contrasting* spirit—the Holy Spirit—a personal being.[25]

Lack of a Personal Name

Jehovah's Witnesses say that if the Holy Spirit was truly a person, it would have a name just as the Father and the Son have. Is this a legitimate argument?

By no means! Spiritual beings are not always named in Scripture. For example, unclean spirits are rarely named in Scripture—and the same Greek word is used for them as is used for the Holy Spirit: *pneuma*. More often than not, they are identified by their particular character (i.e., "unclean," "wicked," and so forth).

In the same way, by contrast, the Holy Spirit is identified by His character, which is *holiness*. To say that the Spirit is not a person because a name is not assigned to Him is clearly fallacious reasoning.

 Ask...

- Were you aware that in most cases unclean spirits are not named in Scripture but are rather described by their particular character, such as *unclean* spirit or *wicked* spirit?

- Does the fact that most unclean spirits are not named in Scripture mean that they are not persons? (The answer is obviously no.)

- By contrast, doesn't it make sense that the designation "Holy Spirit" is intended as a description of character and not as a proof of nonpersonality?

Authorities on the Greek New Testament

The Watchtower Society often cites various Greek scholars in apparent support of their interpretation of the Holy Spirit. For the record, however, let us note that although the following Greek authorities are cited in Watchtower literature, *all of them believe that the Holy Spirit is a person*: F.F. Bruce, A.T. Robertson, John N. Darby, R.C. Trench, J.H. Thayer, Marvin R. Vincent, W.E. Vine, and R. Young.[26] The Watchtower Society is utterly deceptive in citing such individuals in support of their view.

Ask...

- Were you aware that the well-known Greek authorities who are cited in Watchtower literature as *allegedly* supporting the view that the Holy Spirit is a force in fact *all* believe that the Holy Spirit is a person? (Mention some of the names.)

Matthew 3:11 (cf. Mark 1:8)—*Baptized with Holy Spirit*

The Watchtower Teaching. According to the *New World Translation*, John the Baptist said: "I, for my part, baptize you *with water* because of your repentance; but the one coming after me is stronger than I am, whose sandals I am not fit to take off. That one will baptize you people *with holy spirit* and with fire" (emphasis added).

The Jehovah's Witnesses argue that the spirit and the water are *direct parallels* in this verse, and hence the spirit must be an impersonal entity just as the water is.[27] They reason that since the Holy Spirit is so closely associated with impersonal things in Scripture—in this case, water—the Spirit must itself be impersonal.[28]

The Biblical Teaching. It is utterly unwarranted to say that because *water* is not a person, then the Holy Spirit is not a person. Not only does this go against the massive evidence for the Holy Spirit's personality in the New Testament (*see* the discussion under Genesis 1:1,2), there is also virtually no justification for drawing such a strict and wooden parallel between two obviously dissimilar nouns.

Former Jehovah's Witness David Reed suggests that this same baptism argument can be used to "disprove" the personality of Jesus Christ, who clearly walked on this earth as a person. He points to Romans 6:3: "Don't you know that all of us who were *baptized into Christ Jesus* were *baptized into His death*?" (emphasis added). It could be argued that since death is not a person, Jesus Christ must not be a person either.[29] But such logic is clearly ridiculous.

——— *Ask...* ———————

• Since Romans 6:3 tells us that "all of us who have been *baptized into Christ Jesus* have been *baptized into His death*," does this mean that Jesus is not a person since—with these "parallel" baptisms—death is not a person?

(The answer will be no. Likewise, simply because water is not a person [Matthew 3:11] does not mean the Holy Spirit is not a person.)

Acts 2:4—*Filled with Holy Spirit*

The Watchtower Teaching. The *New World Translation* renders Acts 2:4, "And they all became filled with holy spirit and started to speak with different tongues, just as the spirit was granting them to make utterance." The Jehovah's Witnesses argue that since all the disciples were filled with the Holy Spirit, He must not be a person. *You Can Live Forever in Paradise on Earth* asks, "Were they 'filled' with a person? No, but they were filled with God's active force. . . . How could the holy spirit be a person, when it filled about 120 disciples at the same time?"[30]

An Old Testament example of someone being filled with God's Spirit is Samson, who had supernatural strength as a result of that infilling (Judges 14:6). Jehovah's Witnesses ask, Did a divine person enter Samson, manipulating his body to do what he did?[31] No, they answer. It was really God's active force that made Samson so strong.

The Jehovah's Witnesses also point out that Ephesians 5:18 instructs people to be filled with the Holy Spirit instead of with wine. Now, wine is obviously not a person.[32] Likewise, the Holy Spirit is not a person. Rather, it is God's active force. Wine and the Holy Spirit are seen as antithetical parallels in this verse.

The Biblical Teaching. As you respond to the Jehovah's Witnesses you will want to point out that Ephesians 3:19 speaks of being filled with *God Himself*.[33] The fact that God can fill all things does not mean He is not a person. In the same way, the fact that the Holy Spirit can fill numerous people does not prove He is not a person.

Likewise, Ephesians 4:10 speaks of *Christ* filling all things. Ephesians 1:23 speaks of Christ as the One who "fills all in all" (NASB). The fact that Christ can fill all things does not mean He is not a person. And once again, the same applies to the Holy Spirit. Clearly, then, the Watchtower's logic on this issue is faulty.

_____ *Ask...* _____

- Does the fact that God the Father and Christ can fill all things mean that they are not persons? (The answer will be no.)

- Then why does the Watchtower Society argue that the Holy Spirit cannot be a person simply because the Spirit fills numerous people?

_____

As to the wine being an antithetical parallel proving the impersonal nature of the Holy Spirit (Ephesians 5:18), we again must respond that this is a weightless argument. There is no warrant whatsoever for drawing this type of wooden parallel in the context. And it goes against the overwhelming evidence in the New Testament that the Holy Spirit *is* a person (*see* the discussion under Genesis 1:1,2). The point of Paul's argument in Ephesians 5:18 is that as Christians we should not give control of ourselves over to an impersonal substance (such as wine) that can cause us to do bad things. Rather, we are to be filled with the person of the Holy Spirit, who not only personally guides us and teaches us but also produces specific fruit in our lives (Galatians 5:22ff.).[34]

1 John 5:6-8—*Three "Witnesses"*

The Watchtower Teaching. The *New World Translation* renders 1 John 5:6-8, "This is he that came by means of water and blood, Jesus Christ; not with the water only, but with the water and with the blood. And the spirit is that which is bearing witness, because the spirit is the truth. For there are *three witness bearers*, the *spirit* and the *water* and the *blood*, and the three are in agreement" (emphasis added).

The Jehovah's Witnesses argue that since water and blood are obviously not persons, then neither is the holy spirit a person.[35] The three items in this verse—the water, blood, and Holy Spirit—are seen as personifications.

The Biblical Teaching. It is true that water and blood are used in this text in a metaphorical sense, being personified as witnesses. But this does not mean that the Holy Spirit is a personification. That is yet another example of faulty reasoning on the part of the Watchtower Society.

A little historical background helps us to understand what is going on in 1 John 5:6-8. A false teacher by the name of Cerinthus set forth the heretical idea that the "Christ" (a kind of cosmic spiritual being) came upon a human Jesus at His baptism but departed before His crucifixion. First John 5:6-8 refutes this idea. "Water" is a reference to Jesus' baptism while "blood" is a reference to His crucifixion. Both of these act as metaphorical witnesses to the fact that Jesus the Christ experienced *both* the baptism *and* death by crucifixion. And the Holy Spirit (elsewhere known as the Spirit of truth—1 John 2:27; 4:2) is the third witness testifying to this fact. The mention of three witnesses reflects the requirement of Jewish law (Deuteronomy 19:15; John 8:17,18). Simply because water and blood are not persons is no reason to interpret the Holy Spirit as being impersonal.

Though it is true that personifications occur often in Scripture, people generally do not get confused as to whether the item under discussion is personal or impersonal. As Robert Bowman points out, "wherever impersonal realities are personified . . . the fact that they are impersonal is already well known."[36] By contrast, "most people (including most anti-trinitarians) who have read the New Testament have thought the Holy Spirit to be a person, and for good reason."[37] In view of this, it seems legitimate to charge that if the Holy Spirit *is not* a person, then the Bible is misleading since there are so many occasions in Scripture where He is portrayed to have personality and to function as a person.[38]

We might also mention that there are many times in Scripture where Jesus is associated with impersonal items, yet this does not argue against His personality. On different occasions Jesus is called *bread* (John 6:35), a *door* (John 10:7 NASB), a *light* (John 8:12), a *rock* (1 Corinthians 10:4), a *stone* (1 Peter 2:4-8), the *truth* (John 14:6), the *vine* (John 15:1), the *way* (John 14:6), and the *Word* (John 1:1). Clearly, Jesus' personality is not canceled out simply because these kinds of terms are used in association with Him.

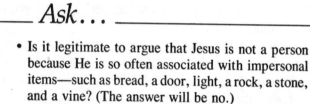

_____ Ask... _____

- Is it legitimate to argue that Jesus is not a person because He is so often associated with impersonal items—such as bread, a door, light, a rock, a stone, and a vine? (The answer will be no.)

- To be consistent, then, isn't it illegitimate to say the Holy Spirit is not a person simply because He is seen in close association with impersonal items like water and blood?

John 14–16—*The "Other Helper"*

The Watchtower Teaching. As Jesus talks to the disciples in the Upper Room, He refers to the Holy Spirit as a "helper"—and in that capacity the Spirit is said to "teach," "guide," "bear witness," "speak," and "hear" (John 14:16, 17, 26; 15:26; 16:13). Do such statements demand that the Holy Spirit be interpreted as being a person?

By no means, according to the Watchtower Society. In this and other passages that *seem* to portray the Holy Spirit as a person, the Holy Spirit is merely being *personified*, they say.[39] That is why in John 14–16 Jesus used the personal pronoun "he" to refer to the Holy Spirit. Use of this personal pronoun in such situations *does not* demand personality, we are told. Moreover, because the Holy Spirit is personified in Scripture, figurative expressions such as "speak" or "hear" do not prove that the Holy Spirit is a person.[40]

Related to this, the Watchtower Society notes that the word "helper" in John 14–16 is in the masculine gender. And, they argue, that is why Jesus used masculine personal pronouns (such as "he") to speak of the Holy Spirit (John 16:7,8). In other words, the use of masculine pronouns ("he") in this passage does not prove personality but is dictated by Greek grammar, since the Greek word for "helper" (*parakletos*) is a masculine noun.

Elsewhere, the Watchtower Society points out, the *neuter* Greek word for Spirit is used of the Holy Spirit. And in these cases, the neuter pronoun "it" is used in reference to the Spirit. Hence, the Society concludes, "When the Bible uses masculine personal pronouns in connection with [the word 'helper'] at John 16:7-8, it is conforming to rules of grammar, not expressing a doctrine."[41]

The Biblical Teaching. In answering the Watchtower claim that the Holy Spirit is a force that is personified in Scripture, David Reed suggests pointing the interested Jehovah's Witness to an article that appeared in a 1973 issue of *Awake!* magazine. There we read, "Is the Devil a personification or a person? . . . Can an unintelligent 'force' carry on a conversation with a person? . . . only an intelligent person could. . . . 'Every quality, every action, which can indicate personality, is attributed to him in language which cannot be explained away.'"[42]

If such an argument can be used to prove the devil's personhood, then it can also be used (with much more substantial evidence) to prove the Holy Spirit's personhood. For, indeed, the Holy Spirit can carry on a conversation with others (Acts 8:29; 13:2), has all the qualities of personality (*see* 1 Corinthians 2:10; 12:11; Ephesians 4:30), and performs all the actions of personality (*see* John 14:26; 15:26; Acts 8:29;

Romans 8:14). Clearly, personality is attributed to the Holy Spirit *in language that cannot be explained away.*

Watchtower expert Marian Bodine suggests the following approach:

_____ *Ask...* _____

- *Christian:* "Do you believe Satan is a spirit person?"

- *JW:* "Yes."

- *Christian:* "Do you believe Satan is a person because he has the qualifying attributes of a person?"

- *JW:* "I suppose so, but what do you mean?"

- *Christian:* "Would you agree that in order to qualify as an intelligent being or person, one must be able to think, act, communicate, and have a will?"

- *JW:* "Yes, Satan can do all those things."

- *Christian:* "Then why don't you believe the Holy Spirit is a person? The Bible teaches that He has *all* the attributes of a person." (Then share some of the specific attributes of personality that the Holy Spirit manifests in Scripture.)[43]

_____

Now, it is one thing to say that individuals like Jesus used personal pronouns to speak of the Holy Spirit. It is highly significant, however, that the Holy Spirit used personal pronouns *of Himself*. An example of this is Acts 13:2: "And while they were ministering to the Lord and fasting, the Holy Spirit said, 'Set apart for *Me* Barnabas and Saul for the work to which *I* have called them'" (emphasis added). Regardless of what the Jehovah's Witnesses say, it seems clear that the Holy Spirit considered Himself a person and not a personification!

_____ *Ask . . .* _____

- If the Holy Spirit is a force, as the Watchtower Society argues, then why does He use the personal pronouns "Me" and "I" in reference to Himself (Acts 13:2)?

Regarding the use of personal pronouns in reference to the Holy Spirit, Reformed theologian Charles Hodge concludes that the Holy Spirit "is introduced as a person so often, not merely in poetic or excited discourse, but in simple narrative, and in didactic instructions; and his personality is sustained by so many collateral proofs, that to explain the use of the personal pronouns in relation to Him on the principle of personification, is to do violence to all the rules of interpretation."[44]

Now, in discussing John chapters 14–16, you will want to focus some of your attention on John 14:16: "And I will ask the Father, and He will give you *another Helper*, that He may be with you forever" (NASB, emphasis added). Now there are two words in the Greek language for the English word "another": The first one (*heteros*) means "another of a different kind." The other Greek word (*allos*) means "another of the same kind." It is this second word, *allos*, that is used in John 14:16. So Jesus is saying that He will ask the Father to send another Helper of the *same kind as Himself*—that is, personal! Just as Jesus was a personal advocate/representative who helped the disciples for three years during His earthly ministry, so now the disciples would have another personal advocate/representative—the Holy Spirit—who would be with them throughout their lives.

The purpose of this personal advocate/representative is to bear witness to Christ (John 15:26,27). *This is something that only a person can do.* Indeed, it is noteworthy that the disciples are told to bear witness after receiving the witness borne by the Holy Spirit. Clearly, the act of bearing witness is a *personal* act.[45]

John 16:13 also tells us that the Holy Spirit "will not speak on his own; he will speak only what he hears." It would be truly ridiculous to interpret this as meaning that a force repeats what "it" hears.[46] It's just as ridiculous as saying that the electricity in my home will repeat to you all that it hears me say.

What about the neuter nouns and pronouns used of the Holy Spirit? When it comes to discussing masculine, feminine, and neuter words in Greek, we are entering a realm that many people would probably prefer to avoid. However, because the Jehovah's Witnesses enter this realm to argue against the Holy Spirit's personality, we must take a brief look at how we should respond.

Let us begin by noting that in the Greek language, all nouns are one of three genders—masculine, feminine, or neuter. These genders are not indicators of sex. In *The Elements of New Testament Greek*, J.W. Wenham notes that "in Greek, gender has to do with the form of the words and has little to do with sex. There are masculine, feminine, and neuter forms, but 'bread' [in the Greek] is masculine, 'head' is feminine, and 'child' is neuter."[47] Thus, simply because a term is grammatically masculine does not mean that it is actually masculine in gender. Simply because a term is grammatically feminine does not mean that it is feminine in gender. And simply because a term is grammatically *neuter* does not mean that the item is an "it."

The primary reason the Jehovah's Witnesses say the Holy Spirit is an "active force" is that the Greek word for "Spirit" (*pneuma*) is neuter. However, as noted above, this is faulty reasoning, since the gender of the word has to do with the *grammatical form* of the word and not actual physical gender. For example, one will find that in Scripture, neuter terms are used in reference to *infants* (Luke 1:41,44; 2:16; 18:15), *children* (Mark 5:39-41), *girls* (Matthew 9:24,25; Mark 5:41,42), *unclean spirits* (Matthew 12:24,27,28; Mark 7:26, 29,30), and *angels* (Hebrews 1:14). Obviously, each of these beings have personality, even though a neuter term is used in reference to them. We can safely conclude, then, that the use of a neuter term does not indicate a lack of personality.

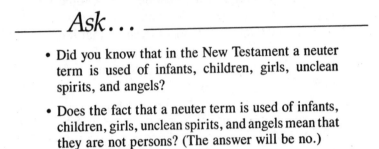

_____ *Ask...* _____

- Did you know that in the New Testament a neuter term is used of infants, children, girls, unclean spirits, and angels?

- Does the fact that a neuter term is used of infants, children, girls, unclean spirits, and angels mean that they are not persons? (The answer will be no.)

- Then is it legitimate for the Watchtower Society to argue that the Holy Spirit is not a person simply because a neuter term is used in reference to Him?

Though a neuter word does not indicate a lack of personality, it is noteworthy that the Scripture writers nevertheless used *masculine* pronouns in referring to the *neuter* word for "spirit" (*pneuma*).[48] Theologian Charles Ryrie explains:

> According to every normal rule of grammar, any pronoun that would be substituted for this neuter noun [*pnuema*] would itself have to be neuter. However, in several places the biblical writers did not follow this normal procedure of grammar, and instead of using a neuter pronoun in place of the neuter noun *pneuma*, they deliberately contradicted the grammatical rule and used masculine pronouns....This shows that they considered the Spirit to be a person and not merely a thing.[49]

_____ *Ask...* _____

- In Scripture, a neuter noun would normally call for a neuter pronoun in reference to it. Why do you think the Scripture writers deliberately contradicted this grammatical rule and used *masculine* pronouns to refer to the neuter noun for "spirit" (when referring to the Holy Spirit)?

Matthew 28:19—*The "Name" of the Holy Spirit*

The Watchtower Teaching. The *New World Translation* renders Matthew 28:19, "Go therefore and make disciples of people of all the nations, baptizing them in the name of the Father and of the Son and of the holy spirit." Upon reading this verse, it would seem clearly evident that the Holy Spirit is a person since the Father and Son are both persons, and because the word "name" is used of the Spirit as well as the Father and the Son. But Jehovah's Witnesses will not agree to that.

They argue that the word "name" does not always mean a personal name. For instance, when we say, "In the name of the law," we are not referring to a person. Rather we are communicating that which the law stands for—its authority. In *Should You Believe in the Trinity?*, it is argued that "name" is a common way of pointing to "power and authority."[50] This is allegedly the sense in which the word is used in Matthew 28:19. Hence, this verse cannot be used to support belief in the personhood of the Holy Spirit.

The Biblical Teaching. One must begin by addressing the Watchtower claim that the word "name" does not always mean a personal name. In actuality the reverse is true: In the New Testament, the Greek word for "name" is almost always used of real persons. As Robert Bowman points out, "The Greek word for 'name' (*onoma*) is used some 228 times in the New Testament, and except for four place-names (Mark 14:32; Luke 1:26; 24:13; Acts 28:7; *see* also Revelation 3:12) always refers to persons."[51] Especially since the word "name" in Matthew 28:19 is used in conjunction with the Father, Son, *and* Holy Spirit, it seems rather obvious that the personal element is present because the Father and the Son are undeniably persons. Likewise, the Holy Spirit must be a person.

Ask...

- Did you know that the Greek word for "name" is used some 228 times in the New Testament, and except for four place-names, the word *always* refers to persons?

- In view of this—and the fact that no place names are mentioned in Matthew 28:19—doesn't this mean that the Watchtower is in error by insisting that "name" used in association with the Holy Spirit does not indicate personality?

What about the Watchtower claim that the word "name" can be used to represent power and authority? An examination of Scripture is clear that the word can indeed represent power and authority—but the power and authority *of persons* is always meant.[52] Never does it represent the power and authority of a force or a thing.

That the word "name" can represent power and authority not only does not support the Watchtower position, it strongly argues against it.

The Holy Spirit: A Person

We have seen that the Holy Spirit speaks of Himself as a person (using the pronouns "I" and "Me"); He is addressed as a person by others; He has all the attributes of personality (mind, emotions, and will); He does things that only a person can do (pray and intercede); He is treated by others as only a person can be treated (He can be lied to), and He interacts with others on a personal basis—including the Father and Son. Very clearly, then, the Watchtower position that the Holy Spirit is a force goes against the clear, consistent testimony of the whole of Scripture.

9

The Trinity: Biblical Doctrine or Pagan Lie?

We worship one God in the Trinity, and the Trinity in unity; we distinguish among the persons, but we do not divide the substance....The entire three persons are coeternal and coequal with one another, so that...we worship complete unity in Trinity and Trinity in unity.

—The Athanasian Creed[1]

The Watchtower publication *Should You Believe in the Trinity?* asks, "If people were to read the Bible from cover to cover without any preconceived idea of a Trinity, would they arrive at such a concept on their own? Not at all."[2]

Rather, the publication says, the Bible student would consistently find "monotheism" set forth—the belief that God is *one*. Jesus Himself emphasized this kind of monotheism in John 17:3 where He referred to the Father as the "only true God." Since Jesus called the Father the *only* true God, then Jesus Himself could not be that God.

The Watchtower Society argues that Jesus never taught any concept of the Trinity. In *"Let God Be True,"* we read that "it is passing strange that this complicated, confusing doctrine received no attention by Christ Jesus, by way of explanation or teaching."[3]

This same publication then raises what it apparently considers a "knock-out-punch" argument against the Trinity. "One of the most mysterious things is the question, Who ran the universe during the three days that Jesus was dead and in the grave. . . . If Jesus was God, then during Jesus' death God was dead and in the grave. What a wonderful opportunity for Satan to take complete control! . . . If Jesus was the immortal God, he could not have died."[4]

Another common Watchtower argument against the Trinity is that because God is not a God of disorder or confusion (1 Corinthians 14:33), it is impossible that Scripture would speak of a God that cannot be understood by human reason. The idea that the Father is God, the Son is God, and the Holy Spirit is God—along with the parallel idea that there is *just one God*—is incomprehensible and unreasonable. Since God is not a God of confusion, this concept of Him cannot be correct. Jesus said, "We worship *what we know*" (John 4:22, emphasis added). Besides, the word "trinity" is not even in the Bible. It is a concept that is *read into* the Bible rather than *derived from* the Bible.

Throughout its history, the Watchtower Society has misrepresented the doctrine of the Trinity in order to make its denial more plausible to "reasonable" people. For example, the Watchtower publication *Studies in the Scriptures* (1899) said that "this doctrine of three Gods in one God . . . [is] one of the *dark mysteries* by which Satan, through the Papacy, has beclouded the Word and character of the plan of God."[5] (Trinitarians, however, do not believe in "three Gods in one God"; they believe in *one* God, and that there are three co-equal *persons* in the one Godhead.)

Elsewhere in this same volume, we find reference to "the unreasonable and unscriptural doctrine of the Trinity—three Gods in *one person*."[6] (Yet Trinitarians do not believe the Trinity is "three Gods in one person"; they believe in three co-equal *persons* in the one Godhead.)

One Watchtower publication went so far as to refer to the Trinity as a freakish being:

> When the clergy are asked by their followers as to how such a combination of three in one can possibly exist, they are obliged to answer, "That is a mystery." Some will try to illustrate it by using triangles, trefoils, or images with three heads on one neck. Nevertheless, sincere persons who want to know the true God and serve him find it a bit difficult to love and worship a complicated, *freakish-looking, three-headed God*. The clergy who inject such ideas will contradict themselves in the very next breath by stating that God made man in his own image; for certainly no one has ever seen a three-headed human creature.[7]

Regarding the alleged satanic origin of this doctrine, the Watchtower book *Reconciliation* (1928) elaborates: "Never was there a more deceptive doctrine advanced than that of the trinity. It could have originated only in one mind, and that the mind of Satan the Devil."[8] The book *Riches* (1936) likewise says, "Another lie made and told by Satan for the purpose of reproaching God's name and turning men away from God is that of the 'trinity.' "[9]

Besides having satanic origins, the Watchtower Society argues that the doctrine of the Trinity is a pagan concept. They cite a book entitled *The Paganism in Our Christianity,* which says, "The origin of the [Trinity] is entirely pagan."[10] It is argued that many centuries before the time of Christ, there were triads or trinities of gods in ancient Babylonia, Egypt, and Assyria.[11] Citing historian Will Durant, "Christianity did not destroy paganism; it adopted it."[12] "It follows then," the Watchtower Society says, "that God was not the author of this doctrine."[13] Rather, this satanic/pagan concept was assimilated into Christian theology in the early centuries of the church.

To be more specific, the Watchtower Society says the concept of the Trinity was adopted by the church some three hundred years after Christ died.[14] According to the 1990 Watchtower publication *Mankind's Search for God*, the emperor Constantine wanted unity in his realm, and in A.D. 325 he called for a council of his bishops at Nicaea. Between 250 and 318 bishops (a minority of bishops) were said to have attended. "After fierce debate, out of that unrepresentative council came the Nicene Creed with its heavy bias toward Trinitarian thought. Yet it failed to settle the doctrinal argument. . . . It was a victory for theology and a defeat for those who held to the Scriptures."[15]

The Watchtower Society argues that this "deviation" from what the early church believed was prophesied by Christ and His apostles. They spoke of a "falling away" or an apostasy that would take place prior to Christ's return. Indeed, besides the pagan doctrine of the Trinity, other pagan concepts such as hellfire, immortality of the soul, and idolatry became a part of Christendom—bringing about a spiritual "dark ages" dominated by a growing "man of lawlessness" clergy class.[16]

The Watchtower Society thus concludes: "To worship God on his terms means to reject the Trinity doctrine. It contradicts what the prophets, Jesus, the apostles, and the early Christians believed and taught. It contradicts what God says about himself in his own inspired Word."[17]

REASONING FROM THE SCRIPTURES

The Word "Trinity"—An Unbiblical Term?

Does the fact that the word "Trinity" is not in the Bible constitute evidence that the doctrine is a false one? By no means! Though the word is not mentioned in the Bible, the concept of the Trinity is clearly derived from Scripture (as will become evident in this chapter).

You might point out to the Jehovah's Witness that the word Jehovah does not appear as such in the Bible.[18] In fact, Jehovah does not appear in *any* legitimate Hebrew or Greek manuscript of the Bible. The word was originally formed by superstitious Jewish scribes who joined the consonants *YHWH* with the vowels from "Adonai." The result was Yahowah, or Jehovah. So if one is going to argue that the doctrine of the Trinity is unbiblical because the word "Trinity" does not appear in the Bible, then by that same logic the doctrine of Jehovah must be considered false since that term does not appear anywhere in the Bible either.

We can also illustrate this point with the word "theocracy." Former Jehovah's Witness Duane Magnani presents the following conversation between Chris (a Christian) and Jay (a Jehovah's Witness):

> *Chris*: Take "theocracy" for instance. While the word is not found in the Bible, the Roman Empire had a theocracy of a sort wherein the emperor was considered a god himself, a deified king. This is true again in Egypt, where the pharaoh was a god ruling the nation. This is very similar to the Watchtower structure
>
> *Jay*: How's that?
>
> *Chris*: The Society claims to be a theocracy, governed from the "Divine Ruler" down, across the whole of God's people [all the Jehovah's Witnesses], right?
>
> *Jay*: Oh, yes, the Watchtower Society is a theocratic organization.
>
> *Chris*: Well, the fact that a "theocracy" is found in pagan structures, and that the word is not found in the Bible, doesn't rule out the fact that the concept might be biblical, does it?[19]

Of course, the answer to the question is no. And, in the same way, simply because the word "Trinity" is not found in the Bible does not mean that the concept of the Trinity is unbiblical.

Ask...

- Does the fact that the word "theocracy" is not in the Bible rule out the possibility that it is a biblical concept? (The answer will be no.)

- To be fair and consistent, then, does the fact that the word "Trinity" is not in the Bible rule out the possibility that it is a biblical concept?

A Pagan Concept?

Is there any substance to the Watchtower claim that the doctrine of the Trinity is a pagan concept? By no means! First, it is critical to recognize that the Babylonians and Assyrians believed in *triads* of gods who headed up a pantheon of many other gods.[20] But these triads constituted three separate gods (polytheism), which is utterly different from the doctrine of the Trinity—which maintains that there is *only one God* (monotheism) with three persons within the one Godhead.

Ask...

- Can you see the difference between a *triad* of gods who headed up a pantheon of many gods and the doctrine of the *Trinity*, which holds that there is one God with three persons within the one Godhead?

Moreover, it has been pointed out that such pagan ideas predate Christianity by some two thousand years and were far removed from the part of the world where Christianity developed.[21] From a historical and geographical perspective, then, the suggestion that Christianity borrowed the Trinitarian concept from pagans is quite infeasible.

You might say to the Jehovah's Witness that pagans taught the concept of a great flood that killed much of humankind.

They also taught the idea of a messiah-like figure (named *Tammuz*) who was resurrected. Hence, as Bible scholar Paul G. Weathers argues, "If the Watchtower uses the same method of reasoning, it follows that the Christian belief in the flood, the Messiah (Jesus), and his resurrection are pagan. After all, the pagans believed these things before the Christians!"[22]

The point is, simply because pagans spoke of a concept remotely resembling something found in Scripture does not mean that the concept was stolen from outside Christianity. If you can effectively demonstrate this to the Jehovah's Witness, he or she will be faced with a choice: "Either admit that the Watchtower argument is false, or conclude that the flood, the Messiah, and the resurrection of Christ are also derived from paganism."[23]

_____ *Ask...* _____

- Did you know that pagans taught the concept of a great flood that killed much of humankind and the concept of a messiah-figure named *Tammuz* who was allegedly resurrected? (They will probably answer no.)

- Are the biblical doctrines of the flood and the Messiah false simply because pagans taught remotely similar accounts long ago?

---

1 Corinthians 14:33—*Jehovah: Not a God of Confusion*

The Watchtower Teaching. The *New World Translation* renders 1 Corinthians 14:33, "God is [a God], not of disorder, but of peace." Jehovah's Witnesses say that because God is not a God of disorder or of confusion, the doctrine of the Trinity cannot possibly be true since it is so unreasonable. After all, how can the Father, the Son, and the Holy Spirit each be God and yet there be only one God? It just doesn't make sense.[24]

In *"Let God Be True,"* we read this of the Trinity: "To excuse it with the word 'Mystery!' is not satisfying. If one has in mind the apostle's words, 'God is not the author of confusion' (1 Corinthians 14:33), it is at once seen that such a doctrine is not of God. Well, one might ask, if God is not the author of this confusing doctrine, who is?"[25] The implication is that the doctrine originated with Satan.

The Biblical Teaching. Just because one is unable to fully comprehend a doctrine does not mean that it is false. For humans to be able to understand everything about God, they would have to have the very mind of God.

You will want to show a Jehovah's Witness key verses in the Bible that show human beings cannot possibly understand everything about God or His ways. For example:

- "Oh, the depth of the riches of the wisdom and knowledge of God! How unsearchable his judgments, and his paths beyond tracing out!" (Romans 11:33).
- " 'For My thoughts are not your thoughts, neither are your ways my ways,' declares the LORD. 'As the heavens are higher than the earth, so are my ways higher than your ways and my thoughts than your thoughts' " (Isaiah 55:8,9).
- "Now we see but a poor reflection; then we shall see face to face. Now I know in part; then I shall know fully, even as I am fully known" (1 Corinthians 13:12).

Such verses make it clear that human reasoning has limitations. Finite minds cannot possibly understand all there is to know about an infinite being. Creatures cannot know everything there is to know about the sovereign Creator. Just as a young child cannot understand everything his father says, so also we as God's children cannot understand all there is to know about our heavenly Father.

_____ *Ask . . .* _____

• Do you think it is possible for human beings to understand *everything* about the nature of God? (They will probably answer no. But if he or she says yes, ask him or her to explain why, in view of Isaiah 55:8,9, Romans 11:33, and 1 Corinthians 13:12.)

Regardless of how a Witness answers, you will want to point out that according to the Watchtower book *Reasoning from the Scriptures*, human beings cannot fully understand that God did not have a beginning. After quoting Psalm 90:2, which addresses God's eternal nature, this book asks:

Is that reasonable? Our minds cannot fully comprehend it. But that is not a sound reason for rejecting it. *Consider examples:* (1) *Time.* No one can point to a certain moment as the beginning of time. And it is a fact that, even though our lives end, time does not. We do not reject the idea of time because there are aspects of it that we do not fully comprehend. Rather, we regulate our lives by it. (2) *Space.* Astronomers find no beginning or end to space. The farther they probe into the universe, the more there is. They do not reject what the evidence shows; many refer to space as being infinite. The same principle applies to the existence of God.[26]

Now, emphasize to the Jehovah's Witness the Watchtower statement that *simply because one cannot comprehend something about God is not a sound reason for rejecting it.* Apply this statement to the doctrine of the Trinity. Simply because we cannot fully comprehend the concept is no reason to reject it.

Ask...

> • _Reasoning from the Scriptures_ says we should not
> reject a doctrine simply because we cannot fully
> comprehend it. Can we agree, then, that we should
> not reject the doctrine of the Trinity simply because
> we cannot fully understand it?

Let's look now at 1 Corinthians 14:33 in its proper context. When Paul said, "God is not a God of confusion but of peace" (NASB), what was he communicating to the Corinthian believers?

Consulting the context of 1 Corinthians makes everything clear. This was a church plagued by internal divisions and disorder (1 Corinthians 1:11). One issue that was causing disorder in the worship services at Corinth had to do with the proper usage of spiritual gifts. Apparently there were situations in which too many people were speaking in tongues and giving prophecies—all at the same time. This led to disarray in the church.

Thus, Paul tells the believers in this church that only one person at a time should speak in tongues, and only two or three people should do this in any one service (1 Corinthians 14:27). Moreover, so the entire church can benefit, there must be an interpreter present. If no such interpreter is available, then the person must remain quiet (verse 28).

Likewise, Paul tells the Corinthian believers that only two or three prophets should speak in any given service—and only one should speak at a time (1 Corinthians 14:29,30). He then states the underlying principle of these instructions: "God is not a God of confusion but of peace" (verse 33). The Greek word for "confusion" has to do with parts of a whole who are at strife with one another. And the Greek word for "peace" refers to parts of a whole who act in concert with one another.[27] Thus, in context, Paul's statement about God deals with a specific situation in the Corinthian church where individual members were at strife with one another, causing disorder and confusion.

Since God is a God of peace (harmony) and not a God of confusion, Paul says, the church itself must seek to imitate God by seeking peace and avoiding disharmony in its services. By so doing, the church honors God.

John 17:3—*Jehovah: The "Only True God"*

The Watchtower Teaching. According to the *New World Translation*, Jesus said in John 17:3: "This means everlasting life, their taking in knowledge of you, *the only true God*, and of the one whom you sent forth, Jesus Christ" (emphasis added). Based on this verse, Watchtower literature argues that one's eternal destiny hinges on knowing the true nature of God, and hence, one must ascertain whether or not the doctrine of the Trinity is true or false.[28]

The Watchtower Society says that Jesus clearly distinguished Himself from God, calling the Father "the only true God" (John 17:3). *Reasoning from the Scriptures* puts it this way: "He [the Father] cannot be 'the only true God' ... if there are two others who are God to the same degree as he is, can he?"[29]

The Watchtower publication *Should You Believe in the Trinity?* tells us that "time and again, Jesus showed that he was a creature separate from God and that he, Jesus, had a God above him, a God whom he worshiped, a God whom he called 'Father.' In prayer to God, that is, the Father, Jesus said, 'You, *the only true God*' (John 17:3)."[30] Indeed, "since Jesus *had* a God, his Father, he could not at the same time *be* that God"[31] (emphasis added).

The Biblical Teaching. When discussing John 17:3 with a Jehovah's Witness, it is important to raise the issue: *Is Jesus a* *true God or a false god?* If Jesus is a true god, then this forces the Jehovah's Witness to believe in more than one true God (which is polytheism). If Jesus is not such a true God, then He must be a false god. In a "Witnessing Tips" article in the *Christian Research Journal* entitled "Is Jesus a True or a False God?" Robert Bowman suggests the following line of logic in conversing with a Jehovah's Witness:

_____ *Ask...* _____

- *Christian*: According to John 17:3, how many *true* Gods are there?

- *JW*: Only one: Jehovah the Father is "the only true God."

- *Christian*: Quite right. Now, would you agree that whatever is not true must be false?

- *JW*: Yes, I suppose so.

- *Christian*: Then, if there is only one true God, all other gods must be false gods, right?

- *JW*: Yes, I can see that.

- *Christian*: Now, according to John 1:1 in the *New World Translation*, Jesus is a god. Do you agree with that?

- *JW*: Of course.

- *Christian*: Well then, is Jesus a true god or a false god?

- *JW*: Hmm... I don't know.

- *Christian*: He can't be a false god, can he, since that would mean the apostle John was guilty of falsely honoring Jesus as a god? Therefore he must be a true God. But Jehovah is the only true God. Therefore, Jesus must be Jehovah.[32]

After making the above points, emphasize that the phrase "only true" (in "only true God") in John 17:3—in both grammar and context—is not intended to contrast the Father and the Son, but rather the one true God's nature with that of false gods.[33] The Greek word for "true" in this verse carries the meaning "real" or "genuine." Hence, Jesus in this verse is simply saying that the Father is the "only true God"—the only real or genuine God—as opposed to the many false gods and idols (*see* 2 Chronicles 15:3; Isaiah 65:16; 1 Thessalonians 1:9; 1 John 5:20; Revelation 3:7). John 17:3 does not take away from Christ's deity in any way. And John firmly establishes Christ's deity (as the *true* God) elsewhere in his gospel (John 1:1; 8:58; 20:28).

Deuteronomy 6:4 and Mark 12:29—*The Greatest Commandment*

The Watchtower Teaching. The *New World Translation* renders Deuteronomy 6:4, "Listen, O Israel: Jehovah our God is one Jehovah." In the New Testament, when Jesus was asked what the greatest commandment was, He answered: "Hear, O Israel, Jehovah our God is one Jehovah" (Mark 12:29 NWT).

Jehovah's Witnesses reason that since God is "one," He cannot possibly be triune at the same time. Because Jehovah is God, and because there is only "one Jehovah," then Jesus cannot possibly be God in the same sense that Jehovah is; nor can the doctrine of the Trinity be true. Thousands of times in the Bible, God is spoken of as a single person. And when He speaks, He speaks as a single, undivided person.[34]

Along these lines, *Should You Believe in the Trinity?* asks, "Why would all the God-inspired Bible writers speak of God as one person if he were actually three persons? . . . Surely, if God were composed of three persons, he would have had his Bible writers make it abundantly clear so that there could be no doubt about it."[35]

The Biblical Teaching. That there is only one true God is the consistent testimony of Scripture from Genesis to Revelation. That truth is like a thread that runs through every page of the Bible. Though there are several possible translations of Deuteronomy 6:4, I believe it is best rendered from the Hebrew text in this way: "Hear, O Israel! The Lord is our God, *the Lord alone.*" Using God's names, we could translate this verse, "Hear, O Israel! Yahweh is our Elohim, Yahweh alone." This affirmation of faith was known as the *Shema* among the ancient Jews.

In a culture saturated with false gods and idols, the *Shema* would have been particularly meaningful for the Israelites. The Jews made a habit of reciting this affirmation twice a day—once in the morning and again in the evening. The importance of the *Shema* is reflected in the Hebrew practice of requiring children to memorize it at a very early age.

Now, while it is true that Yahweh (the Lord) is our Elohim (God), the key identification we must now make is this: Who is Yahweh? Is it the Father alone, as Jehovah's Witnesses assume, or is Jesus also Yahweh? Indeed, is the triune God Yahweh?

Scripture does not come right out and say, "The Father is Yahweh." But we know the Father is Yahweh because He is called "God" and the "only true God" in Scripture (John 6:27; 17:3). By that same virtue, however, Jesus must also be recognized as Yahweh: He is called "God" (John 1:1), "Mighty God" (Isaiah 9:6; cf. 10:21), "our great God and Savior" (Titus 2:13), and "Lord" (Romans 10:9; 1 Corinthians 12:3; Philippians 2:11).[36]

Clearly, then, Jesus is Yahweh just as the Father is Yahweh. The Holy Spirit, as well, must be recognized as Yahweh in view of His deity (*see* Acts 5; 1 Corinthians 3:16; 6:19; 2 Corinthians 3:17; Ephesians 2:22). In light of these facts, we must conclude that in no way does Deuteronomy 6:4 argue against the doctrine of the Trinity. Trinitarians gladly affirm that this verse proves there is one and only one God. And that does not contradict the idea that there are three persons within the one Godhead—a truth that is clearly revealed in other passages, such as Matthew 28:19 and 2 Corinthians 13:14.

_____ *Ask...* _____

- Do you understand that Trinitarians agree with the teaching of Deuteronomy 6:4 that there is only one God—*yes or no*?

- Do you understand that Trinitarians teach *not* that there are three gods in the Trinity but that there is only *one* God and that there are three persons within the one Godhead—*yes or no*?

(These questions will help you clarify to the Jehovah's Witness what Trinitarians really believe, as opposed to the Watchtower's *distortions* of what Trinitarians believe.)

It is interesting to observe that the early Christians—who had a solidly Jewish background—did not hesitate to refer to Jesus as "Lord" and "God," despite their unbending monotheism (Romans 10:13; 1 Thessalonians 5:2; 1 Peter 2:3; 3:15).[37] Indeed, despite their commitment to the *Shema* in Deuteronomy 6:4, they had no scruple about applying to Jesus many Old Testament texts that were originally written in reference to Yahweh. For example:

- In Revelation 1:7 Jesus is seen to be the pierced Yahweh who is described in Zechariah 12:10.
- The reference to Yahweh and Elohim in Isaiah 40:3 is seen to be fulfilled in the person of Jesus Christ in Mark 1:2-4.
- Calling upon Yahweh in Joel 2:32 is seen as identical and parallel to calling upon Jesus in Romans 10:13.
- The glory of Yahweh in Isaiah 6:1-5 is said to be the glory of Jesus in John 12:41.
- Yahweh's voice "like the roar of rushing waters" (Ezekiel 43:2) is identical to Jesus' voice "like the sound of rushing waters" (Revelation 1:15).
- The description of Yahweh as an everlasting light in Isaiah 60:19,20 is seen as identical to the statement about Jesus as an everlasting light in Revelation 21:23.

After sharing the above with the Jehovah's Witness:

_____ *Ask...* _____

- How do you explain that the early Jewish Christians—who were clearly committed to the *Shema* in Deuteronomy 6:4—had no scruple about applying to Jesus many Old Testament texts that were originally written in reference to Yahweh?

- How do you explain that the early Jewish Christians called Jesus "Lord" and "God" in the same sense that Jehovah is called "Lord" and "God"?

Now, while speaking to the Jehovah's Witness about Deuteronomy 6:4, it is important to emphasize that in the course of God's self-disclosure to humankind, He revealed His nature to man in progressive stages. First, God revealed His essential unity and uniqueness—that is, He revealed that He is *one* and that He is the only true God. This was a necessary starting point, for throughout history Israel was surrounded by nations deeply engulfed in polytheism (the belief in many gods). Through the prophets, God communicated and affirmed to Israel the truth of monotheism (the belief that there is only one true God).

While God's unity and oneness—as affirmed in the *Shema*—is the clear emphasis in Old Testament revelation, this is not to say that there are no hints or shadows of the doctrine of the Trinity there, for indeed there are (Genesis 1:26; 3:22; 11:7; Proverbs 30:4; Isaiah 6:8; 48:16). But God did not reveal the *fullness* of this doctrine until New Testament times (*see* Matthew 3:16,17; 28:19; 2 Corinthians 13:14; Ephesians 2:13; 4:4). It is by reading the Old Testament under the illumination of the New Testament that we find supporting evidences for the Trinity there. Indeed, as theologian Benjamin Warfield notes,

The Old Testament may be likened to a chamber richly furnished but dimly lighted; the introduction of light brings into it nothing which was not in it before; but it brings out into clearer view much of what is in it but was only dimly or even not at all perceived before. The mystery of the Trinity is not [explicitly] revealed in the Old Testament; but the mystery of the Trinity underlies the Old Testament revelation, and here and there almost comes into view. Thus the Old Testament revelation of God is not corrected by the fuller revelation which follows it, but only perfected, extended and enlarged.[38]

The teaching that there is one God but three persons within the Godhead is the clear testimony of Scripture. One key New Testament verse illustrating that truth is Matthew 28:19.

Matthew 28:19—*The "Name" of the Father, the Son, and the Holy Spirit*

The Watchtower Teaching. Matthew 28:19 in the *New World Translation* reads, "Go therefore and make disciples of people of all the nations, baptizing them in the name of the Father and of the Son and of the holy spirit."

Does this verse prove that the Father, Son, and Holy Spirit are equal in substance, power, and eternity? No, answers the Watchtower Society—"no more than listing three people, such as Tom, Dick, and Harry, means that they are three in one."[39] Jehovah's Witnesses say that Trinitarians are reading something into the text that simply is not there. The doctrine of the Trinity, they say, is imposed upon the text, not derived from it.

The Biblical Teaching. In the New American Standard Bible, Matthew 28:19 reads, "Go therefore and make disciples of all the nations, baptizing them in the name of *the* Father and *the* Son and *the* Holy Spirit" (emphasis added). It is critical to note that the word "name" is singular in the Greek text, indicating that there is one God, but three distinct persons within the Godhead—the Father, the Son, and the Holy Spirit.[40] Theologian Robert Reymond draws our attention to the importance of this verse for the doctrine of the Trinity:

> Jesus does not say, (1) "into the names [plural] of the Father and of the Son and of the Holy Spirit," or what is its virtual equivalent, (2) "into the name of the Father, and into the name of the Son, and into the name of the Holy Spirit," as if we had to deal with three separate Beings. Nor does He say, (3) "into the name of the Father, Son, and Holy Spirit," (omitting the three recurring articles), as if "the Father, Son, and Holy Ghost" might be taken as merely three designations of a single person. What He does say is this: (4) "into the name [singular] of *the* Father, and of *the* Son, and of *the* Holy Spirit," first asserting the unity of the three by combining them all within the bounds of the single Name, and then throwing into emphasis the distinctness of each by introducing them in turn with the repeated article.[41]

Hence, contrary to what the Watchtower Society says, Matthew 28:19 definitely does support the doctrine of the Trinity, and in a very emphatic manner.

After explaining the above to the Jehovah's Witness:

 *Ask...*

- Can you see that because the word "name" is singular in the Greek—and definite articles are placed in front of Father, Son, and Holy Spirit—that plurality within unity is thereby indicated?

You will also want to point out that there are many other scriptural indications for three-in-oneness in the Godhead. For example, when God was about to create man, He said, "Let *us* make man in *our* image, in *our* likeness, and let them rule over the fish of the sea and the birds of the air, over the livestock, over all the earth, and over all the creatures that move along the ground" (Genesis 1:26, emphasis added). Though scholars have offered different suggestions as to what may be meant by the plural pronouns in this verse,[42] there is good reason to interpret them as references to the Trinity.[43] (Note that the phrase "our image" in Genesis 1:26 is explained in verse 27 as God's image.) Commenting on this verse, Bible scholar Gleason Archer notes that "the one true God subsists in three Persons, Persons who are able to confer with one another and carry their plans into action together—without ceasing to be one God."[44]

After Adam and Eve had fallen into sin, God said, "The man has now become like *one of us*, knowing good and evil. He must not be allowed to reach out his hand and take also from the tree of life and eat, and live forever" (Genesis 3:22, emphasis added). Note that the phrase "like one of us" refers back to verse 5, "like God." As is true with Genesis 1:26, this verse supports plurality within the Godhead.

Later, when sinful mankind was attempting to erect the Tower of Babel, God said, "Come, let *us* go down and confuse their language so they will not understand each other" (Genesis 11:7, emphasis added). Again, we see plurality within the Godhead.

Many centuries later, Isaiah had a vision in the temple during which God commissioned him to service. God asked Isaiah, "Whom shall *I* send? And who will go for *us*?" And Isaiah said, "Here am I. Send me!" (Isaiah 6:8, emphasis added).

Just prior to His crucifixion, Jesus spoke of the three persons of the Trinity in His Upper-Room discourse. Jesus said to the disciples, "And I will ask the Father, and he will give you another Counselor to be with you forever—the Spirit of truth. The world cannot accept him, because it neither sees him nor knows him. But you know him, for he lives with you and will be in you" (John 14:16,17). Jesus also said that "the Counselor, the Holy Spirit, whom the Father will send in my name, will teach you all things and will remind you of everything I have said to you" (14:26). Still again, Jesus said, "When the Counselor comes, whom I will send to you from the Father, the Spirit of truth who goes out from the Father, he will testify about me" (15:26).

Trinitarian language virtually permeates the writings of Paul. Consider this brief excerpt from his first letter to the Thessalonians:

> We always thank *God* [the Father] for all of you, mentioning you in our prayers. We continually remember before our *God and Father* your work produced by faith, your labor prompted by love, and your endurance inspired by hope in our *Lord Jesus Christ*.
>
> For we know, brothers loved by *God* [the Father], that he has chosen you, because our gospel came to you not simply with words, but also with power, with *the Holy Spirit* and with deep conviction. You know how we lived among you for your sake. You became imitators of us and of *the Lord* [Jesus Christ]; in spite of severe suffering, you welcomed the message with the joy given by *the Holy Spirit*. And so you became a model to all the believers in Macedonia and Achaia. The *Lord's* [Christ's] message rang out from you not only in Macedonia and Achaia— your faith in *God* [the Father] has become known everywhere. Therefore we do not need to say anything about it, for they themselves report what kind of reception you gave us. They tell how you turned to *God* [the Father] from idols to serve the *living and true God* [the Father], and to wait for his *Son* from heaven, whom he raised from the dead—*Jesus*, who rescues us from the coming wrath (1 Thessalonians 1:2-10, emphasis added, inserts mine).

It is interesting to observe that Paul and the other New Testament writers felt no incongruity whatever between their doctrine of the Trinity and the Old Testament concept of God. "The New Testament writers certainly were not conscious of being 'setters forth of strange gods.' . . . The God of the Old Testament was their God, and their God was a Trinity, and their sense of the identity of the two was so complete that no question as to it was raised in their minds."[45] In other words, we do not find in the New Testament the birth of a new and novel concept of God. Indeed, "the doctrine of the Trinity does not appear in the New Testament in the making, but as already made."[46]

2 Corinthians 13:14—*Paul's Benediction*

The Watchtower Teaching. The *New World Translation* records Paul's benediction in 2 Corinthians 13:14: "The undeserved kindness of the Lord *Jesus Christ* and the love of *God* and the sharing in the *holy spirit* be with all of you" (emphasis added). The Watchtower Society says that this verse supports only the idea that the three subjects mentioned—Father, Son, and Holy Spirit—*exist*; it says nothing about their relationship to each other or their alleged equality or the doctrine of the Trinity.

The Watchtower Society argues that one cannot justly infer from 2 Corinthians 13:14 that the Father, Son, and Holy Spirit possess equal authority or the same nature.[47] Indeed, references such as this prove "only that there are the three subjects named . . . but it does not prove, by itself, that all the three belong necessarily to the divine nature, and possess equal divine honor."[48]

The Biblical Teaching. No Trinitarian bases his belief in the Trinity on a single verse, but rather on the accumulative evidence of the whole of Scripture. It is true that 2 Corinthians 13:14 by itself does not conclusively prove the doctrine of the Trinity. But when considered with other scriptures, there is no doubt that the doctrine is true.

Though Scripture is clear that there is only one God (as pointed out earlier), in the unfolding of God's revelation to humankind it also becomes clear that there are *three distinct persons* who are called God. For example, Peter refers to the saints "who have been chosen according to the foreknowledge of God *the Father*" (1 Peter 1:2, emphasis added). When Jesus made a postresurrection appearance to doubting Thomas, the disciple worshipfully responded by addressing him, "My Lord and *my God*" (John 20:28, emphasis added). The Father also said of the Son, "Your throne, *O God*, will last for ever and ever" (Hebrews 1:8, emphasis added). In Acts 5:3,4, we are told that lying to the Holy Spirit is equivalent to lying to God: Peter said, "Ananias, how is it that Satan has so filled your heart that you have lied to the Holy Spirit and have kept for yourself some of the money you received for the land? Didn't it belong to you before it was sold? And after it was sold, wasn't the money at your disposal? What made you think of doing such a thing? *You have not lied to men but to God*" (emphasis added).

After going through the above verses:

_____ *Ask...* _____

- Do you agree that the Father, Son, and Holy Spirit are each called God in the New Testament?

  (If the Jehovah's Witness says no—which is a likelihood—have him or her slowly read aloud each of the above verses and ask:)

- Is the Father called God in 1 Peter 1:2?

- Is Jesus called God in John 20:28? (The Jehovah's Witness may try to argue about this verse. See my discussion of John 20:28 later in this chapter.)

- Is the Holy Spirit recognized as God in Acts 5:3,4?

Besides being called God, each of the three persons are seen on different occasions to possess the attributes of deity. For example:

- All three persons possess the attribute of omnipresence (everywhere-present): the Father (1 Kings 8:27), the Son (Matthew 28:20), and the Holy Spirit (Psalm 139:7).

• All three have the attribute of omniscience (all-knowingness): the Father (Psalm 147:5), the Son (John 16:30), and the Holy Spirit (1 Corinthians 2:10).

• All three have the attribute of omnipotence (all-powerful): the Father (Psalm 135:6), the Son (Matthew 28:18), and the Holy Spirit (Romans 15:19).

• *Holiness* is ascribed to each of the three persons: the Father (Revelation 15:4), the Son (Acts 3:14), and the Holy Spirit (Romans 1:4).

• *Eternity* is ascribed to each of the three persons: the Father (Psalm 90:2), the Son (Micah 5:2; John 1:2; Revelation 1:8,17), and the Holy Spirit (Hebrews 9:14).

• Each of the three persons is individually described as the truth: the Father (John 7:28), the Son (Revelation 3:7), and the Holy Spirit (1 John 5:6).

• Each of the three is called Lord (Luke 2:11; Romans 10:12; 2 Corinthians 3:17), everlasting (Romans 16:26; Hebrews 9:14; Revelation 22:13), almighty (Genesis 17:1; Romans 15:19; Revelation 1:8), and powerful (Jeremiah 32:17; Zechariah 4:6; Hebrews 1:3).[49]

After going through the above references:

_____ *Ask...* _____

• Can we agree that the Father, Son, and Holy Spirit each exercise the attributes of deity on different occasions?
(If he or she says no, start looking up some of the above verses with him or her and read each one aloud. Be patient; it will be worth it. Then ask:)

• Can anyone other than God have the *attributes* of God? (Use this question to point to the deity of Jesus and the Holy Spirit.)

In addition to having the attributes of deity, each of the three persons were involved in doing the *works* of deity. For example, all three were involved in the creation of the world: the Father (Genesis 2:7; Psalm 102:25), the Son (John 1:3; Colossians 1:16; Hebrews 1:2), and the Holy Spirit (Genesis 1:2; Job 33:4; Psalm 104:30).

A fact often overlooked in theological discussions is that all three persons of the Trinity were sovereignly involved in the incarnation. In Luke 1:35 we find an angel informing Mary, "The Holy Spirit will come upon you, and the power of the Most High will overshadow you. So the holy one to be born will be called the Son of God." Though the Holy Spirit was the agent through whom the incarnation was brought about, we are told in Hebrews 10:5 that it was the Father who prepared a human body for Christ. Moreover, Jesus is said to have taken upon Himself flesh and blood—as if it were an act of His own individual will (Hebrews 2:14).

The three persons of the Trinity were also involved in Jesus' resurrection from the dead. God the Father is often said to have raised Christ (Acts 2:32; 13:30; Romans 6:4; Ephesians 1:19,20). But without diminishing the Father's key role in the resurrection, it is just as clear from Scripture that Jesus raised Himself. Recall that in John 2:19 Jesus told some Jews who were looking for a divine sign, "Destroy this temple [My physical body], and I will raise it again in three days" (insert mine). Then, in John 10:17,18, Jesus said of His life, "I lay down my life—only to take it up again. No one takes it from me, but I lay it down of my own accord. I have authority to lay it down and authority to take it up again." The Holy Spirit was also involved in Christ's resurrection, for it was "through the Spirit of holiness" that Jesus was "declared with power to be the Son of God by his resurrection from the dead" (Romans 1:4).

Each of the three persons in the Trinity also sanctify (Hebrews 2:11; 1 Peter 1:2, Jude 1), are life (Deuteronomy 30:20; Romans 8:10; Colossians 3:4), give eternal life (John 10:28; Romans 6:23; Galatians 6:8), raise the dead (John 5:21a,

John 5:21b, 1 Peter 3:18), and divinely inspire God's prophets and spokesmen (Mark 13:11; 2 Corinthians 13:3; Hebrews 1:1).[50]

After making some of the points above:

_____ *Ask...* _____

- Can we agree that the Father, Son, and Holy Spirit are all involved in doing the *works* of deity?
  (If he or she says no, look up some of the above verses and read them aloud. Then ask:)

- Can anyone other than God do the works of deity?
  (Use this question to point to the deity of Jesus and the Holy Spirit.)

In view of all the above, it seems clear that within the triune Godhead, never is a single act performed by one person without the instant acquiescence of the other two. This is not to deny that each of the three persons have distinctive ministries unique to themselves. But clearly, the three always act in harmonious unity in all the mighty works wrought by God throughout the universe.

Matthew 3:16,17—*Jesus' Baptism*

The Watchtower Teaching. The *New World Translation* renders Matthew 3:16,17, "After being baptized Jesus immediately came up from the water; and, look! the heavens were opened up, and he saw descending like a dove God's spirit coming upon him. Look! Also, there was a voice from the heavens that said: 'This is my Son, the beloved, whom I have approved.'"

Making mockery of the Trinitarian interpretation of this verse, the Watchtower Society asks, "Was God saying that he was his own son, that he approved himself, that he sent himself? No, God the Creator was saying that he, as the superior, was approving a lesser one, his Son Jesus, for the work ahead."[51]

The Watchtower Society argues that Matthew 3:16,17 does not prove that the Father, Son, and Holy Spirit are one. The booklet *Should You Believe in the Trinity?* notes that Abraham, Isaac, and Jacob are mentioned together a number of times, but this does not make them one. Likewise, Peter, James, and John are mentioned together, but this does not make them one.[52] Hence, Matthew 3:16,17 does not support the doctrine of the Trinity.

The Biblical Teaching. As is true with 2 Corinthians 13:14, Matthew 3:16,17 *by itself* does not prove the doctrine of the Trinity. No Trinitarian bases his belief in the Trinity on a single verse, but rather on the accumulative evidence of the whole of Scripture. When Matthew 3:16,17 is considered with other passages, there can be no doubt that the doctrine of the Trinity is true. (*Be sure to consult as well the detailed scriptural arguments for the Trinity listed in the discussions of Matthew 28:19 and 2 Corinthians 13:14.*)

Though Matthew 3:16,17 may not by itself prove the doctrine of the Trinity, it definitely supports the doctrine. It can be shown *theologically* that the three persons mentioned in this verse—the Father, Son, and Holy Spirit—are God. The Jehovah's Witnesses do not challenge that the Father is God, so we will not seek to establish that. However, as I have noted earlier, the fact that Jesus is called the "Son of God" proves that He has the same divine nature as the Father.

You may remember that though the term "son of . . ." can refer to "offspring of" in some contexts, the more important theological meaning is "of the order of."[53] For example, "sons of the prophets" means "of the order of prophets" (1 Kings 20:35). "Sons of the singers" means "of the order of singers" (Nehemiah 12:28). Likewise, the phrase "Son of God" means "of the order of God," and represents a claim to undiminished deity.

Ancient Semitics and Orientals used the phrase "son of . . ." to indicate *likeness or sameness of nature* and *equality of being*.[54] Hence, when Jesus claimed to be the Son of God, His Jewish contemporaries fully understood that He was making a claim to be God in an unqualified sense. Benjamin Warfield affirms that, from the earliest days of Christianity, the phrase "Son of God" was understood to be fully equivalent to God.[55] This is why when Jesus made His claim, the Jews insisted, "We have a law, and according to that law he [Christ] must die, because he claimed to be the Son of God" (John 19:7, insert mine). Recognizing that Jesus was identifying Himself as God, the Jews wanted to put Him to death for committing blasphemy (*see* Leviticus 24:16).

_____ *Ask . . .* _____

- If the phrase "son of . . ." meant *sameness of nature* and *equality of being* among the ancients, as historical records prove to be true, then what does this tell us about the meaning of the phrase "Son of God"?

Further evidence for Christ's *eternal* sonship is found in Hebrews 1:2, which says God created the universe *through* His "Son"—implying that Christ was the Son of God *prior* to His work of Creation. Moreover, Christ *as the Son* is explicitly said to have existed "before all things" (Colossians 1:17; compare with verses 13,14). Also, Jesus, speaking as the Son of God (John 8:54-56), asserts His eternal preexistence before Abraham (verse 58).

In view of those facts, we must conclude that when the Father and the Son are mentioned in Matthew 3:16,17, they are spoken of in terms of their eternal deity. This adds supportive evidence for the doctrine of the Trinity. And since we know from other passages that the Holy Spirit is God (cf. Acts 5; 1 Corinthians 3:16; 6:19; 2 Corinthians 3:17; Ephesians 2:22), it is clear that Matthew 3:16,17 is an excellent support text for affirming the reality of the Trinity.

John 20:28—*"My Lord and My God"*

The Watchtower Teaching. When doubting Thomas beheld the risen Christ, he responded, "My Lord and my God!" (John 20:28 NWT). Some Jehovah's Witnesses have dismissed this verse as simply recording Thomas's surprise at seeing the risen Christ. The modern parallel to Thomas's words would be something like, "Oh, my God."

Another possible explanation of Thomas's words is suggested in *Should You Believe in the Trinity?*: Jesus seemed "like" *a* god to Thomas—especially in view of the miracle Thomas was presently witnessing. Or perhaps Thomas was making an emotional exclamation that was directed to Jehovah-God though spoken to Jesus.[56] Either way, the verse need not be interpreted as portraying Jesus as God in the same sense that the Father is God.

Reasoning from the Scriptures suggests that Thomas's calling Jesus "a god" is in perfect accord with other Scripture passages. For example, in John 1:18 Jesus is called "the only-begotten god"—indicating that He is a lesser god than Jehovah. Isaiah 9:6 calls Jesus a "mighty god," which is a lesser title than Almighty God. And in John 1:1 Jesus is described as "a god" or "divine."[57]

The Biblical Teaching. Was Thomas just expressing surprise at seeing the risen Christ, exclaiming something to the effect, "Oh, my God"? By no means! Indeed, if Thomas had done this he would have been guilty of taking God's name in vain. Jews of the first century believed that any careless use of God's name amounted to blasphemy.[58]

Now, if Thomas *had* taken God's name in vain, Jesus surely would have rebuked him for doing so. But not only did Jesus *not* rebuke Thomas, He *commended* Thomas for finally coming to believe He was who He said He was (both "Lord" and "God"). Jesus affirmed Thomas, not corrected him.

If the Jehovah's Witness explains John 20:28 in the above way:

Ask...

- If Thomas was just expressing surprise at seeing the risen Christ, wouldn't his words be equivalent to taking God's name in vain?

- If Thomas took God's name in vain in the presence of Jesus, don't you think Jesus would have rebuked him?

- Why do you think Jesus _commended_ Thomas instead of _rebuking_ him?

What about the view that Jesus was "like" a god to Thomas? There is no way that can be correct. A response such as _"my_ Lord and _my_ God" at seeing the risen Christ would have called for a rebuke in first-century Judaism _unless Jesus truly was God (see_ Acts 14:11-15).[59] Thomas wasn't just calling Jesus "a" god; he called Jesus _his_ Lord and _his_ God. And if Jesus was not God Almighty in the same sense the Father is, He surely would have corrected Thomas by saying something like, "No. I am just _a_ god—a lesser god. Jehovah is the only true God. You must not put Me in Jehovah's place. Only Jehovah can be called '_my_ Lord and _my_ God.'" But Jesus said nothing of the sort. Instead, He _commended_ Thomas for recognizing His true identity.

To drive this point home to the Jehovah's Witness:

Ask...

- What precisely was it that Thomas "believed," according to John 20:29? (The obvious answer is that Thomas had finally come to believe that Jesus was "Lord" and "God.")

By the way, in Psalm 35:23 the phrase "my God and my Lord" (NASB) is used of Yahweh.[60] This makes one wonder whether Thomas—a Hebrew believer quite familiar with the Old Testament—had this verse in mind when addressing Jesus as "my Lord and my God."

We may conclude that John 20:28 constitutes an excellent support text for the doctrine of the Trinity. The Father is fully God; the Son is fully God; and yet there is only one true God. *This makes sense only within a Trinitarian framework.* Within the unity of the one Godhead, there are three persons—the Father, Son, and Holy Spirit—and each of the three are co-equal and co-eternal.

John 10:30—*"I and the Father Are One"*

The Watchtower Teaching. In John 10:30 Jesus told a group of Jews, "I and the Father are one" (NWT). What did He mean by this? Jehovah's Witnesses answer by pointing to John 17:21,22, where Jesus prayed to the Father that the disciples "may all be *one*, just as you, Father, are in union with me and I am in union with you, that they also may be in union with us...that they may be *one* just as we are *one*" (emphasis added). It is of great significance, we are told, that Jesus used the same Greek word (*hen*) for "one" in all of those instances.[61]

Clearly, Jesus was not praying for all the disciples to become a single entity. Nor was He praying that they would become a part of the Trinity.[62] Instead, He was praying that they would have unity of thought and purpose, just as He and the Father had.[63] Indeed, "just as Christ and his body members are regarded as one, so are Jehovah and Christ regarded as one. They are all one in *agreement*, *purpose*, and *organization*."[64]

The Biblical Teaching. As any first-year Greek student can tell you, the context is always determinative in how a given word is to be interpreted in a sentence. In different contexts, the same word can carry different nuances of meaning. One must keep this in mind when interpreting the Greek word for "one" (*hen*).

_____ *Ask*... _____

> • Do you understand the consistent teaching of Greek
>   scholars that context is always determinative in how
>   a given word is to be interpreted in a particular
>   sentence?

_____

While the Greek word *hen* by itself does not have to refer to
more than unity of purpose, the context of John 10 makes it
clear that much more is meant.[65] How do we know this? By the
way the Jews responded to Jesus' affirmation that "I and my
Father are one." They immediately picked up stones to put
Him to death. They understood Jesus was claiming to be God
in an unqualified sense. Indeed, according to verse 33, the
Jews said, "For a good work we do not stone You, but for
blasphemy; and because You, being a man, *make Yourself out to
be God*" (emphasis added). The penalty for blasphemy,
according to Old Testament law (Leviticus 24), was death by
stoning.

_____ *Ask*... _____

> • Why would the Jews pick up stones to kill Jesus if all
>   He was affirming was His unity of purpose with the
>   Father?
>
> • Didn't the Jews also have unity of purpose with the
>   Father?
>
> • Why would the Jews—who had unity of purpose
>   with the Father—try to kill Jesus for affirming unity
>   of purpose with the Father?
>
> • If Jesus was just affirming unity of purpose with the
>   Father by saying, "I and the Father are one," then
>   why did the Jews understand His words to be an
>   affirmation that *He was God* (John 10:33)? (If the
>   Jehovah's Witness says that the Jews were mistaken
>   in interpreting Jesus' statement to be an affirmation

of deity, ask him or her why Jesus didn't correct their "misunderstanding," but rather indicated that they understood Him correctly [*see* John 10:34-38].)

Now, the context in John 17:21—where Jesus prays that the disciples "may all be *one*; even as Thou, Father, art in Me, and I in Thee" (NASB)—is entirely different. In this context, the Greek word for "one" refers to unity among people in the midst of their diversity. Just like today, believers back then had a tendency to be divisive over various issues. That's why Christ prayed for their unity. Among other things, this kind of unity can be expressed in the proper exercise of spiritual gifts (Ephesians 4:3-16) as well as in praying for one another and exhorting one another (2 Corinthians 1:11; Hebrews 10:25).

It is critical to emphasize that one cannot adopt a wooden methodology in which a particular word's usage in one verse determines how it is to be interpreted in another distant verse. That is, the way the word "one" is used in John 17:21 does not determine its meaning in John 10:30. We are dealing with two entirely different contexts.

Watchtower expert Marian Bodine says that if the oneness that Christ shares with the Father is identical to the oneness that believers have with Christ, then all believers should be able to say:

- "I [*your name*] and the Father are one" (John 10:30).
- "He who has seen [*your name*] has seen the Father" (John 14:9).
- "Whatever the Father does, these things [*your name*] also does in like manner" (John 5:19).
- "He who does not honor [*your name*] does not honor the Father who sent Him" (John 5:23).
- "All things that the Father has are Mine [*your name*]" (John 16:15).[66]

_____ Ask . . . _____

> • If the Watchtower interpretation of John 10:30 is correct—and the oneness that Christ shares with the Father is *identical* to the oneness that believers have with Christ—are you willing to insert your personal name in John 10:30? In John 14:9? In John 5:23? In John 16:15? (Look up each verse and read it aloud.)

Revelation 1:8 and 22:13—*The "Alpha and Omega"*

The Watchtower Teaching. The *New World Translation* renders Revelation 1:8, " 'I am the Alpha and the Omega,' says Jehovah God, 'the One who is and who was and who is coming, the Almighty.' " Revelation 22:13 also records the words, "I am the Alpha and the Omega, the first and the last, the beginning and the end" (NWT).

According to *Reasoning from the Scriptures,* the references to the "Alpha and Omega" in the Book of Revelation deal not with Jesus Christ but with God Almighty, the Father. Among the evidences cited in support of this view are: 1) In Revelation 1:8 God Almighty is said to be the Alpha and Omega. This is the Father. Now, it is true that in the King James Version, that title "is applied to one whose description thereafter shows him to be Jesus Christ."[67] But the reference to Alpha and Omega in verse 11 is *spurious*, and does not appear in most other translations. 2) "Many translations" of the Bible into Hebrew insert the name Jehovah in Revelation 1:8—in recognition that Almighty God is being referred to.[68]

And 3) overcoming Christians are said to be "sons" of the Alpha and Omega in Revelation 21:6,7. However, the relationship of spirit-anointed believers to Jesus Christ is that of *brothers*, not *sonship*.[69] For these and other reasons, then, references to the Alpha and Omega in Revelation are interpreted to be God Almighty, not Jesus Christ.

The Biblical Teaching. If you can demonstrate to the Jehovah's Witness that Jesus is indeed the "Alpha and Omega" and the "First and the Last," he or she will really have no other option than to admit that Revelation 1:8 and 22:13 say Jesus is Jehovah-God. And demonstrating this fact is not difficult to do. David Reed, a former Jehovah's Witness, suggests using the following line of reason—using the *New World Translation*—to demonstrate that Jesus is the Alpha and Omega:

> Revelation 1:7-8 . . . says that someone "is coming." Who? Verse 7 says it is someone who was "pierced." Who was it that was pierced when he was nailed up to die? Jesus! But verse 8 says that it is Jehovah God who "is coming." Could it be that there are two who are coming? No! Verse 8 refers to "the One who . . . is coming."
>
> Revelation 1:8 states clearly that Jehovah God is the Alpha and the Omega. Now note what he says at Revelation 22:12-13: " 'Look! I am coming quickly . . . I am the Alpha and the Omega, the first and the last. . . . ' " So, Jehovah God is coming quickly. But notice the response when he says it again: " ' "Yes; I am coming quickly." Amen! Come, Lord Jesus' " (22:20, NWT). . . .
>
> Then, again referring to the *New World Translation*, continue like this: Who is speaking in Revelation 2:8? "These are the things that he says, 'the First and the Last,' who became dead and came to life again. . . ." Obviously, it is Jesus. Who was Jesus identifying himself as being, when he called himself "the First and the Last"? This is how Almighty God described himself in the Old Testament (Isa. 48:12-13).[70]

Isaiah 44:6 records Jehovah-God as saying. "I am the first and I am the last; apart from me there is no God." Again, in Isaiah 48:12, God said, "I am he; I am the first and I am the last." God said this right after His pronouncement that "I will not yield my glory to another" (verse 11b). Christ's use of this title in Revelation 22:12,13 was undoubtedly intended to be taken as a claim to be Jehovah-God. No other conclusion is acceptable.

Now, after establishing that Jesus indeed is the Alpha and

the Omega, you need to help the Jehovah's Witness understand what these words really mean. To the modern ear, the claim to be the Alpha and the Omega may seem strange. But for the ancient Jew, Christ was describing Himself in a way he would have readily understood. Though the letters alpha and omega are the first and last letters of the Greek alphabet, John recorded the Book of Revelation for Jewish readers who were also familiar with the Hebrew language and alphabet. And therein lies the significance of Christ's claim: In Jewish thinking, a reference to the first and last letters of an alphabet (*aleph* and *tau* in Hebrew) was regarded as including all the intermediate letters, and came to represent totality or entirety.

It is with this idea in mind that the Jews in their ancient commentaries on the Old Testament said that Adam transgressed the whole law from *aleph* to *tau*. Abraham, by contrast, observed the whole law from *aleph* to *tau*. The Jews also believed that when God brings blessing upon Israel, He does so abundantly, from *aleph* to *tau*.

When used of God (or Christ), the first and last letters express eternality and omnipotence. Christ's claim to be the Alpha and the Omega is an affirmation that He is the all-powerful One of eternity past and eternity future (Jehovah-God). "In describing Himself as 'the first and the last' Christ is relating Himself to time and eternity. He is the eternal God who has always existed in the past and who will always exist in the future."[71] For any created being, however exalted, to claim to be the Alpha and the Omega as these terms are used of Jesus Christ would be utter blasphemy.

_____ *Ask...* _____

• Since Jesus is clearly claiming to be the "first and the last" in Revelation 22:12,13—and since Isaiah 44:6 records Jehovah-God as saying, "I am the first and I am the last; apart from me there is no God"— what must we conclude about Jesus' true identity?

10

The Great Divide:
The "Anointed Class"
and the "Other Sheep"

If anyone serves Me, let him follow Me; and
where I am, *there shall My servant also be* (John
12:26 NASB, emphasis added).

—Jesus Christ

According to Watchtower theology, only 144,000 Jehovah's
Witnesses go to heaven, and these make up what is known as
the "Anointed Class" (Revelation 7:4; cf. 14:1-3). All the
remaining Jehovah's Witnesses are a part of God's "other
sheep," and will live forever on a paradise earth.

Speaking of this "great divide," *Reasoning from the Scriptures* tells us that "God has purposed to associate a limited
number of faithful humans with Jesus Christ in the heavenly
Kingdom."[1] This book teaches that only those who become
"born again"—thereby becoming "sons" of God—can share
in this heavenly Kingdom (John 1:12,13; Romans 8:16,17;
1 Peter 1:3,4).[2]

These individuals look forward not to *physical* but to *spiritual* existence in heaven. The book *"Your Will Be Done On
Earth"* says that "in the resurrection from the dead they expect
to be born like Jesus Christ into the fullness of spirit life in
heaven, changed, transformed indeed."[3]

We are told that "since 'flesh and blood cannot inherit God's kingdom,' these must become the spiritual sons of God."[4] *"Let God Be True"* likewise says that "Christ Jesus was put to death in the flesh and was resurrected an invisible spirit creature. Therefore the world will see him no more. He went to prepare a heavenly place for his associate heirs, 'Christ's body,' for they too will be invisible spirit creatures. Their citizenship exists in the heavenlies."[5]

Now, the Watchtower Society teaches that only a "few" find entrance into this spiritual kingdom—and they are truly a "little flock" when compared with earth's population.[6] This little flock of true believers (Luke 12:32) allegedly began with the 12 apostles and was completely filled by the year 1935 (Judge Rutherford received a "revelation" to this effect). According to current statistics, less than 5,000 of these "anointed" believers are still alive today. Since most of these individuals are currently very old, this number is expected to drop dramatically in the coming decade.

Watchtower literature teaches that to be saved, these individuals must believe in God, repent of their sins, dedicate themselves to God, be baptized by immersion, and undergo the "sacrifice" of all human rights and hopes, even as Jesus did. This is very clearly a works-oriented salvation. These individuals must "set their affections and keep their minds fixed on the things above."[7]

Members of the Anointed Class have spiritual blessings and privileges that the average Jehovah's Witness does not have (most Jehovah's Witnesses are not members of the Anointed Class). The Watchtower Society teaches that *only* members of the Anointed Class:

- become born again (John 3:3-8; Titus 3:5; 1 Peter 1:3; 1 John 5:1);
- become adopted as "sons" of God (John 1:12,13; Romans 8:14-17; Galatians 4:6,7; Ephesians 1:5);
- are brothers with Christ (Romans 8:29; Hebrews 2:11-17; 3:1);

• are conformed to Christ's image (Romans 8:29; 2 Corinthians 3:18);

• are in union with Christ (2 Corinthians 5:17; Ephesians 1:3);

• are heirs with Christ (Romans 8:17);

• are members of the New Covenant (Luke 22:20; Hebrews 12:20-22);

• can partake of the Lord's Supper (Luke 22:15-20; 1 Corinthians 11:20-29);

• are baptized into Christ's death (Romans 6:3-8; Philippians 3:10,11; Colossians 2:12, 20; 2 Timothy 2:11,12);

• are baptized in the Holy Spirit (1 Corinthians 12:13);

• are members of the church (Ephesians 1:22,23; Colossians 1:18);

• are members of Christ's body (Romans 12:5; 1 Corinthians 12:13; Ephesians 4:4);

• are members in God's temple (1 Corinthians 3:16; Ephesians 2:20-22; 1 Peter 2:5);

• are members of Abraham's seed (Galatians 3:26-29; 6:15,16);

• are members of the royal priesthood (1 Peter 2:4-9; Revelation 1:6; 5:10);

• are justified by faith (Romans 3:22-28; 5:1; Titus 3:7);

• are sanctified (1 Corinthians 1:2; 6:11; Ephesians 1:4; Hebrews 12:14);

• receive glorified bodies (1 Corinthians 15:40-54; Philippians 3:21);

• enjoy life in heaven (John 14:2,3; 1 Corinthians 15:50; 1 Peter 1:4);

• will rule with Christ (1 Corinthians 6:2; 2 Timothy 2:12; Revelation 20:6);

• and will see Christ and God (Matthew 5:8; 1 John 3:2).[8]

With these and other such privileges belonging only to the Anointed Class, it is clear that the vast majority of New

Testament blessings and privileges are rendered irrelevant for a great number of Jehovah's Witnesses, since most of them are not members of the Anointed Class.

What will be the primary activity of the Anointed Class in heaven? According to Watchtower literature, these individuals will rule with Christ. Indeed, "they will be priests of God and of the Christ, and will rule as kings with him for the thousand years" (Revelation 20:6 NWT). And, obviously, if the Anointed Class is made up of "kings," then there must be others over whom the Anointed Class will rule.[9] These are the "other sheep" who have an earthly destiny.

Jehovah's Witnesses who are not members of the Anointed Class look forward not to a heavenly destiny but to living eternally on an earthly paradise. *The Watchtower* magazine says that "the heavenly hope was held out, highlighted, and stressed until about the year 1935. Then as 'light flashed up' to reveal clearly the identity of the 'great crowd' of Revelation 7:9, the emphasis began to be placed on the earthly hope."[10] Since the required number of 144,000 members for the Anointed Class became a reality in 1935, all Jehovah's Witnesses since that year have looked forward to an earthly destiny.

The book *"Your Will Be Done On Earth"* assures us that "the heavenly hope of the 144,000 faithful ones of the true Christian congregation does not leave the rest of mankind with nothing to hope for. That gleaming hope of an earthly Paradise, where God's will is to be done on earth as well as in heaven, is the blessed hope reserved for them according to God's unchanged loving purpose."[11]

In support of this, the Watchtower Society says the Bible consistently sets forth the idea that "the earth will remain 'to time indefinite, or forever' (Psalm 104:5; Ecclesiastes 1:4). So the Paradise earth was meant to serve permanently as a delightful home for perfect humans, who would live there forever."[12] These "perfect humans" are Jehovah's Witnesses who are not a part of the Anointed Class. They make up what Revelation 7:9 calls the "great multitude/crowd," or what

John 10:16 calls the "other sheep." These are followers of Jesus Christ but are not in the "New Covenant sheepfold" with a hope of heavenly life (this heavenly "sheepfold" is for the Anointed Class only).[13]

Those who make up the "other sheep" hope to survive the approaching Great Tribulation and Armageddon, and to enjoy perfect human life on earth under the rule of Christ.[14] The Watchtower Society says that "just as Noah and his family survived the global deluge and formed the nucleus of the new human society on earth, so the 'great crowd' will survive the approaching 'great tribulation' and will form the permanent nucleus of the new human society, the symbolic 'new earth.'"[15]

Watchtower literature tells us that after Armageddon, "in all parts of the globe will the 'other sheep' and their righteously trained offspring be found. They will set themselves to the carrying out of God's will, to subdue the earth as well as to have the lower animal creatures in subjection.... After Armageddon all 'those ruining the earth' will have been brought to ruin. Only those eager to upbuild the earth and to 'cultivate it and to take care of it' will remain."[16]

The book *Mankind's Search for God* tells us that "in that new world, there will be no room for exploitation of fellow humans or of animals. There will be no violence or bloodshed. There will be no homelessness, no starvation, no oppression."[17]

Salvation for the "other sheep" is a works-oriented salvation, just as it is for the so-called Anointed Class. The main "work" of each Jehovah's Witness would seem to be witnessing door to door and distributing Watchtower literature. "In this day they delight to share in the obligation resting on every Christian, that of preaching this good news of God's kingdom. Gladly they go, from house to house, on the streets, and in public-meeting places, making known to righteously disposed Catholics, Protestants, Jews, and those professing other religious beliefs, or none at all, God's way to life."[18]

The Watchtower Society tells us that those of the "other sheep" who have died will experience a "resurrection of life."

They will not be denied the full enjoyment of the many earthly blessings promised to this class.[19]

REASONING FROM THE SCRIPTURES

The "Anointed Class"

Luke 12:32—*The "Little Flock" as the "Anointed Class"*

The Watchtower Teaching. The *New World Translation* renders Luke 12:32, "Have no fear little flock because your Father has approved of giving you the kingdom." The little flock, according to the Jehovah's Witnesses, is made up of 144,000 people who have a heavenly destiny (*see* Revelation 7:4). Indeed, the Watchtower Society teaches that "the Revelation limits to 144,000 the number that become a part of the Kingdom and stand on heavenly Mount Zion. Thus it is seen that God never purposed to convert this old world and take *all* the good to heaven. There are only a few that find entrance into this kingdom—only a 'little flock' when compared with earth's population."[20]

The Watchtower Society also teaches that pre-Christian saints such as Abraham, Isaac, Jacob, and the Old Testament prophets are not a part of this little flock. Rather, they are part of the "other sheep" Jesus spoke of in John 10:16. Therefore they have an earthly hope and not a heavenly one.

The Biblical Teaching. The Watchtower interpretation of Luke 12:32 violates the context of the passage. A look at the context shows that Luke 12:22-34 (all thirteen verses!) is a *single* unit. It begins this way: "Then Jesus said *to his disciples...*" (verse 22, emphasis added). The entire unit—from verses 22 to 34—contains words spoken by Jesus *directly to His earthly disciples* in the first century. By no stretch of the imagination, then, can Luke 12:32 be made to relate to a select group of 144,000 members of an anointed class that would develop from the first century to 1935. The Jehovah's Witnesses are reading something into the text that simply is not there.

Jesus elsewhere referred to His disciples as sheep in His flock. For example, when He was giving the twelve disciples instructions for their future service, He said, "I am sending you out *like sheep* among wolves. Therefore be shrewd as snakes and as innocent as doves" (Matthew 10:16, emphasis added). Later, Jesus told the disciples that His crucifixion would cause them to scatter: "This very night you will all fall away on account of Me, for it is written, 'I will strike the shepherd, and *the sheep of the flock* will be scattered'" (Matthew 26:31, emphasis added). Just as the disciples are called "sheep" in Jesus' flock in Matthew 10:16 and 26:31, so also are they called Jesus' "little flock" in Luke 12:32.[21] Jesus called them a "little flock" because they were a small, defenseless group that could be easily preyed upon. But there was no cause to worry, for the divine Shepherd would take care of them.

More specifically, in Luke 12:22-34 Jesus is instructing the disciples not to worry about food, clothing, and other things. Worry is senseless because it doesn't really accomplish anything (verses 25,26). It will not extend anyone's life a single day, and the root of worry is a lack of faith (verse 29). The disciples were to keep in mind that God the Father knew what they needed (verse 30). Jesus therefore said that if they would simply commit to making the kingdom their consuming passion, then God would take care of all their other needs (verse 31). Disciples are not to fear but to trust in God, for God "has been pleased to give you the kingdom" (verse 32). Clearly, then, in context, there is no warrant whatsoever for relating these verses to 144,000 members of a so-called anointed class.

_____ *Ask*... _____

- According to Luke 12:22, who is Jesus speaking to in the thirteen verses that span Luke 12:22-34?

- Where specifically is there any indication in the text of Luke 12:32 that the 144,000 of Revelation chapters 7 and 14 are being spoken of?

> • Where does Scripture indicate that entrance
>   into this so-called "little flock" of anointed
>   believers would be closed in the year 1935?[22]

It is important to bring up this last question to a Jehovah's Witness, for he must come to recognize that his view is not based upon Scripture but upon an alleged "revelation" given to J.F. Rutherford. Be sure to remind the Jehovah's Witness that the Watchtower Society says they are the only group on earth that truly follows the Bible.

Speaking of the Bible, point out that the Gospels portray Jesus as incessantly speaking of the kingdom of heaven and the kingdom of God during His three-year ministry. And *never once* did He restrict the kingdom to a mere 144,000 people. He taught that *all* people should seek the kingdom, and said that whoever sought it would find it (e.g., Matthew 9:35-38; Mark 1:14,15; Luke 12:22-34).[23]

Ask...

> • Can you think of a single verse in the Bible where
>   Jesus limits the citizenship of heaven to 144,000
>   people? (If he or she points you to Revelation 7 or 14,
>   ask him or her to show you a single verse in those
>   chapters where it *explicitly* says that the kingdom is
>   limited to 144,000. The fact is, there is no such
>   verse!)

You might also point the Jehovah's Witness to Jesus' words in John 3:5: "Truly, truly, I say to you, unless one is born of water and the Spirit, he cannot enter into the kingdom of God" (NASB). Now, as noted earlier, the Watchtower Society teaches that only members of the Anointed Class are "born again" and thus can enter heaven. But that is not what Scripture teaches. Open your Bible to 1 John 5:1 and read aloud to the Jehovah's

Witness, "*Whoever believes* that Jesus is the Christ is born of God; and whoever loves the Father loves the child born of Him" (emphasis added). Emphasize the words "whoever believes" to the Jehovah's Witness. These words are all-inclusive, and are not limited to a mere 144,000 people.[24]

_____ Ask... _____

- First John 5:1 says that "*whoever* believes that Jesus is the Christ is born of God." Doesn't the "whoever" include *everyone* and not just a select 144,000 people?

- If becoming "born of God" is open to "*whoever* believes"—and if the requirement for entering the kingdom of heaven is being "born of God" or "born again" (John 3:5)—then isn't the kingdom of heaven open to "whoever believes" and not just 144,000 people?

What about the Watchtower teaching that the Old Testament saints are not part of the little flock or Anointed Class and therefore do not have a heavenly hope? The best way to answer that is to turn to Hebrews 11, where we read the names of those who are in the Faith Hall of Fame.[25] As you read through highlights of this chapter, notice that many Old Testament saints are mentioned—including Abel, Enoch, Noah, and Abraham. Now, invite the Jehovah's Witness to read aloud verses 13 through 16:

> All these died in faith, without receiving the promises, but having seen them and having welcomed them from a distance, and having confessed that they were strangers and exiles on the earth.
> For those who say such things make it clear that they are seeking a country of their own.

And indeed if they had been thinking of that country from which they went out, they would have had opportunity to return.

But as it is, they desire a better country, *that is a heavenly one.* Therefore God is not ashamed to be called their God; for He has prepared a city for them [emphasis added].

Clearly, these Old Testament saints looked forward to a *heavenly* destiny, not an earthly one. This blows a wide hole in the Watchtower theory that only 144,000 select believers of a so-called Anointed Class will live eternally in heaven.

Besides, we have clear references in Scripture that prove that certain Old Testament saints went to heaven. For example, in 2 Kings 2:1 we read, "When the LORD was about to take Elijah up to heaven in a whirlwind, Elijah and Elisha were on their way from Gilgal." Then in verse 11 we read, "As they were walking along and talking together, suddenly a chariot of fire and horses of fire appeared and separated the two of them, and *Elijah went up in a whirlwind to heaven*" (emphasis added). Elijah bypassed the experience of death and went directly to God's presence in heaven. Here is an undeniable example of an Old Testament saint with a heavenly destiny!

There are other examples as well. Matthew 8:11 specifically refers to Abraham, Isaac, and Jacob being in the Kingdom of heaven. And all the Old Testament prophets are said to be with Abraham, Isaac, and Jacob in Luke 13:28.

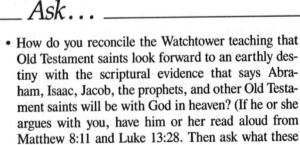

_____ *Ask...* _____

- How do you reconcile the Watchtower teaching that Old Testament saints look forward to an earthly destiny with the scriptural evidence that says Abraham, Isaac, Jacob, the prophets, and other Old Testament saints will be with God in heaven? (If he or she argues with you, have him or her read aloud from Matthew 8:11 and Luke 13:28. Then ask what these verses mean.)

Revelation 7:4 and 14:1-3—*144,000 in the "Anointed Class"?*

The Watchtower Teaching. The *New World Translation* renders Revelation 7:4, "And I heard the number of those who were sealed, *a hundred and forty-four thousand*, sealed out of every tribe of the sons of Israel" (emphasis added). This verse, the Jehovah's Witnesses say, refers to the Anointed Class of believers who have a heavenly destiny (cf. Revelation 14:1-3).

According to Watchtower literature, these 144,000 are the ones referred to as the "little flock" in Luke 12:32. This "little flock" of 144,000 makes up the body of Christ and will reign with Him. The Watchtower Society says they will participate in the "first resurrection"—receiving spirit bodies just as Jesus did.[26] They must have spirit bodies because "flesh and blood cannot inherit God's kingdom" (1 Corinthians 15:50 NWT).

Though the Book of Revelation says the 144,000 represent the twelve tribes of Israel with 12,000 people from each tribe, the Watchtower Society says this is actually a metaphorical reference to the Anointed Class of Jehovah's Witnesses. Indeed, "the heavenly congregation is likened to twelve tribes of 12,000 members each, under the Greater Moses, Christ Jesus."[27]

How do we know that literal tribes of Israel are not meant in Revelation 7:4-8? The Watchtower Society says these cannot be the tribes of natural Israel because there never was a tribe of Joseph in the Old Testament, even though it is mentioned in Revelation 7:4-8. Also, the tribes of Ephraim and Dan—which are listed in the Old Testament—are not included in Revelation 7. And the Levites—who are mentioned as being a tribe in Revelation 7—were set aside for service in connection with the temple in the Old Testament but were not reckoned as one of the 12 tribes.[28] Clearly, then, the 144,000 in Revelation 7 are not *literally* the twelve tribes of Israel. This passage refers not to natural Israelites but to the Anointed Class of 144,000 consecrated Jehovah's Witnesses.

The Biblical Teaching. There are a number of important points you can make in disproving the Watchtower's interpretation of Revelation 7:4 and 14:1-3. First, point out that the Watchtower Society switches interpretive methodology right in the middle of Revelation 7:4. Notice that they interpret the first half of the verse using a *literal* method of interpretation: "Then I heard the number of those who were sealed: *144,000...*" (emphasis added). They conclude from this that the so-called Anointed Class will have *precisely* 144,000 people.

But then, the second half of the verse *is not* interpreted literally: "...from all the tribes of Israel." In other words, the Watchtower Society says there are literally 144,000 people, but this refers not to the literal tribes of Israel but to the Anointed Class of Jehovah's Witnesses. Within the confines of a single verse, then, they use both a literal *and* a figurative means of interpreting Scripture.

After pointing this out to the Jehovah's Witness:

_____ *Ask...* _____

- What justification is there for switching methods of interpretation—from *literal* to *figurative*—right in the middle of Revelation 7:4?

Second, you will want to show that women are clearly excluded from the 144,000 in the Book of Revelation.[29] In referring to this group, Revelation 14:4 says, "These are those who did *not defile themselves with women*, for they kept themselves pure" (emphasis added). This means either that the 144,000 men are unmarried, or celibate (cf. 2 Corinthians 11:2). Either way, the fact that they "did not defile themselves with women" and that masculine pronouns are used of this group shows that they are men. For the Watchtower Society to say that women are a part of this group is to ignore the clear teaching of Scripture.

_____ *Ask*... _____

- Are there women in the "Anointed Class" of 144,000 believers? (They will say yes.)

- How do you reconcile that with Revelation 14:4, which clearly indicates that the 144,000 are *all men* who have not been defiled with women?

_____

Third, and most important, it is the clear testimony of Scripture that a heavenly destiny awaits *all* who believe in Jesus Christ, not just a select group of 144,000 anointed believers (Ephesians 2:19; Philippians 3:20; Colossians 3:1; Hebrews 3:1; 12:22; 2 Peter 1:10,11). Drawing a dichotomy between those with a heavenly destiny and those with an earthly one has absolutely no warrant in Scripture. *All* who believe in Christ are heirs of the eternal kingdom (Galatians 3:29; 4:28-31; Titus 3:7; James 2:5). The righteousness of God that leads to life in heaven is available "through faith in Jesus Christ *for all those who believe; for there is no distinction*" (Romans 3:21 NASB, emphasis added). Jesus promised, "If *any one* serves Me, let him follow Me; and *where I am, there shall My servant also be* [i.e., heaven]" (John 12:26 NASB, emphasis added). Jesus clearly affirmed that all believers will be together in "one flock" under "one shepherd" (John 10:16). There will not be two "folds"—one on earth and one in heaven. Scripture is clear: *one fold, one Shepherd!*

_____ *Ask*... _____

- How do you reconcile the Watchtower teaching that there will be an "Anointed Class" in heaven and the "other sheep" on earth when John 10:16 clearly says that *all* believers will be together in "one flock" under "one shepherd"?

_____

Literal Tribes of Israel? We must now address the Watchtower contention that the tribes mentioned in Revelation 7 cannot be literal tribes of Israel. One key observation is that the very fact that specific tribes are mentioned along with specific numbers for those tribes removes all possibility that this is a figure of speech. Nowhere else in the Bible does a reference to twelve tribes of Israel mean anything but twelve tribes of Israel. Apologist Norman Geisler rightly says that "the word 'tribes' is never used of anything but a literal ethnic group in Scripture."[30] Besides, as the *Expositor's Bible Commentary* points out, the word "Israel" is normally used in the New Testament as referring to the physical descendants of Jacob.[31] The Watchtower view is thus against the normal New Testament usage of "Israel."

_____ *Ask...* _____

- Did you know that the word "tribes" is never used in Scripture of anything but a literal ethnic group?

- Did you know that the word "Israel" is almost always used in Scripture in reference to the physical descendants of Jacob?

- Can you see that the Watchtower interpretation of Revelation 7:4 goes against common usage of those words?

Next we must address the question, Why are the Old Testament tribes of Dan and Ephraim omitted in Revelation 7? It's important to know that the Old Testament "has no fewer than twenty variant lists of the tribes, and these lists include anywhere from ten to thirteen tribes, though the number twelve is predominant (cf. Gen. 49; Deut. 33; Ezek. 48)."[32] Thus, no list of the twelve tribes must be identical. However, since twelve seems to be the ideal number when listing Israel's tribes, it seems clear that John wanted to maintain this ideal figure in Revelation 7 and 14.

Most scholars today agree that Dan's tribe was omitted because they were guilty of idolatry on many occasions and, as a result, were largely obliterated (Leviticus 24:11; Judges 18:1,30; cf. 1 Kings 12:28,29). To engage in unrepentant idolatry is to be cut off from God's blessing. There was also an early tradition that the Antichrist would come from the tribe of Dan. Bible scholar Robert H. Mounce comments on all this:

> Apparently Dan was omitted because of an early connection with idolatry. When the tribe of Dan migrated to the north and settled at Laish, they set up for themselves the graven image (Judg. 18:30). Later Dan became one of the two great shrines in the northern kingdom (1 Kings 12:29). In the *Testament of Dan* (5:6) Satan is said to be the prince of the tribe. Irenaeus, writing in the latter part of the second century, noted that the omission of Dan was due to a tradition that the Antichrist was to come from that tribe (*Adv. Haer.* v.30.2.).[33]

What about the tribe of Ephraim? Why was it omitted in Revelation 7? Well, keep in mind that Ephraim and Manasseh were both sons of Joseph. In the Old Testament, the tribe of Joseph is "always mentioned in the other lists by either including Joseph and excluding his two sons, Ephraim and Manasseh (Gen. 49), or by omitting Joseph and counting the two sons as one tribe each (Ezek. 48)."[34] In Revelation 7, however, the tribes of Joseph and Manasseh are listed and Ephraim is omitted. The question is, then, *Why?*

An examination of Scripture indicates that the tribe of Ephraim—like the tribe of Dan—was involved in idolatry and paganized worship (Judges 17; Hosea 4:17). Apparently, Ephraim was omitted from the list in Revelation 7 for the same reason Dan was. And, as the *Expositor's Bible Commentary* points out, if idolatry is the reason for omitting both Dan and Ephraim, "the readjustment of the list to include Joseph and Manasseh to complete the twelve can be understood."[35]

Ask...

- What is the Watchtower Society's position on idolatry? (The Society condemns all forms of idolatry.)

- If the tribes of Dan and Ephraim were guilty of idolatry, as Scripture clearly indicates, do you think these tribes should still be listed in Revelation 7 as God's servants? (They'll say no.)

- So you agree there is good reason for omitting these tribes in Revelation 7?

- In view of what we've learned about why the tribes of Dan and Ephraim are not listed in Revelation 7, isn't it obvious that the Watchtower Society's non-literal interpretation of the tribes is _illegitimate_, since it is based upon the _legitimate_ omission of Dan and Ephraim?

One final question remains: Why was the tribe of Levi included in the listing of tribes in Revelation 7? Remember that in the Old Testament they were not a part of the twelve tribes because of their special status as a priestly tribe under the Mosaic Law. It is probable that they are included here because the priestly functions of their tribe _ceased_ with the coming of Christ—the ultimate High Priest.[36] Indeed, the Levitical priesthood was fulfilled in the Person of Christ (Hebrews 7–10).[37] Because there was no further need for their services as priests, there was no reason for keeping them distinct and separate from the others; hence, they were properly included in the tribal listing in the Book of Revelation.

The Watchtower Society's objections to interpreting the tribes of Revelation 7 and 14 as literal tribes of Israel are thus seen to be completely unwarranted. Their view that the 144,000 refers to an Anointed Class represents a gross and heinous distortion of Scripture.

The "Other Sheep"

John 10:16—*The "Other Sheep"*

The Watchtower Teaching. The *New World Translation* renders John 10:16, "And I have *other sheep*, which are not of this fold; those also I must bring, and they will listen to my voice, and they will become one flock, one shepherd" (emphasis added). The Jehovah's Witnesses teach that though there are only 144,000 spirit-anointed believers who go to heaven, God has "other sheep"—that is, other true believers— who will receive eternal life and live on an earthly paradise. As noted earlier, the opportunity to become part of the 144,000 ended in 1935.

According to *"Let God Be True,"* these other sheep "remember their Creator, hold fast their faith, and break clean away from the satanic elements that now reign. Zealously they preach of Armageddon's approach and of the Kingdom blessings to follow. Continuing faithful till Armageddon, the other sheep who seek righteousness and meekness will, like the flood survivors of Noah's day, be hid in the antitypical ark, Jehovah's theocratic system of things, and come through into an earth cleansed of evil."[38]

These "other sheep" will have the privilege of subduing, beautifying, and populating the paradise earth. Though they do not go to heaven, their existence is a blissful one on a perfect and restored earth.[39] Because these "sheep" are busy proclaiming the kingdom to people all over the world—bringing even more sheep into the "fold"—they are a continually growing group, as opposed to the set number of those in the Anointed Class (144,000).

The Biblical Teaching. It is very clear from the context that the phrase "other sheep" in John 10:16 is referring to *Gentile* believers as opposed to *Jewish*. As a backdrop, it is critical to recognize that in the Gospels the Jews were called "the lost sheep of Israel" (Matthew 10:6; 15:24), and those Jews who followed Christ were called His "sheep" (John 10).

Jesus often referred to His Jewish disciples as sheep in His flock. For example, when He was giving the twelve instructions for their future service, He said, "I am sending you out like *sheep* among wolves. Therefore be as shrewd as snakes, and as innocent as doves" (Matthew 10:16, emphasis added). Later, Jesus told them that His crucifixion would cause them to scatter: "You will all fall away on account of me, for it is written: 'I will strike the shepherd, and *the sheep of the flock will be scattered*'" (Matthew 26:31, emphasis added).

Now, when Jesus said, "I have *other sheep*, which are not of this fold" (John 10:16 NASB, emphasis added), He was clearly referring to non-Jewish, Gentile believers. These Gentiles, along with the Jewish believers, "shall become *one flock* with *one shepherd*" (John 10:16 NASB, emphasis added). This is in perfect accord with Ephesians 2:11-22, where we are told that in Christ, Jews and Gentiles are reconciled in *one body*. Galatians 3:28 tells us that "there is neither Jew nor Greek [Gentile], slave nor free, male nor female; for *you are all one* in Christ Jesus" (emphasis added). Likewise, Colossians 3:11 speaks of "a renewal in which there is no distinction between Greek [Gentiles] and Jew, circumcised and uncircumcised, barbarian, Scythian, slave and freeman, but Christ is all, and in all."

You must emphasize to the Jehovah's Witness what the latter part of John 10:16 says: "They shall become *one flock* with *one shepherd*." There will not be one flock of God's people in heaven and another flock on earth. There will be no distinction between an Anointed Class and the "other sheep." Rather, all will dwell together as "one flock" under "one shepherd."

_____ *Ask...* _____

- How do you reconcile the Watchtower teaching that there will be an "Anointed Class" in heaven that remains forever distinct from the "other sheep" on earth when Scripture clearly says that *all God's people* are "one" in Christ and are a part of "one flock" under "one shepherd"?

Revelation 7:9 — *The "Great Multitude" as the "Other Sheep"*

The Watchtower Teaching. Revelation 7:9 in the *New World Translation* reads, "After these things I saw, and, look! A *great crowd, which no man was able to number*, out of all nations and tribes and peoples and tongues, standing before the throne and before the Lamb, dressed in white robes; and there were palm branches in their hands" (emphasis added).

The Watchtower Society argues that this verse refers to the "other sheep" mentioned in John 10:16. And, as noted earlier, those who are part of this group *cannot* become members of the body of Christ, be born again, share in Christ's heavenly kingdom, receive the baptism of the Holy Spirit, participate in communion, or be included in the New Covenant mediated by Christ. Clearly, the "other sheep" are an underprivileged group.

In the Watchtower publication *Mankind's Search for God*, we read the following summary of the Book of Revelation's "great crowd":

> In 1935 the Witnesses came to a clearer understanding regarding the heavenly Kingdom class, who will reign with Christ, and their subjects on the earth. They already knew that the number of anointed Christians called to rule with Christ from the heavens would be only 144,000. So, what would be the hope for the rest of mankind? A government needs subjects to justify its existence. This heavenly government, the Kingdom, would also have millions of obedient subjects here on earth. These would be the "great crowd, which no man was able to number, out of all nations and tribes and peoples and tongues." . . .

> This understanding about the great crowd helped Jehovah's Witnesses to see that they had before them a tremendous challenge—to find and teach all those millions who were searching for the true God and who would form the "great crowd."[40]

The Watchtower Society anticipates a possible theological objection to their interpretation of the Book of Revelation by addressing a particular phrase in Revelation 7:9, where the 144,000 are described as "standing before the throne and in front of the Lamb." Doesn't this mean that this group is in heaven and not on earth?

No, the Watchtower Society says. This phrase indicates not necessarily a location but "an approved condition." The expression "before the throne" is said to be literally "in sight of the throne." Such a phrase does not require that the group be in heaven. The position of the crowd is simply "in sight of the throne." This is in keeping with how God sometimes says that from heaven He beholds the sons of men (Psalm 11:4).[41]

The Biblical Teaching. Should you talk to a Jehovah's Witness about Revelation 7:9, Watchtower expert Marian Bodine suggests you begin by asking these key questions:

_____ *Ask...* _____

- Where in the text does it say the great multitude is exempt from heaven?

- Where does it say the great multitude is relegated to live on earth?[42]

The fact is, *nowhere* in the text of Revelation does it say this great multitude is exempt from heaven. This is something the Watchtower Society reads into the Scripture. Request the Jehovah's Witness to read the passage aloud and keep asking the above questions until he or she answers.

Now, Revelation 7:9 clearly refers to this great multitude as "standing before the throne and in front of the Lamb." Though Jehovah's Witnesses try to argue that "before the throne" simply means "in sight of the throne," this is not at all what is being communicated in this verse. The picture is of a great multitude that is *physically present* before God's throne in heaven, just as the angels are before His throne (verse 11).

The Greek word for "before" (*enopion*) in Revelation 7:9 is used a number of times in that book to speak of those who are in the physical presence of God's throne. For example, the word is used in Revelation 5:8, where we are told that "the four living creatures and the twenty-four elders fell down *before* the Lamb. Each one had a harp and they were holding golden bowls full of incense, which are the prayers of the saints." The Greek word is used again in Revelation 7:11, where we read, "All the angels were standing around the throne and around the elders and the four living creatures. They fell down on their faces *before* the throne and worshiped God." The word is also used in Revelation 14:3, where we read this of the 144,000: "And they sang a new song *before* the throne and *before* the four living creatures and the elders."

Now, *enopion* is used in the *exact same sense* in Revelation 7:9, which says that the great multitude is "*before* the throne" of God. According to the authoritative *Greek-English Lexicon of the New Testament and Other Early Christian Literature*, this Greek word is used in Revelation 7:9 not in the sense of "in sight of" but in the sense "*of place*, before someone or something."[43] In other words, it refers to being in the physical presence of God's throne.

_____ *Ask . . .* _____

- Since the Greek word for "before" is used in Revelation of the 144,000 being before God's throne (14:3), the angels before God's throne (7:11), and the twenty-four elders before God's throne (5:8), doesn't it make sense to use the word in the same way of the great multitude before God's throne (7:9)?

Notice what is said about this great multitude in Revelation 7:15: "They are before the throne of God, and they serve Him day and night *in his temple*" (emphasis added). And where is God's "temple" located? Point out to the Jehovah's Witness that Revelation 11:19 refers to "the temple of God *which is in heaven*" (NASB, emphasis added). Revelation 14:17 likewise says, "And another angel came out of the temple *which is in heaven*" (NASB, emphasis added).

If the great multitude serves God day and night in His temple (Revelation 7:15), and if the temple is in heaven (Revelation 11:19; 14:17), then clearly the great multitude is in heaven and not on earth, as the Watchtower Society tries to argue.[44] The great multitude is "before the throne," "in front of the Lamb," and they serve God day and night "in his temple" which is "in heaven." What could be clearer? To say that the great multitude is on earth is to completely ignore the context of Revelation chapters 7 and 14.

_____ *Ask*... _____

- Since the "great multitude" serves God day and night *in* His temple (Revelation 7:15), and since God's temple is *in heaven* (Revelation 11:19; 14:17), then doesn't this mean that the great multitude is in heaven?

There is one other argument that may be effective in your conversation with the Jehovah's Witness. A good cross-reference for Revelation 7:9 is Revelation 19:1,2: "After these things I heard, as it were, a loud voice of *a great multitude in heaven*, saying, "Hallelujah! Salvation and glory and power belong to our God" (NASB). Note that the great multitude is said to be "in heaven" in this passage.[45]

After asking the Jehovah's Witness to read aloud from Revelation 19:1,2:

_____ *Ask...* _____

- According to Revelation 19:1, is the great multitude in heaven or on earth?

Matthew 6:10—*A Paradise on Earth?*

The Watchtower Teaching. The *New World Translation* renders Matthew 6:10, "Let your kingdom come. Let your will take place, as in heaven, also upon earth." This verse is often cited by the Watchtower Society in support of their view that the "other sheep" or "great multitude" will spend eternity in an earthly paradise, not in heaven.

The book *Reasoning from the Scriptures* asks, "What is God's will regarding the earth?"[46] In answer to this question, two Bible verses are cited:

- "God blessed them and God said to them: 'Be fruitful and become many and fill the earth and subdue it, and have in subjection the fish of the sea and the flying creatures of the heavens and every living creature that is moving upon the earth" (Genesis 1:28 NWT).
- "For this is what Jehovah has said, the Creator of the heavens, He the [true] God, the Former of the earth and the Maker of it, He the One who firmly established it, who did not create it simply for nothing, who formed it even to be inhabited: 'I am Jehovah, and there is no one else'" (Isaiah 45:18 NWT).

Since it is God's will that the earth be inhabited and subjugated by man—and because Matthew 6:10 asks that God's will be done on earth—then, clearly (it is argued), this is a prayer for the establishment of an earthly paradise in which man will dwell forever.

The Biblical Teaching. When Jesus taught the disciples to pray, "Your will be done on earth as it is in heaven," was He really teaching them to pray for an earthly paradise in which man will dwell forever? Not at all! This is an example of what is known as *eisegesis* (reading a meaning *into* the text) as opposed to *exegesis* (deriving the meaning *out of* the text). A person who reads this verse without consulting biased Watchtower literature would never in a million years come up with such an interpretation and relate it to Genesis 1:28 and Isaiah 48:15! Matthew 6:10 simply does not refer to an earthly paradise.

_____ *Ask...* _____

- What contextual evidence can you provide me that proves that Matthew 6:10 was intended to be connected with Genesis 1:28 and Isaiah 48:15?

A plain reading of Matthew 6:10 (in context) indicates that Jesus was teaching the disciples to pray that just as God's will is *already* being perfectly done in heaven, so should God's will be done on earth—the sphere on which fallen, sinful humanity dwells. As Alva J. McClain notes, "Although the Kingdom of God [in a spiritual sense] was already ruling over all, there was nevertheless a difference between the exercise of its rule 'in heaven' and 'on earth.' This difference arises out of the fact that rebellion and sin exist upon the earth."[47] This part of the Lord's Prayer thus addresses a very relevant need for Christians who live on earth. That need is for God to deal with all those who resist and rebel against His will and bring about a multitude of negative consequences.

_____ *Ask...* _____

> • Doesn't it make sense that because earth is the
> dwelling place of fallen and sinful man, a legitimate
> prayer request would be for God's will to be done on
> earth just as it is already done in heaven?

Eventually, this prayer—which has been uttered untold millions of times by Christians all over the world since the first century—will be completely and perfectly fulfilled. This will take place when God at last puts down all human rebellion with its evil results, thus finally bringing in the fullness of God's Kingdom in which the will of God shall be done just as much *on earth* as it is *in heaven*.[48] In that future time, God's will shall be universally obeyed by all.

That Christ the Lord will ultimately fulfill this prayer is clear from what He says elsewhere in Scripture. He affirmed in Matthew 28:18, "All authority *in heaven* and *on earth* has been given to me" (emphasis added). Christ is sovereign over *both* realms. And when He comes again in glory as the King of kings and Lord of lords (Revelation 19), He will squash all resistance to His sovereign will.

Psalm 37:9,11,29—*A Paradise on Earth?*

The Watchtower Teaching. The *New World Translation* renders Psalm 37:9,11,29: "For evildoers themselves will be cut off, but those hoping in Jehovah are the ones that *will possess the earth*. . . . But the meek ones themselves *will possess the earth*, and they will indeed find their exquisite delight in the abundance of peace. . . . The righteous themselves *will possess the earth*, and they will reside forever upon it" (emphasis added).

According to *Reasoning from the Scriptures*, these verses prove that not all good people go to heaven.[49] Some will live forever on earth. These verses also show that a person does not have to go to heaven in order to have a truly happy life. Many will live happily forever on a paradise earth.[50]

The Biblical Teaching. A look at the context of Psalm 37 makes it clear that the Psalm is not referring to a distant future time when God will remove all wicked people and allow the good to live on a paradise earth. Rather, the psalmist was speaking of something that people *in his own lifetime* (and the following generations) would experience. Evil people *in his time* would be cut off; righteous people *in his time* would experience blessing in the promised land.[51]

It is critical to recognize that the Hebrew word for "earth" in this context has reference to *land*—more specifically, "the land of Judea, given by God himself as an inheritance to their fathers and their posterity forever."[52] Though the Hebrew word (*'eres*) is often translated "earth" in the Old Testament, it also often carries the meaning of "land." *Vine's Expository Dictionary of Biblical Words* explains,

> *'Eres* does not only denote the entire terrestrial planet, but is also used of some of the earth's component parts. English words like *land*, *country*, *ground*, and *soil* transfer its meaning into our language. Quite frequently, it refers to an area occupied by a nation or tribe. . . . Israel is said to live "in the *land* of the Lord" (Lev. 25:33f.; Hos. 9:13). When the people arrived at its border, Moses reminded them that it would be theirs only because the Lord drove out the other nations to "give you their *land* for an inheritance" (Deut. 4:38). Moses promised that God would make its soil productive, for "He will give rain for your *land*" so that it would be "a fruitful *land*," "a *land* flowing with milk and honey, and *land* of wheat and barley" (Deut. 11:13-15; 8:7-9; Jer. 2:7).[53]

Clearly, the Hebrew word *'eres* is used in the present context of the *promised land* and not to a future paradise earth. Indeed, the central issue addressed in this psalm is as follows:

> Who will "inherit the land" (vv. 9,11,22,29), i.e., live on to enjoy the blessings of the Lord in the promised

land? Will the wicked, who plot (v. 12), scheme (vv. 7,32), default on debts (v. 21), use raw power to gain advantage (v. 14) and seem thereby to flourish (vv. 7,16,35)? Or will the righteous, who trust in the Lord (vv. 3,5,7,34) and are humble (v. 11), blameless (vv. 18,37), generous (vv. 21,26), upright (v. 37) and peaceable (v. 37), and from whose mouth is heard the moral wisdom that reflects meditation on God's law (vv. 30-31)?[54]

The obvious answer given in the psalm is that the righteous will inherit the promised land and experience God's blessing there.

_____ *Ask...* _____

- Did you know that the Hebrew word for "earth" in Psalm 37 often means "land" in the Old Testament, and is the actual word used in the Old Testament in reference to the promised land God gave Israel?

- Can you see how the contrast between the righteous and the wicked makes a great deal of sense when interpreted in terms of "inheriting" or being "cut off" from the promised land?

If this interpretation is correct, then what does verse 29 mean when it says that "the righteous will inherit the land and dwell in it *forever*" (emphasis added)? Contrary to what the Watchtower Society teaches, it does not mean that there will be an earthly class of people who will forever live in an earthly paradise, separate from the Anointed Class that lives in heaven.

According to the most highly respected authorities on the Hebrew language, the Hebrew word for "forever" (*'ad*) often denotes the unforeseeable future in the Old Testament.[55] Hence, the phrase "dwell in it forever" simply means "dwell in it from the present through the unforeseeable future." The

phrase is a Hebraistic way of saying that the *then-living* Israelites would dwell in the promised land their entire lives *as
would their children and their children's children*, and so forth.
From one generation to the next, the righteous would experience blessing in the promised land into the unforeseeable
future. This is in noted contrast to the wicked; for, as the
previous verse points out, "the offspring of the wicked will be
cut off" (verse 28b).

Psalm 115:16—*A Paradise on Earth?*

The Watchtower Teaching. Psalm 115:16 in the *New World
Translation* reads, "As regards the heavens, to Jehovah the
heavens belong, but the earth he has given to the sons of men."
Again, the destiny of the average Jehovah's Witness—the
"other sheep," not part of the Anointed Class—is said to be an
earthly paradise.

After citing this psalm, *"Let Your Name Be Sanctified"*
comments, "So the purpose set before Adam and Eve was
exclusively earthly, to live to see the whole earth filled with
their big family, with billions of descendants, and then to keep
on living with them forever in perfect happiness in a paradise
that covered all the earth. Jehovah God told them that this was
his purpose for them."[56]

The Biblical Teaching. It is true that God has given the
earth to man. But what is the context of the statement in Psalm
115:16? Is this verse written in regard to only a portion of
humankind—an earthly class of believers as distinct from an
Anointed Class? Clearly this is not the case; Psalm 115:16 is
saying that God has given the earth to the whole race of man—
with no distinctions or exclusions mentioned.

_____ *Ask...* _____

- Where in Psalm 115:16 is there any proof that this
  verse applies only to a portion of humankind as
  opposed to the entire human race?

If Psalm 115:16 applies to *all* human beings, as the context clearly indicates, then in what sense has God given the earth to them? It seems rather clear that He has given *mortal* human beings the earth as a dwelling place and a place over which to rule. Genesis 1:28 tell us, "God blessed them and said to them, 'Be fruitful and increase in number; fill the earth, and subdue it. Rule over the fish of the sea and the birds of the air, and over every living creature that moves on the ground.'"

We see this same basic thought reflected in Psalm 8:6-8: "Thou dost make him [man] to rule over the works of Thy hands; Thou hast put all things [on earth] under his feet, all sheep and oxen, and also the beasts of the field, the birds of the heavens, and the fish of the sea, whatever passes through the paths of the seas."[57] In view of such passages, it seems obvious that Psalm 115:16 is dealing with mortal man and mortal life on earth (prior to death).

After making the above points to the Jehovah's Witness, point him or her to New Testament passages that indicate that all true believers look forward to a heavenly destiny. It is the clear testimony of Scripture that heaven awaits *all* who believe in Jesus Christ, not just a select group of 144,000 anointed believers (Ephesians 2:19; Philippians 3:20; Colossians 3:1; Hebrews 3:1; 12:22; 2 Peter 1:10,11). Jesus promised, "If *any one* serves Me, let him follow Me; and *where I am, there shall My servant also be* [i.e., heaven]" (John 12:26 NASB, emphasis added). *All* who believe in Christ are heirs of the eternal kingdom (Galatians 3:29; 4:28-31; Titus 3:7; James 2:5).

You might request the Jehovah's Witness to read John 12:26 aloud and then:

___ *Ask...* ___

- In view of John 12:26—"If *any one* serves Me, let him follow Me; and *where I am, there shall My servant also be* [i.e., heaven]" (NASB, emphasis added)—isn't it clear to you that *any* who follow Christ can look forward to a heavenly destiny?

11

Salvation the Watchtower Way

> *The difference between faith and works is just this: In the case of faith, God does it; in the case of works, we try to do it ourselves; and the difference is measured simply by the distance between the infinite and the finite, the Almighty God and a helpless worm.*

> —Albert Benjamin
> Simpson
> (1843-1919)[1]

The Jehovah's Witnesses often give "lip service" to the idea of salvation by grace through faith in Christ.[2] In reality, however, they believe in a works-oriented salvation. Salvation for a Jehovah's Witness is impossible apart from total obedience to the Watchtower Society and vigorous participation in the various programs prescribed by the Society. By such obedience and participation, Jehovah's Witnesses take part in "working out" their salvation (Philippians 2:12 NWT).

Regarding the centrality of the Watchtower Society, *The Watchtower* magazine urges readers to "come to Jehovah's organization [the Watchtower Society] for salvation."[3] Indeed, we read that "unless we are in touch with this channel of communication [the Watchtower Society] that God is using, we will not progress along the road to life, no matter how much Bible reading we do."[4] We are told that "to receive everlasting life in the earthly Paradise we must identify that organization [the Watchtower Society] and serve God as part of it."[5]

The importance of doing works for salvation becomes evident in perusing Watchtower literature. For example, *The Watchtower* magazine says that "to get one's name written in that Book of Life will depend upon one's works."[6] Another issue of this magazine makes reference to "working hard for the reward of eternal life."[7] This "works" concept of salvation has implications for how parents raise their kids: "Parents who love their children and who want to see them alive in God's new world will encourage and guide them toward goals of increased service and responsibility."[8]

How do Jehovah's Witnesses understand *grace*? In reading Watchtower literature, it becomes evident that grace is more or less the *opportunity* for human beings to "work out" or earn their salvation. It does not involve a free gift of salvation. The Society teaches that obeying "God's commandments . . . can mean an eternal future."[9] Indeed, "in all areas of life, we should be prepared to give our very best. We should not be half-hearted about such vital matters. What is at stake is Jehovah's approval and our being granted life."[10]

Part of "working out" one's salvation depends upon one's faithfulness in distributing the literature of the Watchtower Society door to door. *The Watchtower* magazine says, "God requires that prospective subjects of his Kingdom support his government by *loyally advocating his Kingdom rule to others*."[11] The magazine asks: "Will you meet this requirement by telling others about God's Kingdom?"[12]

With this concept of salvation, it is not surprising that the Watchtower Society also teaches that Jehovah's Witnesses cannot know for sure if they have salvation during this life.[13] Indeed, only a constant, unbending stance against sin and total obedience to God (through obedience to the Watchtower Society) gives the Witness any hope of salvation. Even then, the Witness is told that if he or she should fail during the future millennium, he or she will be annihilated. However, if he or she faithfully serves God throughout this 1000-year period, eternal life may finally be granted.[14]

If salvation is by works, then how does it relate to the person and work of Jesus Christ in Watchtower theology? Well, the Society teaches that Jesus *did* die (not on a cross but on a torture stake) as a sacrifice for sin. But they do not interpret Christ's sacrificial death the same way evangelical Christians do. In a capsule, the Society teaches that the human life Jesus laid down in sacrifice was *exactly equal* to the human life Adam fell with. "Since one man's sin (that of Adam) had been responsible for causing the entire human family to be sinners, the shed blood of another perfect human (in effect, a second Adam), being of corresponding value, could balance the scales of justice."[15] If Jesus had been God, the Watchtower Society says, then the ransom payment would have been *way too much.*

Now, Jehovah's Witnesses *do* speak of the need for grace and faith in Christ to be saved. And they speak of salvation as a "free gift." But, obviously, grace and faith are not enough, according to Watchtower literature. Nor is salvation really a free gift in Watchtower theology. Former Jehovah's Witness Duane Magnani explains:

> What the Watchtower means by "free gift" is that Christ's death only wiped away the sin inherited from Adam. They teach that without this work of atonement, men could not *work their way toward* salvation. But the "gift" of Christ's ransom sacrifice is freely made available to all who desire it. In other words, without Christ's sacrifice, the individual wouldn't have a chance to get saved. But in view of His work, the free gift which removed the sin inherited from Adam, the individual now has a *chance.*[16]

Jehovah's Witnesses also speak of being "born again" (John 3:3-5). But they do not mean what evangelical Christians mean by this phrase. They say that the new birth is for the Anointed Class only. This new birth is necessary for them so they can enjoy spirit life in heaven. *The Watchtower* magazine says that "the 'other sheep' do not need any such rebirth, for their goal is life everlasting in the restored earthly Paradise as subjects of the Kingdom."[17]

It is clear from the above that the Jehovah's Witnesses use many of the same words evangelical Christians do when describing salvation, but they attach entirely different meanings to those words. This is a common mark of the cults.

Let's examine the Bible passages the Watchtower Society uses to support its distorted view of salvation.

_____REASONING FROM THE SCRIPTURES_____

1 Timothy 2:5,6—*The Ransom Sacrifice of Jesus*

The Watchtower Teaching. The *New World Translation* renders 1 Timothy 2:5,6, "For there is one God, and one mediator between God and men, a man, Christ Jesus, who gave himself a corresponding ransom for all."

The Watchtower Society argues that because Jesus is said to mediate "between God and men," it is clear that He cannot be viewed as God. After all, "since by definition a mediator is someone separate from those who need mediation, it would be a contradiction for Jesus to be one entity with either of the parties he is trying to reconcile. That would be a pretending to be something he is not."[18] Their conclusion, then, is that Christ as a mediator cannot be viewed as God. How could Jesus mediate between God and man if He Himself was God?

Regarding the "corresponding ransom" Jesus paid, the Watchtower Society teaches that the human life Jesus laid down in sacrifice was exactly equal to the human life Adam fell with. Indeed, "as the human life privileges had been forfeited for the human race by its perfect father Adam, through sin, those life privileges had to be repurchased by the sacrifice of a perfect human life like Jesus."[19] Clearly, then, Christ's ransom corresponded *exactly* to Adam:

> Jesus, no more and no less than a perfect human, became a ransom that compensated exactly for what Adam lost—the right to perfect human life on earth. So Jesus could rightly be called "the last Adam" by the apostle Paul, who said in the same context: "Just as in Adam all are dying, so also in the Christ all will be made alive" (1 Corinthians 15:22,45). The perfect human life of Jesus was the "corresponding ransom" required by divine justice—no more, no less. A basic principle even of human justice is that the price paid should fit the wrong committed.[20]

Watchtower literature argues that if Jesus were a part of a triune Godhead, "the ransom price would have been infinitely higher than what God's own Law required."[21] After all, it was Adam—a *perfect human being*—who sinned in the Garden of Eden, not God. Hence, the ransom that was paid, to be truly in line with God's perfect justice, had to be an exact equivalent to Adam—a perfect human being: "When God sent Jesus to earth as the ransom, he made Jesus to be what would satisfy justice, not an incarnation, not a god-man, but a perfect man."[22] This sacrifice of the second Adam, being of corresponding value, could "balance the scales of justice."[23]

The Biblical Teaching. Is it true that because Jesus is a mediator between God and man, He cannot be God, since "by definition a mediator is someone separate from those who need mediation"?[24] By no means! The folly of this reasoning is at once evident in the fact that if Jesus as mediator cannot be God, then, by the same logic, He cannot be man either.[25]

Ask...

- Since by definition "a mediator is someone *separate* from those who need mediation," and the Watchtower Society says Christ as a mediator cannot be God, then doesn't this also mean that He cannot be man?

- If Christ *as a man* can be a mediator between God and man, then can't Christ *as God* also be a mediator between God and man?

The fact is, Jesus can mediate between God and man precisely because He is both God and man.[26] Indeed, humankind's redemption was completely dependent upon the human-divine union in Christ. If Christ the Redeemer had been *only* God, He could not have died, since God by His very nature cannot die. It was only as a man that Christ could represent humanity and die as a man. As God, however, Christ's death had infinite value sufficient to provide redemption for the sins of all people. Clearly, then, Christ had to be both God *and* man to secure man's salvation (1 Timothy 2:5).

This is related to the Old Testament concept of the kinsman-redeemer. In Old Testament times, the phrase *kinsman-redeemer* was always used of one who was related by blood to someone he was seeking to redeem from bondage. If someone was sold into slavery, for example, it was the duty of a blood relative—the next of kin—to act as that person's kinsman-redeemer and buy him out of slavery (Leviticus 25:47,48).

Jesus is the Kinsman-Redeemer for sin-enslaved humanity. For Jesus to become such, however, He had to become related by blood to the human race. This indicates the necessity of the incarnation. Jesus became a man in order to redeem man (Hebrews 2:14-16). And because He was also fully God, His sacrificial death had infinite value (Hebrews 9:11-28).

Related to Christ's role as Mediator is his role as Savior. A study of the Old Testament indicates that it is only God who saves. In Isaiah 43:11, God asserts, "I, even I, am the LORD, and *apart from me there is no savior*" (emphasis added). This is an extremely important verse, for it indicates that 1) a claim to be Savior is, in itself, a claim to deity; and 2) there is only one Savior—God.

And because the New Testament refers to Jesus Christ as the Savior, we can be certain that He has a divine nature. Following His birth, an angel appeared to some nearby shepherds and said, "Today in the town of David a Savior has been born to you; he is Christ the Lord" (Luke 2:11). John's Gospel records the conclusion of the Samaritans: Jesus "really is the Savior of the world" (John 4:42).

In Titus 2:13, Paul encourages Titus to await the blessed hope, the "glorious appearing of our great God and Savior, Jesus Christ." An examination of Titus 2:10-13, 3:4, and 3:6 reveals that the phrases "God our Savior" and "Jesus our Savior" are used interchangeably four times. The parallel truths that *only God is the Savior* (Isaiah 43:11) and that Jesus Himself is the Savior constitute a powerful evidence for Christ's deity. In the incarnation, God the Savior became a human being—and this enabled Him to fulfill His role as Mediator between God and man (since He Himself was both God and man).

_____ *Ask...* _____

- Can you see how the parallel truths that *only God is the Savior* (Isaiah 43:11) and that *Jesus Himself is the Savior* (Luke 2:11) requires that Jesus be God Almighty?
  (If the Jehovah's Witness responds by saying that Jesus is just a "mighty god," then ask the following:)

- Who is speaking in Isaiah 43:11? (He will say Jehovah-God.)

- So only Jehovah-God can be Savior? (He will have to say yes.)

- Since Jesus is called Savior in the New Testament, and since only Jehovah-God can be Savior, then doesn't this mean that Jesus is Jehovah-God?

A "Corresponding Ransom"?

In answering the Watchtower argument that Jesus was a "corresponding ransom" to Adam, we begin by addressing what the Greek text for 1 Timothy 2:6 indicates. The New American Standard Bible says that Jesus "gave Himself *as a ransom* for all" (emphasis added). The Greek word for "ransom" is *antilutron*. The question is, Does this word point to a "corresponding ransom" in the sense of "no more and no less" as the Watchtower Society argues? By no means! This is a case of *over*translation, and the Jehovah's Witnesses are reading more into this word than is really there.[27]

Thayer's Greek lexicon says that *antilutron* means "what is given in exchange for another as the price of his redemption, ransom."[28] The "ransom" is here called *antilutron* "in order to stress the fact of Christ's coming and suffering in the place of all and for their advantage."[29] *Vine's Expository Dictionary of Biblical Words* points out that the preposition *anti* "has a vicarious significance, indicating that the 'ransom' holds good for those who, accepting it as such, no longer remain in death since Christ suffered death in their stead."[30]

Watchtower expert Robert Bowman points out that "although the word [*antilutron*] is very rare in Greek, and it appears only here in the Bible, the meaning is certainly the same as Christ's statement in Mark 10:45 that he came to give his life as 'a ransom in exchange for [*lutron anti*] many' (NWT). The idea in both passages is simply that of substitution—of Christ's taking our place. The idea that this required that Christ be 'no more' than a perfect human is absent."[31] So the Greek text solidly militates against the Watchtower understanding of 1 Timothy 2:6.

_____ *Ask...* _____

• Did you know Greek language authorities universally agree that the meaning of the Greek word for "ransom" simply involves the idea of *substitution* and not a strict "no more/no less" type of correspondence?

Bowman makes another point worth mentioning: The Jehovah's Witnesses can "give no reason why God needed to send his Son to earth as a man at all. Since all that was required was a perfect human, God could simply have created one 'from scratch,' if he had wanted."[32] You might mention this to the Jehovah's Witness and ask him or her to comment. The response should be interesting!

Acts 16:30-32—*Believing on the Lord Jesus*

The Watchtower Teaching. Acts 16:30,31 in the *New World Translation* reads, "And he [the jailer] brought them [Paul and Silas] outside and said: 'Sirs, what must I do to get saved?' They said: 'Believe on the Lord Jesus and you will get saved, you and your household.' And they spoke the word of Jehovah to him together with all those in his house."

Jehovah's Witnesses acknowledge that faith is necessary for salvation, but they always add works to this faith. Commenting on Acts 16:30,31, *Reasoning from the Scriptures* says, "If that man [the jailer] and his household truly believed, would they not *act* in harmony with their belief? Certainly."[33] In other words, works play a central role.

In *Make Sure of All Things*, we are told that "faith must be demonstrated by consistent works."[34] Watchtower literature makes it very clear that to really be saved one must be an active Jehovah's Witness, consistently following all of the rules and regulations of the Society.[35]

The Biblical Teaching. As you discuss Acts 16:30-32 with Jehovah's Witnesses, you will want to point out that this passage represents a strong argument for the deity of Christ. When the jailer asked Paul and Silas how to become saved, they responded, "Believe in the Lord Jesus, and you will be saved—you and your household" (Acts 16:31). Then, after he became saved, we are told that the jailer "was filled with joy because he had come to believe in God [*Theos*]—he and his whole family" (verse 34). *Believing in Christ* and *believing in God* are seen as identical acts.

___ Ask... _____

- What do you think it says about Christ's nature that *believing in Him* (Acts 16:31) and *believing in God* (verse 34) are seen as identical acts?

Moving on to the next question: Is believing in Christ sufficient for salvation? Or must we combine believing in Christ with doing good works? Emphasize to the Jehovah's Witness that close to 200 times in the New Testament salvation is said to be *by faith alone*—with no works in sight. Acts 16:31 is just one of many verses that say we are to believe in the Lord Jesus for salvation. Consider the following:

- John 3:15 tells us that *"everyone who believes in him may have eternal life"* (emphasis added).
- John 5:24 says, "I tell you the truth, *whoever hears my word and believes* him who sent me *has eternal life* and will not be condemned; he has crossed over from death to life" (emphasis added).
- In John 11:25 Jesus says, "I am the resurrection and the life. *He who believes in me* will live, even though he dies" (emphasis added).
- John 12:46 says: "I have come into the world as a light, so that *no one who believes in me should stay in darkness*" (emphasis added).

• John 20:31 says: "But these are written *that you may believe* that Jesus is the Christ, the Son of God, and that *by believing* you may have life in his name" (emphasis added). Clearly, salvation is by faith in Christ!

Related to belief in Christ is the issue of grace versus works. Consider the following:

• Ephesians 2:8,9 says, "For it is by grace you have been saved, through faith—and this not from yourselves, it is the gift of God—not by works, so that no one can boast."

• Titus 3:5 says, "He saved us, not because of righteous things we had done, but because of his mercy."

• Romans 3:20 tells us that "by the works of the Law no flesh will be justified in His sight" (NASB).

• In Galatians 2:16 Paul tells us, "knowing that a man is not justified by the works of the Law but through faith in Christ Jesus, even we have believed in Christ Jesus, that we may be justified by faith in Christ, and not by the works of the Law; since by the works of the Law shall no flesh be justified" (NASB).

We have merely touched upon the tip of an iceberg in dealing with the passages that speak of salvation by grace through faith. Suffice it to say that the entire weight of the New Testament stands against the Watchtower's works-oriented view of Acts 16:30-32 and other similar passages.

You might want to read all the above verses to the Jehovah's Witness and then:

_____ *Ask...* _____

• Does salvation as described in these verses sound like the concept of salvation that is set forth in Watchtower literature, or do you see a difference?

Romans 10:13—*Calling Upon Yahweh*

The Watchtower Teaching. In the *New World Translation*, Romans 10:13 reads, "Everyone who calls on the name of Jehovah will be saved." In citing this passage (and others like it), the Jehovah's Witnesses say that the proper use of God's "correct" name—Jehovah—is absolutely essential to one's salvation.[36] As noted earlier, more than a few converts have been won to this cult by utilizing such an approach.

The Watchtower Society often says that the time left to call upon Jehovah for salvation is very short because Armageddon is near. The Watchtower book *Man's Salvation Out of World Distress At Hand!* states:

> Since we have been living in the "time of the end" of this worldly system of things since the year 1914 C.E., the time that is left during which Jehovah may be found in a favorable way is by now very short. So *now* is the favorable time in which to search for him. A person does not have to go far in this search in order to find him. He is still near, within reach of sincere searchers for him. So *now* is also the time to call to him. He is not beyond hearing distance. Now, before "the great and fear-inspiring day of Jehovah," is when the reassuring words apply: "It must occur that everyone who calls on the name of Jehovah will get away safe."[37]

The Biblical Teaching. The *New World Translation* blatantly mistranslates Romans 10:13. The original Greek text has no reference to "Jehovah." This word was inserted into the passage by the Watchtower Society's translators. The verse correctly reads, "Everyone who calls on the name *of the Lord* [Greek: *kurios*] will be saved" (NIV, emphasis added, insert added). And, in the broader context of our passage (Romans 10:9-13), "Lord" is referring to Jesus Christ (*see* verse 9, where Jesus is explicitly identified as the "Lord" of these five verses[38]).

_____ *Ask...* _____

- Did you know that the word "Jehovah" is not in any New Testament Greek manuscript, but was inserted in Romans 10:13 and elsewhere by the Watchtower Society?

- Did you know that while the Watchtower puts the word "Jehovah" in Romans 10:13, all the Greek manuscripts have the word *kurios*, which means "Lord"?

- Did you know that the broader context of this verse—Romans 13:9-13—makes it clear that the "Lord" being referred to is Jesus, especially since He is explicitly identified as the "Lord" in verse 9?

Romans 10:13 is actually a quote from Joel 2:32: "And everyone who calls on the name of the LORD [Yahweh] will be saved." This *does not* give justification, however, for using the words Yahweh or Jehovah in Romans 10:13. As noted earlier, the word used in the Greek manuscripts for "Lord" in Romans 10:13 is *kurios*, not Yahweh. Thus the Watchtower's translation is unwarranted.

Here is what is significant about Joel 2:32: As much as the Jehovah's Witness may want to deny it, the apostle Paul is quoting Joel 2:32 ("calling upon the LORD [Yahweh]") in the context of *being fulfilled* by calling upon Jesus Christ for salvation. "Calling upon Yahweh" and "calling upon Jesus Christ" are here equated. This is a clear evidence pointing to Christ's identity as Yahweh.

The apostle Peter cites this same verse from Joel 2:32 when preaching to the crowd on the day of Pentecost: "And everyone who calls on the name of the Lord will be saved" (Acts 2:21). A look at verses 22 through 36 shows beyond any question that the "Lord" Peter is speaking of is none other than Jesus Christ. (This "Lord" was attested by miracles and wonders on earth, was nailed to a cross, was raised from the dead, and ascended to the right hand of the Father.)

Commenting on Acts 2:21, theologian Robert Reymond says, "It is difficult to avoid the conclusion that [Peter] was urging [the crowd] to avail themselves of the remedy Joel himself had prescribed in his prophecy when he said, 'And everyone who calls on *the name of the Lord* will be saved' (Acts 2:21). But then this means, in turn, that for Peter Jesus was the Lord of Joel 2:32a (cf. Rom. 10:9-13), which means in turn that Jesus was the Yahweh who spoke through Joel."[39]

With that in mind, you might want to request the Jehovah's Witness to read aloud from Joel 2:32 and Acts 2:21, and then:

_____ *Ask...* _____

- Who is the "Lord" of Joel 2:32? (He'll say Jehovah.)

- Since the "Lord" of Acts 2:21 was nailed to a cross, raised from the dead, and ascended to heaven, who, then, is this "Lord" of Acts 2:21? (Obviously Jesus.)

- Since Peter is quoting Joel 2:32 in Acts 2:21 as being fulfilled in Jesus Christ, what does this say about Jesus' true identity?

It is interesting to note that the February 1, 1980, issue of *The Watchtower* magazine (page 61) said that Romans 10:13 was referring to Jehovah. However, the May 1, 1978, issue of *The Watchtower* magazine (page 12) said this verse was referring to Jesus Christ. If the Watchtower organization is God's prophet and "channel of truth" today, one must wonder how God's prophet can virtually reverse itself regarding the interpretation of this important Bible verse.

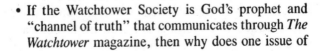

_____ *Ask...* _____

- If the Watchtower Society is God's prophet and "channel of truth" that communicates through *The Watchtower* magazine, then why does one issue of the magazine (in 1980) say Romans 10:13 refers to *Jehovah* while another issue (1978) says it refers to *Jesus Christ*?

John 3:5—*Becoming "Born Again"*

The Watchtower Teaching. The *New World Translation* renders John 3:5,6: "Jesus answered: 'Most truly I say to you, unless anyone is born from water and spirit, he cannot enter into the kingdom of God. What has been born from the flesh is flesh, and what has been born from the spirit is spirit.'"

According to Watchtower literature, being "born again" enables one to become a "son of God" with the prospect of sharing in the Kingdom of God. "When Jesus spoke about being born again he said that it was necessary in order to enter the Kingdom of God, that is, to be part of God's Kingdom, his heavenly government."[40] Jesus experienced being born again, and the 144,000 people that make up the Anointed Class are also born again, sharing with Him a spirit existence in heaven.[41]

Mortal human beings cannot take part in this spirit existence in heaven. After all, Paul tells us that "flesh and blood cannot inherit God's kingdom, neither does corruption inherit incorruption" (1 Corinthians 15:50 NWT). John 3:6 is clear that "what has been born from the flesh is flesh, and what has been born from the spirit is spirit."[42] Only those born of the spirit ("born again") can take part in spirit life in heaven. Those born of the flesh are suited only for life on earth.

This is not to say that one who is not born again cannot be saved. After all, Scripture teaches that a "great crowd" of Jehovah's Witnesses look forward to eternal life on a paradise earth (Revelation 7:9). These individuals are not born again but are nevertheless saved and enjoy Jehovah's favor.

How does this earthly class relate to the Anointed Class in heaven? The Anointed Class (those who *are* born again) will rule over those who live on earth (those who *are not* born again).[43] Being born again clearly has its benefits!

The Biblical Teaching. Scripture is clear that the opportunity to become born again is not limited to 144,000 people in the so-called Anointed Class but is open to *all* who believe in Jesus Christ. First John 5:1, for example, states, *"Everyone who believes that Jesus is the Christ is born of God"* (emphasis added). There are no exceptions. Any and all who believe in Jesus Christ are "born again."[44]

This is consistent with Jesus' discussion on being "born again" with Nicodemus (John 3:1-21). After saying that one must be born again (verses 3,7), Jesus said, "For God so loved the world, that He gave His only begotten Son, that *whoever believes in Him* should not perish, but have eternal life" (verse 16 NASB, emphasis added). John 1:12,13 agrees: "But as many as received Him, to them He gave the right to become children of God, *even to those who believe in His name*, who were born not of blood, nor of the will of the flesh, nor of the will of man, but of God" (NASB, emphasis added).

_____ *Ask...* _____

- Why is it that every passage in the New Testament that speaks of being born again says that *all who believe in Jesus* can be born again, with no mention of limiting this experience to a mere 144,000 people? (If he or she argues about this, ask him or her to show you a single passage that limits this experience to the 144,000.)

Being "born again" (literally, "born from above") simply refers to the act in which God gives eternal life to the one (*anyone!*) who believes in Christ (Titus 3:5). Being born again thus places one in God's eternal family (1 Peter 1:23) and gives the believer a new capacity and desire to please the Father (2 Corinthians 5:17).

This fits with what we read in John 3:6: "That which is born of the flesh is flesh; and that which is born of the Spirit is spirit" (NASB). The "flesh" includes not only what is natural but what is sinful in man—that is, man as he is born into this fallen world and lives his life apart from God's grace. "Flesh can only reproduce itself as flesh, and this cannot pass muster with God (cf. Rom. 8:8). The law of reproduction is 'after its kind.' So likewise the Spirit produces spirit, a life born, nurtured, and matured by the Spirit of God."[45] This experience of fallen man receiving eternal life from God is open to all who believe in Christ.

In Nicodemus's case, we find a Pharisee who would have been trusting in his physical descent from Abraham for entrance into the Messiah's kingdom. The Jews believed that because they were physically related to Abraham, they were in a specially privileged position before God. Christ, however, denied such a possibility. As Bible scholar J. Dwight Pentecost says, "Parents can transmit to their children only the nature which they themselves possess. Since each parent's nature, because of Adam's sin, is sinful, each parent transmits a sinful nature to the child. What is sinful cannot enter the kingdom of God (v. 5)."[46] The only way one can enter God's kingdom is to experience a spiritual rebirth, and this is precisely what Jesus is emphasizing to Nicodemus.

Now, what about the Watchtower claim that Jesus Himself was born again? This position is as ridiculous as it is untenable. In the incarnation, Jesus (who is eternal God) took on a human nature (Luke 1:35; 1 Timothy 3:16; Hebrews 2:14; 1 John 4:2,3). Christ's development as a human being was normal in every respect, with two major exceptions: 1) He always did the will of God, and 2) He never sinned. As Hebrews 4:15 tells us, in Christ "we do not have a high priest who is unable to sympathize with our weaknesses, but we have one who has been tempted in every way, just as we are—*yet was without sin*" (emphasis added). Indeed, Christ is intrinsically "holy," "blameless," and "pure" (Hebrews 7:26).

In light of that, and since Christ is fully God (John 1:1; 8:58; 20:28), there is no need for Jesus to be born again. Jesus came to *provide* redemption (1 Timothy 2:5,6); He—as the Redeemer—did not Himself need to be redeemed. The One who possesses life in Himself (John 5:26) does not need to receive such life from another.

_____ Ask... _____

- Can you show me a single passage anywhere in Scripture that says that Jesus became born again?

Philippians 2:12—*Working Out Your Own Salvation*

The Watchtower Teaching. The *New World Translation* renders Philippians 2:12, "Consequently, my beloved ones, in the way that you have always obeyed, not during my presence only, but now much more readily during my absence, keep working out your own salvation with fear and trembling." Commenting on this verse, *Reasoning from the Scriptures* says, "This [Book of Philippians] was addressed to 'the saints,' or holy ones, at Philippi, as stated in Philippians 1:1. Paul urged them not to be overly confident but to realize that their final salvation was not yet assured."[47]

In the book *"Let God Be True,"* we are told that before members of "Christ's body" can receive their heavenly inheritance, "they must be set apart more and more from this world and to the holy service of Jehovah God, demonstrating their dependability by carrying out their dedication faithfully until death."[48] *Note that there is no security of salvation in Watchtower literature.*

All Jehovah's Witnesses must diligently study God's Word (and Watchtower literature), apply all that they learn to daily life, and seek at all times to be led by God's Holy Spirit. They must be holy even as God is holy. They must be entirely devoted to God and His righteousness. That is why Jehovah's

Witnesses are admonished to "keep working out" their salvation with fear and trembling.[49]

Former Jehovah's Witness Lorri MacGregor's comments are highly revealing: "I was told [that 'working out your salvation'] consisted of 'publishing the good news of God's kingdom' by selling their publications door-to-door, attending five meetings a week, and meeting numerous other quotas."[50] Salvation in Watchtower theology is works-oriented from beginning to end.

The Biblical Teaching. What does Philippians 2:12 mean when it says, "Work out your salvation with fear and trembling"? Was Paul really urging the Philippians "not to be overly confident but to realize that their final salvation was not yet assured"?[51] By no means! In fact, this verse has nothing to do with assurance of final salvation for individual believers.

One must keep in mind the situation in the church at Philippi. This church was plagued by 1) rivalries and individuals with personal ambition (Philippians 2:3,4; 4:2); 2) the teaching of Judaizers (who said that circumcision was necessary for salvation—3:1-3); 3) perfectionism (the view that one could attain sinless perfection in this life—3:12-14); and, 4) the influence of "antinomian libertines" (people who took excessive liberty in how they lived their lives, ignoring or going against God's law—3:18,19).[52] Because of such problems, this church as a unit was in need of "salvation" (that is, salvation in the temporal, experiential sense, not in the eternal sense).

It is critical to recognize that "salvation" in this context is referring to the *community* of believers in Philippi and not to *individuals*. Salvation is spoken of in a *corporate* sense. The Philippians were called by the apostle Paul to "keep on working out" (continuously) the "deliverance of the church into a state of Christian maturity."[53]

The Greek word for "work out" (*katergazomai*) is a compound verb that indicates *achievement* or *bringing to a conclusion*. Paul was calling the Philippians to solve all the church's problems, thus bringing corporate "salvation" or deliverance to a state of final achievement. He would not permit things to continue as they were; the problems had to be solved. The Philippians were to "work it out to the finish."[54]

In the phrase "work out your own salvation," the words "your own" are strongly emphatic in the Greek text. As Bible scholar H.C.G. Moule notes, "The Apostle is in fact bidding them 'learn to walk alone,' instead of leaning too much on *his* presence and personal influence. 'Do not make me your proxy in spiritual duties which must be your own.'"[55] This was all the more necessary because the apostle Paul was absent from the church (Philippians 2:12a).

The Philippians were to accomplish their appointed task with an attitude of "fear and trembling." This doesn't mean Paul wanted them to have terror in their hearts as a motivation. Rather, the words "fear and trembling" are an idiomatic expression pointing to great reverence for God and a humble frame of mind. (Remember: Many in Philippi were prideful and had *little* reverence for God.) Such humility and reverence for God would help them overcome the problems they were experiencing in the church (cf. 1 Corinthians 2:3; 2 Corinthians 7:15; Ephesians 6:5).

_____ *Ask*... _____

- Can you see that from a contextual and historical point of view, Philippians 2:12 makes great sense when interpreted as referring to *corporate* salvation of the church in Philippi—a church that had specific problems Paul wanted them to deal with on their own?

It is also significant that in other writings, the apostle Paul clearly sets forth what theologians call "eternal security." For example, in Romans 8:29,30 Paul said, "For those God foreknew he also predestined to be conformed to the likeness of his

Son...and those He predestined, he also called, those he called, those he also justified; those he justified, he also glorified." *Here we find an unbroken progression from predestination to glorification.* And the tense of the word "glorified" (in the Greek text) indicates that our future glorification is *so certain* that it can be said to already be accomplished!

After reading Romans 8:29,30 aloud:

_____ *Ask...* _____

- Can you see that there is an unbroken chain from predestination to glorification in this passage?

- What do you think this means?

We find another Pauline affirmation for eternal security in Ephesians 4:30, where we are told that believers are "sealed" by the Holy Spirit for the day of redemption. A seal indicates *possession* and *security.* "The presence of the Holy Spirit, the seal, is the believer's guarantee of the security of his salvation."[56] The believer is thus assured that he will, in fact, be with God in heaven for all eternity.

_____ *Ask...* _____

- What do you think it means to be "sealed" by the Holy Spirit for the day of redemption?

To recap our discussion on Philippians 2:12, the Watchtower Society is way off base in teaching that Paul was urging the Philippians "not to be overly confident but to realize that their final salvation was not yet assured."[57] Such an interpretation not only goes against the rest of the Book of Philippians, it goes against the rest of Scripture as well (Psalm 37:23; 138:8;

John 5:24; 6:37-40; 10:27-30; 17:8-11; Romans 5:1-5; 1 Corinthians 1:8.9; 2 Corinthians 1:21,22; Ephesians 1:4,5; Philippians 1:6; 1 Thessalonians 5:24; 2 Timothy 1:12; 4:18; 1 Peter 1:3-5; 5:10; 1 John 2:1,2; 5:10-18; Jude 1). It might be worth your while to go over some of those passages with the Jehovah's Witness.

12

Understanding the Soul and Soul-Sleep

The only alternative to eternal life is eternal punishment.

—Harry W. Post[1]

The Jehovah's Witnesses do not believe that man's soul or spirit is distinct from the physical body. Rather, they believe that man is a combination of body and "breath" that together forms a "living soul."

To be more specific, Jehovah's Witnesses believe that the *soul* refers not to an immaterial part of man that can survive death, but to the very life that a person has. Every person *is* a "soul"—not because he or she possesses an immaterial nature but because he or she is *a living being*. "A soul, heavenly or earthly, consists of a body together with the life principle or life force actuating it."[2]

In support of this view, Jehovah's Witnesses point out that according to 1 Peter 3:20, "In Noah's days...a few people, that is, eight souls, were carried safely through the water" (NWT). In Genesis 9:5, the soul is said to have blood—and only a *living being* has blood, not an immaterial nature. Joshua 11:11 of the *New World Translation* says, "They went striking every soul...with the edge of the sword" (and immaterial natures cannot be touched with swords). Clearly, "soul" is synonymous with "living being" in these verses.

The Watchtower Society finds further support for their view in the lives of Bible characters. For example, as a soul, Adam is said to have lived on the earth for a prolonged time and then died. The Watchtower book *"Let Your Name Be Sanctified"* says, "For nine hundred and thirty years a 'living soul' on earth, [Adam] now became a dead soul in the earth, in the ground."[3]

Likewise, Luke 23:46 informs us that Jesus—after saying to the Father, "Into your hands I entrust my spirit" (NWT)—*expired*. The Watchtower Society thus argues, "Notice that Jesus expired. When his spirit went out he was not on his way to heaven. Not until the third day from this was Jesus resurrected from the dead."[4] Thus, "it is clearly seen that even the man Christ Jesus was mortal. He did not have an immortal soul: Jesus, the human soul, died."[5] So, what did Jesus mean by what He said at the time of His death? "He was saying that he knew that, when he died, his future life prospects rested entirely with God."[6]

Obviously, the doctrine of the soul relates closely to the question of what happens at the moment of death. The Watchtower Society tells us that because we inherited sin from Adam, we die and return to the dust, just as animals do. The Society emphasizes that human beings *do not* possess an immaterial nature (soul or spirit) that goes on living as an intelligent personality after death, when it ceases its association with the body.[7] Man's spirit is interpreted as the "life-force" within him, and at death, the life-force wanes: "After breathing, heartbeat, and brain activity stop, the life-force gradually ceases to function in body cells."[8]

Now, this leads us to a major emphasis in Watchtower theology. Since at death man has no immaterial nature that survives, then obviously he is not *conscious* of anything following death. Like animals, man's consciousness ceases to exist at the death of the physical form. Even for the righteous, the dead remain unconscious and inactive in the grave until the time of the future resurrection.

The Watchtower book *Mankind's Search for God* thus comments, "If, as the Bible says, man does not *have* a soul but *is* a soul, then there is no conscious existence after death. There is no bliss, and there is no suffering. All the illogical complications of the 'hereafter' disappear."[9] Hence, "when a person is dead he is completely out of existence. He is not conscious of anything."[10] Indeed, the dead experience neither pain nor pleasure, since they have no thought processes whatever.[11]

Now, the Watchtower book *Reasoning from the Scriptures* raises the question as to *who* would want people to believe that an immaterial nature of man survives death. In answering the question, the Genesis account is cited to prove that the devil is behind this idea. Consider: After God warned Adam and Eve that disobedience would bring death, who contradicted God's warning? It was Satan acting through the serpent: "You positively will not die" (Genesis 3:4 NWT). Later, of course, Adam and Eve did die. "Reasonably, then, who invented the idea that a spirit part of man survives the death of the body?"[12] The answer, they say, is Satan. The Watchtower book *"Let God Be True"* tells us that "this doctrine is the main one that the Devil has used down through the ages to deceive the people and hold them in bondage. In fact, it is the foundation doctrine of false religion."[13]

Satan is also said to be behind the concept of hell as an eternal place of suffering. The "slanderous" concept of hell is said to have originated "with the chief slanderer of God (the Devil, which name means 'Slanderer'), the one whom Jesus Christ called 'the father of the lie.'"[14] The idea of hell as a place of eternal punishment is a "God-dishonoring religious doctrine."[15]

According to Watchtower literature, "hell" simply refers to the common grave of humankind. This is the grave not just of the wicked but of *all* humankind. "Yes, good people go to the Bible hell. . . . Sheol and Hades refer not to a place of torment but to the common grave of all mankind."[16]

_____ REASONING FROM THE SCRIPTURES _____

Genesis 2:7—Man a "Living Soul"?

The Watchtower Teaching. The *New World Translation* renders Genesis 2:7, "And Jehovah God proceeded to form the man out of dust from the ground and to blow into his nostrils the breath of life, and *the man came to be a living soul*" (emphasis added). Jehovah's Witnesses cite this verse to prove that man does not have a material and immaterial nature that are distinct from one another. Rather, man is a combination of physical material and "breath," which together form a living soul.

The book *"Let God Be True"* tells us that "man is a combination of two things, namely, the 'dust of the ground' and 'the breath of life.' The combining of these two things (or factors) produced a living soul or creature called man."[17] Man was not *given* a soul but rather he *became* a soul, a living person.[18] The Genesis account, then, clearly proves that the idea "that man has an immortal soul and therefore differs from the beast is not Scriptural."[19]

The Biblical Teaching. It is true that in the Old Testament, the Hebrew word for soul (*nephesh*) can be used in reference to a living being.[20] Genesis 2:7 is clearly an example of this. But because the word can be used in this sense does not mean that it is *limited* to this sense, or that man does not have an immaterial nature.

You must emphasize to the Jehovah's Witness that he or she is reading into the text of Genesis 2:7 something that is not there. Indeed, Genesis 2:7 is simply telling us what man *is* (a living being), not what he *is not*.[21] In other words, while Genesis 2:7 affirms that man is a living being, it does not *deny* in any way that man has an immaterial nature. (In fact, Genesis 35:18 may be an example of *nephesh* being used of man's immaterial nature.[22])

Besides referring to "living beings," the word *nephesh* is also used in the Old Testament to speak of the seat of the emotions and experiences. Man's *nephesh* can be *sad* (Deuteronomy 28:65), *grieved* (Job 30:25), in *pain* (Psalm 13:2), *distressed* (Genesis 42:21), *bitter* (Job 3:20), *troubled* (Psalm 6:3), and *cheered* (Psalm 86:4). Clearly, man's soul can experience a wide range of emotional ups and downs.

In this sense, *nephesh* seems to refer to the "inner man" *within* the human being. This is consistent with verses like 2 Kings 4:27, where we read, "The man of God said, 'Let her alone, for her soul is troubled *within her*'" (NASB). Likewise, Psalm 42:6 says, "O my God, my soul is in despair *within me*" (NASB), and Psalm 43:5 says, "Why are you in despair, O my soul? And why are you disturbed *within me*?" (NASB).

_____ *Ask...* _____

- Are you aware that the Hebrew word for soul— *nephesh*—can be used in a variety of ways in Scripture? (Give some examples.)

- Do you concede that the word *nephesh*, for example, can be used to refer to the "inner man" as opposed to man as a living being? (If he or she says no, have him or her read the above verses aloud and ask the question again.)

_____

Now, having said all this, I must mention that one of the most important principles of Bible interpretation is that *Scripture interprets Scripture*. We must ever bear in mind that the interpretation of a specific passage must not contradict the total teaching of God's Word on a given point. Individual texts do not exist as isolated fragments, but as parts of a whole. The exposition of these texts must therefore exhibit them in right relation both to the whole and to each other. Remember, each of the biblical writers wrote within the larger context of previous biblical teaching. And they all assumed that *all of Scripture*—though communicated through human instruments—

had *one Author* (God) who didn't contradict Himself (2 Peter 1:21).

I say this because the Jehovah's Witnesses will argue that Genesis 2:7 teaches that man does not have an immaterial nature. This is a faulty and unwarranted conclusion since, again, the text is telling us what man *is* (a living being), not what he *is not*. The Watchtower view clearly goes against the rest of the Bible on this subject. By comparing Scripture with Scripture, it becomes quite evident that while Genesis 2:7 says only that man became a "living being," other passages clearly point to man's immaterial nature. Let us now turn our attention to some of these. (*Note: The following verses can be used not only to correct the Watchtower misunderstanding of Genesis 2:7 but many other Watchtower "proof texts" regarding the soul and soul-sleep as well.*)

Matthew 10:28—*The Soul Exists After Death*

In Matthew 10:28 Jesus says, "Do not be afraid of those who kill the body but cannot kill the soul. Rather, be afraid of the One who can destroy both soul and body in hell." In this verse, the Greek word used for "soul" is *psuche*. In their authoritative *Greek-English Lexicon of the New Testament*, William Arndt and F. Wilbur Gingrich point out that the word *psuche* can mean "breath of life, life-principle," "earthly life itself," "the soul as seat and center of the inner life of man in its many and varied aspects," and "the soul as seat and center of life *that transcends the earthly*"[23] (emphasis added). The word *psuche* is often used to translate the Hebrew term *nephesh* into Greek. (For example, the Greek translation of the Old Testament—the Septuagint—has *psuche* in place of *nephesh* in Genesis 2:7.)

Now, in Matthew 10:28 *psuche* is clearly being used to designate the part of man that continues on after physical death. It is not being used simply to refer to the "whole person." If that were the case, then the *psuche* (soul) would die when the physical body is killed. This verse clearly indicates that it is possible to kill the body *without* killing the soul (*psuche*). What Jesus is saying, then, is this: "There is something about you which those who kill you [in your physical being] cannot touch! That something is that aspect of man which continues to exist after the body has been lowered into the grave."[24]

You might want to read Matthew 10:28 to the Jehovah's Witness and then:

_____ *Ask...* _____

- If the word *soul* is just another way of referring to the "whole person"—as the Watchtower Society teaches—then wouldn't the soul die when the physical body dies?

- How do you reconcile the Watchtower position with Matthew 10:28, which clearly indicates that it is possible to kill the body *without* killing the soul?

Revelation 6:9,10—*Souls Under God's Altar*

In Revelation 6:9,10 we read, "And when He broke the fifth seal, I saw underneath the altar *the souls of those who had been slain* because of the word of God, and because of the testimony which they had maintained; and they cried out with a loud voice, saying, 'How long, O Lord, holy and true, wilt Thou refrain from judging and avenging our blood on those who dwell on the earth?'" (NASB, emphasis added).

In this passage it is impossible for "souls" to refer to living beings, for then the text would read, "I saw underneath the altar the *living beings* of those who had been slain."[25] Notice that the souls exist and are conscious despite the fact that they had been physically slain. How do we know they are conscious? Scripture says that they "cried out" to God and are spoken to in turn. *That which is unconscious cannot cry out or be spoken to.*

_____ Ask... _____

- Isn't it impossible for the word "soul" to refer to living beings in Revelation 6:9,10 since the text would then read, "I saw underneath the altar the *living beings* of those who had been slain"?

- Since these souls had been physically slain—and since they are obviously conscious in God's presence—doesn't this indicate that they have an immaterial nature that survived their physical slaying (death)?

Luke 23:46—*"Into Thy Hands I Commit My Spirit"*

In Luke 23:46 we read these words Jesus uttered as He died on the cross: "Jesus called out with a loud voice, 'Father, into your hands I commit my spirit.' When he had said this, he breathed his last."

The word translated "spirit" in this verse is *pneuma*. According to Arndt and Gingrich, this word can have a wide range of meanings—including "wind," "breath," "life-spirit," "soul," "the spirit as a part of the human personality," "the spirit of God," "the spirit of Christ," and "the Holy Spirit."[26]

Now, many of the above meanings are disqualified as possible contenders for Luke 23:46 by virtue of the context. It doesn't make any sense for Jesus to commend His "wind" or His "breath" to the Father. Nor does it fit the context for Jesus to commit "the spirit of God" or "the Holy Spirit" to the Father. In fact, the only meanings of *pneuma* that make any sense in this context are "soul" and "spirit as a part of the human personality." It seems clear from a plain reading of the passage that Jesus is committing His *human immaterial soul or spirit* to the Father. And since Christ was not raised from the dead until three days after His crucifixion, we must conclude that Jesus' human soul or spirit went directly to the Father's presence in heaven while His body lay in the tomb.[27]

_____ *Ask...* _____

- Don't you think that a person reading this verse for the first time, without having consulted any Watchtower literature, would conclude that the verse deals with committing Christ's *immaterial* soul or spirit to the Father?

Acts 7:59—*"Lord Jesus, Receive My Spirit"*

In Acts 7:59 we read, "And they went on stoning Stephen as he called upon the Lord and said, 'Lord Jesus, receive my spirit!'" This verse would make virtually no sense if we interpret "spirit" (*pneuma*) as simply the life-force within Stephen that ceased to exist at the moment of his death. Why would Stephen ask Jesus to "receive" that which was about to cease existing?[28] He is clearly asking Jesus to receive and take to Himself that part of his self that would survive the death of his physical body.

_____ *Ask...* _____

- From a plain reading of Acts 7:59, doesn't it seem unlikely that Stephen would appeal to Jesus to "receive my spirit" if the spirit was merely his life-force that was about to be extinguished and cease existing?

1 Thessalonians 4:13-17—*"The Dead in Christ Shall Rise First"*

In 1 Thessalonians 4:13-17 (NASB) we read,

> But we do not want you to be uninformed, brethren, about *those who are asleep*, that you may not grieve, as do the rest who have no hope.

> For if we believe that Jesus died and rose again, even so *God will bring with Him those who have fallen asleep in Jesus.*
>
> For this we say to you by the word of the Lord, that we who are alive, and remain until the coming of the Lord, shall not precede *those who have fallen asleep.*
>
> For the Lord Himself will descend from heaven with a shout, with the voice of the archangel, and with the trumpet of God; and the *dead in Christ* shall rise first.
>
> Then we who are alive and remain shall be caught up together with them in the clouds to meet the Lord in the air, and thus we shall always be with the Lord.

Note that though the term "sleep" is often used to denote death in Scripture, it is never used in reference to the immaterial part of man. Indeed, cult expert Walter Martin explains that "the term *sleep* is always applied in Scripture to the body alone, since in death the body takes on the *appearance* of one who is asleep. But the term *soul sleep* is never found in Scripture. And nowhere does Scripture state that the soul ever passes into a state of unconsciousness."[29]

Walter Martin had this to say about the significance of 1 Thessalonians 4:13-17 in relation to the idea of conscious existence of the soul after death:

> Verse 14 in this passage indicates that Paul, while using the metaphor *sleep* to describe physical death, clearly understood that when Jesus comes again, He will bring *with* (Greek: *sun*) Him those whose bodies are "sleeping." To be more explicit, the souls and spirits of those who are now with Christ in glory (2 Cor. 5:8; Phil. 1:22-23) will be reunited with their resurrection bodies (1 Cor. 15); that is, they will be clothed with immortality, incorruptibility, and exemption from physical decay. The Greek word *sun* indicates that they (i.e., their souls and spirits) will be in a "side by side" position with Christ, and their physical bodies that are "sleeping" will in that

instant be raised to immortality and reunited with their spirits.[30]

_____ *Ask...* _____

- According to 1 Thessalonians 4:14, who will Jesus bring with Him when He comes again?

- Do these believers have bodies yet? (Obviously not, since they don't receive their resurrection bodies until verse 16.)

- If Jesus is bringing some believers with Him (verse 14), but they don't have resurrection bodies yet (verse 16), then doesn't this mean that the immaterial souls/spirits of these believers are with Jesus and will be reunited to their bodies at the resurrection?

Luke 20:38—*The God of the Living*

In Luke 20:38, we read of Jesus' words to the Sadducees regarding the Old Testament saints Abraham, Isaac, and Jacob: "He [God] is not the God of the dead, but *of the living*; for all live to Him" (NASB, emphasis added).

According to first-century Jewish historian Flavius Josephus, "the doctrine of the Sadducees is this: that souls die with the bodies."[31] And in Luke 20:38, Jesus contradicts the view of the Sadducees. In effect, He is saying, "Abraham, Isaac, and Jacob, though they died many years ago, are actually living today. For God, who calls Himself the God of Abraham, Isaac, and Jacob, is not the God of the dead but of the living."[32] Jesus' words clearly indicate that these Old Testament patriarchs are living *at the present moment*, even though they "died " physically many years ago.

Notice the words at the end of Luke 20:38: "for all *live* to Him" (emphasis added). What does this mean? Bible scholar Anthony Hoekema answers:

Though the dead seem to us to be completely nonexistent, they are actually living as far as God is concerned. Note that the tense of the word for live is not *future* (which might suggest only that these dead will live at the time of their resurrection) but *present*, teaching us that they are living now. This holds true not only for the patriarchs but for all who have died. To suggest, now, that Abraham, Isaac, and Jacob are nonexistent between death and the resurrection violates the thrust of these words, and implies that God is, with respect to these patriarchs, for a long period of time the God of the dead rather than the God of the living.[33]

___ *Ask...* _____

- Why do you think Jesus referred to God as the "God... of the living" in reference to Abraham, Isaac, and Jacob (Luke 20:38)?

- Why do you think Jesus said of the dead that "all *live*" to God, using a present tense word for "live"— thereby indicating *present-time* living as opposed to a *future* living?

Philippians 1:21-23—*To Depart and Be with Christ*

In Philippians 1:21-23 we read, "For to me, to live is Christ and to die is gain. If I am to go on living in the body, this will mean fruitful labor for me. Yet what shall I choose?... I am torn between the two: I desire to depart and be with Christ, which is better by far."

Now, here's the question that immediately comes to mind: *How could Paul refer to death as "gain" if death meant non-existence?*[34] What the apostle meant by gain is very clear from the context, for he defines it as departing the physical body *to be with Christ*. Being with Christ is far better, Paul says, than remaining in the physical body. (Being in a state of nonexistence, however, cannot be said to be far better by any stretch of the imagination.)

It is important to note that Philippians 1:21-23 is not speaking of a future resurrection at which time Paul will be with Christ. Rather Paul is saying that the very moment after physical death occurs he will be with Christ. How do we know this? It's clear from the Greek text! Without going into too much detail, suffice it to say that an aorist infinitive ("to depart") is linked by a *single article* with a present infinitive ("*to be* with Christ"). The infinitives thus belong together: "The single article ties the two infinitives together, so that the actions depicted by the two infinitives are to be considered two aspects of the same thing, or two sides of the same coin."[35] So Paul is saying that the very moment after he departs the body or dies, he will be with Christ in heaven.

 Ask...

- How could Paul refer to death as gain if death meant nonexistence?

- Doesn't it seem to you that Paul defines what he means by *gain* by his words in verse 23: "I desire to *depart and be with Christ*, which is better by far"?

- Did you know that the construction of the Greek text in verse 23 indicates that *departing* (dying) and *being with Christ* are two sides of the same coin—that is, *being with Christ* occurs immediately after the *departing* takes place?

2 Corinthians 5:6-8—*Absent from the Body; Home with the Lord*

In 2 Corinthians 5:6-8 we read, "Therefore, being always of good courage, and knowing that *while we are at home in the body we are absent from the Lord*—for we walk by faith, not by sight—we are of good courage, I say, and prefer rather *to be absent from the body and to be at home with the Lord*" (NASB, emphasis added).

In the Greek text of this passage, the phrases "at home in the body" and "absent from the Lord" are both *present tense* (which indicates continuing action). We could paraphrase Paul in this way: "Therefore, being always of good courage, and knowing that while we are *continuing to be at home in the body* we are *continuing to be absent from the Lord*."[36]

By contrast, the latter part of the passage contains two *aorist infinitives*: "absent from the body" and "at home with the Lord." Such aorists indicate a sense of "once-for-all." We might paraphrase it, "We are of good courage, I say, and prefer rather to be . . . *absent from the [mortal, perishable] body* and to be *once-for-all at home with the Lord.*"[37]

Regarding all this, Anthony Hoekema comments, "Whereas the present tenses in verse 6 picture a continuing at-homeness in the body and a continuing away-from-homeness as to the Lord, the aorist infinitives of verse 8 point to a once-for-all momentary happening. What can this be? There is only one answer: *death*, which is an immediate transition from being at home in the body to being away from home as to the body."[38] *The moment a Christian dies, he or she is immediately in the presence of Christ.*

It is also noteworthy that the Greek word *pros* is used for "with" in the phrase "be at home *with* the Lord." This word suggests very close (face-to-face) fellowship or intimate relationships. Paul thereby indicates that the fellowship he expects to have with Christ immediately following his physical death will be one of great intimacy.

_____ *Ask...* _____

- What do you think is meant by the phrase "to be absent from the body and to be at home with the Lord" (2 Corinthians 5:8)?

- Did you know that the Greek word translated "with" (in the phrase "to be absent from the body and to be at home *with* the Lord") is one that indicates intimate fellowship?

From the above Scripture passages, it is clear that human beings do indeed possess an immaterial nature that survives physical death. And this immaterial nature enjoys *conscious* existence following death. Try to share as many of these passages as possible with the Jehovah's Witness. The accumulative effect is devastating to the Watchtower position.

Psalm 146:3,4—*Is Man Conscious After Death?*

The Watchtower Teaching. The *New World Translation* renders Psalm 146:3,4, "Do not put your trust in nobles, nor in the son of earthling man, to whom no salvation belongs. His spirit goes out, he goes back to his ground; In that day *his thoughts do perish*" (emphasis added).

Jehovah's Witnesses say this verse proves there is no conscious existence after death. When the spirit is said to go out of the human body, this simply means that the life-force in that person ceases to be active. That is when a person's thoughts supposedly perish. His thought processes *do not continue on* in another realm.[39]

The Biblical Teaching. The Jehovah's Witnesses have grossly misunderstood what is being said in Psalm 146:3,4. It does not say that people will think no thoughts at all following the moment of death. Rather—in context and in consideration of the original Hebrew, according to the authoritative *Theological Wordbook of the Old Testament*[40]—it means that peoples' *plans*, *ambitions*, and *ideas for the future* will cease and come to nought at the moment of death. That is what the Hebrew word for "thoughts" communicates in Psalm 146:3,4. A person's plans and ideas for the future die with him.

As commentator Albert Barnes has noted, a man's "purposes; his schemes; his plans; his purposes of conquest and ambition; his schemes for becoming rich or great; his plans of building a house, and laying out his grounds, and enjoying life; his design of making a book, or taking a journey, or giving himself to ease and pleasure"[41]—*these are the things that perish when a great prince dies*. And because of this, people are urged by the psalmist to put their trust in the One who is infinitely more powerful than any mortal man, including princes—One whose plans do not fail. Putting trust in a mere mortal man can only lead to disappointment, for mortal men die.

Former Jehovah's Witness David Reed suggests the following analogy from modern times:

> An actual example of the lesson of Psalm 146 is found in the death of President John F. Kennedy. He was a "prince" whom many people trusted to help them improve their lot in life. Yet, when he died, "all his thoughts did perish"—with him gone, *his plans and programs soon collapsed*. People who had put all their trust in him were disappointed. Their primary trust should have been in God, who offers real hope, justice, healing, and salvation—and who remains King forever.[42]

Clearly, Psalm 146 cannot be used to support the erroneous idea that there is no conscious existence after death. It is man's plans and ambitions—not his consciousness—that perishes at death.

_____ Ask... _____

- Since the Hebrew word for "thoughts" carries the idea of plans, doesn't it make sense to interpret the psalmist's words as meaning that peoples' *plans* and *ambitions* cease and come to nought at the moment of death?

Ecclesiastes 9:5—*The Dead Know Nothing?*

The Watchtower Teaching. The *New World Translation* renders Ecclesiastes 9:5, "For the living are conscious that they will die; but as for the dead, *they are conscious of nothing at all*, neither do they anymore have wages, because the remembrance of them has been forgotten" (emphasis added). Since the dead are "conscious of nothing at all," the Watchtower Society argues, it is also obvious that people feel no pain or pleasure whatsoever following death.[43]

The Biblical Teaching. While evangelical scholars interpret Ecclesiastes 9:5 in different ways, *all of them* agree that the verse is *not* teaching that man does not have a conscious existence following death. Let us briefly look at the two major viewpoints:

1) It is well known that the Book of Ecclesiastes presents two contrasting ways of looking at man's plight in the world. One is the secular, humanistic, materialistic viewpoint that interprets all things from a limited earthly perspective—not recognizing God or His involvement in man's affairs. This earthly perspective is one completely unaided by divine revelation.[44]

The other perspective is a godly, spiritual one that interprets life and its problems from a God-honoring viewpoint. This viewpoint takes divine revelation into account when interpreting life and its problems. This perspective triumphs at the end of the book.[45]

Now, this is what I want to emphasize: There are many scholars who interpret Ecclesiastes 9:1-10 as reflecting the *earthly* perspective that is unaided by divine revelation.[46] To prove that these verses express a strictly human perspective, David Reed suggests the following:

> Not only does the writer say in verse 5 that the dead know nothing, but he also adds that "they have no more *for ever* any share in all that is done under the sun" (v. 6, RSV, emphasis added). (Ask the Jehovah's Witness if he

believes that the dead are gone *forever*. He will answer *no*, because he believes in a future resurrection to this earth under the sun.) Verse 2 (RSV) expresses the thought that "one fate comes to all, to the righteous and the wicked, to the good and the evil," an idea contradictory to all the rest of Scripture. (Ask the Witness if he believes that he will receive the same fate, whether he is righteous or wicked. His answer will have to be *no*.) . . . We conclude that verse 5 is located in the midst of a section expressing the faithless, secular viewpoint—not God's.[47]

Since Ecclesiastes 9:1-10 expresses a strictly human perspective, then verse 5 indicates that *from a strictly human viewpoint*, the dead are conscious of nothing at all. This being the case, the verse does not teach *God's truth*. And this being so, the verse cannot be used to support the contention that there is no conscious existence after death.

_____ *Ask* . . . _____

- Did you know that the Book of Ecclesiastes presents two contrasting viewpoints—one that is strictly humanistic, and another that is spiritual and God-honoring?

- If, as many scholars believe, Ecclesiastes 9:1-10 reflects the strictly humanistic viewpoint, can you see how the statement in verse 5 reflects not *God's* perspective but *fallen humanity's* perspective?

Watchtower expert Marian Bodine raises one further point (which is similar to David Reed's) regarding this verse. She says, "If the phrase, 'know not anything,' means the dead are unconscious in the grave or spirit world, then [the phrase] 'neither have they anymore reward' means there will be no resurrection or rewards after 'this' life."[48] If the Jehovah's Witnesses are consistent, this is what one must conclude.

Ask...

- If the phrase "know not anything" (Ecclesiastes 9:5 NASB) means the dead are unconscious in the grave, then doesn't the phrase "nor have they any longer a reward" mean there will be no resurrection or rewards after this life—even for Jehovah's Witnesses?

You can use this question to strengthen your point that the statement in Ecclesiastes 9:5 reflects not *God's* perspective but an *earthly, human* perspective.

2) There are other evangelical scholars who interpret Ecclesiastes 9:5 as meaning that the dead are not conscious of events taking place *in the physical realm.* In their commentary, Robert Jamieson, A.R. Fausset, and David Brown say that the dead know nothing "so far as their bodily senses and worldly affairs are concerned (Job 14:21; Isa. 63:16)."[49] We likewise read in H.C. Leupold's commentary on Ecclesiastes that the writer in this verse "is only expressing the relation of the dead to this world."[50] Nevertheless, the dead *are still* conscious of things not associated with the physical, earthly realm.

Whichever interpretation you choose, it is clear that Ecclesiastes 9:5 cannot be cited as a proof of the Watchtower view. The Watchtower Society is reading something into the text that simply is not there.

Ezekiel 18:4—*Death for the Soul?*

The Watchtower Teaching. Ezekiel 18:4 in the *New World Translation* reads, "Look! All the souls—to me they belong. As the soul of the father so likewise the soul of the son—to me they belong. *The soul that is sinning—it itself will die*" (emphasis added). *Reasoning from the Scriptures* cites this verse in answer to the question, Is there some part of man that lives on when the body dies? The answer, of course, is no.[51]

The Watchtower Society points out that some translations of this verse say, "*The man* that is sinning . . . will die" or, "*the one* that is sinning . . . will die" or, "*the person* that is sinning . . . will die."[52] Hence, the word "soul" (Hebrew: *nephesh*) refers not to the immaterial nature of man but to the actual living person. The soul is *not* something that survives the death of the body, we are told.

The Biblical Teaching. The statement in Ezekiel 18:4 that "the soul who sins . . . will die" does not go against the idea that man has an immaterial nature that consciously survives death. In the present context, it is true that the Hebrew word for soul (*nephesh*) is used in the sense of "living being" or "person." This is not disputed by evangelicals. (As noted earlier, in certain contexts *nephesh* means "living being"; it can also have other meanings—such as the "inner person" of a human being.)

Evangelicals point out that since man's immaterial nature is not discussed in Ezekiel 18:4, we cannot draw *conclusions* about it, pro or con, from this verse. All Ezekiel was intending to do was to combat a false teaching that had arisen in his day—a teaching related to the doctrine of inherited guilt. Some people were arguing that children were suffering and dying because of the sins of their fathers. While it is true that there is an accumulative effect of sin (*see* Exodus 20:5,6), Ezekiel's point in this verse was to emphasize that each individual is accountable for his *own* sin. That's why he said that the soul (or person) who sins will die. He wasn't attempting to teach anything about man's *possession* or *lack of* an immaterial nature.

Though the Hebrew word *nephesh* is used in Ezekiel 18:4 in reference to a "living being" or "person," there are other passages in the Old Testament where the word is used in a different sense. For example, in Genesis 35:18 *nephesh* can be interpreted to refer to man's immaterial nature: "And it came about *as her soul was departing* (for she died), that she named him Ben-oni; but his father called him Benjamin"[53] (emphasis added). This verse seems to recognize the soul as distinct from the physical body, which dies. Remember too in our discussion of Genesis 2:7 (see pages 308-19) we saw there are many, many New Testament passages that prove beyond any doubt that man has an immaterial nature (*see*, for example, 2 Corinthians ians 5:8-10 and Revelation 6:9-11).

For Ezekiel 18:4, ask the Jehovah's Witness the same questions that are listed in the extensive discussion under Genesis 2:7 (pages 308-19).

Luke 16:22-28—*Abraham's Bosom*

The Watchtower Teaching. In Luke 16:22-28 we read Jesus' words about the rich man and Lazarus. Both men died and went to Hades. Lazarus was in peace in the "paradise" compartment of Hades (Abraham's bosom), while the rich man was in the "torments" compartment. They were separated by a great gulf. The rich man, who was suffering, requested Father Abraham to "send Lazarus to dip the tip of his finger in water and cool my tongue" (verse 24). Abraham refused the request, for the rich man was suffering justly.

Jehovah's Witnesses say this teaching of Jesus is entirely symbolic and does not indicate conscious existence after death. They argue that this passage is a parable. Indeed, *The Jerusalem Bible* is cited, which says, This is a "parable in story form without reference to any historical personage."[54] If taken literally, this passage would mean that all of God's people could fit at the bosom of one man—Abraham. Also, the water on a man's fingertip is portrayed as not being evaporated by the fire of Hades—and this single drop of water is supposed to bring relief to a suffering man. The Watchtower Society asks, *Does this sound reasonable to you?*[55] Obviously this is not to be taken literally.

If this parable is not to be taken literally, what, then, does it mean? The Watchtower Society says that the rich man symbolizes the Jewish religious leaders—the Pharisees. Lazarus is a picture of the Jewish followers of Jesus—people who had been despised by the Pharisees and who repented to follow Jesus. (Some of these became the apostles of Jesus.) Abraham pictures Jehovah-God.

The death of each of these "people" pictures a change of conditions for each group while here on earth.[56] Those who had once been despised came into a position of divine favor. By contrast, those who had been seemingly favored were rejected by Jehovah-God, and became "tormented" by the proclamations delivered by the ones they had despised (the apostles).[57] In other words, the torments of the rich man pictures the *public exposure* of the hypocritical Jewish religious leaders by the preaching of the apostles.

The Biblical Teaching. The Watchtower interpretation of Luke 16:22-28 shows the lengths the Jehovah's Witnesses are willing to go to deny that man has an immaterial nature that consciously survives death. Think about it for a minute: If at death people simply lapse into a state of nonexistence or unconsciousness, then *what is the point of Luke 16:22-28?* Are we to conclude that Jesus was teaching something based entirely on a *falsehood*—something that is wholly untrue in every way? If the rich man and Lazarus were not conscious after death, then the answer would have to be yes.

Scholars have noted that when Jesus taught people using parables or stories, *He always used real-life situations*. For example, as David Reed notes, "a prodigal son returned home after squandering his money; a man found a buried treasure in a field, hid it again, and sold everything he had in order to buy that field; a king put on a wedding feast for his son; a slave-owner traveled abroad and then returned home to his slaves; a man constructed a vineyard, leased it out to others, but had difficulty collecting what they owed him; and so on."[58] All of these were common occurrences in biblical days!

Clearly, Jesus never illustrated His teaching with a falsehood. We must conclude that Luke 16 portrays a real-life situation and should be taken as solid evidence for conscious existence after death. Any other interpretation makes an absurdity of the text.

After sharing the above with the Jehovah's Witness:

_____ *Ask...* _____

- Do you believe Jesus illustrated His teachings with falsehoods? (The answer will be no.)

- Since Jesus was *absolutely consistent* in using real-life situations to illustrate His teachings, what does this tell you about His words in Luke 16?

- If the Watchtower's interpretation of Luke 16 is correct, then how can we *not* conclude that Jesus was being utterly deceptive with His words—since at face value they indicate conscious existence after death?

Luke 23:43—*With Christ in Paradise*

The Watchtower Teaching. The *New World Translation* renders Luke 23:43, "And he said to him: 'Truly I tell you today, you will be with me in Paradise.'" This is in contrast to, for example, the New American Standard Bible, which renders this verse, "Truly I say to you, today you shall be with Me in Paradise."

Notice that in the *New World Translation* the comma is placed after the word "today," not after "you," as in the New American Standard Bible (and all other translations). Jehovah's Witnesses do this to keep the thief from being with Jesus in Paradise "today" (which would mean that there is conscious existence after death). Instead, they make it appear that Jesus' *statement* to the thief about Paradise took place "today."[59]

How do we determine which translation is correct? Jehovah's Witnesses answer that the teachings of Christ and of the rest of Scripture must determine which is right. And since Scripture is clear that there is no conscious existence after death (Psalm 146:3,4), it is obvious that Jesus did not say, "Today you will be with me in Paradise," as if He and the thief would be in

Paradise the same day as their deaths.[60] Rather, Jesus' *statement* to the thief took place "today."

The Biblical Teaching. This is a clear case of the Jehovah's Witnesses changing the Bible in order to fit their doctrines. Without any warrant whatsoever, they have forced a comma into a part of the sentence that changes entirely the intended meaning of Jesus' words.

It is helpful to observe how the phrase, "Truly, I say to you" is used elsewhere in Scripture. This phrase—which translates the Greek words *amen soi lego*—occurs 74 times in the Gospels and is always used as an introductory expression. It is somewhat similar to the Old Testament phrase, "Thus says the Lord."[61] Jesus used this phrase to introduce a truth that was very important.

Now here's the important point: In 73 out of the 74 times the phrase occurs in the Gospels, the *New World Translation* places a break—such as a comma—immediately after the phrase, "Truly, I tell you."[62] Luke 23:43 is the *only* occurrence of this phrase in which the *New World Translation* does not place a break after it. Why? Because if a break—such as a comma— was placed after "Truly, I say to you," the word "today" would then belong to the second half of the sentence, indicating that "today" the thief would be with Jesus in Paradise. But this would go against Watchtower theology. Hence, the relocated comma.

_____ *Ask* . . . _____

- Did you know that 73 out of 74 times in the New Testament, the *New World Translation* correctly places a break—such as a comma—immediately after the phrase, "Truly, I tell you"?

- Don't you think it's best to be consistent when translating Scripture?

- To be consistent, don't you think Luke 23:43 should be translated, "Truly I say to you, today you shall be with Me in Paradise"?

Apologist Robert Bowman notes that if Jesus had really wanted to say, "Truly, I say to you *today*," He could have done this very clearly by using a different construction in the Greek language.[63] But based upon the usage of *amen soi lego* throughout Scripture, it is clear that the word "today" belongs with the second part of the sentence, not the first.

_____ *Ask*... _____

- Did you know that if Jesus had really wanted to say, "Truly I say to you *today*," He could have done this very easily by using a different construction in the Greek language?

Related to all this, Watchtower expert Marian Bodine points out that the phrase, "Truly, I say to you *today*," does not make good sense: "It would have been needless to say, 'Today, I am telling this to you.' Of course He was! What other day would He have been speaking to the thief on? Jesus never added the word 'today' when speaking to anyone."[64]

Now, according to orthodox scholars, this thief apparently believed that Jesus would eventually come into His kingdom *at the end of the world*. He therefore asked to be remembered by Jesus at that time. Jesus' reply, however, promised him more than he had asked for: "*Today* [not just at the end of the world] you will be with me in Paradise."[65]

And what is this "Paradise"? First-century Jews believed Paradise was a place of blessedness occupied by the souls of righteous people who had physically died.[66] This place of blessing was considered to be a compartment in Hades. Thus, when Jesus promised the thief that he would go to Paradise, He was promising the thief that he would be in the blessed resting place of the righteous dead. Later, at the Ascension, Christ took the occupants of this compartment to heaven with Him (2 Corinthians 12:4).[67]

From the above, it is clear that Luke 23:43 argues strongly against the Watchtower position that there is no immaterial nature that consciously survives death. As is true with other Bible verses, a thorough look at the text unmasks the Watchtower deception.

Matthew 25:46—Everlasting "Cutting Off"?

The Watchtower Teaching. Matthew 25:46 in the *New World Translation* reads, "And these will depart *into everlasting cutting-off*, but the righteous ones into everlasting life" (emphasis added). This is in contrast to, for example, the New American Standard Bible, which renders this verse, "And these will go away *into eternal punishment*, but the righteous into eternal life" (emphasis added). Jehovah's Witnesses conclude from this verse, based on the *New World Translation*, that there is no eternal conscious punishment for the wicked. Rather, they are forever "cut off."

The Watchtower Society argues that one meaning of the Greek word *kolasin* is "to cut off; as lopping off branches of trees, to prune."[68] Hence, "to cut off an individual from life, or society . . . is esteemed as *punishment*."[69] Indeed, the punishment of the wicked will be "a wiping out of existence as an eternal punishment."[70]

The Biblical Teaching. As noted above, the New American Standard Bible translates Matthew 25:46, "And these will go away into eternal punishment, but the righteous into eternal life." Notice that this translation has the words "eternal punishment" instead of the *New World Translation*'s "everlasting cutting-off." The Greek words in question are *aionios* (eternal) and *kolasis* (punishment).

Regarding the second word, it is true that the stem of *kolasis* (*kolazoo*) originally meant "pruning." But Greek scholars universally agree that there is no justification for the translation "cutting-off" in Matthew 25:46. The authoritative *Greek-English Lexicon of the New Testament* by William Arndt and

F. Wilbur Gingrich says the meaning of *kolasis* in Matthew 25:46 is "punishment."[71] This meaning is confirmed by Moulton and Milligan's *The Vocabulary of the Greek New Testament*,[72] Joseph Thayer's *Greek-English Lexicon of the New Testament*,[73] Gerhard Kittel's *Theological Dictionary of the New Testament*,[74] and many others.

_____ *Ask...* _____

- Did you know that Greek scholars universally agree that "punishment" is the correct rendering in Matthew 25:46, not "cutting-off"?

The punishment spoken of in Matthew 25:46 cannot be defined as a nonsuffering extinction of consciousness. Indeed, if actual suffering is lacking, then so is punishment. Let us be clear on this: *punishment entails suffering*. And suffering necessarily entails consciousness.[75] Bible scholar John Gerstner comments, "One can exist and not be punished; but no one can be punished and not exist. Annihilation means the obliteration of existence and anything that pertains to existence, such as punishment. Annihilation avoids punishment, rather than encountering it."[76]

_____ *Ask...* _____

- Doesn't it seem reasonable to you that punishment and suffering must necessarily involve consciousness?

- Doesn't annihilation *avoid* punishment rather than *encountering* it?

How do we know that the punishment in Matthew 25:46 does not entail an extinction of consciousness and annihilation?

There are many evidences. For example, consider the fact that there are no *degrees* of annihilation. As Bible scholar Alan Gomes explains it, "one is either annihilated or one is not. In contrast, the Scripture teaches that there will be degrees of punishment on the day of judgment (Matt. 10:15; 11:21-24; 16:27; Luke 12:47-48; John 15:22; Heb. 10:29; Rev. 20:11-15; 22:12, etc.)."[77] The very fact that people will suffer varying degrees of punishment in hell shows that annihilation or the extinction of consciousness is not taught in Matthew 25:46 or anywhere else in Scripture. These are incompatible concepts.

_____ *Ask...* _____

- How do you reconcile the clear scriptural teaching that the wicked will suffer varying degrees of punishment with the Watchtower teaching of the annihilation of the wicked?

Moreover, one cannot deny that for a person who is suffering excruciating pain, the extinction of his or her consciousness would actually be a blessing, not a punishment (cf. Luke 23:30,31; Revelation 9:6). As theologian William Shedd notes, "The guilty and remorseful have, in all ages, deemed the extinction of consciousness after death to be a blessing; but the advocate of conditional immortality explains it to be a curse."[78] Any honest seeker after truth must admit that one cannot define eternal punishment as an extinction of consciousness.

Torment cannot, by definition, be anything *but* conscious torment. One cannot torment a tree, a rock, or a house. By its very nature, being tormented requires consciousness. Alan Gomes comments, "A punishment [such as torment] that is not felt is not a punishment. It is an odd use of language to speak of an insensate (i.e., unfeeling), inanimate object receiving punishment. To say, 'I punished my car for not starting by slowly plucking out its sparkplug wires, one by one,' would evoke laughter, not serious consideration."[79] We repeat, then, that punishment entails consciousness!

Note also in Matthew 25:46 that this punishment is said to be *eternal*. There is no way that annihilationism or an extinction of consciousness can be forced into this passage. Indeed, the adjective *aionion* in this verse means "everlasting, without end." You might want to point out to the Jehovah's Witness that this same adjective is predicated of God (the "eternal" God) in Romans 16:26, 1 Timothy 1:7, Hebrews 9:14, 13:8, and Revelation 4:9. *The punishment of the wicked is just as eternal as the forever existence of our eternal God.* Moreover, as Professor Gomes notes,

> What is particularly determinative here is the fact that the duration of punishment for the wicked forms a parallel with the duration of life for the righteous: the adjective *aionios* is used to describe both the length of punishment for the wicked and the length of eternal life for the righteous. One cannot limit the duration of punishment for the wicked without at the same time limiting the duration of eternal life for the redeemed. It would do violence to the parallel to give it an unlimited signification in the case of eternal life, but a limited one when applied to the punishment of the wicked.[80]

___ *Ask . . .* ___

- Since the same Greek word for "eternal" in the phrase "eternal punishment" is used to describe the eternality of God (Romans 16:26; 1 Timothy 1:7; Hebrews 9:14; 13:8; Revelation 4:9), doesn't it make sense that the punishment of the wicked will be just as eternal as God is?

- Since the same Greek word for "eternal" in the phrase "eternal punishment" in Matthew 25:46 is used in the phrase "eternal life" (same verse), doesn't this indicate that the punishment of the wicked is just as eternal as the life of the righteous?

In view of the above factors, the Watchtower's view that Matthew 25:46 teaches annihilationism must be rejected. In fact, we must conclude this is one of the clearest passages in the Bible that teaches eternal punishment of the wicked.

2 Thessalonians 1:9—*Everlasting Destruction?*

The Watchtower Teaching. The *New World Translation* renders 2 Thessalonians 1:9, "These very ones will undergo the judicial punishment of *everlasting destruction* from before the Lord and from the glory of his strength" (emphasis added). The destruction of the wicked, Jehovah's Witnesses say, is everlasting in the sense that they are forever annihilated and cease to exist.[81] They do not suffer eternal torment.

The Biblical Teaching. The New American Standard Bible translates this verse, "And these will pay the penalty of *eternal destruction*, away from the presence of the Lord and from the glory of His power" (emphasis added). Contrary to the Watchtower's understanding of this verse, annihilation is not in view here. The Greek word translated "destruction" in this verse is *olethros*, and carries the meaning "sudden ruin," or "loss of all that gives worth to existence."[82] New Testament scholar Robert L. Thomas says that *olethros* "does not refer to annihilation . . . but rather turns on the thought of separation from God and loss of everything worthwhile in life. . . . Just as endless life belongs to Christians, endless destruction belongs to those opposed to Christ."[83]

Along these same lines, commentator David A. Hubbard notes that "annihilation is not the thought but rather total ruin, the loss of everything worthwhile. Specifically, it is separation from the presence (*face*) of the Lord, the true source of all good things."[84] Hence, the "destruction" suffered by the wicked does not involve a cessation of existence, but rather a continual and perpetual state of ruination.

_____ *Ask* . . . _____

- Did you know that the Greek word translated "destruction" in 2 Thessalonians 1:9 carries the idea of a perpetual state of *ruination*, not annihilation?

Notice too that the word "eternal" (*aionion*) is used in conjunction with "destruction." Now, it is obvious that annihilation, by definition, must take place *instantly*—in a mere moment. It makes virtually no sense to say that the wicked will suffer "endless annihilation."[85] Rather, 2 Thessalonians 1:9 is saying that the wicked will suffer a ruin which is everlasting— a punishment that will never end.

_____ *Ask* . . . _____

- Since by definition annihilation must take place in an instant, wouldn't it be senseless to say that the wicked will suffer "endless annihilation"?

Revelation 14:9-11—*Tormented with Fire?*

The Watchtower Teaching. The *New World Translation* renders Revelation 14:9-11, "And another angel, a third, followed them, saying in a loud voice: 'If anyone worships the wild beast and its image, and receives a mark on his forehead or upon his hand, he will also drink of the wine of the anger of God that is poured out undiluted into the cup of his wrath, and he shall be *tormented with fire and sulphur* in the sight of the holy angels and in the sight of the Lamb. And *the smoke of their torment ascends forever and ever, and day and night they have no rest*, those who worship the wild beast and its image, and whoever receives the mark of its name'" (emphasis added).

The book *Reasoning from the Scriptures* asks, What is the "torment" to which this passage refers? The book answers by pointing to Revelation 11:10, where reference is made to "prophets that torment those dwelling on the earth." Ungodly people on earth experience torment as a result of the humiliating exposure they go through because of the message the prophets proclaim.

It is true, Jehovah's Witnesses say, that worshipers of the "beast" are said to be "tormented with fire and brimstone." However, this cannot refer to eternal conscious torment after death because, as Ecclesiastes 9:5 tells us, "the dead know not any thing." Revelation 14, then, is explained as referring to the torment individuals suffer while *still living*. And what causes the torment? It is simply *the message of God's servants* that worshipers of the beast will experience the second death—represented by the "lake which burnest with fire and brimstone."[86]

Does the smoke that rises forever mean that the suffering of these individuals must be eternal? Not at all, the Watchtower Society says. This symbolic reference simply indicates that their destruction will be eternal and will never be forgotten.[87]

The Biblical Teaching. A look at the Greek text of Revelation 14 shows that the torment is not related to a mere message of God's prophets, but to real, genuine physical pain. The Greek word for "torment" in this verse is *basanizo*. Joseph Thayer's lexicon says the word means "to vex with grievous pains... to torment."[88] Likewise, Arndt and Gingrich's lexicon says the word means "to torture, torment."[89] When one examines the way this word is used throughout Scripture, it becomes plain that it is always used in contexts of great pain and conscious misery.

You might mention to the Jehovah's Witness that the same word for "torment" is used to speak of the pains of childbirth in Revelation 12:2. It is also used of the centurion's sick servant being grievously tormented by palsy in Matthew 8:6. It is used in Luke 16:23 and 28 to describe the physical suffering of the rich man in Hades.[90] Clearly, the word communicates the idea of horrendous physical pain.

Now, the "torment" in Revelation 14 is described as a *never-ending* torment: "And the smoke of their torment rises *for ever and ever*. There is no rest day or night" (verse 11). The words "for ever and ever" translate an emphatic Greek phrase, *eis aionas aionon* ("unto the ages of the ages"). The twofold use of the term *aionas* is used in Scripture to emphasize the concept of eternity. And the plural forms ("unto the *ages* of the *ages*") reinforces the idea of never-ending duration. Lutheran scholar R.C.H. Lenski comments,

> The strongest expression for our "forever" is *eis tous aionan ton aionon*, "for the eons of eons"; many eons, each of vast duration, are multiplied by many more, which we imitate by "forever and ever." Human language is able to use only temporal terms to express what is altogether beyond time and timeless. The Greek takes its greatest term for time, the eon, pluralizes this, and then multiplies it by its own plural, even using articles which make these eons the definite ones.[91]

This same emphatic construction is used to speak of the never-ending worship of God in Revelation 1:6, 4:9, and 5:3. It is also used to describe the eternality of God in Revelation 4:10 and 10:6. We cannot emphasize too strongly that this phrase shows beyond doubt that the physical torment of the wicked is forever and ever and ever.

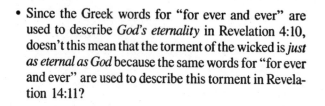

_____ *Ask...* _____

- Since the Greek words for "for ever and ever" are used to describe *God's eternality* in Revelation 4:10, doesn't this mean that the torment of the wicked is *just as eternal as God* because the same words for "for ever and ever" are used to describe this torment in Revelation 14:11?

The use of the words "day and night" (NASB) is also significant (in the phrase "they have no rest day and night" [NASB]). Gomes comments: "The expression 'day and night' is indicative of ceaseless activity. This same phrase is used of the never-ending worship of God in Revelation 4:8 and 7:15. By juxtaposing the words 'day and night' with 'forever and ever' in 20:10 [another passage dealing with eternal torment], we have the most emphatic expression of unending, ceaseless activity possible in the Greek language."[92]

Note, also, that if annihilation is the fate of the wicked, they indeed would experience "rest." But our text in Revelation 14:11 specifically says they have no rest *forever*. Clearly, then, the language of Revelation 14 emphatically points to the eternal, *conscious* suffering of the wicked.

_____ *Ask...* _____

- How can a person who has been annihilated experience "no rest" *forever*?

In closing, it is vital to note that many of the most graphic descriptions we have of the eternal perdition of the lost come from the very lips of Jesus.[93] And what He taught on the eternal suffering of the lost, He communicated very clearly. One must therefore ask, "Had Christ wished to teach the annihilation of the wicked, is it reasonable that He would have selected language guaranteed to lead His church astray?"[94] Jehovah's Witnesses must be made to face the implications of that question.

13

Prophecy and the Watchtower Society: A History of Failures

When a prophet speaks in the name of the LORD, if the thing does not come about or come true, that is the thing which the LORD has not spoken.

—Deuteronomy 18:22
(NASB)

Throughout its history, the Watchtower Society has claimed to be God's prophet on earth today. According to *The Watchtower* magazine, "the 'prophet' whom Jehovah has raised up has been, not an individual man as in the case of Jeremiah, but a class."[1] The Watchtower Society is God's "prophetlike organization."[2]

Is there a way to really be sure that the Watchtower Society is God's prophet on earth? In answer to this question, the Watchtower Society itself invites people to test the prophecies of the organization. *The Watchtower* magazine boasts, "Of course, it is easy to say that this group acts as a 'prophet' of God. It is another thing to prove it. The only way that this can be done is to review the record. What does it show?"[3] Another issue of the magazine says that "the best method of proof is to put a prophecy to the test of time and circumstances. The Bible invites such a test . . . the Bible . . . established the rules for testing a prophecy at Deuteronomy 18:20-22."[4]

339

Deuteronomy 18:20-22 reads, "The prophet who shall speak a word presumptuously in My name which I have not commanded him to speak, or which he shall speak in the name of other gods, that prophet shall die. And you may say in your heart, 'How shall we know the word which the LORD has not spoken?' When a prophet speaks in the name of the LORD, if the thing does not come about or come true, that is the thing which the LORD has not spoken. The prophet has spoken it presumptuously; you shall not be afraid of him." Hence, a true prophet of God will be known by his prophecies that come to pass.

Jehovah's Witnesses in the past have affirmed that if a prophet utters prophecies that do not come to pass, then that means he is a false prophet. The Watchtower publication *Light*, for example, says that for prophets whose prophecies fail to come to pass, "that alone is strong evidence that they are false prophets."[5] Another Watchtower publication notes that "if these prophecies have not been fulfilled, and if all possibility of fulfillment is past, then these prophets are proven false."[6]

God will make sure that false prophets are exposed, we are told. Indeed, the Watchtower publication *Paradise Restored to Mankind—By Theocracy* tells us: "Jehovah . . . will put all false prophets to shame either by not fulfilling the false prediction of such self-assuming prophets or by having His own prophecies fulfilled in a way opposite to that predicted by the false prophets."[7]

However, the Watchtower Society now admits that it was wrong in its prediction for 1874 (the second coming of Christ), 1925 (the coming of select Old Testament saints to earth), 1975 (the end of human history), and other times.[8] Yet in the Watchtower's *1975 Yearbook* the Society makes the claim that for over a century the Jehovah's Witnesses have "enjoyed spiritual enlightenment and direction."[9] How can this be? The Watchtower Society itself has told us how a false prophet can be recognized, and by that criteria, the Society has proven itself a false prophet. How, then, can it be said that Jehovah's Witnesses have "enjoyed spiritual enlightenment and direction" by following the Society?

_____ *Ask...* _____

- How can it be said that Jehovah's Witnesses have "enjoyed spiritual enlightenment and direction" by following the Watchtower Society when the Society was wrong in its predictions for 1874, 1925, 1975, and other times?

_____

Despite its many failed predictions, the Watchtower Society refuses to concede that it is a false prophet. The Society argues that "the need to revise our understanding somewhat does not make us false prophets."[10] Besides, Watchtower leaders point out, they are not *infallible* or *inspired* prophets.[11] Thus, some mistakes are allowable. Some of the biblical prophets held mistaken views and yet they were not condemned as false. Neither should the Watchtower Society be condemned for its errors, we are told.

In this chapter we will see that prophecy in Watchtower literature focuses primarily on the spiritual/invisible "second coming" of Christ, the preaching of the "good news of the Kingdom" (which is the "good news" that Christ has spiritually come again in 1914), and that all the prophecies in Scripture—including those dealing with Armageddon—will take place before "this [1914] generation" passes away (Matthew 24:34). But we cannot discuss the Watchtower's history of prophetic speculation without touching on the Great Pyramid of Egypt. Let us turn briefly to this prophetic embarrassment in Watchtower history.

The Great Pyramid of Egypt

An examination of early Watchtower literature reveals that the Witness leaders once believed that the Great Pyramid of Egypt contained prophetic wisdom from God. Indeed, Charles Taze Russell was convinced that God had purposely designed the pyramid as an indicator of the end times. The pyramid was likened to a "Bible in stone." In his *Studies in the Scriptures*, Russell wrote,

> Then measuring *down* the "Entrance Passage" from that point, to find the distance to the entrance of the "Pit," representing the great trouble and destruction with which this age is to close, when evil will be overthrown from power, we find it to be 3416 inches, symbolizing 3416 years from the above date, B.C. 1542. This calculation shows A.D. 1874 as marking the beginning of the period of trouble; for 1542 years B.C. plus 1874 was the *chronological* beginning of the time of trouble such as was not since there was a nation—no, nor ever shall be afterward.[12]

As noted earlier, Watchtower leaders now admit that the 1874 date was wrong.

Upon his death in 1916, Russell was buried underneath a massive pyramid-shaped grave marker.[13] Following Russell's death, the pyramid doctrine continued to be taught by the Watchtower Society. For those who doubt this, one might want to consult the May 15, 1925, issue of *The Watchtower* magazine, in which we read of the pyramid: "Its testimony speaks with great eloquence concerning the divine plan."[14]

It wasn't until 1928 that Joseph Rutherford, Russell's successor, renounced this "Bible in stone" doctrine. This means that the doctrine was taught by the Watchtower Society for almost fifty years before it was discarded (1879 to 1928).

In 1928, the Society completely reversed its teaching. Instead of calling it a "Bible in stone," it was now called "Satan's Bible." The November 15, 1928, issue of *The Watchtower* magazine comments, "It is more reasonable to conclude that the great pyramid of Gizeh, as well as the other pyramids thereabout, also the sphinx, were built by the rulers of Egypt and under the direction of Satan the Devil. . . . Then Satan put his knowledge in dead stone, which may be called Satan's Bible, and not God's stone witness."[15]

_____ *Ask...* _____

- Did you know that Charles Taze Russell and the Watchtower Society in its early years said the Great Pyramid in Egypt was God's "Bible in stone," and that later the Watchtower Society changed its position, calling the Great Pyramid "Satan's Bible"?

- How do you reconcile this with the Watchtower's claim to be a true prophet of God and "channel of truth"?

A History of Errors

The Watchtower Society's history of prophetic speculation can be summed up in two words: consistent error. Former Jehovah's Witness David Reed reflects, "Although condemning others as false prophets, they themselves predicted that the world would end in 1914; later, that the patriarchs Abraham, Isaac, and Jacob would rise from the grave in 1925; and, more recently, that the world would end and the thousand-year-reign of Christ would begin in 1975."[16]

Most Jehovah's Witnesses today are unaware of the magnitude of these false predictions. Indeed, Reed says, "Most Jehovah's Witnesses have no idea that these things happened, or else, they have heard a vague, sugar-coated version."[17]

Let us now examine how the Watchtower Society has consistently been wrong in its prophetic speculations. In your witnessing encounters with Jehovah's Witnesses, some of the following facts will help you to undermine the Watchtower Society's claim to be a "prophet of God."

1874—The Second Coming of Christ?

Early in its history, the Watchtower Society declared that the Second Coming of Christ occurred in October 1874. Jehovah's Witnesses do not like to admit this, since the Society now teaches that Christ "returned" invisibly in 1914. But the evidence is irrefutable. The original date for Christ's return, according to Watchtower literature, was undeniably 1874.

For those who may be skeptical of this, the following references are a representative sampling of early Watchtower literature on this subject:

- Charles Taze Russell's *Studies in the Scriptures* (volume 4) says, "Our Lord, the appointed King, is now present, since October 1874 A.D. . . . and the formal inauguration of his kingly office dates from April 1878, A.D."[18]
- The Watchtower publication *Creation* said that "the second coming of the Lord therefore began in 1874. . . ."[19]
- The Watchtower publication *Prophecy* says that "the Scriptural proof is that the second presence of the Lord Jesus Christ began in 1874 A.D."[20]
- A 1922 issue of *The Watchtower* magazine said, "No one can properly understand the work of God at this time who does not realize that since 1874, the time of the Lord's return in power, there has been a complete change in God's operations."[21]

1914—The Invisible Coming of Christ

Despite the fact that early Watchtower literature assured people that Christ returned in 1874, the Society later argued that the invisible Second Coming of Christ occurred in 1914. The following quotations are a sampling of the Watchtower books that reflect this date switch:

- *The Truth Shall Make You Free* states that "Christ Jesus came to the Kingdom in A.D. 1914, but unseen to men."[22]
- *"Let God Be True"* tells us that "Jesus foretold many things that would mark the time of his invisible presence and the setting up of God's kingdom. The end of the Gentile Times or 'appointed times of the nations' in 1914 was the time for these to begin appearing."[23]

• *Man's Salvation Out of World Distress At Hand!* speaks of people who "refuse to discern the invisible, spiritual 'presence' of Jesus Christ in Kingdom power since the close of the Gentile Times in 1914."[24]

_____ *Ask...* _____

• Why did early Watchtower literature teach that the Second Coming of Christ occurred in 1874, while later literature from the Society taught that it happened in 1914?

• Do true prophets of God change their minds like this?

Watchtower literature was also very clear that 1914 would mark the overthrow of human governments and the full establishment of the Kingdom of God on earth. Note the following damning quotes:

• Charles Taze Russell's *Studies in the Scriptures* (volume 2, 1888) said that "within the coming twenty-six years all present governments will be overthrown and dissolved. . . . The full establishment of the Kingdom of God will be accomplished by the end of A.D. 1914."[25] (Note that in later editions of this publication—after 1914—the phrase "*by* the end of A.D. 1914" was changed to "*near* the end of A.D. 1915."[26])

• *Studies in the Scriptures* (volume 3, 1891) refers to "the full establishment of the Kingdom of God in the earth at A.D. 1914."[27]

• *Studies in the Scriptures* (volume 3—1913 edition) states, "That the deliverance of the saints must take place *some time before 1914* is manifest. . . . Just how long *before* 1914 the last living members of the body of Christ will be glorified, we are not directly informed."[28] (Note that the 1923 edition reads, "That the deliverance of the saints must take place *very soon after 1914* is manifest. . . . Just how long *after* 1914 the last living members of the body of Christ will be glorified, we are not directly informed"[29] [emphasis added].)

Ask...

- Why didn't the overthrow of human governments and the full establishment of God's Kingdom occur in 1914 like the Watchtower Society predicted?

- Since the prophecy did not come to pass, doesn't this mean the Society is a false prophet?

Because the overthrow of human governments and the full establishment of God's Kingdom did not occur in 1914, many Jehovah's Witnesses were greatly disappointed. Indeed, the Watchtower publication *Light* said, "All of the Lord's people looked forward to 1914 with joyful expectation. When that time came and passed there was much disappointment. . . . They were ridiculed by the clergy and their allies in particular, and pointed to with scorn, because they had said so much about 1914, and what would come to pass, and their 'prophecies' had not been fulfilled."[30] The history of error continues . . .

1925—The Return of Abraham, Isaac, Jacob, and the Prophets?

Watchtower leaders once taught that Abraham, Isaac, Jacob, and the Old Testament prophets would return as "princes" and live in an estate in San Diego, California known as Beth-Sarim ("House of Princes"). This was to occur in 1925. The book *Salvation* said that "the purpose of acquiring that property and building the house was that there might be some tangible proof that there are those on earth today . . . who believe that faithful men of old will soon be resurrected by the Lord, be back on earth, and take charge of the visible affairs of earth."[31] The publication *The New World* affirmed that "those faithful men of old may be expected back from the dead any day now...in this expectation the house was built....It is now held in trust for the occupancy of those princes on their return."[32]

The year 1925 was definitely when these Old Testament saints were expected to come on the scene. This expectancy is reflected in the following Watchtower publications:

> • *Millions Now Living Will Never Die* (1920) said that "we may expect 1925 to witness the return of these faithful men of Israel from the condition of death, being resurrected....1925 will mark the return of Abraham, Isaac, Jacob, and the faithful prophets of old."[33]
> • A 1917 issue of *The Watchtower* magazine said, "There will be no slip-up....Abraham should enter upon the actual possession of his promised inheritance in the year 1925 A.D."[34]
> • A 1923 issue of *The Watchtower* said, "1925 is definitely settled by the Scriptures."[35]
> • A 1924 issue of *The Watchtower* said, "The year 1925 is a date definitely and clearly marked in the Scriptures, even more clearly than that of 1914."[36]

 Ask...

- Why didn't Abraham, Isaac, Jacob, and other Old Testament "princes" show up in 1925 like the Watchtower Society said they would?

- Since this prophecy did not come to pass, doesn't this mean the Society is a false prophet?

It is obvious that Abraham, Isaac, Jacob, and the Old Testament prophets never showed up in 1925, and this led to great disappointment for many Jehovah's Witnesses. The *1975 Yearbook of Jehovah's Witnesses* reflected, "The year 1925 came and went. Jesus' anointed followers were still on earth as a class. The faithful men of old times—Abraham, David, and others—had not been resurrected to become princes in the earth (Ps. 45:16). So, as Anna MacDonald recalls: '1925 was a sad year for many brothers. Some of them were stumbled; their hopes were dashed. . . . Instead of its being considered a "probability," they read into it that it was a "certainty," and some prepared for their own loved ones with expectancy of their resurrection.' "37

Sadly but truly, the pattern of disappointment was not over . . .

1975—The End of Human History?

The Watchtower Society continued its pattern of false predictions by telling its followers that 6,000 years of human history would come to an end in 1975. Armageddon was to occur that year and Christ was to set up the Millennial Kingdom of earthly paradise. Note the following Watchtower publications:

• A 1966 issue of *Awake!* magazine said, "In what year, then, would the first 6,000 years of man's existence and also the first 6,000 years of God's rest day come to an end? The year 1975."38 (Note, however, that a much earlier issue of *The Watchtower* magazine [1894] had said that the 6,000 years of man's history had ended in 1873.39)

• In 1968, the Watchtower publication *Our Kingdom Ministry* claimed, "There are only about ninety months [7 and 1/2 years] left before 6,000 years of man's existence on earth is completed. . . . The majority of people living today will probably be alive when Armageddon breaks out."40

• In 1969 *Our Kingdom Ministry* said, "In view of the short time left, a decision to pursue a career in this system of things is not only unwise but extremely dangerous. . . . Many young brothers and sisters were offered scholarships or employment that promised fine pay. However, they turned them down and put spiritual interests first."[41]

• In a similar vein, the 1974 *Our Kingdom Ministry* said, "The end of this system is so very near! Is that not reason to increase our activity? . . . Reports are heard of brothers selling their homes and property and planning to finish out the rest of their days in this old system in the pioneer service. Certainly this is a fine way to spend the short time remaining before the wicked world's end."[42]

• Notice, however, that a late-1974 issue of *The Watchtower* magazine began to soften its stance just a little: "The publications of Jehovah's Witnesses have shown that, according to Bible chronology, it appears that 6,000 years of man's existence will be completed in the mid-1970's. But these publications have never said that the world's end would come then. Nevertheless, there has been considerable individual speculation on the matter."[43]

___ *Ask* . . . _____

• Did you know that the Watchtower Society originally taught that 6,000 years of human history would come to an end in 1873, and later changed the year to 1975?

• Since the Watchtower Society was wrong *both times*, doesn't this mean the Society is a false prophet?

_____

As was true with the earlier false predictions by the Watchtower Society, many Jehovah's Witnesses were greatly disappointed when 1975 came and went without anything happening. A 1976 issue of *The Watchtower* magazine tells us, "It is not advisable for us to set our sights on a certain date. . . . If anyone has been disappointed through not following this line of thought, he should now concentrate on adjusting his viewpoint, seeing that it was not the word of God that failed or deceived him and brought disappointment, but that *his own understanding was based on wrong premises*"[44] (emphasis added). Amazingly, the Society led its followers along for years, making them think 1975 would bring about the end of human history. Then, when that didn't happen, the Society lectured its followers for setting their sights on a certain date and basing their beliefs on wrong premises!

Understandably, hundreds of thousands of Jehovah's Witnesses left the Watchtower organization worldwide between 1976 and 1978.[45] "Enough was enough" for these people.

_____ *Ask. . .* _____

- Why didn't human history come to an end in 1975—culminating in the outbreak of Armageddon—like the Watchtower Society said it would?

- Do you really think the Watchtower Society is a true prophet of God?

No Condemnation for the Watchtower Society?

Those who have followed Watchtower literature over the years can attest to the fact that the Society has consistently changed its prophecies in order to cover up its many errors. Former Jehovah's Witness William J. Schnell observed that "*The Watchtower* magazine changed our doctrines between 1917 and 1928 no less than 148 times."[46]

Incredibly, the Watchtower Society argues that it should not be criticized for its past errors regarding prophecy. After all, the biblical prophets and apostles made mistakes, and they were not condemned as being false.

One example Jehovah's Witnesses cite in support of this is the prophet Nathan. When King David wanted to build a house of worship for God, Nathan told David to do as he wished. But later God told Nathan to inform David that he was not to be the one who would build the temple. Despite Nathan's error, however, Nathan was not condemned by God or by anyone else. Indeed, God continued to use Nathan because he humbly corrected the matter when God made it plain to him.[47]

Orthodox Christians point out, however, that Nathan's original message to David about building the house *was not* claimed by Nathan to be instruction from God (1 Chronicles 17:2). His subsequent message about not building the house *was* claimed to be instruction from God (17:3-15).[48] Hence, again, we find the Watchtower Society twisting Scripture to suit its own ends.

Amazingly, despite its many failed predictions, the Watchtower Society has not learned its lesson. Even since 1981 it continues to say that Armageddon and the world's end is very near.

You might remind the Jehovah's Witness that *The Watchtower* magazine says that when one discovers false prophets, "the people should no longer trust them as safe guides."[49]

_____ Ask... _____

- Do you agree with the Watchtower instruction that when one discovers false prophets, then "the people should no longer trust them as safe guides"?

- Since the Watchtower Society was wrong in 1874, 1914, 1925, and 1975, do you think you should still trust the Society as a "safe guide"?

_____ REASONING FROM THE SCRIPTURES _____

Matthew 24:3—A "Spiritual" Second Coming?

The Watchtower Teaching. The *New World Translation* renders Matthew 24:3, "While he was sitting upon the Mount of Olives, the disciples approached him privately, saying: 'Tell us, when will these things be, and what will be the sign of your *presence* and of the conclusion of the system of things?' " (emphasis added). Note that the Watchtower Society substitutes the word "presence" for "coming." The Society uses this distorted translation as a basis for teaching Jehovah's Witnesses that Jesus returned invisibly in 1914 and has been spiritually present with man ever since.[50]

Why is the Second Coming an invisible coming? In *The Greatest Man Who Ever Lived*, we read, "Humans cannot see angels in their heavenly glory. So the arrival of the Son of man, Jesus Christ, with the angels must be invisible to human eyes."[51]

Now, keep in mind that (according to the Watchtower Society) Jesus was "resurrected" from the dead as a spirit creature—as the archangel Michael. He was not *physically* raised from the dead. Obviously, then, Jesus could never return in physical, visible form. Because Jesus arose an invisible, spirit creature, His return would be as an invisible spirit creature.

Now, according to Jehovah's Witnesses, we have been in the last days and Christ has been spiritually "present" since 1914.[52] What are some of the signs of being in the last days? Well, no *single* sign proves we are near the end, but all the signs together make this clearly evident. They form what is called a "composite" sign—and the composite sign that we are living in the last days includes the following elements: nations are rising against nations (Matthew 24:7); food shortages (Matthew 24:7); great earthquakes (Luke 21:11); deadly pestilences (Luke 21:11); an increase in lawlessness (Matthew 24:11,12); men are becoming "faint out of fear" of the things coming upon the earth (Luke 21:25,26); Christ's followers are being persecuted (Matthew 24:9); and the good news of the kingdom is being preached around the world (Matthew 24:14).

The Watchtower publication *The Greatest Man Who Ever Lived* tells us that "a careful review of world events since 1914 reveals that Jesus' momentous prophecy has been undergoing its major fulfillment since that year."[53] Indeed,

> We would be blinding ourselves to the ominous "sign" if we did not discern that the end of the global system of things is marked by such things occurring since 1914 C.E. From that never-to-be-forgotten year onward this world system of things can be impeached before all humanity for the most gory wars of all human history, for food shortages humanly induced to a large extent, for pestilences traceable to human misconduct, for increase of law-lessness, for the cooling off of the divine quality of love, for betrayal of mankind, for outright hatred and persecution in all the nations toward those Christians who were counteracting false prophets by preaching in all the inhabited earth "this good news of the kingdom" for a "witness to all the nations"![54]

Watchtower authorities conclude that because world-shattering events have followed one another in quick succession since 1914, it is clear that this is the year Christ came and began His spiritual rule.[55] Consequently, the end of this world system must be very near.

The Biblical Teaching. Let's begin by noting that the Greek word for "coming" (*parousia*) has a number of slight variations of meaning—including "present," "presence," "being physically present," "coming to a place," and "arriving."[56] *Vine's Expository Dictionary of Biblical Words* says that *parousia* "denotes both an 'arrival' and a consequent 'presence with.' For instance, in a papyrus letter a particular lady speaks of the necessity of her *parousia* in a place in order to attend to matters relating to her property there."[57] *Parousia* is also used to describe the physical "presence" of Christ with His disciples on the Mount of Transfiguration (2 Peter 1:16).

The word *parousia* is used elsewhere in the New Testament with no invisibility implied or required. For example:

- The apostle Paul says in 1 Corinthians 16:17, "And I rejoice over the *coming* of Stephanas and Fortunatus and Achaicus; because they have supplied what was lacking on your part" (NASB, emphasis added).
- Paul says in 2 Corinthians 7:6,7, "But God, who comforts the downcast, comforted us by the *coming* of Titus, and not only by his *coming* but also by the comfort you had given him."
- In 2 Corinthians 10:10 Paul relays what some people had said about him: "For they say, 'His letters are weighty and strong, but his personal *presence* is unimpressive, and his speech contemptible' " (NASB).
- Paul tells the Philippians that "I know that I shall remain and continue with you all for your progress and joy in the faith, so that your proud confidence in me may abound in Christ Jesus through my *coming* to you again" (1:25,26 NASB).
- Paul also tells the Philippians: "Therefore, my dear friends, as you have always obeyed—not only in my *presence*, but now much more in my absence, work out your salvation with fear and trembling" (2:12). (Note the contrast here between physical *presence* and *absence*.)

Greek scholar Joseph Thayer in his lexicon defines *parousia*: "In the [New Testament the word is used] especially of the advent, [that is] the future, *visible, return from heaven of Jesus*, the Messiah, to raise the dead, hold the last judgment, and set up formally and gloriously the kingdom of God."[58] There is no hint of invisibility here.

In biblical times, the word *parousia* was used to refer to the visit of a king or another official. It may be that the disciples are using the term in this sense in Matthew 24:3. As Bible expositor Stanley Toussaint notes, the disciples "were convinced that Jesus was the Messiah who would yet manifest Himself as the King of Israel in His coming."[59] In keeping with this, exegete Robert Gundry notes that the word *parousia* is used in Matthew 24:3 "in accord with its use for visits of dignitaries ... it connotes the *publicness* of the Son of man's coming."[60]

___ *Ask...* _____

- Did you know that the Greek word for "presence" in Matthew 24:3 (*parousia*) is used of the *physical, visible coming* of Stephanas, Fortunatus, and Achaicus to the apostle Paul (1 Corinthians 16:17); of the *physical, visible coming* of Titus to Paul (2 Corinthians 7:6,7); of Paul's *physical, visible presence* in Corinth (2 Corinthians 10:10); and of Paul's *physical, visible coming* to the church at Philippi (Philippians 1:25,26)?

- Did you know that Greek experts say the term is to be used in the same way in Matthew 24:3—pointing to the *physical, visible* Second Coming of Jesus Christ?

_____

There are other Greek words besides *parousia* used to describe the Second Coming of Christ in the New Testament. One of these is *apokalupsis*, which carries the basic meaning of "revelation," "visible disclosure," "unveiling," and "removing the cover" from something that is hidden. The word is used of pulling a cover off a sculpture so everyone can see it. The word is also used to speak of the Second Coming in 1 Peter 4:13: "But to the degree that you share the sufferings of

Christ, keep on rejoicing; so that also at the *revelation* of His glory, you may rejoice with exultation" (emphasis added). The use of *apokalupsis* in regard to the Second Coming makes it absolutely clear that it will be a *visible* coming that all humankind will see.

_____ *Ask...* _____

- Since the Greek word *apokalupsis*—which means "revelation," "visible disclosure," "unveiling," and "removing the cover" from something that is hidden—is used of Christ's Second Coming in 1 Peter 4:13, doesn't this indicate that it will be a *visible* coming?

Related to the Greek word *apokalupsis* is the concept of *glory*. As we consider the glory of Christ, it is important to note that this word, when used of God/Christ, refers to the luminous manifestation of God's person, His glorious revelation of Himself to man.[61] This definition is borne out by the many ways the word is used in Scripture. For example, *brilliant light* consistently accompanies the divine manifestation in His glory (Matthew 17:2,3; 1 Timothy 6:16; Revelation 1:16). Moreover, the word "glory" is often linked with verbs of *seeing* Exodus 16:7; 33:18; Isaiah 40:5) and verbs of *appearing* (Exodus 16:10; Deuteronomy 5:24), both of which emphasize the visible nature of God's glory. It is this visible glory of Christ that will be revealed (*apokalupsis*) at the Second Coming (*see* 1 Peter 4:13).

Another Greek word used of Christ's Second Coming is *epiphaneia*, which carries the basic meaning of "to appear." *Vine's Expository Dictionary of Biblical Words* says this word literally means "a shining forth." The dictionary provides several examples from ancient literature of how the word points to a physical, visible appearance of someone.[62]

The word *epiphaneia* is used several times by the apostle Paul in reference to Christ's visible Second Coming.[63] For example, in Titus 2:13 Paul speaks of looking "for the blessed hope—the glorious *appearing* of our great God and Savior, Jesus Christ" (emphasis added). In 1 Timothy 6:14 Paul urges Timothy to "keep this commandment without spot or blame until the *appearing* of our Lord Jesus Christ" (emphasis added).

Significantly, Christ's first coming—which was both *bodily* and *visible* ("the Word become flesh")—was called an *epiphaneia* (2 Timothy 1:10). In the same way, Christ's Second Coming will be both *bodily* and *visible*. It is the consistent testimony of Scripture—whether the word *parousia*, *apokalupsis*, or *epiphaneia* is used—that Christ's Second Coming will be visible to all humankind (*see* Daniel 7:13; Zechariah 9:14; 12:10; Matthew 16:27,28; 24:30; Mark 1:2; John 1:51; 2 Timothy 4:1).

_____ *Ask. . .* _____

• Since the Greek word *epiphaneia* (meaning "to appear") is used of Christ's first coming (which was *physical* and *visible*), and the same word is also used of Christ's Second Coming, shouldn't we conclude that the Second Coming is just as visible and physical as the first?

Now, in arguing against the Watchtower view that Christ's (invisible) Second Coming has already occurred (in 1914), point him or her to Matthew 24:29,30: "Immediately after the distress of those days 'the sun will be darkened, and the moon will not give its light; the stars will fall from the sky, and the heavenly bodies will be shaken.' At that time the sign of the Son of Man will appear in the sky, and all the nations of the earth will mourn. They will see the Son of Man coming on the clouds of the sky, with power and great glory."

After reading this passage aloud, Watchtower expert Marian Bodine suggests asking the Jehovah's Witness the following questions:

_____ *Ask . . .* _____

- Did any of the above events happen in 1914? How about 1874?

- Did the moon refuse to give its light during those years?

- How about the stars? Did they fall from heaven?

- Did ALL the tribes of earth mourn at that time?[64]

Acts 1:9-11—An "Invisible" Second Coming?

The Watchtower Teaching. The *New World Translation* renders Acts 1:9-11, "And after he had said these things, while they were looking on, he was lifted up and a cloud caught him up from their vision. And as they were gazing into the sky while he was on his way, also, look! two men in white garments stood alongside them, and they said: 'Men of Galilee, why do you stand looking into the sky? This Jesus who was received up from you into the sky will come thus in the same manner as you have beheld him going into the sky.'"

Jehovah's Witnesses argue that the "manner" of Jesus' ascent was that He disappeared from view, and His departure was observed only by His disciples. The world was not aware of what had happened. Acts 1:9-11 indicates that the same would be true of Christ's Second Coming—that is, the world would be unaware of Christ's invisible coming.[65] And, indeed, the world *was* largely unaware of Christ's invisible coming in 1914.

The Biblical Teaching. In Acts 1:9-11, the Watchtower Society confuses "manner" with "result." The *manner* of Jesus' ascent was not "disappearing from view"; rather, the *result* of Jesus' ascent was "disappearing from view." The actual *manner* of Jesus' ascent was *visible* and *bodily*. Jesus visibly and bodily ascended, with the end result of disappearing from view. Likewise, at the Second Coming, Christ will come visibly and bodily and will *appear* into view.

_____ *Ask...* _____

- Instead of describing the *manner* of Jesus' ascent as "disappearing from view," doesn't it make more sense to say that the *manner* of His ascent was physical and visible with the *end result* of "disappearing from view"?

- In the same way, is it not clear from Acts 1:9-11 that at the Second Coming Christ will come *physically* and *visibly* and will *appear* into view?

The mention of a cloud in Acts 1:9 is significant, for clouds are often used in the New Testament in association with God's visible glory. For example:

- We read that while Jesus was speaking on the Mount of Transfiguration, "a *bright cloud* enveloped them; and a voice from the cloud said, 'This is my Son, whom I love; with him I am well pleased. Listen to Him!' " (Matthew 17:5, emphasis added).
- Speaking of His future Second Coming, Jesus said, "At that time the sign of the Son of Man will appear in the sky, and all the nations of the earth will mourn. They will see the Son of Man coming on *the clouds of the sky,* with power and great glory" (Matthew 24:30, emphasis added).
- When Jesus replied to the high priest at His trial, He said, "In the future you will see the Son of Man sitting at the right hand of the Mighty One and coming on the *clouds of heaven*" (Matthew 26:64, emphasis added).

God's visible glory is often associated with clouds in the Old Testament as well. For example:

• Recall that "while Aaron was speaking to the whole Israelite community, they looked toward the desert, and there was the glory of the LORD *appearing in the cloud*" (Exodus 16:10, emphasis added).

• When the tabernacle in the wilderness was completed, the glory cloud settled upon it, preventing human entrance: "Then *the cloud* covered the Tent of Meeting, and the glory of the LORD filled the tabernacle. Moses could not enter the Tent of Meeting because *the cloud* had settled upon it, and the glory of the LORD filled the tabernacle" (Exodus 40:34,35, emphasis added).

• God's glory was also seen in a cloud when Solomon's temple was dedicated: "When the priest withdrew from the Holy Place, *the cloud* filled the temple of the LORD. And the priests could not perform their service because of *the cloud*, for the glory of the LORD filled his temple" (1 Kings 8:10-11, emphasis added).

Now, here is my point in saying all this: Christ's *transfiguration* (Matthew 17), His *ascension* to heaven (Acts 1), and His *Second Coming* (Matthew 24) are *three successive manifestations* of Christ's divine (visible) glory to humankind. Thus, the mention of a cloud in Acts 1 points to a manifestation of Christ's *visible glory* at the Second Coming.[66] Bible scholar F.F. Bruce explains: "The cloud in each case [at the transfiguration, ascension, and Second Coming] is probably to be interpreted as the cloud of the Shekinah—the cloud which, resting above the tent of meeting in the days of Moses, was *the visible token to Israel* that the glory of the Lord dwelt within (Ex. 40:34). So, in the last moment that the apostles saw their Lord with outward vision [at the ascension in Acts 1], they were granted 'a theophany: Jesus is enveloped in the cloud of the divine presence.'"[67]

Just as Jesus left with a *visible* manifestation of the glory of God, so Christ will return with a *visible* manifestation of the glory of God.[68] There is no way Acts 1:9-11 can be twisted to mean that Christ will come again invisibly, as the Watchtower attempts to teach.

_____ *Ask . . .* _____

- Since clouds are often used in Scripture in reference to the *visible glory* of God—and since Christ both ascended with clouds and will come again with clouds—doesn't this indicate the visible nature of His Second Coming?

_____

Revelation 1:7—*An "Invisible" Second Coming?*

The Watchtower Teaching. Revelation 1:7 in the *New World Translation* reads, "Look! He is coming with the clouds, and every eye will see him, and those who pierced him; and all the tribes of the earth will beat themselves in grief because of him. Yes, Amen."

Jehovah's Witnesses say that the reference to "coming with the clouds" means *invisibility*. After all, when an airplane is in a thick cloud, people on the ground usually cannot see it. Since Christ is coming "with the clouds," this means that human beings will not be able to see it.[69] It will be an invisible event.

If Christ's Second Coming is invisible, then in what sense will "every eye" see him? Well, this is not to be taken literally. Jehovah's Witnesses say that people will *discern* from events on earth that Christ is invisibly present and is spiritually ruling.[70] Especially when judgments are poured out on the wicked, it will be clear that these come from the hand of Christ. This will be a striking evidence of his "presence." With this in mind, the book *"Let God Be True"* tells us, "His return is recognized by the eyes of one's understanding, such eyes being enlightened by God's unfolding Word. Christ's arrival and presence are not discerned because of a visible bodily nearness, but by the light of his acts of judgment and the fulfillment of Bible prophecy."[71]

The Biblical Teaching. The Watchtower argument that Christ's "coming with the clouds" means an invisible coming is a complete distortion of Scripture. As noted earlier, clouds are often used in association with God's visible glory (Exodus 16:10; 40:34,35; 1 Kings 8:10,11; Matthew 17:5; 24:30; 26:64). John F. Walvoord explains that just "as Christ was received by a cloud in His ascension (Acts 1:9), so He will come in the clouds of heaven (Matt. 24:30; 26:64; Mark 13:26; 14:62; Luke 21:27)."[72] Just as Jesus left with a *visible* manifestation of the glory of God (clouds were present), so Christ will return with a *visible* manifestation of the glory of God (clouds will be present).

Now, what about the Watchtower Society's interpreting the statement "every eye will see him" to mean "every eye of understanding will see him"? A plain, unbiased reading of the text indicates that *every eye* on earth will see Christ coming in glory. This is consistent with numerous other Scripture passages. For example, Matthew 24:30 says of the Second Coming, "At that time the sign of the Son of Man will *appear in the sky*, and *all the nations of the earth* will mourn. They *will see the Son of Man* coming on the clouds of the sky with power and great glory" (emphasis added).

In Revelation 1:7 the Greek word for "see" is *horao*. In the *Greek-English Lexicon of the New Testament*, William Arndt and F. Wilbur Gingrich say the word in Revelation 1:7 means "see, catch sight of, notice *of sense perception*."[73] Likewise, Thayer's *Greek-English Lexicon of the New Testament* says *horao* is used in Revelation 1:7 in the sense of "to see with the eyes [physical organs]."[74] *Vine's Expository Dictionary of Biblical Words* defines *horao* as "bodily vision."[75] In the context of Revelation 1:7, then, there is virtually no possibility that the intended meaning is "see with the eyes of one's understanding, such eyes being enlightened by God's unfolding Word." Clearly this passage is referring to an observation made with the eyes—the physical, bodily organs.

_____ *Ask...* _____

- Assuming that the Bible contains normal, readable, understandable words used in a cognizant, intelligent way, what would a person conclude from Revelation 1:7 regarding the visibility of the Second Coming of Christ without having consulted Watchtower literature?

- In keeping with Revelation 1:7, did "all the tribes of the earth beat themselves in grief" (NWT) at Christ's alleged invisible Second Coming in 1914?

Matthew 24:34—*The 1914 Generation*

The Watchtower Teaching. The *New World Translation* renders Matthew 24:34, "Truly I say to you that *this generation* will by no means pass away until all these things occur" (emphasis added). The Watchtower Society teaches Jehovah's Witnesses that "this generation" is the 1914 generation. It is *this* group of people that will not pass away, they say, until all these things (prophecies, including Armageddon) come to pass.

Now, it is an enlightening experience to study how the Watchtower Society has dealt with this verse throughout its history. Back in 1968, the Society was teaching its followers that Jehovah's Witnesses who were 15 years of age in 1914 would be alive to see the consummation of all things. Indeed, a 1968 issue of *Awake!* magazine said of "this generation":

> Jesus was obviously speaking about those who were old enough to witness with understanding what took place when the "last days" began. . . . Even if we presume that *youngsters 15 years of age* would be perceptive enough to realize the import of what happened in 1914, it would still make the youngest of "this generation" nearly 70 years old today. . . . Jesus said that the end of this

wicked world would come before that generation passed
away in death (emphasis added).[76]

Some ten years later, a 1978 issue of *The Watchtower* magazine said: "Thus, when it comes to the application in our time,
*the 'generation' logically would not apply to babies born during
World War I*"[77] (emphasis added). It is clear that at this time,
the Watchtower Society was still holding out to the view that
those who were teenagers during 1914 would see the culmination of all things.

However, as David Reed points out, "one need only calcu-
late that someone fifteen years old in 1914 would be twenty-
five years old in 1924, thirty-five years old in 1934—and
eighty-five years old in 1984—to realize that the Watchtower's
'generation that will not pass away' was almost gone by the
mid-1980s. The prophecy was about to fail. But, rather than
change the prophecy, [Watchtower] leaders simply stretched
the generation."[78]

A 1980 issue of *The Watchtower* magazine said of "this
generation": "It is the generation of people who saw the
catastrophic events that broke forth in connection with World
War I from 1914 onward. . . . *If you assume that 10 is the age* at
which an event creates a lasting impression"[79] (emphasis
added). The Watchtower leaders reduced the age from 15 to 10
in order to allow for five more years for a "generation" that
was quickly dying off.

The 1980 solution didn't alleviate the problem. Another
step had to be taken. So, in a 1984 issue of *The Watchtower*
magazine, we read, "If Jesus used 'generation' in that sense
and we apply it to 1914, then *the babies of that generation* are
now 70 years old or older. . . . Some of them 'will by no means
pass away until all these things occur' "[80] (emphasis added).

Along these same lines, a 1985 issue of *The Watchtower*
said, "Before the 1914 generation completely dies out, God's
judgment must be executed."[81] More recently, a 1988 issue of
Awake! magazine said, "Most of the generation of 1914 has
passed away. However, there are still millions on earth who

were born in that year or prior to it. . . . Jesus' words will come true, 'this generation will not pass away until all these things have happened.' "[82]

Reasoning from the Scriptures (1989) tells us that time is running short: "The 'generation' that was alive at the beginning of the fulfillment of the sign in 1914 is now well along in years. The time remaining must be very short. World conditions give every indication that this is the case."[83]

The Biblical Teaching. When discussing Matthew 24:34 with a Jehovah's Witness, you might begin by asking him or her:

___ *Ask...* ___

- Where is there an explicit, direct statement in Scripture indicating that 1914 is the precise year around which prophetic calculations are to be made regarding end-time chronology?

He or she will probably say that there have been many signs in the world indicating that 1914 is the critical year. Don't accept this evasion. Insist on biblical support—chapter and verse!

You might also ask the Jehovah's Witness about the age changes regarding those living during 1914—those who would allegedly see the consummation of all things:

___ *Ask...* ___

- Regarding the "generation" that was alive in 1914—the generation that is supposed to see the culmination of all things prophetically—did you know that over the past fifteen years the Watchtower Society has changed the age of that group from *fifteen* years old, to *ten* years old, and now to *babies*?

- Does the Society sound like a true prophet of God to you?

Evangelical Christians have generally held to one of two interpretations of Matthew 24:34. The first is that Christ is simply saying that those who witness the signs stated earlier in Matthew 24 (signs which deal with the future Tribulation period) will see the coming of Jesus Christ within that very generation. Since it was common knowledge among the Jews that the future tribulation would last *only seven years* (Daniel 9:24-27), it is obvious that those who were living at the beginning of this time would likely live to see the Second Coming *seven years later* (except for those who lose their lives during this tumultuous time).

Bible scholar Norman Geisler says,

> The generation alive when these things (the abomination of desolation [v. 15], the great tribulation such as has never been seen before [v. 21], the sign of the Son of Man in heaven [v. 30], etc.) begin to come to pass will still be alive when these judgments are completed. Since it is commonly believed that the tribulation is a period of some *seven years* (Dan. 9:27; cf. Rev. 11:2) at the end of the age, then Jesus would be saying that "this generation" alive at the beginning of the tribulation will still be alive at the end of it.[84]

Other evangelicals hold that the word "generation" is to be taken in its basic usage of "race, kindred, family, stock, or breed." If this is what is meant, then Jesus is promising in Matthew 24:34 that the nation of Israel will be preserved— despite terrible persecution during the Tribulation—until the consummation of God's program for Israel at the Second Coming. Norman Geisler comments,

> Jesus' statement could mean that the Jewish race would not pass away until all things are fulfilled. Since there were many promises to Israel, including the eternal inheritance of the land of Palestine (Gen. 12; 14–15; 17) and the Davidic kingdom (2 Sam. 7), then Jesus could be

referring to God's preservation of the nation Israel in order to fulfill His promises to them. Indeed, Paul speaks of a future of the nation of Israel when they will be reinstated in God's covenantal promises (Rom. 11:11-26).[85]

Whichever interpretation one chooses, there is no indication in Matthew 24 (or any other passage) that prophetic things must come to a culmination some specified time after 1914 or any other year. The Jehovah's Witnesses are reading something into the text that simply is not there.

Is the Watchtower Society a False Prophet?

I noted earlier that the Watchtower Society has made numerous predictions throughout its history and has been severely criticized because of so many failed prophecies. As a result, many have defected from the cult.

I also mentioned that the Watchtower Society has responded by arguing that even biblical prophets made some mistakes. Therefore, the Jehovah's Witnesses should not be condemned. *Reasoning from the Scriptures* tells us that "the apostles and other early Christian disciples had certain wrong expectations, but the Bible does not classify them with the 'false prophets.'"[86]

Of the passages cited by the Watchtower Society in support of this view, three come up quite often: Luke 19:11, Acts 1:6, and Jonah 3:4-10; 4:1,2. We shall examine these shortly. But first, let me tell you briefly about how one Jehovah's Witness dealt with the Watchtower's false prophecies.

While we were talking, this Witness admitted that the Watchtower Society had been in error on some prophecies in the past. As expected, he argued that some of the biblical prophets had also been in error. But he added that the "light" (presumably from God) is getting brighter and brighter today, and things are much more clear now. Hence, the Watchtower Society understands things more than ever before, and the light is getting brighter *with each passing day.*

I responded, "So, conceivably, if the light is getting brighter every day, it is possible that ten years from now you might discover that everything you presently believe is in error, since the light ten years from now will be so much brighter, right?"

He squirmed a little, but acknowledged the legitimacy of my point. What else could he do?

I then said, "Now, what if you should die tomorrow? Does this mean you will die having believed the wrong thing, and thus be lost forever and ever?" He quickly changed the subject, not wanting to continue the discussion. But the point was made.

I left one final thought with him. An early Watchtower publication called *Zion's Watch Tower* said that a new view of truth can never contradict a former truth. "New light" never extinguishes older "light" but merely adds to it.[87] I told the Witness that the Watchtower's "older light" (false prophecies) was clearly in error, and now the Watchtower was trying to say that "new light" is *correcting* this "older light." I then asked him, "Do you really want to base your eternal destiny on the Watchtower Society as God's 'channel of truth'"?

One other thing: When you specify the prophetic errors of the Watchtower Society to a Jehovah's Witness, he or she will sometimes say, "Well, we've admitted our mistakes; therefore, we're not false prophets." If a Witness says this to you during a witnessing encounter:

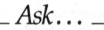

_____ *Ask...* _____

- Where does the Bible teach that after a prophecy fails, if the prophet *admits* he made a mistake, he is no longer a false prophet?[88]

Luke 19:11—*The Disciples: Wrong Expectations?*

The Watchtower Teaching. Luke 19:11 in the *New World Translation* reads, "While they [the disciples] were listening to these things he spoke in addition an illustration, because he was near Jerusalem and they were imagining that the kingdom of God was going to display itself instantly."

Jehovah's Witnesses point out that the disciples' "imagining" was clearly in error. The kingdom of God was not going to display itself instantly. The disciples were thinking wrong; they made a mistake. Yet, they were still disciples of Christ.

Though the Jehovah's Witnesses once claimed that the Watchtower Society is an inspired prophet (just like Ezekiel), they have altered this claim in recent years. Now they say that the Society *does not* claim to be an inspired prophet. It has made mistakes. Like the disciples of Christ in Luke 19:11, the Society at times has had some wrong expectations.[89]

The Watchtower Society explains it this way: "True, the brothers preparing these publications are not infallible. Their writings are not inspired as those of Paul and the other Bible writers (2 Tim. 3:16). And so, at times, it has been necessary, as understanding became clearer, to correct views (Prov. 4:18)."[90]

The Biblical Teaching. Evangelical Christians concede that Christ's disciples occasionally held false notions as human beings. However, there is no indication in Luke 19:11 or any other text of Scripture that the disciples or prophets ever taught such false notions as part of God's "Thus-saith-the-Lord" revelation to humankind.[91]

We must emphasize that whenever the prophets or apostles were speaking *as God's mouthpieces* to humanity, they never communicated any false notions. No true prophet of God ever made a mistake while uttering a prophecy because he was delivering *God's words* to humankind, not his own.

It is utter folly for the Watchtower Society (which claims to be God's voice to humanity) to draw a parallel between its many and consistent false prophecies and the occasional false notions of God's disciples or prophets when they were not speaking authoritatively for God. There is no legitimate comparison between the two.

_____ *Ask. . .* _____

> • Can you point me to a single example in Scripture in which a prophet was issuing a "Thus-saith-the-Lord" prophecy direct from the Lord and was subsequently shown to be in error?
>
> (If he or she cites Jonah and his prophecy regarding Nineveh, see below. Emphasize that when speaking prophecies *from God*, the prophets were *never* in error.)
>
> • How can the Watchtower Society claim to be God's prophetic voice to the world and yet issue prophetic statements that in many cases have proven to be in error?

It is critical to recognize that simply because the Bible *records* an erroneous statement by a particular individual does not mean that statement came directly from God. Sometimes the disciples did or said something *as human beings* and not *as God's mouthpieces*. This is illustrated in Luke 19:11 when the disciples were "imagining" that the kingdom was going to display itself instantly.[92]

By contrast, when the apostles or prophets spoke as God's mouthpieces, there was no possibility of error—for they were communicating direct revelation from God. Note the following passages:

> • "I will raise up for them a prophet like you from among their brothers; I will put my words in his mouth, and he will tell them everything I command him" (Deuteronomy 18:18).
>
> • "The Spirit of the LORD spoke through me; his word was on my tongue" (2 Samuel 23:2).
>
> • "When they heard this, they raised their voices together in prayer to God. 'Sovereign Lord,' they said. . . . 'You spoke by the Holy Spirit through the mouth of your servant, our father David' " (Acts 4:24,25).

> • "We speak, not in words taught us by human wisdom but in words taught by the Spirit, expressing spiritual truths in spiritual words" (1 Corinthians 2:13).

_____ *Ask...* _____

- • If God puts His words in a prophet's mouth, can that prophet utter error when he speaks forth?

- • Since the Watchtower Society has uttered error, what must we conclude regarding the source of those words?

Regarding Luke 19:11, one must keep in mind that the disciples had already been told that the kingdom of God had *arrived* in some sense and was *present* in Jesus' ministry (Luke 11:20). So when Jesus and the disciples came "near Jerusalem" (the capital city), some thought that the completion of God's kingdom purposes was near at hand—despite Jesus' continued warnings of the coming cross. He dealt with the disciples' wrong "imagining" or thinking by telling them a parable (19:12-27) that showed there would be an interval of time before the kingdom was consummated. Jesus used the parable to correct their thinking and dispel their overeager hopes.

Acts 1:6—*The Apostles: Erroneous Views?*

The Watchtower Teaching. The *New World Translation* renders Acts 1:6, "When, now, they had assembled they went asking him: 'Lord, are you restoring the kingdom to Israel at this time?'" This is yet another verse cited by the Watchtower Society in support of the contention that the disciples made mistakes or had erroneous views (since the kingdom was not being restored to Israel at this time). Jehovah's Witnesses use this verse to justify (or at least excuse) their own errors. Since the disciples held wrong views and were not condemned, so the

Watchtower Society should not be condemned for its errors in the past.

The Biblical Teaching. As we saw in Luke 19:11, Christ's disciples occasionally held false notions as human beings. However, this does not mean that the disciples or apostles ever taught such false notions as part of God's "Thus-saith-the-Lord" revelation to humankind. No true prophet of God ever made a mistake while uttering a prophecy because he was delivering *God's* words to humankind, not his own.[93]

Again, the Watchtower Society (which has claimed to be God's voice to humanity) cannot legitimately draw a parallel between its many and consistent false prophecies and the occasional false notions of God's prophets or apostles. There is no rightful comparison between the two.

_____ *Ask...* _____

- Can you point me to a single example in Scripture in which a prophet was issuing a "Thus-saith-the-Lord" prophecy direct from the Lord and was subsequently shown to be in error?

- How can the Watchtower Society claim to be God's prophetic voice to the world when so many of its prophecies have been shown to be in error?

What happened, then, in Acts 1:6? When the disciples heard Jesus speak of the coming gift of the Holy Spirit (Acts 1:5)— and they knew that the coming of the Spirit was the "mark" of a new age[94]—they understandably concluded that this may be the occasion for restoring the kingdom to Israel. This sparked the question to Jesus in Acts 1:6.

Certainly the disciples had, to some extent, bought into some of the common political expectations of their day regarding the coming of the Messiah. The common thought was that the Messiah would deliver the Jews from Roman domination and establish a political kingdom in which the people would be free at last.

It would also seem, as F.F. Bruce notes, that the disciples "had in earlier days been captivated by the idea that in such a restored order they themselves would have positions of authority (cf. Mark 10:35ff.; Luke 22:24ff.)."[95] Hence, some of the disciples' questions to Jesus may have been motivated by personal interests.

Jesus' answer in Acts 1:7 was, in effect, "This is not your concern." The timing of establishing the kingdom was in the Father's hands. Jesus instructed the disciples that their primary concern was to be His witnesses, accurately reporting to other people what they had seen regarding Jesus' life and teachings. They were to accomplish this in the power of the Holy Spirit.

Simply because the disciples held a false notion does not excuse or justify the consistent false predictions of the Watchtower Society. The disciples were *simply asking a question* of Jesus; they were not speaking a "Thus-saith-the-Lord" revelation to anyone. Thus, there is no parallel between these disciples and the Watchtower Society.

Jonah 3:4-10; 4:1,2—*The Prophets: Erroneous Prophecies?*

The Watchtower Teaching. The *New World Translation* renders Jonah 3:4-10 and 4:1,2, "Finally Jonah started to enter into the city the walking distance of one day, and he kept proclaiming and saying: 'Only forty days more, and Nineveh will be overthrown.' . . . And the [true] God got to see their works, that they had turned back from their bad way; and so the [true] God felt regret over the calamity that he had spoken of causing to them; and he did not cause [it]."

The Jehovah's Witnesses cite this verse to prove that biblical prophets sometimes made mistakes in their predictions. After all, what Jonah predicted about Nineveh's destruction did not come to pass. And Jonah was not condemned for this. The Watchtower Society, then, should not be condemned for its prophetic errors.

The Biblical Teaching. In response to the Watchtower position, you must point out that Jonah *did not make a mistake*. After all, Jonah told the Ninevites *exactly* what Jehovah-God told him to say (*see* Jonah 3:1).

_____ *Ask...* _____

- Since Jonah was speaking the very words of God (Jonah 3:1), how can the Watchtower Society say he was in error?

Apparently there was a "repentance clause" built into Jonah's prophecy to the Ninevites. In view of how the Ninevites responded, it seems clear that they understood the final outcome of things to be dependent on *how they responded*. The Ninevites understood that their city would be toppled in forty days *unless they repented* (Jonah 3:5-9).[96] Based on how the Ninevites responded to Jonah's prophecy, God withdrew the threatened punishment—thus making it clear that even He Himself viewed the prophecy as hinging on how the Ninevites responded.[97]

This seems related to what God said in the Book of Jeremiah: "If at any time I announce that a nation or kingdom is to be uprooted, torn down and destroyed, and if that nation I warned repents of its evil, then I will relent and not inflict on it the disaster I had planned" (Jeremiah 18:7,8). This principle is clearly illustrated for us in the case of Nineveh. It is noteworthy that God is often seen showing mercy where repentance is evident (Exodus 32:14; 2 Samuel 24:6; Amos 7:3,7).[98]

We must conclude, based on the account of Jonah, that God sometimes chooses to withdraw a punishment when the people in danger of judgment decide to repent and the grounds for the threatened punishment have disappeared. As Old Testament scholar Walter C. Kaiser notes, "for God *not* to change in such cases would go against his essential quality of justice and his responsiveness to any change that he had planned to bring about."[99]

It is clear that Jonah's prophecy does not in any way lessen the guilt of the Watchtower Society in its numerous false predictions—none of which were akin to the *conditional* prophecy in the Book of Jonah.[100] And inasmuch as Jonah himself spoke *exactly* the words God gave him to say, it is clear that the Watchtower Society is wrong in saying that Jonah made a mistake. This passage thus lends no support to the Watchtower Society.

After reading aloud from Jeremiah 18:7,8:

 Ask...

- Can you see that God showed mercy to the Ninevites because of His stated policy in Jeremiah 18:7,8?

- Since Jonah spoke only the words God gave him— and since God relented of His judgment against Nineveh based on the principle in Jeremiah 18:7,8— can you see that it is illegitimate for the Watchtower Society to cite Jonah's prophecy as justification for continuously setting forth false prophecies?

14

Controversial Issues: Blood Transfusions, Birthdays, and Wearing Crosses

The Devil can cite Scripture for his purpose.

—William Shakespeare
(1564-1616)

This chapter will focus on three of the more controversial issues in Watchtower theology: blood transfusions, the celebration of birthdays, and the wearing of crosses as a symbol of Christianity. Jehovah's Witnesses make much of these issues in their witnessing endeavors. It is accordingly important for Christians to know what Scripture truly teaches on these matters.

Blood Transfusions

According to the teachings of the Watchtower Society, a Jehovah's Witness must refuse blood transfusions in every and all circumstances—even when doctors say death is inevitable without such a transfusion. The Watchtower Society also requires that parents see to it that their children never receive blood transfusions.[1]

Jehovah's Witnesses believe that references to "eating blood" in the Bible prohibit receiving blood via transfusion.

For this reason, many Witnesses carry a signed card with them stating that they are not to receive a blood transfusion in the event that they are found unconscious.[2]

The Jehovah's Witnesses point out that our first parents, Adam and Eve, were forbidden to eat of the fruit of the tree in the Garden of Eden. As everyone knows, Adam and Eve disobeyed God and lost everything. Today, we are not forbidden to eat of any trees. We are, however, forbidden to eat blood. So, the real issue is: Will we obey God and do as He asks, or disobey God like Adam and Eve did and lose everything?[3]

The backdrop to the Watchtower position is that blood is sacred. The book *Aid to Bible Understanding* tells us, "Life is sacred. Therefore, blood, in which the creature's life resides, is sacred and is not to be tampered with. Noah, the progenitor of all persons today living on the earth, was allowed by Jehovah to add flesh to his diet after the Flood, but he was strictly commanded not to eat blood."[4]

Because God commanded this abstinence (which includes transfusions), followers of Jehovah have no choice but to obey. Jehovah's Witnesses point out that even if a person dies as a result of not having the needed blood, God promises resurrection.[5] The Watchtower Society accordingly asks: If you are a person who is near death, is it wise to abandon God at that point by not obeying what He has said about blood?[6] Those who *truly* trust Jehovah will have no trouble refusing a blood transfusion, because their confidence is in the future resurrection promised by Jehovah.

Watchtower theology teaches that a proper view toward blood is critical to a right relationship with Jehovah. The Watchtower publication *Jehovah's Witnesses and the Question of Blood* says, "The issue of blood for Jehovah's Witnesses, therefore, involves the most fundamental principles. . . . Their relationship with their Creator and God is at stake."[7] Along these same lines, the publication *Blood, Medicine, and the Law of God* points out that a blood transfusion "may result in the immediate and very temporary prolongation of life, but that at the cost of eternal life for a dedicated Christian."[8]

Jehovah's Witnesses like to point out that, even apart from what Scripture teaches on this subject, getting a blood transfusion is bad for one's health. The book *Man's Salvation Out of World Distress At Hand!* tells us, "Unknown to many, the widespread resort to blood transfusions has resulted in the spread of crippling disease, fatal in many cases, not to speak of deaths directly caused by this medical practice, still pursued by many."[9]

Is the Watchtower position on blood transfusions legitimate? Among the key passages Jehovah's Witnesses cite in favor of their view are Genesis 9:4, Leviticus 7:26,27; 17:11,12, and Acts 15:28,29. Let us now reason from the Scriptures with a look at these passages.

_____ REASONING FROM THE SCRIPTURES _____

Genesis 9:4—*No Blood Transfusions*

The Watchtower Teaching. The *New World Translation* renders Genesis 9:4, "Only flesh with its soul—its blood—you must not eat." This verse, the Jehovah's Witnesses say, forbids blood transfusions. They argue that a blood transfusion is the same as eating blood because it is so similar to intravenous feeding.[10]

The Watchtower Society argues that if a person is sick and is in a hospital and cannot eat through the mouth, that person is "fed" intravenously. They ask, Would the person who refused to partake of blood through the mouth be obeying God's command regarding abstaining from blood if he accepted blood by transfusion?[11] Or, to use a comparison, "consider a man who is told by the doctor that he must abstain from alcohol. Would he be obedient if he quit drinking alcohol but had it put directly into his veins?"[12]

The point is that there is no essential difference between eating blood and a blood transfusion. Hence, Genesis 9:4 prohibits not only eating blood but blood transfusions as well.

The Biblical Teaching. In response to the Jehovah's Witness you might begin by mentioning the often-tragic consequences of their position. The fact is, many people have died as a result of heeding the Watchtower's prohibition of blood transfusions. Former Jehovah's Witnesses Leonard and Marjorie Chretien comment:

> [One man told of] the heartrending decision he was forced to make between his religion and the life of his child. His baby boy was born with a serious hernia. An immediate operation was required to save the child's life, but that would require a blood transfusion. Jehovah's Witnesses are taught that this is against God's law, and the penalty for not obeying this rule is removal from the organization and isolation from all friends and family members who are Witnesses. The heartbroken father chose to obey "God's law," and two days later his baby died. [13]

It is truly tragic to note that hundreds and even thousands of Jehovah's Witnesses and their children have died because they have put their confidence in this distorted Watchtower interpretation of "blood" passages in the Bible. The Watchtower's disallowal of a transfusion for the above-mentioned baby reminds one of how the harsh-minded and heartless Pharisees condemned and chastised Jesus for healing someone on the Sabbath (Luke 6:6-11). [14]

Ask...

- Would you _really_ allow your baby to die because of instructions from the Watchtower Society?

Now, having said all this, you will want to point out to the Jehovah's Witness that the Watchtower Society has a very bad track record regarding changing its position on medical issues. Take vaccinations as an example. *The Golden Age* magazine (1931) said that a "vaccination is a direct violation of the everlasting covenant that God made with Noah after the flood."[15] Vaccinations were hence forbidden by the Watchtower Society for twenty years. However, the Watchtower Society dropped this prohibition in the 1950s, and since this time children in the sect have been openly vaccinated.[16] The August 22, 1965, issue of *Awake!* magazine even acknowledged that vaccinations seem to have caused a decrease in diseases.[17] One must wonder how the parents of children who had died as a result of *not* being vaccinated felt when the Watchtower Society suddenly reversed its view.

We find another example in the Watchtower's change of position on organ transplants.[18] The November 15, 1967, issue of *The Watchtower* magazine said that organ transplants amounted to cannibalism and are not appropriate for Christians.[19] The next year's issue of *Awake!* magazine agreed that *all* organ transplants are cannibalism.[20] Hence, organ transplants were forbidden for some thirteen years. During this time, many Jehovah's Witnesses died or suffered greatly as a result of not having such a transplant. But then the Watchtower Society changed its view when the medical benefits of such transplants became a proven fact. The March 15, 1980, issue of *The Watchtower* magazine said that organ transplants are *not necessarily* cannibalistic[21] and began allowing them.

In light of the above changes, former Jehovah's Witness David Reed comments: "Given the Watchtower's track record of prohibiting vaccinations for over twenty years, then reversing itself, and later banning organ transplants for thirteen years before again changing the interpretation, one can only wonder how long it will be until the Society reinterprets the Bible verses it now uses to forbid transfusions."[22]

Ask...

- Did you know that the Watchtower Society prohibited vaccinations in the early 1930s but then reversed its position and began allowing them in the 1950s?

- Did you know that the Watchtower Society prohibited organ transplants in 1967 but then reversed its position in 1980 and began allowing them?

- How do you think Jehovah's Witness parents whose children had died as a result of not having a vaccination or an organ transplant felt when the Watchtower Society reversed its positions?

- In view of the Watchtower Society's inconsistent track record on medical issues, do you think it is possible that the Society may reverse itself on the issue of blood transfusions in the not-too-distant future?

- What do you think accounts for the Watchtower's inconsistency on medical issues?

- Is such inconsistency fitting for a prophet of God, as the Watchtower Society claims to be?

Now, before going any further, we must address the question: Why was the dietary law in Genesis 9:4 given to the Israelites in the first place? Many scholars relate the law to the blood sacrifices that would become a regular part of Israel's religious life. Bible scholar H.C. Leupold comments:

> These restrictions are given in view of the ordinances that are later to govern the use of blood in sacrifices. This provision, then, of Noah's time prepares for the sacrificial use of blood, and that which is to be sacred in sacrifice... should hardly be employed that a man may glut his appetite with it.

> In fact, it is not an overstatement of the case to remark that ultimately this restriction is made in view of the sanctity of the blood of our Great High Priest, who is both priest and sacrifice.[23]

It is understandable why such a dietary regulation would be necessary. After all, some of the pagan nations surrounding Israel had no respect whatsoever for blood. These pagans ate blood on a regular basis. Sometimes they did this as part of the worship of false gods; at other times they did this because they thought it might bring them supernatural power. In any event, the prohibition against eating blood set Israel apart from such ungodly nations.

But now we must ask, *Is there no essential difference between eating blood and receiving a blood transfusion?* In answering this question, we must first affirm that evangelical Christians agree that Genesis 9:4 and other such passages prohibit the eating of blood. That is not the issue of debate. The debate focuses on whether eating blood is the same as a blood transfusion. It is here that the Jehovah's Witnesses have erred.

In his excellent book *Scripture Twisting*, James Sire argues that the Watchtower's attempt to ban blood transfusions based on Genesis 9:4 is a clear example of a cultic distortion of Scripture. Indeed, he rightly points out that "a transfusion replenishes the supply of essential, life-sustaining fluid that has otherwise drained away or become incapable of performing its vital tasks in the body. A blood transfusion is not even equivalent to intravenous feeding because the blood so given does not function *as food*."[24] Walter Martin agrees, commenting, "When one gives a transfusion, it is not a sacrifice of life, and the eating of forbidden blood, but a *transference of life from one person to another*, a gift of strength offered in a spirit of mercy and charity."[25]

Apologist Norman Geisler further points out that "even though a doctor might give food to a patient intravenously and call this 'feeding,' it is simply not the case that giving blood intravenously is also 'feeding.' This is clear from the fact that blood is not received into the body as 'food.' "[26] Indeed, "to refer to the giving of food directly into the blood stream as 'eating' is only a figurative expression. . . . Eating is the *literal* taking in of food in the normal manner through the mouth and into the digestive system. The reason intravenous injections are referred to as 'feeding' is because the ultimate result is that, through intravenous injection, the body receives the nutrients that it would normally receive by eating."[27] Thus, Genesis 9:4 and other such passages cannot be used to support a prohibition on blood transfusions, since transfusions are not a form of "eating."

_____ *Ask . . .* _____

- Since the medical profession is unanimous that blood is not taken into the body *as food to digest* but simply replenishes essential, life-sustaining fluid, is it not patently clear that a transfusion is different from eating?

- Have you considered the possibility that blood transfusions use blood for the *same purpose that God intended*—as a life-giving agent in the bloodstream?[28]

There is one final point worth making. In the context of Genesis 9, it is the eating of *animal* blood that is prohibited, not the transfusion of *human* blood. As Walter Martin and Norman Klann have observed, "This verse, as it appears in context, has not the remotest connection with human blood, much less transfusions. In the previous verse of the same chapter, Jehovah clearly tells Noah that He is speaking in reference to animals and *their* flesh and that he should not eat *their* blood. God told Noah that animal flesh was for food with but one provision—that he *eat not of the blood*."[29] Hence, this verse does not prohibit the transfusion of human blood.

Leviticus 7:26,27—"*Cutting Off*" *from God's People?*

The Watchtower Teaching. Leviticus 7:26,27 in the *New World Translation* reads, "And you must not eat any blood in any places where you dwell, whether that of fowl or that of beast. Any soul who eats any blood, that soul must be cut off from his people." So serious is the "crime" of receiving blood transfusions that the penalty for doing so is "cutting off" from God's people. *Aid to Bible Understanding* says that "deliberate violation of this law regarding the sacredness of blood meant 'cutting off' *in death*."[30]

God, then, considers the eating of blood a very serious violation. Today, if a Jehovah's Witness is caught having a transfusion, he or she is disfellowshipped. The Jehovah's Witness is shunned by family and friends, who are forbidden to even greet the offender.

The Biblical Teaching. As was true in the section on Genesis 9:4, you will want to emphasize that you agree that Leviticus 7:26,27 forbids the eating of blood—but *this has nothing to do with blood transfusions*. These are two different issues. As *The New Treasury of Scripture Knowledge* puts it, "The provision against eating blood has no bearing upon the modern day medical practice of blood transfusion, which was not in view; and, as it does not have anything to do with eating or digesting of the blood, has no possible legitimate connection with this law."[31]

Now, invite the Jehovah's Witness to open up the *New World Translation* and read aloud from Leviticus 3:17: "You must not eat any fat or any blood at all." Then:

_____ *Ask...* _____

- Why do Watchtower leaders prohibit blood transfusions but allow for the eating of fat?[32]

To be consistent, if one of these is condemned and forbidden, then why not condemn and forbid the other? Of course, your point is simply to show the Jehovah's Witness that he or she is not being consistent in interpreting the Bible.

You might also want to mention, as David Reed does in his book *How to Rescue Your Loved One from the Watchtower*, that even orthodox Jews "to whom the law was originally given and who meticulously drain blood from their kosher food, will accept a transfusion."[33] Certainly orthodox Jews do not consider eating blood the same as a blood transfusion.

_____ *Ask* . . . _____

- Did you know that orthodox Jews—to whom this law was originally given and who meticulously drain blood from their kosher food—will nevertheless accept a blood transfusion?

_____

One further point: As was true with Genesis 9:4, Leviticus 7:26,27 specifically prohibits the eating and digesting of *animal* blood ("bird" or "animal"). It has nothing to do with the transfusion of *human* blood.[34]

Leviticus 17:11,12—*The Soul of the Flesh Is in the Blood*

The Watchtower Teaching. The *New World Translation* renders Leviticus 17:11,12, "For *the soul of the flesh is in the blood*, and I myself have put it upon the altar for you to make atonement for your souls, because it is the blood that makes atonement by the soul [in it]. That is why I have said to the sons of Israel: '*No soul of you must eat blood* and no alien resident who is residing as an alien in your midst should eat blood'" (emphasis added).

Since "the soul of the flesh is in the blood" (Leviticus 17:11), then human blood is intimately involved in man's very life processes. And since God is the source of life, we must follow His clear instructions regarding the use to which blood may be put.[35] One of the uses that blood may *not* be put is eating it. This prohibition directly forbids the "eating" of blood by intravenous feeding, the Watchtower Society says.

The Biblical Teaching. Norman Geisler notes that the prohibition in Leviticus 17:11,12 is primarily directed "at eating flesh that was still pulsating with life because the lifeblood was still in it. But, the transfusion of blood is not eating flesh with the lifeblood still in it."[36] Hence, there is no violation of Leviticus 17 when you take part in a blood transfusion.

Again, you must emphasize that you agree that Leviticus 17:11,12 prohibits the eating of blood. Blood is not something to be profaned by eating it via the mouth, as the ancient pagans did.

However, eating blood is not the same as a blood transfusion. As noted earlier, a transfusion treats the blood not with disrespect but with reverence. A transfusion simply replenishes the supply of essential, life-sustaining fluid that has in some way been drained away or has become incapable of performing its vital tasks in the body. In this context, blood does not function as food.[37] A transfusion simply represents a *transference of life from one person to another*, and as such is an act of mercy.[38]

To emphasize your point, you might ask the Jehovah's Witness the following questions (similar to those listed earlier):

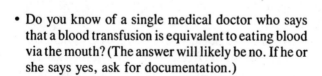

_____ *Ask...* _____

- Do you know of a single medical doctor who says that a blood transfusion is equivalent to eating blood via the mouth? (The answer will likely be no. If he or she says yes, ask for documentation.)

- Do you know of a single orthodox Jew who says that a blood transfusion is equivalent to eating blood via the mouth? (The answer will likely be no.)

- Despite medical and theological evidence to the contrary on the issue of blood transfusions, are you

> going to continue trusting the Watchtower—an
> organization that once prohibited vaccinations
> and organ transplants and then reversed its
> teaching on both?
>
> • Would you *really* allow your baby to die
> because of this Watchtower prohibition?

Finally, as was true with Genesis 9:4 and Leviticus 7:26,27, the prohibition in Leviticus 17:11,12 has to do with eating *animal* blood, not a transfusion of human blood. Jehovah's Witnesses often quote verses 11 and 12 in Leviticus 17, but omit mentioning verse 13, which limits the context to animal blood: "So when any man from the sons of Israel, or from the aliens who sojourn among them, in hunting catches a *beast* or a *bird* which may be eaten, he shall pour out its blood and cover it with earth" (NASB, emphasis added).

Acts 15:28,29—*The Jerusalem Council*

The Watchtower Teaching. Acts 15:28,29 in the *New World Translation* reads, "For the holy spirit and we ourselves have favored adding no further burden to you, except these necessary things, to keep *abstaining* from things sacrificed to idols and *from blood* and from things strangled and from fornication. If you carefully keep yourselves from these things, you will prosper. Good health to you" (emphasis added).

The Watchtower Society says that the Jerusalem Council in New Testament times (Acts 15) *reaffirmed* the Old Testament teaching regarding abstaining from blood. Thus, the prohibition against eating blood (including intravenous feeding) is not just based on an Old Testament commandment. It is a New Testament teaching as well.[39]

Notice also that in this verse "the eating of blood is equated with idolatry and fornication, things that we should not want to engage in."[40] Hence, to take part in a blood transfusion is just as bad as engaging in idolatry or fornication.

The Biblical Teaching. Begin by emphasizing that you do not disagree that Acts 15:28,29 addresses the issue of *eating* blood. That is not an issue of dispute. In Acts 15:28,29, we find that the Jerusalem Council had convened to consider whether Gentile converts should be obligated to adopt the ceremonial requirements of Judaism in order to become Christians. As president of the council, James said he didn't want to burden the Gentile converts with anything beyond a few simple points—one of which was not *eating* blood.

But—*again*—eating blood is not the same as a blood transfusion. You must keep driving this point home: A transfusion treats the blood not with disrespect but with reverence. And a transfusion replenishes the supply of essential, life-sustaining fluid that has in some way been drained away or has become incapable of performing its vital tasks in the body. In such a context, the blood does not function as food.[41] A transfusion uses blood for the same purpose that God intended—as a life-giving agent in the bloodstream.[42]

Now, open your Bible and read aloud to the Jehovah's Witness from Acts 15 verses 9 and 11 (note that this is the same chapter in Acts that contains the instruction about blood): "He made no distinction between us and them [Jews and Gentiles], for he purified their hearts *by faith*. . . . We believe it is *through the grace of our Lord Jesus* that we are saved, just as they also are" (emphasis and insert added).

_____ *Ask* . . . _____

- Is it not clear in Acts 15 that salvation is entirely based on *"faith"* through "the *grace* of the Lord Jesus"?

- Is salvation by *any other means* mentioned anywhere in Acts 15? (The answer will be no.)

- Is the *loss* of salvation mentioned anywhere in Acts 15? (The answer will be no.)

• Is there an explicit statement *anywhere* in Acts 15 that one's salvation depends upon how one responds to the "blood" instruction? (The answer is no.)[43]

One final point worth making is that the reason Gentile Christians were asked to abstain from blood—according to Acts 15 verses 20 and 29—was so they could avoid offending the Jewish Christians (who were horrified at the thought of drinking blood). Hence, the instruction about abstaining from blood involved a matter of *fellowship* between the Jewish and Gentile Christians.[44] Theologian George Ladd comments: "This decree was issued to the Gentile churches not as a means of salvation but as a basis for fellowship, in the spirit of Paul's exhortation that those who were strong in faith should be willing to restrict their liberty in such matters rather than offend the weaker brother (Rom. 14:1ff.; 1 Cor. 8:1ff.)."[45]

Clearly, we must conclude that the Watchtower is in gross error in trying to support a prohibition of blood transfusions from the above-mentioned Bible passages. Jehovah's Witnesses are reading something into these texts that simply is not there.

Birthdays

The Watchtower Society strictly forbids Jehovah's Witnesses to celebrate birthdays. Even the act of sending a birthday card to someone can bring discipline by a judicial committee. Punishment for one who disobeys the Watchtower Society on this issue is disfellowshipping.[46]

Jehovah's Witnesses argue that there are only two references in the Bible to birthday celebrations: Genesis 40:20-22 and Matthew 14:6-10. And in both cases they are presented in an extremely negative light. Indeed, both individuals were pagans and both had someone put to death on their birthdays.[47] In view of this, it is clear that no follower of Jehovah should ever celebrate a birthday. To do so would be an affront against God Himself.

Genesis 40:20-22—*Are Birthdays Evil?*

The Watchtower Teaching. The *New World Translation* renders Genesis 40:20-22, "Now on the third day it turned out to be Pharaoh's birthday, and he proceeded to make a feast for all his servants and to lift up the head of the chief of the cupbearers and the head of the chief of the bakers in the midst of his servants. Accordingly he returned the chief of the cupbearers to his post of cupbearer, and he continued to give the cup into Pharaoh's hand. But the chief of the bakers he hung up [killed], just as Joseph had given the interpretation."

Jehovah's Witnesses argue that everything in the Bible is there for a reason (2 Timothy 3:16,17)—even historical accounts of what particular pagans did in biblical times. And since the Bible presents birthdays in an unfavorable light, then Christians should avoid them.[48] To be more specific, Jehovah's Witnesses argue that since the horribly evil Pharaoh celebrated a birthday and had someone put to death on that day, then birthdays are evil and Christians should not celebrate them.

The Biblical Teaching. The Watchtower position is a clear case of what is known as "guilt by association." Concluding that a particular day is evil simply because something bad happened on that day is truly warped logic. Genesis 40:20-22 proves only that the *Pharaoh* was evil, not *birthdays*. Certainly there is no scriptural command to celebrate birthdays, but there is no warrant for saying that to do so is *forbidden* from Genesis 40:20-22 or any other passage.

_____ *Ask...* _____

- Based on a reading of Genesis 40:20-22, isn't it more logical to conclude that it is the *Pharaoh* that is portrayed as evil and not *birthdays*?

(If the Jehovah's Witness argues about this, ask:)
- What is the source of the evil in Genesis 40:20-22—
the Pharaoh or the birthday?

You might also want to point out to the Jehovah's Witness that the Pharaoh actually did something nice on his birthday as well—that is, he declared amnesty for the chief cupbearer (Genesis 40:21). He set the man free!

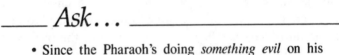 *Ask...*

- Since the Pharaoh's doing *something evil* on his birthday means birthdays are bad (according to the Watchtower), then does the fact that the Pharaoh did *something nice* on his birthday mean there is something nice about birthdays too (using the same logic)?

Regarding birthdays in general in biblical times, Bible scholar E.M. Blaiklock comments:

> The celebration of the anniversary of one's birth is a universal practice, for in most human cities the privileges and responsibilities of life are attached to the attainment of a certain age. The surviving census documents, dating back to A.D. 48, carefully record the age of those described and enrolled according to the requirements of the Roman census law, which implies an observance and counting of birthdays. The birth of a child, according to Leviticus 12, occasioned certain rites and ceremonies. Under the Mosaic law age was the chief qualification for authority and office. The blind man's parents declared that their son was "of age" (John 9:21). There was significance in Jesus' visit to the Temple at twelve years of

age. In spite of the absence of documentary material, it seems obvious that birthdays held their annual importance.[49]

From a historical perspective, it would seem that the birthdays spoken of above had no evil whatsoever associated with them.

_____ *Ask . . .* _____

- In view of the historical evidence that many ancient birthdays had no evil associated with them, do you really think it is legitimate to formulate a legalistic and unbending policy on birthdays based upon two isolated individuals who executed people not just on their birthdays but on a variety of other occasions throughout the year?[50]

A number of scholars—including Albert Barnes, Adam Clarke, Robert Jamieson, Andrew Fausset, and David Brown—believe that birthdays are mentioned in Job 1:4[51] : "And [Job's] sons used to go and hold a feast in the house of each one *on his day*, and they would send and invite their three sisters to eat and drink with them" (NASB, emphasis added; cf. 3:1-3). Adam Clarke notes, "It is likely that a birthday festival is here intended. When the birthday of one arrived, he invited his brothers and sisters to feast with him; and each observed the same custom."[52] (Note that Job seems to define the "day" as a birthday in Job 3:1-3.)

Note that nothing in the text indicates that Job's children did evil things on this day. Their celebration is not portrayed as a pagan practice. And certainly Job does not condemn the celebration. If the observance of birthdays was offensive to Jehovah, then Job—a man who "was blameless, upright, fearing God, and turning away from evil" (Job 1:1 NASB)—would have prevented this practice among his own children.

Matthew 14:6-10—*Are Birthdays Evil?*

The Watchtower Teaching. The *New World Translation* renders Matthew 14:6-10, "But when Herod's birthday was being celebrated the daughter of Herodias danced at it and pleased Herod so much that he promised with an oath to give her whatever she asked. Then she, under her mother's coaching, said: 'Give me here upon a platter the head of John the Baptist.' Grieved though he was, the king out of regard for his oaths and for those reclining with him commanded it to be given; and he sent and had John beheaded in the prison."

Jehovah's Witnesses say that since Herod the pagan celebrated a birthday and had John the Baptist executed on that day, then Christians shouldn't celebrate birthdays. To take part in celebrating a birthday is to associate oneself with a pagan practice and violate God's holy law. Hence, no true follower of Jehovah will celebrate a birthday.

The Biblical Teaching. Again, the Watchtower position is a clear case of guilt by association. Concluding that a particular day is evil simply because something bad happened on that day is warped logic. Matthew 14:6-10 proves only that *Herod* was evil, not birthdays.

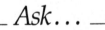 _____ *Ask. . .* _____

- Based on a reading of Matthew 14:6-10, isn't it more logical to conclude that it is *Herod* that is portrayed as evil and not *birthdays*?

  (If the Jehovah's Witness argues about this, ask:)
- What is the source of the evil in Matthew 14:6-10— Herod or the birthday?

_____

Wearing Crosses

The Jehovah's Witnesses teach that the cross is a pagan religious symbol. Christians adopted this symbol, we are told, when Satan took control of ecclesiastical authority in the early centuries of Christianity.[53] The Witnesses say that Christ was not crucified on a cross but on a stake. Thus, for people to wear crosses today dishonors God and constitutes a form of idolatry.

It is interesting to note that early Watchtower literature indicated a belief that Christ was crucified on a *cross*, not on a *stake*, as the Watchtower Society currently teaches.[54] Illustrations in early Watchtower literature even contained pictures of Jesus crucified on a cross. Examples of this include a 1927 Watchtower publication entitled *Creation*[55]; the January 1, 1891, issue of *The Watchtower* magazine[56]; a 1921 Watchtower book entitled *The Harp of God*; and the Watchtower book *Reconciliation* (1928).

However, according to the *1975 Yearbook of Jehovah's Witnesses*, "beginning with its issue of October 15, 1931, *The Watchtower* no longer bore the cross and crown symbol on its cover."[57] The November 8, 1972, issue of *Awake!* magazine said that "no biblical evidence even intimates that Jesus died on a cross."[58] Along these same lines, the August 15, 1987, issue of *The Watchtower* magazine said, "Jesus most likely was executed on an upright stake without any crossbeam."[59]

_____ *Ask…* _____

• Does a true prophet of God—who speaks with the voice of Jehovah—change position on important topics like this?

Jehovah's Witnesses argue that the Greek word for cross (*stauros*) in classical Greek meant "upright stake" or "pale." The Watchtower Society cites *The Imperial Bible Dictionary*: "The Greek word for cross [*stauros*], properly signified a *stake*, an upright pole, or piece of paling, on which anything might be hung, or which might be used in impaling [fencing in] a piece of ground."[60] Therefore, the traditionally accepted view that Christ died on a cross is incorrect.

Besides all this, the Watchtower Society says, the cross was actually a symbol used in pre-Christian times and by non-Christian peoples. Indeed, the cross was a symbol of the false god Tammuz in ancient Chaldea. Thus if a person cherishes a cross, he is honoring a symbol that is opposed to the true God.[61]

Cross or Stake?

The Jehovah's Witnesses fail to point out that the Greek word *stauros* was used to refer to a *variety* of wooden structures used for execution in ancient days. Robert Bowman notes that *stauros* as a wooden structure could represent shapes "similar to the Greek letter *tau* (T) and the plus sign (+), occasionally using two diagonal beams (X), as well as (infrequently) a simple upright stake with no crosspiece. To argue that only the last-named form was used, or that *stauros* could be used only for that form, is contradictory to the actual historical facts and is based on a naive restriction of the term to its original or simplest meaning."[62]

___ *Ask* ... _____

- Are you aware that historical evidence affirms that the Greek word for cross (*stauros*) was used to represent a variety of wooden structures used for execution, including ones resembling the shapes of a T, +, X, and an upright stake?

To support the view that Jesus died on a cross and not a stake, you might want to ask the Jehovah's Witness to open the *New World Translation* and read aloud from John 20:25: "Consequently the other disciples would say to him: 'We have seen the Lord!' But he [Thomas] said to them: 'Unless I see in his hands the print *of the nails* and stick my finger into the print *of the nails* and stick my hand into his side, I will certainly not believe'" (emphasis added).

Now, if Jesus was crucified not on a cross but on a stake, then *only one nail would have been used for His hands*. Our text, however, says that *nails* were used (one for each hand).[63] This verse is extremely problematic for the Watchtower position—especially since their own *New World Translation* has the plural form of "nails."[64]

_____ *Ask. . .* _____

• If Jesus was crucified on an upright stake, then why does John 20:25 say that "nails" were used as opposed to a single "nail"?

It is also significant that when Jesus spoke of Peter's *future* crucifixion, He indicated that Peter's arms would be *outstretched*, not above his head.[65] Jesus told Peter: " 'I tell you the truth, when you were younger you dressed yourself and went where you wanted; but when you are old, *you will stretch out your hands*, and someone else will dress you and lead you where you do not want to go.' Now Jesus said this to indicate the kind of *death* by which Peter would glorify God" (John 21:18,19, emphasis added).

After reading aloud from John 21:18,19:

_____ *Ask. . .* _____

• In view of John 21:18,19, how can a crucifixion be on an upright stake if the hands are outstretched?

In keeping with a cross-crucifixion instead of a stake-crucifixion, we read in Matthew 27:37, "*Above his head* they placed the written charge against him: THIS IS JESUS, THE KING OF THE JEWS" (emphasis added). If Jesus had died on a stake, the text would have said, "Above His *hands*." But it clearly says, "Above His head," showing that a cross-crucifixion is meant.

_____ *Ask* . . . _____

- If Jesus was crucified on an upright stake, then why does Matthew 27:37 say a sign was put above Jesus' head instead of His hands?

_____

Is Wearing a Cross Idolatrous?

Jehovah's Witnesses say that wearing a cross is a form of idolatry. Among the passages they cite in support of this view are 1 Corinthians 10:14 and Exodus 20:4,5. Let us now examine these passages and reason from the Scriptures.

_____ REASONING FROM THE SCRIPTURES _____

1 Corinthians 10:14—*Is Wearing a Cross a Form of Idolatry?*

The Watchtower Teaching. The *New World Translation* renders 1 Corinthians 10:14, "Therefore, my beloved ones, flee from idolatry." In view of verses such as this, the Watchtower Society has taken a stand against all forms of idolatry. This same stand against idolatry was clearly evident in the early church, we are told.[66]

Based on 1 Corinthians 10:14, the Jehovah's Witnesses say that wearing a cross and venerating it as a symbol of Christianity is forbidden because it involves a form of idolatry.[67] Besides, as *Reasoning from the Scriptures* asks, "How would you feel if one of your dearest friends was executed on the basis of false charges? Would you make a replica of the instrument of execution? Would you cherish it, or would you rather shun it?"[68] The whole idea of venerating a cross is preposterous, Jehovah's Witnesses say.

The Biblical Teaching. You might begin by saying that you agree with what 1 Corinthians 10:14 says (in context)—that is, that we are to flee from idolatry. Emphasize that you believe that anyone who thinks a cross is intrinsically holy or is to be worshiped or venerated in and of itself is clearly in the wrong. But simply because one *wears* a cross does not mean that person is engaging in idolatry.

One must keep in mind that the Corinthian Christians (to whom the apostle Paul wrote 1 Corinthians) came out of a pagan culture in which idolatry was quite rampant. Indeed, there were temples of Apollo, Asclepius, Demeter, Aphrodite, and other pagan gods and goddesses that were objects of worship in Corinth. Hence, Paul was addressing a very real problem when he wrote these words to the Corinthians.[69]

Now, in context, it is clear that 1 Corinthians 10:14 has no application regarding the wearing of crosses. Indeed, when Christians wear crosses, they are not venerating or worshiping them. Rather, they are simply acknowledging outwardly that they believe in the *message* of the cross—*that Christ died for our sins and was raised from the dead*. The cross, then, *represents* a worshipful attitude toward Christ. For this reason, wearing a cross cannot be viewed as a form of idolatry.

After explaining this to the Jehovah's Witness:

_____ *Ask. . .* _____

- Are you aware that when a Christian wears a cross, it is not because he or she worships or venerates it but because the cross represents a worshipful attitude toward Christ and His work of salvation?

Exodus 20:4,5—*Is Wearing a Cross a Form of Idolatry?*

The Watchtower Teaching. The *New World Translation* renders Exodus 20:4,5, "You must not make for yourself a carved image or a form like anything that is in the heavens above or that is on the earth underneath or that is in the waters under the earth. You must not bow down to them nor be induced to serve them, because I Jehovah your God am a God exacting exclusive devotion, bringing punishment for the error of fathers upon sons, upon the third generation and upon the fourth generation, in the case of those who hate me."

Jehovah's Witnesses say Exodus 20:4,5 forbids the wearing of a cross because it is a "carved image" and as such is idolatrous. *"Let God Be True"* tells us, "This law [regarding carved images] was given them out of clouds and thick darkness and fire, and no form of any kind was discernible, for the very purpose of preventing man's attempt at making an image of the Almighty God. Thus his law became a hedge, a safeguard to a people constantly surrounded by image-worshiping nations."[70] Therefore, we are told, it would be pure folly to use the cross as a symbol of Christianity.

The Biblical Teaching. In context, Exodus 20:4,5 is dealing with idols before which one bows down and worships.[71] In this passage, it is only objects of worship or veneration that are prohibited.[72] Since Christians do not bow down before and worship crosses, Exodus 20:4,5 does not apply to them. Rather, they exalt Christ and Him alone, and for that reason wear a cross, which points to their worshipful attitude toward Him.

___ *Ask...* ___

- Do you think that Christians bow down and worship the cross?

  (If they answer yes, set them straight. Then ask:)
- Since Christians do not bow down and worship crosses, then the prohibition in Exodus 20:4,5 is not relevant to a discussion of crosses, is it?

The reason Exodus 20:4,5 says, "You shall not make for yourself an idol in the form of *anything in heaven above or on the earth beneath or in the waters below*" (emphasis added) is obvious from Israel's previous experience in Egypt. You see, the Egyptians made idols and images of false gods that resembled things in heaven (angelic beings), on the earth (humans and animals), and in the sea (sea creatures). The true God said that such images should not be made. One must be faithful to Him alone. No competing deities will be tolerated.

Clearly, in context, such a prohibition has nothing to do with the symbol of the cross, since it is not worshiped or venerated.

15

Witnessing to the Jehovah's Witnesses

Christianity is not devotion to work, or to a cause, but devotion to a person, the Lord Jesus Christ.

—Oswald Chambers
(1874-1917)

In this book a great deal of space has been devoted to answering Watchtower arguments from specific passages in the Bible. In this closing chapter—which will be short and to the point—my intention is not to offer further arguments against Watchtower theology but to offer some brief hints on witnessing to the Witnesses.

The hints in the following pages are largely gleaned from the many years of experience in which Dr. Walter Martin personally witnessed to the Jehovah's Witnesses and other cultists. I have adopted his methods as my own, and I acknowledge my indebtedness to him for these insights.

During one of his many speaking engagements, Dr. Martin made the point that there are some do's and don'ts when it comes to witnessing to cultists like the Jehovah's Witnesses.[1] Without going into detail, we shall now look at four do's and two don'ts.

• *Do identify with the Jehovah's Witness.* Martin says you must "convince him (or her) that you consider him to be a person in his own right—worthwhile, basically honest, and not trying to put something over on you. Cultists are *people* before they're *cultists*. They have families, they have children, they have needs, they have frustrations and fears, and they are brothers and sisters *in Adam*, though not *in Christ*."[2]

Acts 17:26 tells us that all people on earth—by virtue of being created by God—are "offspring" of God. In Adam, then, all of us share a common heritage. In view of this, Martin suggests, let's talk to Jehovah's Witnesses from the *"family-of-Adam* perspective," prayerfully hoping to bring them to the *"family-of-God* perspective."[3]

I remember one Sunday afternoon a Jehovah's Witness—a man about 35 years of age—stopped by my house with his son, who appeared to be about five years old. Several times during our conversation, the young boy looked up at his father admiringly. He seemed so proud to be with his father, going door to door talking to people about God. I could picture him thinking, *I'm going to be just like my dad when I grow up!*

This experience, more than any other, showed me that Jehovah's Witnesses are *people* before they're *cultists*. They have families and children and all the other things that are important to normal human beings. This man loved his son, and his son loved him. No doubt this man was trying to set a good example for his son. In my mind's eye, I can see this young boy running up to his mother upon returning home, telling her all about how he and daddy had talked to many people about God. This Jehovah's Witness family—though spiritually misled—was a normal human family in every respect.

If you can keep in mind that Jehovah's Witnesses are people before they're cultists—people with families and children, people who have the need for friendship, love, and security, people who laugh and cry, and so forth—you will find it much easier to treat them with respect and kindness when they show up on your doorstep.

• *Do labor persistently with the Jehovah's Witness.* Never give up unless he or she decisively refuses further contact. Martin says, "Until they pull the plug, we need to hang in there—remembering that the Lord blesses His Word."[4] Remember what God said in the Book of Isaiah: "My word that goes out from my mouth: It will not return to me empty, but will accomplish what I desire and achieve the purpose for which I sent it" (Isaiah 55:11).

You must keep in mind that God's Word is alive and powerful. Hebrews 4:12 says, "For the word of God is *living and active*. Sharper than any double-edged sword, it penetrates even to dividing soul and spirit, joints and marrow; it judges the thoughts and attitudes of the heart" (emphasis added). As you persist in sharing insights on the Word of God with the Jehovah's Witness, you can be sure that God is at work in his or her heart.

I know from personal experience that it's not always easy to labor persistently with the Jehovah's Witnesses. Sometimes when a Witness with whom you have previously spoken pays you another visit *unexpectedly*, the temptation is to say, "This is not a good time; would you mind coming back later?" (This is especially true if you've already got your day planned.) The problem is, he or she may not come back later—and hence, this may be your last opportunity to share the truth with him or her. Let's face it: If you're going to be an effective witness for Christ, you need to *expect* unexpected interruptions.

• *Do exhaust every effort to answer the questions of Jehovah's Witnesses.* We must share not only *what* we believe as Christians, but *why* we believe it as well. We must be able to give convincing reasons for our beliefs. Dr. Martin notes that "the apostles were apologists [defenders of the faith] as well as evangelists. They not only proclaimed Christ, but when they were questioned, they had good, solid reasons for their faith."[5] This is why the apostle Peter said, "Always be prepared to give an answer to everyone who asks you to give the reason for the hope that you have" (1 Peter 3:15).

What happens if you don't know the answer to a question brought up by a Jehovah's Witness? Following Walter Martin's lead (from his early days of witnessing to cultists), just say, "That's a good question. I'm not sure what the answer is, but

I'm going to do some research this week and find the answer. Can we talk about this the next time you stop by?" The Jehovah's Witness will invariably go along with your request. Hopefully, the book you're holding in your hand will go a long way toward providing the answers you need.

• *Do allow the Jehovah's Witness to save face.* When you share the gospel with a Jehovah's Witness and defend your position from Scripture, there will come a time in your encounter when you'll know that you've "won the argument." When that moment arrives, you must make every effort to let love shine through and allow him or her to save face. Otherwise, the Witness will resent you, even though he knows in his heart that you're right.

Dr. Martin suggests handling it this way: "When you sense that the person has lost the argument and is deflated, that's the time to be magnanimous and say to the person, lovingly: 'I realize that we can get awfully uptight in these areas if we let ourselves. Let's just forget that you're a Jehovah's Witness and I'm a Baptist (or whatever you are). And let's just think of ourselves as two people who want more than anything else to know the whole truth and the whole counsel of God. *Right?'* I haven't met a cultist yet who wouldn't say 'Right' in response."[6] Disarming the situation in this way will help lower defensive barriers and will create an atmosphere in which the Jehovah's Witness will actually *want* to hear what you have to say.

Former Jehovah's Witness David Reed attests to the importance of taking a loving, disarming approach. He points out that "empathy is so very important when reaching out to these misled individuals. Try to think of how you would want others to speak to you, if you were the one who was misled. Then remember that 'all things whatsoever ye would that men should do to you, do ye even so to them' (Matt. 7:12)."[7]

Now, there are also two *don'ts* to keep in mind when witnessing to the Witnesses.

• *Don't approach a Jehovah's Witness with a spiritual chip on your shoulder.* Martin says that "a spiritual chip is the communication of the feeling that you are looking down on the cultist because you have something he or she doesn't have. Such an attitude will turn them off as fast as anything you could imagine."[8]

For Christians who have thoroughly prepared themselves by learning hard-hitting scriptural answers to Watchtower errors (such as those contained in this book), the temptation may be to intellectually talk down at the Jehovah's Witness instead of conversing with him or her. Don't let this happen. Be on your guard and make every effort, with God's help, to remain humble during your witnessing encounter. Watch out for spiritual pride; it's deadly!

• *Don't lose your patience, regardless of how dense you may think the Jehovah's Witness is.* This is an extremely important point. Dr. Martin advises, "Remember how dense you and I were—until the Lord managed to break through. Because cultists are bound in the chains of slavery to sin, you need to be patient. And being patient means being willing to go over something ten times if necessary, believing that the Lord will bless your efforts."[9]

If you should lose your patience and raise your voice at the Jehovah's Witness, the likelihood is that the Witness will not come to your house again. This is something you don't want to happen. After all, it may take multiple exposures to the truth before the Jehovah's Witness comes to see that the Watchtower Society has led him astray. You need to maintain a witnessing environment such that the Witness will feel free to stop by your house without fearing a verbal assault.

I can personally attest that the above *do's* and *don'ts* will help you as you seek to share the gospel with Jehovah's Witnesses. But as important as these are, you must not forget the Holy Spirit's central role in effective evangelism—with Jehovah's Witnesses and everyone else. After all, it is *He* who touches their souls; it is *He* who convinces them of sin, righteousness, and judgment (John 16:8). And we become *in His hands* effective instruments for the Master's use (cf. 1 Corinthians 6:19; 12:11; Ephesians 5:18).[10]

Remember, only God can lift the veil of darkness that Watchtower theology has cast over the hearts of individual Jehovah's Witnesses. Hence, your success in bringing a Jehovah's Witness to Christ depends in a big way on God the Holy Spirit's work in that person's life. For this reason, be sure to pray fervently for the Holy Spirit's involvement in *all* your witnessing encounters (1 Corinthians 7:5; Philippians 4:6; 1 Thessalonians 5:17).

I close with an invitation: If I can be of help in your work of witnessing for Christ, please feel free to contact me at the address below:

Ron Rhodes
Christian Research Institute
P.O. Box 500
San Juan Capistrano, CA 92693

Notes

Introduction

1. *Draper's Book of Quotations for the Christian World* (Wheaton, IL: Tyndale House Publishers, 1992), p. 628.
2. *The Watchtower*, 1 January 1993, p. 16.
3. "The Growth of Jehovah's Witnesses," *Christian Research Newsletter*, January/February 1992, p. 2; cf. *The Watchtower*, 1 January 1993, p. 6.
4. *The Watchtower*, 1 January 1993, p. 11.
5. *Ibid.*, p. 20.
6. Don Nelson, "That Hideous Strength: The Watchtower Society," *Christian Research Newsletter*, March/April 1991, p. 1.
7. *Ibid.*
8. *Ibid.*
9. *Ibid.*
10. *Ibid.*, pp. 1-2.
11. *Ibid.*, p. 2.
12. "I Was an Elder with the Jehovah's Witnesses: The Personal Testimony of Chuck Love," interviewed by Dan Kistler, *Christian Research Newsletter*, 2:3, p. 1.
13. *Reasoning from the Scriptures* (Brooklyn: Watchtower Bible and Tract Society, 1989), pp. 15-24.
14. David A. Reed, *How to Rescue Your Loved One from the Watchtower* (Grand Rapids: Baker Book House, 1989), p. 44.
15. *Ibid.*, p. 29.
16. *Ibid.*, pp. 43-44.
17. *Ibid.*, p. 37.
18. *You Can Live Forever in Paradise on Earth* (Brooklyn: Watchtower Bible and Tract Society, 1982), pp. 22-23.
19. Reed, *How to Rescue Your Loved One from the Watchtower*, pp. 23-24.
20. *Ibid.*, p. 33.
21. *The Watchtower*, 15 March 1986, p. 14.
22. Reed, *How to Rescue Your Loved One from the Watchtower*, p. 46.
23. *The Watchtower*, 15 July 1963, pp. 443-44.
24. "I Was an Elder with the Jehovah's Witnesses: The Personal Testimony of Chuck Love," p. 2.
25. Nelson, "That Hideous Strength: The Watchtower Society," p. 2.
26. *The Watchtower*, 15 August 1950, p. 263.
27. *Awake!*, 22 October 1973, p. 6.
28. David Reed, *Jehovah's Witnesses: Answered Verse by Verse* (Grand Rapids: Baker Book House, 1992), p. 116; cf. Duane Magnani, *The Watchtower Files: Dialogue with a Jehovah's Witness* (Minneapolis: Bethany House Publishers, 1985), p. 10.
29. Reed, *Jehovah's Witnesses: Answered Verse by Verse,* p. 116.
30. *Ibid.*, p. 114.
31. Peter Barnes, *The Truth About Jesus and the Trinity* (San Diego: Equippers, Inc., 1989), p. 2.
32. Reed, *Jehovah's Witnesses: Answered Verse by Verse*, p. 115.
33. *See* Robert M. Bowman, "Is Jesus a True or a False God?" *Christian Research Journal*, Winter/Spring 1990, p. 7; cf. Magnani, pp. 125-26.
34. Reed, *How to Rescue Your Loved One from the Watchtower*, pp. 29, 53.

Chapter One—The Watchtower Society: God's Organization or Cultic Tyrant?

1. *Draper's Book of Quotations for the Christian World* (Grand Rapids: Baker Book House, 1992), p. 629.
2. *Ibid.*
3. *Reasoning from the Scriptures* (Brooklyn: Watchtower Bible and Tract Society, 1989), p. 199.
4. *The Watchtower*, 15 January 1917, p. 6033.
5. *The Watchtower*, 1 April 1919, p. 6414.
6. *The Watchtower*, 1 May 1938, p. 169.
7. *The Watchtower*, 1 June 1985, p. 19.
8. *The Watchtower*, 1 July 1973, p. 402.
9. *The Watchtower*, 15 June 1957, p. 370.
10. *The Watchtower*, 1 March 1983, p. 25.
11. *The Watchtower*, 15 March 1969, p. 172.
12. *The Watchtower*, 1 May 1957, p. 274.
13. *The Watchtower*, 1 December 1981, p. 27.

410

14. *Studies in the Scriptures*, vol. 1: *The Divine Plan of the Ages* (Brooklyn: Watchtower Bible and Tract Society, 1924-27 editions), p. 7; vol. 7: *The Finished Mystery* (1917), pp. 5, 418.
15. *The Harp of God* (Brooklyn: Watchtower Bible and Tract Society, 1921), p. 239.
16. *The Watchtower*, 1 April 1920, p. 100.
17. *Ibid.*, p. 101.
18. David Reed, *Jehovah's Witnesses Answered Verse by Verse* (Grand Rapids: Baker Book House, 1992), p. 59.
19. *Ibid.*
20. *God's Kingdom of a Thousand Years Has Approached* (Brooklyn: Watchtower Bible and Tract Society, 1973), p. 346.
21. *"Let God Be True"* (Brooklyn: Watchtower Bible and Tract Society, 1952), p. 200; *Reasoning from the Scriptures*, p. 206, emphasis added.
22. Robert M. Bowman, *Understanding Jehovah's Witnesses* (Grand Rapids: Baker Book House, 1991), p. 59.
23. *The Watchtower*, 15 January 1969, p. 51.
24. *The Watchtower*, 15 February 1981, p. 19.
25. *The Watchtower*, 1 May 1964, p. 277.
26. *The Watchtower*, 1 August 1972, p. 460.
27. *The Watchtower*, 1 October 1967, p. 590.
28. *Ibid.*
29. *The Watchtower*, 1 December 1981, p. 14.
30. *The Watchtower*, 1 May 1957, p. 274.
31. *The Watchtower*, 15 January 1983, p. 22.
32. *Ibid.*, p. 27.
33. *The Watchtower*, 15 September 1911, p. 4885.
34. *The Watchtower*, 1 October 1967, p. 587.
35. *Qualified to be Ministers* (Brooklyn: Watchtower Bible and Tract Society, 1955), p. 156.
36. *The Watchtower*, 1 July 1965, p. 391.
37. Reed, p. 121.
38. *Man's Salvation Out of World Distress At Hand!* (Brooklyn: Watchtower Bible and Tract Society, 1975), p. 329; cf. *"Let Your Name Be Sanctified"* (Brooklyn: Watchtower Bible and Tract Society, 1961), pp. 245, 361; *"Let God Be True,"* p. 200.
39. James W. Sire, *Scripture Twisting: 20 Ways the Cults Misread the Bible* (Downers Grove, IL: InterVarsity Press, 1980).
40. Bowman, p. 61.
41. Reed, p. 45.
42. *"Your Will Be Done on Earth"* (Brooklyn: Watchtower Bible and Tract Society, 1958), p. 362, insert mine.
43. Bowman, p. 62.
44. *Ibid.*
45. *"Let God Be True,"* p. 43.
46. Edmond Gruss, *We Left Jehovah's Witnesses* (Nutley, NJ: Presbyterian & Reformed, 1974), p. 41, insert mine.
47. *Studies in the Scriptures*, cited by Leonard & Marjorie Chretien, *Witnesses of Jehovah* (Eugene, OR: Harvest House Publishers, 1988), p. 33.
48. *The Bible Knowledge Commentary*, New Testament, eds. John F. Walvoord and Roy B. Zuck (Wheaton, IL: Victor Books, 1983), p. 757.
49. Bowman, p. 62; F.W. Thomas, *Masters of Deception* (Grand Rapids: Baker Book House, 1983), p. 146.
50. *Vine's Expository Dictionary of Biblical Words*, eds. W.E. Vine, Merrill F. Unger, and William White (Nashville: Thomas Nelson Publishers, 1985), p. 330.
51. Michael Green, *The Second Epistle of Peter and the Epistle of Jude*, Tyndale New Testament Commentaries (Grand Rapids: Wm. B. Eerdmans Publishing Co., 1979), p. 91.
52. *The Watchtower*, 15 August 1950, p. 263.
53. Reed, pp. 92-93.
54. *Reasoning from the Scriptures*, p. 327, emphasis added.
55. *The Watchtower*, 1 November 1961, p. 668, insert added.
56. *The Watchtower*, 1 August 1960, p. 474.
57. *Reasoning from the Scriptures*, p. 283.
58. Bowman, p. 55, emphasis added.
59. *Ibid.*, p. 56.
60. *The International Bible Commentary*, ed. F.F. Bruce (Grand Rapids: Zondervan, 1986), p. 1351.
61. *The Wycliffe Bible Commentary*, eds. Charles F. Pfeiffer and Everett F. Harrison (Chicago: Moody Press, 1974), p. 1231.
62. Reed, p. 93.
63. *Ibid.*, p. 81.
64. *The Watchtower*, 15 November 1981, p. 21.
65. Bowman, p. 81.
66. *The Bible Knowledge Commentary*, p. 331.
67. Reed, p. 81.
68. *"Let God Be True,"* p. 222.
69. *The Bible Knowledge Commentary*, p. 413.
70. Robert L. Saucy, *The Church in God's Program* (Chicago: Moody Press, 1972), p. 175.

Chapter 2—Jehovah's Witnesses and the Divine Name

1. Marian Bodine, *Christian Research Newsletter*, "Bible Answer Man" column, May/June 1992, p. 3.
2. *Ibid.*
3. Robert M. Bowman, *Understanding Jehovah's Witnesses* (Grand Rapids: Baker Book House, 1991), p. 114.
4. This is not to deny that the Jehovah's Witnesses point to some manuscripts that contain the name *Jehovah* (a few copies of the Septuagint—the Greek translation of the Hebrew Old Testament—use "Jehovah"). But such manuscripts are not held to be reliable. The majority of the manuscripts know nothing of this name.
5. Bowman, p. 110.
6. *Reasoning from the Scriptures* (Brooklyn: Watchtower Bible and Tract Society, 1989), p. 195.
7. David Reed, *Jehovah's Witnesses Answered Verse by Verse* (Grand Rapids: Baker Book House, 1992), p. 34.
8. Bowman, p. 110.
9. *The Watchtower*, 15 May 1969, p. 307.
10. *The Watchtower*, 15 December 1984, p. 29.
11. *Reasoning from the Scriptures*, p. 150.
12. *The Watchtower*, 15 March 1975, p. 174.
13. *"Let Your Name Be Sanctified"* (Brooklyn: Watchtower Bible and Tract Society, 1961), p. 88.
14. Bowman, p. 113.
15. *See* Reed, pp. 28-29.
16. Bowman, p. 117.
17. Reed, p. 29.
18. *Ibid.*, p. 52.
19. *See* Ron Rhodes, *Christ Before the Manger: The Life and Times of the Preincarnate Christ* (Grand Rapids: Baker Book House, 1992).
20. *"Let God Be True"* (Brooklyn: Watchtower Bible and Tract Society, 1952), p. 28.
21. *"Let Your Name Be Sanctified."*
22. *Ibid.*, p. 12, insert added.
23. *Ibid.*, pp. 374-75.
24. Bowman, p. 118.
25. *Reasoning from the Scriptures*, p. 64.
26. Bodine, p. 3.
27. *Ibid.*
28. Bowman, p. 119.
29. *Ibid.*
30. *Ibid.*
31. Robert L. Reymond, *Jesus, Divine Messiah: The Old Testament Witness* (Scotland, Great Britain: Christian Focus Publications, 1990), pp. 78-84.
32. Jon A. Buell and O. Quentin Hyder, *Jesus: God, Ghost or Guru?* (Grand Rapids: Zondervan Publishing House, 1978), p. 27; cf. Josh McDowell and Bart Larson, *Jesus: A Biblical Defense of His Deity* (San Bernardino, CA: Here's Life Publishers, 1983), pp. 21-24.
33. Robert L. Reymond, *Jesus, Divine Messiah: The New Testament Witness* (Phillipsburg, NJ: Presbyterian and Reformed, 1990), pp. 92-94.
34. Millard J. Erickson, *The Word Became Flesh: A Contemporary Incarnational Christology* (Grand Rapids: Baker Book House, 1991), pp. 28-29.
35. David F. Wells, *The Person of Christ* (Westchester, IL: Crossway Books, 1984), pp. 64-65.
36. This chart is adapted from Josh McDowell and Bart Larson, *Jesus: A Biblical Defense of His Deity* (San Bernardino, CA: Here's Life Publishers, 1983), pp. 62-64.

Chapter 3—The Christ of the *New World Translation*

1. Bruce M. Metzger; cited by Erich and Jean Grieshaber, *Redi-Answers on Jehovah's Witnesses Doctrine* (Tyler, TX: n.p., 1979), p. 30.
2. *The Watchtower*, 15 May 1969, p. 307.
3. *The Watchtower*, 15 December 1984, p. 29.
4. *Aid to Bible Understanding* (Brooklyn: Watchtower Bible and Tract Society, 1971), p. 391.
5. *Reasoning from the Scriptures* (Brooklyn: Watchtower Bible and Tract Society, 1989), p. 150.
6. *The Watchtower*, 15 March 1975, p. 174.
7. *The Watchtower*, 1 November 1964, p. 671.
8. *Awake!*, 8 November 1972, p. 28.
9. *The Watchtower*, 15 August 1987, p. 29.
10. *Studies in the Scriptures*, vol. 7 (Brooklyn: Watchtower Bible and Tract Society, 1917), p. 57.
11. *You Can Live Forever in Paradise on Earth* (Brooklyn: Watchtower Bible and Tract Society, 1982), p. 143.
12. *"The Kingdom Is at Hand"* (Brooklyn: Watchtower Bible and Tract Society, 1944), p. 259.
13. *You Can Live Forever in Paradise on Earth*, p. 145.
14. *The Watchtower*, 1 September 1953, p. 518.
15. *"Things in Which It Is Impossible for God to Lie"* (Brooklyn: Watchtower Bible and Tract Society, 1965), p. 354.
16. *"Let God Be True"* (Brooklyn: Watchtower Bible and Tract Society, 1952), p. 33.

412

17. *Aid to Bible Understanding*, p. 1669.
18. *Ibid.*, p. 918.
19. *Reasoning from the Scriptures*, pp. 408-09.
20. *New World Translation* (Brooklyn: Watchtower Bible and Tract Society, 1981), p. 6.
21. Robert M. Bowman, *Understanding Jehovah's Witnesses* (Grand Rapids: Baker Book House, 1991), p. 66.
22. Robert L. Reymond, *Jesus, Divine Messiah: The New Testament Witness* (Phillipsburg, NJ: Presbyterian and Reformed, 1990), p. 248.
23. Jerry and Marian Bodine, *Witnessing to the Witnesses* (Irvine, CA: n.p., n.d.), pp. 39-40.
24. *Ibid.*, p. 40.
25. Bruce M. Metzger, "The Jehovah's Witnesses and Jesus Christ," *Theology Today*, 10 (April 1953), p. 70.
26. *Ibid.*
27. Robert M. Bowman, *Why You Should Believe in the Trinity* (Grand Rapids: Baker Book House, 1989), p. 68.
28. Ron Rhodes, *Christ Before the Manger: The Life and Times of the Preincarnate Christ* (Grand Rapids: Baker Book House, 1992), pp. 57-58.
29. John Eadie, *A Commentary on the Greek Text of the Epistle of Paul to the Colossians* (Grand Rapids: Baker Book House, 1979), p. 51.
30. Curtis Vaughan, "Colossians," in *The Expositor's Bible Commentary*, vol. 11, ed. Frank E. Gaebelein (Grand Rapids: Zondervan Publishing House, 1978), p. 182.
31. Norman Geisler, *Christian Apologetics* (Grand Rapids: Baker Book House, 1976), p. 338.
32. Eadie, p. 56.
33. Rhodes, p. 71.
34. Cited by Marvin R. Vincent, *Word Studies in the New Testament*, vol. 3 (Grand Rapids: Wm. B. Eerdmans Publishing Co., 1975), p. 471.
35. John F. Walvoord, *Jesus Christ Our Lord* (Chicago: Moody Press, 1980), p. 50.
36. Eadie, p. 57.
37. Walvoord, p. 50.
38. *Reasoning from the Scriptures*, p. 421.
39. J.B. Lightfoot, *St. Paul's Epistles to the Colossians and to Philemon* (Grand Rapids: Zondervan Publishing House, 1979), p. 181.
40. Walter Martin and Norman Klann, *Jehovah of the Watchtower* (Minneapolis: Bethany House Publishers, 1974), p. 55.
41. J.H. Thayer, *A Greek-English Lexicon of the New Testament* (Grand Rapids: Zondervan Publishing House, 1963), p. 288.
42. R.C. Trench; cited in *The New Treasury of Scripture Knowledge* (Nashville: Thomas Nelson Publishers, 1992), p. 1401.
43. John A. Bengel; *New Testament Word Studies*, Vol. 2 (Grand Rapids: Kregel Publications, 1978), p. 460.
44. H.C.G. Moule, *Studies in Colossians & Philemon* (Grand Rapids: Kregel Publications, 1977), p. 102.
45. Reymond, p. 250.
46. Benjamin B. Warfield, *The Person and Work of Christ* (Philadelphia: Presbyterian and Reformed Publishing, 1950), p. 46.
47. R.C. Trench; cited in Kenneth S. Wuest, "Ephesians and Colossians in the Greek New Testament," *Wuest's Word Studies* (Grand Rapids: Wm. B. Eerdmans Publishing Co., 1953), p. 203.
48. David Reed, *Jehovah's Witnesses Answered Verse by Verse* (Grand Rapids: Baker Book House, 1992), p. 98.
49. Reymond, pp. 79-80.
50. *Ibid.*, p. 80.
51. *Reasoning from the Scriptures*, p. 418.
52. Robert H. Countess, *The Jehovah's Witnesses' New Testament* (Phillipsburg, NJ: Presbyterian and Reformed Publishing Co., 1982), p. 61.
53. *Ibid.*
54. A.T. Robertson, *Word Pictures in the New Testament*, vol. 3 (Nashville: Broadman Press, 1930), p. 353.
55. Warfield, p. 63.
56. *Ibid.*, p. 80.
57. Robert G. Gromacki, *The Virgin Birth: Doctrine of Deity* (Grand Rapids: Baker Book House, 1984), p. 113, emphasis added.
58. Spiros Zodhiates, *The Complete Word Study Dictionary* (Chattanooga, TN: AMG Publishers, 1992), p. 94.
59. *Reasoning from the Scriptures*, p. 421.
60. Bruce Metzger; cited by John Ankerberg and John Weldon, *The Facts on Jehovah's Witnesses* (Eugene, OR: Harvest House Publishers, 1988), p. 24.
61. H.E. Dana and Julius R. Mantey, *A Manual Grammar of the Greek New Testament* (New York: Macmillan and Co., 1957), p. 147.
62. Wuest, vol. 3, p. 31.
63. Bowman, *Why You Should Believe in the Trinity*, p. 105.
64. *Ibid.*, p. 105.
65. Reymond, p. 276.
66. *The International Bible Commentary*, ed. F.F. Bruce (Grand Rapids: Zondervan Publishing House, 1979), p. 1495.
67. *See*, for example, Bruce M. Metzger, "The Jehovah's Witnesses and Jesus Christ," *Theology Today*, 10 (April 1953), p. 75f.

68. Bowman, *Why You Should Believe in the Trinity*, p. 105.
69. Reymond, p. 276.
70. *The New Treasury of Scripture Knowledge*, p. 1440.
71. Reymond, p. 121.
72. *Aid to Bible Understanding*, p. 1597.
73. *Reasoning from the Scriptures*, p. 422.
74. Bowman, *Why You Should Believe in the Trinity*, p. 107.
75. *Ibid.*
76. Millard J. Erickson, *The Word Became Flesh: A Contemporary Incarnational Christology* (Grand Rapids: Baker Book House, 1991), p. 459.
77. Ruth Tucker, *Another Gospel* (Grand Rapids: Zondervan Publishing House, 1989), p. 142.
78. Countess, p. 91.
79. H.H. Rowley, "How Not to Translate the Bible," *The Expository Times*, No. 1953, pp. 41-42.
80. *Ibid.*
81. Julius R. Mantey; cited in Grieshaber, p. 30.
82. Bruce Metzger; *ibid.*
83. William Barclay; cited in Grieshaber, p. 31.
84. Reed, p. 71.
85. Erich and Jean Grieshaber, *Exposé—of Jehovah's Witnesses* (Tyler, TX: Jean Books, 1982), p. 100.
86. *Ibid.*

Chapter 4—Jehovah's Witnesses and the Gospel of John

1. Charles L. Feinberg; cited by Erich and Jean Grieshaber, *Redi-Answers on Jehovah's Witnesses Doctrine* (Tyler, TX: n.p., 1979), p. 31.
2. *Aid to Bible Understanding* (Brooklyn: Watchtower Bible and Tract Society, 1971), p. 919.
3. *The Watchtower*, 1 July 1986, p. 31.
4. *Reasoning from the Scriptures* (Brooklyn: Watchtower Bible and Tract Society, 1989), p. 212.
5. *Ibid.*, pp. 416-17.
6. *Aid to Bible Understanding*, p. 919.
7. *"Let God Be True"* (Brooklyn: Watchtower Bible and Tract Society, 1952), p. 33.
8. *Aid to Bible Understanding*, p. 919.
9. *Ibid.*
10. *See* Walter R. Martin, "The New World Translation," *Christian Research Newsletter*, 3:3, p. 5.
11. *Reasoning from the Scriptures*, pp. 416-17.
12. *Ibid.*, p. 417.
13. *Aid to Bible Understanding*, pp. 1134, 1669; *The Watchtower*, 15 September 1962, p. 554; *The Watchtower*, 15 October 1975, p. 640; *The Watchtower*, 15 April 1976, p. 231.
14. David Reed, *Jehovah's Witnesses Answered Verse by Verse* (Grand Rapids: Baker Book House, 1992), p. 72.
15. *See The Watchtower*, 15 February 1956, p. 111.
16. *See* Lorri MacGregor, *Coping with the Cults* (Eugene, OR: Harvest House Publishers, 1992), p. 21.
17. *The Watchtower*, 1 April 1983, p. 31; cf. Reed, p. 72.
18. Lorri MacGregor, *What You Need to Know about Jehovah's Witnesses* (Eugene, OR: Harvest House Publishers, 1992), p. 63.
19. *The Watchtower*, 15 February 1956, pp. 110-11; cf. Reed, p. 73.
20. Julius Mantey; cited by Walter R. Martin, "The New World Translation," *Christian Research Newsletter*, 3:3, p. 5.
21. *Ibid.*
22. *Ibid.*
23. *Ibid.*
24. *Ibid.*
25. *Ibid.*
26. Robert M. Bowman, *Jehovah's Witnesses, Jesus Christ, and the Gospel of John* (Grand Rapids: Baker Book House, 1989), pp. 70-73.
27. Robert M. Bowman, *Why You Should Believe in the Trinity* (Grand Rapids: Baker Book House, 1989), p. 95.
28. Bowman, *Jehovah's Witnesses, Jesus Christ, and the Gospel of John*, pp. 70, 72.
29. *Ibid.*, pp. 80-81.
30. *Ibid.*
31. Bowman, *Why You Should Believe in the Trinity*, p. 95.
32. William F. Arndt and F. Wilbur Gingrich, *A Greek-English Lexicon of the New Testament and Other Early Christian Literature* (Chicago: The University of Chicago Press, 1957), p. 357, emphasis added.
33. *See* Bowman, *Why You Should Believe in the Trinity*, p. 93.
34. Bowman, *Jehovah's Witnesses, Jesus Christ, and the Gospel of John*, pp. 39-53.
35. Julius Mantey made this clear in a personal letter to the Watchtower Society dated July 11, 1974.
36. I recommend Bowman, *Jehovah's Witnesses, Jesus Christ, and the Gospel of John*.
37. James W. Sire, *Scripture Twisting: 20 Ways the Cults Misread the Bible* (Downers Grove, IL: InterVarsity Press, 1980), p. 163.

414

38. Walter Martin and Norman Klann, *Jehovah of the Watchtower* (Minneapolis: Bethany House Publishers, 1974), p. 49.
39. *Ibid.*, p. 50.
40. *The New Treasury of Scripture Knowledge*, ed. Jerome H. Smith (Nashville: Thomas Nelson Publishers, 1992), p. 1181.
41. Robert L. Reymond, *Jesus, Divine Messiah: The New Testament Witness* (Phillipsburg, NJ: Presbyterian and Reformed, 1990), p. 303.
42. Leon Morris, *The Gospel According to John* (Grand Rapids: Eerdmans, 1971), p. 77.
43. F.F. Bruce, *The Gospel of John* (London: Pickering & Inglis, 1983), p. 31.
44. Morris, p. 73; Bruce, p. 33; *see* also Bowman, *Jehovah's Witnesses, Jesus Christ, and the Gospel of John*, pp. 21-22.
45. R.C.H. Lenski, *Hebrews* (Minneapolis, MN: Augsburg Publishing House, 1961), p. 36.
46. F.F. Bruce, *The Epistle to the Hebrews* (Grand Rapids: Wm. B. Eerdmans Publishing Co., 1979), p. 4.
47. Harold B. Kuhn, "Creation," in *Basic Christian Doctrines*, ed. Carl F. Henry (Grand Rapids: Baker Book House, 1983), p. 61.
48. Louis Berkhof, *Manual of Christian Doctrine* (Grand Rapids: Wm. B. Eerdmans Publishing Co., 1983), p. 96.
49. R.C.H. Lenski, *The Interpretation of St. John's Gospel* (Minneapolis: Augsburg Publishing House, 1961), p. 27.
50. Morris, p. 73.
51. Benjamin B. Warfield, *The Person and Work of Christ* (Philadelphia: Presbyterian and Reformed Publishing Co., 1950), p. 53.
52. David J. Ellis, "John," in *The International Bible Commentary*, ed. F.F. Bruce (Grand Rapids: Zondervan Publishing House, 1986), p. 1232.
53. Morris, p. 79.
54. Lenski, *The Interpretation of St. John's Gospel*, p. 33.
55. *Reasoning from the Scriptures*, pp. 417-18.
56. *The Greatest Man Who Ever Lived* (Brooklyn: Watchtower Bible and Tract Society, 1991), preface.
57. Ron Rhodes, *Christ Before the Manger: The Life and Times of the Preincarnate Christ* (Grand Rapids: Baker Book House, 1992), pp. 160-65.
58. *Evangelical Commentary on the Bible*, ed. Walter A. Elwell (Grand Rapids: Baker Book House, 1989), p. 43, emphasis in original, inserts added.
59. John J. Davis, *Moses and Gods of Egypt* (Grand Rapids: Baker Book House, 1986), p. 72, emphasis added.
60. *Cambridge Bible*, cited in *The Wycliffe Bible Commentary*, eds. Charles F. Pfeiffer and Everett F. Harrison (Chicago: Moody Press, 1974), p. 55.
61. Carl F. Keil and Franz Delitzsch, cited in *The Wycliffe Bible Commentary*, p. 55, emphasis added.
62. *The Wycliffe Bible Commentary*, p. 55.
63. Bowman, *Jehovah's Witnesses, Jesus Christ, and the Gospel of John*, pp. 90-98.
64. Reed, p. 27.
65. Jon A. Buell and O. Quentin Hyder, *Jesus: God, Ghost or Guru?* (Grand Rapids: Zondervan Publishing House, 1978), p. 27.
66. Morris, p. 473.
67. Bowman, *Why You Should Believe in the Trinity*, p. 99.
68. *Ibid.*
69. Reymond, pp. 92-94.
70. Millard J. Erickson, *The Word Became Flesh: A Contemporary Incarnational Christology* (Grand Rapids: Baker Book House, 1991), pp. 28-29.
71. Bowman, *Why You Should Believe in the Trinity*, p. 100.
72. *Ibid.*
73. Bowman, *Jehovah's Witnesses, Jesus Christ, and the Gospel of John*, p. 99.
74. William Barclay, *The Gospel of John*, vol. 2 (Philadelphia: Westminster Press, 1956), pp. 42-43.
75. Erickson, p. 434.

Chapter 5—Is Christ Inferior to the Father?—Part 1

1. *"Let God Be True"* (Brooklyn: Watchtower Bible and Tract Society, 1952), p. 200.
2. *Ibid.*, p. 107.
3. *Should You Believe in the Trinity?* (Brooklyn: Watchtower Bible and Tract Society, 1989), p. 14.
4. Spiros Zodhiates, *The Complete Word Study Dictionary* (Chattanooga, TN: AMG Publishers, 1992), p. 260.
5. William F. Arndt and F. Wilbur Gingrich, *A Greek-English Lexicon of the New Testament and Other Early Christian Literature* (Chicago: The University of Chicago Press, 1957), p. 112.
6. Zodhiates, p. 261.
7. Cited in John F. Walvoord, *The Revelation of Jesus Christ* (Chicago: Moody Press, 1980), p. 90.
8. Robert M. Bowman, *Why You Should Believe in the Trinity* (Grand Rapids: Baker Book House, 1989), p. 65.
9. *Ibid.*, p. 66.
10. *Ibid.*, p. 65.
11. *Ibid.*, p. 66.
12. David Reed, *Jehovah's Witnesses Answered Verse by Verse* (Grand Rapids: Baker Book House, 1992), p. 104.
13. Bowman, p. 66.

14. *Should You Believe in the Trinity?*, p. 14.
15. *Aid to Bible Understanding* (Brooklyn: Watchtower Bible and Tract Society, 1971), p. 918, emphasis in original.
16. *The American Heritage Dictionary* (Boston: Houghton Mifflin Co., 1978).
17. *The Bible Knowledge Commentary*, Old Testament, eds. John F. Walvoord and Roy B. Zuck (Wheaton, IL: Victor Books, 1985), p. 922.
18. Bowman, p. 60.
19. *Ibid.*, pp. 60-61.
20. *Ibid.*, p. 61.
21. *Ibid.*
22. *Aid to Bible Understanding*, p. 918.
23. *Reasoning from the Scriptures* (Brooklyn: Watchtower Bible and Tract Society, 1989), p. 408.
24. *"Let God Be True,"* p. 33.
25. *The Greatest Man Who Ever Lived* (Brooklyn: Watchtower Bible and Tract Society, 1991), introduction.
26. Cf. Robert L. Reymond, *Jesus, Divine Messiah: The New Testament Witness* (Phillipsburg, NJ: Presbyterian and Reformed, 1990), p. 247.
27. *See* Bowman, p. 63.
28. Reed, p. 97.
29. Paul G. Weathers, "Answering the Arguments of Jehovah's Witnesses Against the Trinity," *Contend for the Faith*, ed. Eric Pement (Chicago: EMNR, 1992), p. 138.
30. Ray Stedman, *Hebrews* (Downers Grove, IL: InterVarsity Press, 1992), p. 29.
31. F.F. Bruce, in *Inerrancy*, ed. Norman L. Geisler (Grand Rapids: Zondervan, 1979).
32. *Ibid.*
33. J.B. Lightfoot, *Paul's Epistles to the Colossians and to Philemon* (Grand Rapids: Zondervan, 1979), p. 147.
34. Jerry and Marian Bodine, *Witnessing to the Witnesses* (Irvine, CA: n.p., n.d.), p. 40.
35. Bowman, p. 62, emphasis added.
36. *Aid to Bible Understanding*, p. 918, emphasis in original.
37. *Should You Believe in the Trinity?*, p. 16.
38. *Ibid.*, p. 16.
39. *Ibid.*
40. *Ibid.*
41. *See* Bowman, p. 82.
42. *Ibid.*
43. John F. Walvoord, *Jesus Christ Our Lord* (Chicago: Moody Press, 1980), p. 44.
44. Benjamin B. Warfield, *The Person and Work of Christ* (Philadelphia: Presbyterian and Reformed Publishing, 1950), p. 56.
45. James Oliver Buswell, *A Systematic Theology of the Christian Religion* (Grand Rapids: Zondervan Publishing House, 1979), 1:105.
46. Charles C. Ryrie, *Basic Theology* (Wheaton, IL: Victor Books, 1986), p. 248.
47. Warfield, p. 77.
48. *See* Walvoord, *Jesus Christ Our Lord*, pp. 22-25.
49. C.F. Keil and F. Delitzsch, *Commentary on the Old Testament*, vol. 6 (Grand Rapids: Wm. B. Eerdmans Publishing Co., 1986), pp. 273-78; Robert Jamieson, A.R. Fausset, and David Brown, *A Commentary—Critical, Experimental, and Practical—on the Old and New Testaments* (Grand Rapids: Wm. B. Eerdmans Publishing Co., 1973), p. 508.
50. *See* R. Laird Harris, "Proverbs," in *The Wycliffe Bible Commentary*, eds. Charles F. Pfeiffer and Everett F. Harrison (Chicago: Moody Press, 1974), p. 581.
51. I am indebted to Robert Bowman for these evidences.
52. *Aid to Bible Understanding*, p. 918.
53. E.W. Hengstenberg, *Christology of the Old Testament* (Grand Rapids: Kregel, 1970), pp. 586-95.
54. *The Bible Knowledge Commentary*, p. 1486.
55. Jamieson, Fausset, and Brown, p. 600.
56. Robert L. Reymond, *Jesus, Divine Messiah: The Old Testament Witness* (Scotland, Great Britain: Christian Focus Publications, 1990), pp. 60-61.
57. *The Bible Knowledge Commentary*, p. 1486.
58. Reymond, *Jesus, Divine Messiah: The Old Testament Witness*, p. 61.
59. Charles C. Ryrie, *The Ryrie Study Bible* (Chicago: Moody Press, 1986), p. 1247.
60. *Should You Believe in the Trinity?*, p. 20.
61. *Reasoning from the Scriptures*, p. 410.
62. *"Let God Be True,"* p. 104.
63. Josh McDowell and Bart Larson, *Jesus: A Biblical Defense of His Deity* (San Bernardino, CA: Here's Life Publishers, Inc., 1975), p. 90.
64. Bowman, p. 80.
65. *The New Treasury of Scripture Knowledge*, ed. Jerome H. Smith (Nashville: Thomas Nelson Publishers, 1992), p. 1347.
66. *The Wycliffe Bible Commentary*, p. 1257, emphasis added.
67. F.W. Thomas, *Masters of Deception* (Grand Rapids: Baker Book House, 1983), p. 21.

Chapter 6—Is Christ Inferior to the Father?—Part 2

1. *"Let God Be True"* (Brooklyn: Watchtower Bible and Tract Society, 1952), p. 110.
2. *Reasoning from the Scriptures* (Brooklyn: Watchtower Bible and Tract Society, 1989), p. 410.
3. *Aid to Bible Understanding* (Brooklyn: Watchtower Bible and Tract Society, 1971), p. 919.
4. Leon Morris, *The Gospel According to John* (Grand Rapids: Wm. B. Eerdmans Publishing Co., 1971), p. 658.
5. Robert M. Bowman, *Why You Should Believe in the Trinity* (Grand Rapids: Baker Book House, 1989), pp. 14-15.
6. Arthur W. Pink, *Exposition of the Gospel of John*, vol. 3 (Swengel, PA: Bible Truth Depot, 1945), pp. 281-82, inserts added.
7. Walter Martin and Norman Klann, *Jehovah of the Watchtower* (Minneapolis: Bethany House Publishers, 1974), pp. 162-64.
8. *Ibid.*, p. 164.
9. Charles C. Ryrie, *Basic Theology* (Wheaton, IL: Victor Books, 1986), p. 261.
10. Benjamin B. Warfield, *The Person of Christ* (Philadelphia: Presbyterian and Reformed Publishing, 1950), p. 39.
11. *Ibid.*
12. John F. Walvoord, *Jesus Christ Our Lord* (Chicago: Moody Press, 1980), p. 138.
13. *Ibid.*, pp. 138-39.
14. Robert L. Reymond, *Jesus, Divine Messiah: The New Testament Witness* (Phillipsburg, NJ: Presbyterian and Reformed, 1990), p. 258.
15. *See* Millard J. Erickson, *The Word Became Flesh: A Contemporary Incarnational Christology* (Grand Rapids: Baker Book House, 1991), p. 734.
16. Walvoord, *Jesus Christ Our Lord*, p. 144.
17. *Ibid.*
18. Robert P. Lightner, "Philippians," in *The Bible Knowledge Commentary*, New Testament, eds. John F. Walvoord and Roy B. Zuck (Wheaton, IL: Victor Books, 1983), p. 654.
19. Walvoord, *Jesus Christ Our Lord*, p. 143.
20. Lightner, p. 654.
21. J.I. Packer, *Knowing God* (Downers Grove, IL: InterVarsity Press, 1979), p. 50, emphasis added.
22. *Reasoning from the Scriptures*, p. 212.
23. *Ibid.*, p. 411.
24. Paul G. Weathers, "Answering the Arguments of Jehovah's Witnesses Against the Trinity," *Contend for the Faith*, ed. Eric Pement (Chicago: EMNR, 1992), p. 141.
25. Bowman, p. 72.
26. Reymond, *Jesus, Divine Messiah: The New Testament Witness*, pp. 210-11.
27. *Should You Believe in the Trinity?* (Brooklyn: Watchtower Bible and Tract Society, 1989), p. 19.
28. Reymond, *Jesus, Divine Messiah: The New Testament Witness*, p. 80.
29. Quoted in McDowell and Larson, *Jesus: A Biblical Defense of His Deity* (San Bernardino, CA: Here's Life Publishers, Inc., 1975), p. 54.
30. Reymond, *Jesus, Divine Messiah: The New Testament Witness*, p. 122.
31. *Should You Believe in the Trinity?*, p. 17.
32. *Aid to Bible Understanding*, p. 676.
33. Norman Geisler and Thomas Howe, *When Critics Ask: A Popular Handbook of Bible Difficulties* (Wheaton, IL: Victor Books, 1992), p. 350.
34. *The Bible Knowledge Commentary*, New Testament, eds. John F. Walvoord and Roy B. Zuck (Wheaton, IL: Victor Books, 1983), p. 150.
35. Geisler and Howe, p. 350.
36. Jerry and Marian Bodine, *Witnessing to the Witnesses* (Irvine, CA: n.p., n.d.), pp. 41-42.
37. J. Dwight Pentecost, *The Words and Works of Jesus Christ* (Grand Rapids: Zondervan Publishing House, 1982), p. 359.
38. *Reasoning from the Scriptures*, p. 411.
39. *Ibid.*, p. 150.
40. *See* David Reed, *Jehovah's Witnesses Answered Verse by Verse* (Grand Rapids: Baker Book House, 1992), p. 96.
41. Bowman, p. 73.
42. Reed, p. 96.
43. *Reasoning from the Scriptures*, p. 198.
44. *See* Reymond, *Jesus, Divine Messiah: The New Testament Witness*, p. 105.
45. Pentecost, pp. 391-92.
46. *Ibid.*, p. 392.
47. *Reasoning from the Scriptures*, pp. 413-14.
48. Cited in Bowman, p. 97.
49. Bowman, pp. 97-98.
50. Reed, p. 43.
51. *See* Robert P. Lightner, *The God of the Bible* (Grand Rapids: Baker Book House, 1978), pp. 109-10.
52. Gregory A. Boyd, "Sharing Your Faith with a Oneness Pentecostal," *Christian Research Journal* (Spring 1991), p. 7.
53. Albert Barnes, *Notes on the Old Testament—Isaiah* (Grand Rapids: Baker Book House, 1977), p. 193.
54. E.W. Hengstenberg, *Christology of the Old Testament* (Grand Rapids: Kregel, 1970), p. 196.

55. *Ibid.*
56. John Martin, "Isaiah," in *The Bible Knowledge Commentary*, Old Testament, p. 1053.
57. J.F. Stenning, *The Targum of Isaiah* (London: Oxford Press, 1949), p. 32.
58. *The Watchtower*, 1 November 1964.
59. *The Watchtower*, 15 February 1983, p. 18.
60. *The Watchtower*, March 1880, p. 83.
61. *The Watchtower*, 15 May 1892, p. 1410.
62. *The Watchtower*, 1 November 1964, p. 671.
63. *The Watchtower*, 15 July 1959, p. 421.
64. *The Watchtower*, 15 February 1983, p. 18.
65. Reed, p. 101.
66. Ray Stedman, *Hebrews* (Downers Grove, IL: InterVarsity Press, 1992), p. 29.

Chapter 7—Mistaken Identity: Is Christ the Archangel Michael?

1. *The Watchtower*, 15 May 1969, p. 307, emphasis added.
2. *The Watchtower*, 15 December 1984, p. 29.
3. *Aid to Bible Understanding* (Brooklyn: Watchtower Bible and Tract Society, 1971), p. 391.
4. *"Let God Be True"* (Brooklyn: Watchtower Bible and Tract Society, 1952), p. 200.
5. *Ibid.*, p. 40.
6. *Studies in the Scriptures*, vol. 7 (Brooklyn: Watchtower Bible and Tract Society, 1917), p. 57.
7. *Ibid.*, vol. 5 (1899), p. 454.
8. *Aid to Bible Understanding*, p. 1152.
9. *You Can Live Forever in Paradise on Earth* (Brooklyn: Watchtower Bible and Tract Society, 1982), p. 143.
10. *"Let God Be True,"* p. 41.
11. *Aid to Bible Understanding*, p. 1396.
12. *Studies in the Scriptures*, vol. 2 (1888); p. 129, emphasis added.
13. *The Watchtower*, 1 September 1953, p. 518.
14. *The Watchtower*, 1 August 1975, p. 479.
15. *"Things in Which It Is Impossible for God to Lie"* (Brooklyn: Watchtower Bible and Tract Society, 1965), p. 354.
16. *Awake!*, 22 July 1973, p. 4.
17. *"The Kingdom Is At Hand"* (Brooklyn: Watchtower Bible and Tract Society, 1944), p. 259.
18. *Aid to Bible Understanding*, p. 1395.
19. *"Your Will Be Done on Earth"* (Brooklyn: Watchtower Bible and Tract Society, 1958), p. 310.
20. *Ibid.*, p. 313, emphasis added.
21. *Ibid.*, p. 311.
22. David Reed, *Jehovah's Witnesses Answered Verse by Verse* (Grand Rapids: Baker Book House, 1992), p. 48.
23. Ray Stedman, *Hebrews* (Downers Grove, IL: InterVarsity Press, 1992), p. 29.
24. *The Bible Knowledge Commentary*, New Testament, eds. John F. Walvoord and Roy B. Zuck (Wheaton, IL: Victor Books, 1983), p. 782.
25. John F. Walvoord, *Jesus Christ Our Lord* (Chicago: Moody Press, 1980), p. 30.
26. *Aid to Bible Understanding*, p. 1152.
27. Fred Dickason, *Angels: Elect and Evil* (Chicago: Moody Press, 1975), p. 68, emphasis added.
28. *International Standard Bible Encyclopedia*, ed. Geoffrey W. Bromiley, vol. 3 (Grand Rapids: Eerdmans, 1986), p. 347.
29. Reed, p. 47; cf. *The New Treasury of Scripture Knowledge*, ed. Jerome H. Smith (Nashville: Thomas Nelson Publishers, 1992), p. 1412.
30. Lorri MacGregor, *What You Need to Know about Jehovah's Witnesses* (Eugene, OR: Harvest House Publishers, 1992), p. 51.
31. *"Let Your Name Be Sanctified"* (Brooklyn: Watchtower Bible and Tract Society, 1961), p. 266.
32. *"Let God Be True,"* p. 272.
33. *Aid to Bible Understanding*, p. 1395.
34. *Reasoning from the Scriptures* (Brooklyn: Watchtower Bible and Tract Society, 1989), p. 334.
35. Louis A. Barbieri, *First and Second Peter* (Chicago: Moody Press, 1979), p. 69; cf. Walter Martin and Norman Klann, *Jehovah of the Watchtower* (Minneapolis: Bethany House Publishers, 1974), p. 70; Norman Geisler, *When Critics Ask* (Wheaton, IL: Victor Books, 1992), p. 533; *NIV Study Bible* (Grand Rapids: Zondervan, 1985), p. 1893.
36. Barbieri, p. 69, emphasis added.
37. Martin and Klann, p. 70, emphasis added.
38. Norman Geisler, "The Significance of Christ's Resurrection," *Bibliotheca Sacra*, April-June 1989, p. 163.
39. Robert Gundry, *Soma in Biblical Theology* (Cambridge: Cambridge University Press, 1976), p. 168.
40. *Aid to Bible Understanding*, p. 1395.
41. *"Your Will Be Done on Earth,"* p. 50.
42. Geisler, p. 153, emphasis added.
43. Gundry, p. 168.
44. Geisler, p. 153.
45. *Ibid.*

418

46. *Ibid.*, p. 154.
47. Norman Geisler, *When Critics Ask* (Wheaton, IL: Victor Books, 1992), p. 468, emphasis in original.
48. *Ibid.*, p. 469, emphasis in original.

Chapter 8—Identifying the Holy Spirit

1. Millard J. Erickson, *Christian Theology* (Grand Rapids: Baker Book House, 1987), p. 862.
2. Though not reflected in this chapter, please note that Watchtower literature *lowercases* references to the Holy Spirit (i.e., "holy spirit"). As well, the definite article ("the") is rarely used in such references (i.e., "holy spirit," not "*the* holy spirit").
3. *Reasoning from the Scriptures* (Brooklyn: Watchtower Bible and Tract Society, 1989), p. 381.
4. *Should You Believe in the Trinity?* (Brooklyn: Watchtower Bible and Tract Society, 1989), p. 20.
5. *Ibid.*, p. 21.
6. *Ibid.*
7. *Reasoning from the Scriptures*, p. 380.
8. *Ibid.*, p. 407.
9. *Should You Believe in the Trinity?*, p. 22.
10. *Aid to Bible Understanding* (Brooklyn: Watchtower Bible and Tract Society, 1971), p. 1543.
11. *Should You Believe in the Trinity?*, p. 21.
12. *Ibid.*
13. *Ibid.*, p. 23.
14. *Ibid.*, p. 20.
15. *Aid to Bible Understanding*, p. 1544.
16. *New World Translation of the Holy Scriptures*, with footnotes (Brooklyn: Watchtower Bible and Tract Society, 1971), p. 9; cf. *Should You Believe in the Trinity?*, p. 20.
17. *Aid to Bible Understanding*, p. 1542.
18. Francis Brown, S.R. Driver, and Charles A. Briggs, *A Hebrew and English Lexicon of the Old Testament* (Oxford: Clarendon Press, 1980), p. 926.
19. H.C. Leupold, *Exposition of Genesis* (Grand Rapids: Baker Book House, 1968), p. 49.
20. William F. Arndt and F. Wilbur Gingrich, *A Greek-English Lexicon of the New Testament and Other Early Christian Literature* (Chicago: The University of Chicago Press, 1957), p. 874.
21. *Ibid.*, p. 146.
22. Charles C. Ryrie, *The Holy Spirit* (Chicago: Moody Press, 1965), p. 13.
23. Robert M. Bowman, *Why You Should Believe in the Trinity* (Grand Rapids: Baker Book House, 1989), p. 118.
24. *Ibid.*, p. 116.
25. *Ibid.*, p. 48.
26. For example, see Richard Trench, *Synonyms of the New Testament* (Grand Rapids: Eerdmans, 1953), pp. 357-61; A.T. Robertson, *Word Pictures in the New Testament*, vol. 5 (Nashville: Broadman Press, 1932), p. 253; and W.E. Vine, *An Expository Dictionary of New Testament Words*, vol. 4 (Old Tappan, NJ: Revell, 1966), p. 64.
27. *Should You Believe in the Trinity?*, p. 22.
28. *Aid to Bible Understanding*, p. 1543.
29. David Reed, *Jehovah's Witnesses Answered Verse by Verse* (Grand Rapids: Baker Book House, 1992), p. 51.
30. *You Can Live Forever in Paradise on Earth* (Brooklyn: Watchtower Bible and Tract Society, 1982), p. 85.
31. *Should You Believe in the Trinity?*, p. 21.
32. *Ibid.*, p. 22.
33. Bowman, p. 122.
34. *Ibid.*
35. *Should You Believe in the Trinity?*, p. 22.
36. Bowman, p. 121.
37. *Ibid.*, p. 120.
38. *Ibid.*, p. 121.
39. *Reasoning from the Scriptures*, p. 380.
40. *Ibid.*, p. 381.
41. *Should You Believe in the Trinity?*, p. 22.
42. *Awake!*, 8 December 1973, p. 27; cf. David Reed, *Index of Watchtower Errors* (Grand Rapids: Baker Book House, 1990), p. 85.
43. Jerry and Marian Bodine, *Witnessing to the Witnesses*, prepublication manuscript copy of 2d edition (Irvine: n.p., 1993).
44. Charles Hodge, *Systematic Theology* (Grand Rapids: Eerdmans, 1952), I:524.
45. Bowman, p. 116.
46. *Ibid.*, p. 117.
47. J.W. Wenham, *The Elements of New Testament Greek* (Cambridge: Cambridge University Press, 1979), p. 8.
48. *The New Treasury of Scripture Knowledge*, ed. Jerome H. Smith (Nashville: Thomas Nelson Publishers, 1992), p. 1219.
49. Ryrie, p. 14.
50. *Should You Believe in the Trinity?*, p. 22.

51. Bowman, p. 115.
52. *Ibid.*

Chapter 9—The Trinity: Biblical Doctrine or Pagan Lie?

1. Henry C. Thiessen, *Lectures in Systematic Theology* (Grand Rapids: Eerdmans, 1981), p. 90.
2. *Should You Believe in the Trinity?* (Brooklyn: Watchtower Bible and Tract Society, 1989), p. 12.
3. *"Let God Be True"* (Brooklyn: Watchtower Bible and Tract Society, 1952), p. 200.
4. *Ibid.*, p. 109.
5. *Studies in the Scriptures*, vol. 5 (Brooklyn: Watchtower Bible and Tract Society, 1899), pp. 60-61, emphasis in original.
6. *Ibid.*, p. 76.
7. *"Let God Be True,"* p. 102, emphasis added.
8. *Reconciliation* (Brooklyn: Watchtower Bible and Tract Society, 1928), p. 101.
9. *Riches* (Brooklyn: Watchtower Bible and Tract Society, 1936), p. 185.
10. *Should You Believe in the Trinity?*, p. 3.
11. *Ibid.*, p. 9.
12. *Ibid.*, p. 11.
13. *"Let God Be True,"* p. 101.
14. *Should You Believe in the Trinity?*, p. 6.
15. *Mankind's Search for God* (Brooklyn: Watchtower Bible and Tract Society, 1990), p. 276.
16. *Should You Believe in the Trinity?*, p. 12.
17. *Ibid.*, p. 31.
18. Walter Martin and Norman Klann, *Jehovah of the Watchtower* (Minneapolis: Bethany House Publishers, 1974), p. 43.
19. Duane Magnani, *The Watchtower Files* (Minneapolis: Bethany House Publishers, 1985), p. 148.
20. Paul G. Weathers, "Answering the Arguments of Jehovah's Witnesses Against the Trinity," *Contend for the Faith*, ed. Eric Pement (Chicago: EMNR, 1992), pp. 132, 136.
21. Robert M. Bowman, *Why You Should Believe in the Trinity* (Grand Rapids: Baker Book House, 1989), p. 43.
22. Weathers, p. 136.
23. *Ibid.*
24. *Should You Believe in the Trinity?*, p. 4.
25. *"Let God Be True,"* p. 100.
26. *Reasoning from the Scriptures* (Brooklyn: Watchtower Bible and Tract Society, 1989), p. 148.
27. *Vine's Expository Dictionary of Biblical Words*, eds. W.E. Vine, Merrill F. Unger, and William White (Nashville: Thomas Nelson Publishers, 1985), p. 464.
28. *Should You Believe in the Trinity?*, p. 3.
29. *Reasoning from the Scriptures*, p. 411.
30. *Should You Believe in the Trinity?*, p. 17.
31. *Ibid.*
32. Robert M. Bowman, "Is Jesus a True or a False God?, *Christian Research Journal*, Winter/Spring 1990, p. 7.
33. Weathers, p. 141.
34. *Should You Believe in the Trinity?*, p. 13.
35. *Ibid.*
36. Robert M. Bowman, *Understanding Jehovah's Witnesses* (Grand Rapids: Baker Book House, 1991), p. 120.
37. Robert L. Reymond, *Jesus, Divine Messiah: The New Testament Witness* (Phillipsburg, NJ: Presbyterian and Reformed, 1990), p. 287.
38. Benjamin B. Warfield, *Biblical and Theological Studies* (Phillipsburg, NJ: Presbyterian and Reformed Publishing Co., 1968), p. 30.
39. *Should You Believe in the Trinity?*, p. 23.
40. Benjamin B. Warfield, *The Person and Work of Christ* (Philadelphia: Presbyterian and Reformed Publishing Co., 1950), p. 66.
41. Reymond, p. 84.
42. H.C. Leupold, *Exposition of Genesis*, vol. 1 (Grand Rapids: Baker Book House, 1980), pp. 86-88.
43. *Ibid.*
44. Gleason Archer, *Encyclopedia of Bible Difficulties* (Grand Rapids: Zondervan Publishing House, 1982), p. 359.
45. Warfield, *Biblical and Theological Studies*, p. 32.
46. *Ibid.*
47. *Should You Believe in the Trinity?*, p. 23.
48. *Ibid.*
49. *The New Treasury of Scripture Knowledge*, ed. Jerome H. Smith (Nashville: Thomas Nelson Publishers, 1992), pp. 1095-96.
50. *Ibid.*
51. *Should You Believe in the Trinity?*, p. 18.
52. *Ibid.*, p. 23.
53. James Oliver Buswell, *A Systematic Theology of the Christian Religion* (Grand Rapids: Zondervan, 1979), 1:105.

54. Charles C. Ryrie, *Basic Theology* (Wheaton, IL: Victor Books, 1986), p. 248.
55. Warfield, *The Person and Work of Christ*, p. 77.
56. *Should You Believe in the Trinity?*, p. 29.
57. *Reasoning from the Scriptures*, p. 213.
58. David Reed, *Jehovah's Witnesses Answered Verse by Verse* (Grand Rapids: Baker Book House, 1992), p. 84.
59. Bowman, *Why You Should Believe in the Trinity*, pp. 96-97.
60. Robert M. Bowman, *Jehovah's Witnesses, Jesus Christ, and the Gospel of John* (Grand Rapids: Baker Book House, 1989), p. 133.
61. *Reasoning from the Scriptures*, p. 424.
62. *Ibid.*
63. *Should You Believe in the Trinity?*, p. 24.
64. *"Let God Be True,"* p. 104, emphasis added.
65. Bowman, *Why You Should Believe in the Trinity*, p. 88.
66. Jerry and Marian Bodine, *Witnessing to the Witnesses* (Irvine, CA: n.p., n.d.), p. 46.
67. *Reasoning from the Scriptures*, p. 412.
68. *Ibid.*
69. *Ibid.*, pp. 412-13.
70. Reed, p. 102.
71. John F. Walvoord, *The Revelation of Jesus Christ* (Chicago: Moody Press, 1980), p. 60.

Chapter 10—The Great Divide: The "Anointed Class" and the "Other Sheep"

1. *Reasoning from the Scriptures* (Brooklyn: Watchtower Bible and Tract Society, 1989), p. 76.
2. *Ibid.*, p. 77.
3. *"Your Will Be Done On Earth"* (Brooklyn: Watchtower Bible and Tract Society, 1958), p. 50.
4. *"Let God Be True"* (Brooklyn: Watchtower Bible and Tract Society, 1952), p. 200.
5. *Ibid.*, p. 138.
6. *Ibid.*, p. 137.
7. *"Your Will Be Done On Earth,"* p. 50.
8. These points are derived from Robert M. Bowman, "Only for the 144,000?" Fact Sheet, Christian Research Institute.
9. *Reasoning from the Scriptures*, p. 79.
10. *The Watchtower*, 1 February 1982, p. 28.
11. *"Your Will Be Done On Earth,"* p. 50.
12. *Life—How Did It Get Here?* (Brooklyn: Watchtower Bible and Tract Society, 1985), p. 233.
13. *Reasoning from the Scriptures*, p. 166.
14. *Man's Salvation Out of World Distress At Hand!* (Brooklyn: Watchtower Bible and Tract Society, 1975), p. 201.
15. *Ibid.*, p. 325.
16. *"Your Will Be Done On Earth,"* p. 351.
17. *Mankind's Search for God* (Brooklyn: Watchtower Bible and Tract Society, 1990), p. 374.
18. *"Let God Be True,"* pp. 264-65.
19. *Ibid.*, p. 265.
20. *Ibid.*, pp. 136-37, emphasis added.
21. *See* I. Howard Marshall, *Commentary on Luke* (Grand Rapids: Eerdmans, 1983), p. 530.
22. David Reed, *Jehovah's Witnesses Answered Verse by Verse* (Grand Rapids: Baker Book House, 1992), p. 107.
23. Walter Martin and Norman Klann, *Jehovah of the Watchtower* (Minneapolis: Bethany House Publishers, 1974), pp. 150-51.
24. Reed, p. 74.
25. *Ibid.*, p. 79.
26. *"Let God Be True,"* p. 277.
27. *Ibid.*, p. 130.
28. *Reasoning from the Scriptures*, pp. 166-67.
29. *The New Treasury of Scripture Knowledge*, ed. Jerome H. Smith (Nashville: Thomas Nelson Publishers, 1992), p. 1516.
30. Norman Geisler and Thomas Howe, *When Critics Ask* (Wheaton, IL: Victor Books, 1992), p. 553.
31. *Expositor's Bible Commentary*, "Revelation," ed. Frank E. Gaebelein (Grand Rapids: Zondervan Publishing House, 1978), p. 479.
32. *Ibid.*, p. 482.
33. Robert H. Mounce, *The Book of Revelation*, The New International Commentary on the New Testament (Grand Rapids: Eerdmans, 1977), pp. 169-70.
34. *Expositor's Bible Commentary*, p. 482.
35. *Ibid.*, pp. 482-83.
36. Charles C. Ryrie, *Revelation* (Chicago: Moody Press, 1981), p. 51.
37. Geisler and Howe, p. 554.
38. *"Let God Be True,"* p. 264.
39. *Ibid.*, p. 231.
40. *Mankind's Search for God*, pp. 358-59.

41. *Reasoning from the Scriptures*, p. 167.
42. Jerry and Marian Bodine, *Witnessing to the Witnesses* (Irvine, CA: n.p., n.d.), p. 65.
43. William F. Arndt and F. Wilbur Gingrich, *A Greek-English Lexicon of the New Testament and Other Early Christian Literature* (Chicago: The University of Chicago Press, 1957), p. 270.
44. Bodine, p. 64.
45. David Reed, *How to Rescue Your Loved One from the Watch Tower* (Grand Rapids: Baker Book House, 1989), p. 28.
46. *Reasoning from the Scriptures*, p. 165.
47. Alva J. McClain, *The Greatness of the Kingdom* (Grand Rapids: Kregel Publications, 1960), p. 35.
48. *Ibid.*, p. 35.
49. *Reasoning from the Scriptures*, p. 162.
50. *Ibid.*, p. 163.
51. Reed, *Jehovah's Witnesses Answered Verse by Verse*, pp. 33-34.
52. *The New Treasury of Scripture Knowledge*, p. 610.
53. *Vine's Expository Dictionary of Biblical Words*, eds. W.E. Vine, Merrill F. Unger, and William White (Nashville: Thomas Nelson Publishers, 1985), p. 66, emphasis added.
54. *NIV Study Bible*, ed. Kenneth Barker (Grand Rapids: Zondervan Publishing House, 1985), p. 822.
55. *Theological Wordbook of the Old Testament*, ed. R. Laird Harris, vol. 2 (Chicago: Moody Press, 1981), p. 645.
56. *"Let Your Name Be Sanctified,"* p. 34.
57. Inserts added.

Chapter 11—Salvation the Watchtower Way

1. *Draper's Book of Quotations for the Christian World* (Grand Rapids: Baker Book House, 1992), p. 205.
2. *Reasoning from the Scriptures* (Brooklyn: Watchtower Bible and Tract Society, 1989), p. 132.
3. *The Watchtower*, 15 November 1981, p. 21, insert added.
4. *The Watchtower*, 1 December 1981, p. 27, insert added.
5. *The Watchtower*, 15 February 1983, pp. 12-13, insert added.
6. *The Watchtower*, 1 April 1947, p. 204.
7. *The Watchtower*, 15 August 1972, p. 491.
8. *The Watchtower*, 15 March 1962, p. 179.
9. *Making Your Family Life Happy* (Brooklyn: Watchtower Bible and Tract Society, 1978), pp. 182-83.
10. *The Watchtower*, 1 May 1979, p. 20; cf. *The Watchtower*, 1 May 1980, p. 13.
11. *The Watchtower*, 15 February 1983, pp. 12-13.
12. *Ibid.*
13. *Life Everlasting—In Freedom of the Sons of God* (Brooklyn: Watchtower Bible and Tract Society, 1966), p. 398.
14. John Ankerberg and John Weldon, *The Facts on Jehovah's Witnesses* (Eugene, OR: Harvest House Publishers, 1988), p. 18.
15. *Reasoning from the Scriptures*, p. 308.
16. Duane Magnani, *The Watchtower Files* (Minneapolis: Bethany House Publishers, 1985), p. 232.
17. *The Watchtower*, 15 February 1986, p. 14.
18. *Should You Believe in the Trinity?* (Brooklyn: Watchtower Bible and Tract Society, 1989), p. 16.
19. Anthony Hoekema, *The Four Major Cults* (Grand Rapids: Eerdmans, 1978), p. 273.
20. *Should You Believe in the Trinity?*, p. 15.
21. *Ibid.*
22. *Ibid.*
23. *Reasoning from the Scriptures*, p. 308.
24. *Should You Believe in the Trinity?*, p. 16.
25. Robert M. Bowman, *Why You Should Believe in the Trinity* (Grand Rapids: Baker Book House, 1989), p. 73.
26. *Ibid.*
27. *Ibid.*, p. 77.
28. J.H. Thayer, *A Greek-English Lexicon of the New Testament* (Grand Rapids: Zondervan Publishing House, 1963), p. 50.
29. Spiros Zodhiates, *The Complete Word Study Dictionary* (Chattanooga, TN: AMG Publishers, 1992), p. 193.
30. *Vine's Expository Dictionary of Biblical Words*, eds. W.E. Vine, Merrill F. Unger, and William White (Nashville: Thomas Nelson Publishers, 1985), p. 506.
31. Bowman, *Why You Should Believe in the Trinity*, p. 77.
32. *Ibid.*
33. *Reasoning from the Scriptures*, p. 359, emphasis added.
34. *Make Sure of All Things* (Brooklyn: Watchtower Bible and Tract Society, 1953), p. 438.
35. *The Watchtower*, 15 February 1983, pp. 12-13.
36. *Reasoning from the Scriptures*, pp. 149.
37. *Man's Salvation Out of World Distress At Hand!* (Brooklyn: Watchtower Bible and Tract Society, 1975), p. 111, emphasis in original.
38. Robert M. Bowman, *Understanding Jehovah's Witnesses* (Grand Rapids: Baker Book House, 1991), p. 120-21; *Why You Should Believe in the Trinity*, p. 108.
39. Robert L. Reymond, *Jesus, Divine Messiah: The New Testament Witness* (Phillipsburg, NJ: Presbyterian and Reformed, 1990), p. 230, emphasis in original.

40. *Reasoning from the Scriptures*, p. 80.
41. *Ibid.*, p. 76.
42. *Ibid.*, p. 77.
43. *Ibid.*, p. 79.
44. David Reed, *Jehovah's Witnesses Answered Verse by Verse* (Grand Rapids: Baker Book House, 1992), p. 74.
45. *The Wycliffe Bible Commentary*, eds. Charles F. Pfeiffer and Everett F. Harrison (Chicago: Moody Press, 1974), p. 1078.
46. J. Dwight Pentecost, *The Words and Works of Jesus Christ* (Grand Rapids: Zondervan Publishing House, 1982), p. 125.
47. *Reasoning from the Scriptures*, p. 358.
48. *"Let God Be True"* (Brooklyn: Watchtower Bible and Tract Society, 1952), p. 200; *Reasoning from the Scriptures*, p. 301.
49. *Ibid.*, p. 302
50. Lorri MacGregor, *Coping with the Cults* (Eugene, OR: Harvest House Publishers, 1992), pp. 19-20.
51. *Reasoning from the Scriptures*, p. 358.
52. *The Ryrie Study Bible* (Chicago: Moody Press, 1986), p. 1622.
53. *The Wycliffe Bible Commentary*, p. 1325.
54. *The NIV Study Bible*, ed. Kenneth Barker (Grand Rapids: Zondervan Publishing House, 1985), p. 1806.
55. H.C.G. Moule, *Philippians* (Grand Rapids: Kregel Publications, 1977), p. 72, emphasis in original.
56. *The Ryrie Study Bible*, p. 1614.
57. *Reasoning from the Scriptures*, p. 358.

Chapter 12—Understanding the Soul and Soul-Sleep

1. *Draper's Book of Quotations for the Christian World* (Grand Rapids: Baker Book House, 1992), p. 180.
2. Quoted in Anthony Hoekema, *The Four Major Cults* (Grand Rapids: Eerdmans, 1978), p. 265, footnote 191.
3. *"Let Your Name Be Sanctified"* (Brooklyn: Watchtower Bible and Tract Society, 1961), p. 44.
4. *Reasoning from the Scriptures* (Brooklyn: Watchtower Bible and Tract Society, 1989), p. 384.
5. *"Let God Be True"* (Brooklyn: Watchtower Bible and Tract Society, 1952), p. 200; *Reasoning from the Scriptures*, p. 63.
6. *Reasoning from the Scriptures*, p. 384.
7. *Ibid.*, p. 383.
8. *Ibid.*, p. 98.
9. *Mankind's Search for God* (Brooklyn: Watchtower Bible and Tract Society, 1990), p. 128, emphasis in original.
10. *You Can Live Forever in Paradise on Earth* (Brooklyn: Watchtower Bible and Tract Society, 1982), p. 88.
11. *Reasoning from the Scriptures*, p. 103.
12. *Ibid.*, p. 101.
13. *"Let God Be True,"* p. 75.
14. *Reasoning from the Scriptures*, p. 175.
15. *"Let God Be True,"* p. 68.
16. *You Can Live Forever in Paradise on Earth*, p. 83.
17. *"Let God Be True,"* p. 68.
18. *Reasoning from the Scriptures*, p. 375.
19. *"Let God Be True,"* p. 68.
20. Francis Brown, S.R. Driver, and Charles A. Briggs, *A Hebrew and English of the Old Testament* (Oxford: Clarendon Press, 1980), p. 659.
21. Robert M. Bowman, Fact Sheet on the Jehovah's Witnesses, Christian Research Institute.
22. Scholars differ on this issue, but the *possibility* that it refers to man's immaterial nature cannot be denied; cf. *The New Treasury of Scripture Knowledge*, ed. Jerome H. Smith (Nashville: Thomas Nelson Publishers, 1992), p. 5.
23. William F. Arndt and F. Wilbur Gingrich, *A Greek-English Lexicon of the New Testament and Other Early Christian Literature* (Chicago: The University of Chicago Press, 1957), pp. 901-02.
24. Hoekema, p. 347.
25. *Ibid*, emphasis in original.
26. Arndt and Gingrich, pp. 681-83.
27. Hoekema, p. 349.
28. *Ibid.*, p. 350.
29. Walter Martin, "Jehovah's Witnesses and the Doctrine of Death," *Christian Research Newsletter*, 5:3, p. 4, emphasis in original.
30. *Ibid.*, p. 4, emphasis in original.
31. Josephus, *Antiquities*, XVIII, 1, 4.
32. Hoekema, p. 352.
33. *Ibid.*, p. 353.
34. *Ibid.*, p. 354.
35. *Ibid.*
36. *Ibid.*, p. 356.
37. *Ibid.*

38. *Ibid.*
39. *Reasoning from the Scriptures*, p. 383.
40. *Theological Wordbook of the Old Testament*, ed. R. Laird Harris (Chicago: Moody Press, 1980), 2:1056.
41. Albert Barnes, *Barnes' Notes on the Old & New Testaments*, Psalms (Grand Rapids: Baker Book House, 1977), III:326.
42. David Reed, *Jehovah's Witnesses Answered Verse by Verse* (Grand Rapids: Baker Book House, 1992), p. 39, emphasis added.
43. *Reasoning from the Scriptures*, p. 169.
44. Jerry and Marian Bodine, *Witnessing to the Witnesses* (Irvine, CA: n.p., n.d.), p. 59.
45. Reed, p. 40.
46. *Ibid.*
47. *Ibid.*, pp. 40-41, emphasis in original.
48. Bodine, p. 59.
49. Robert Jamieson, A.R. Fausset, and David Brown, *A Commentary—Critical, Experimental, and Practical—on the Old and New Testaments* (Grand Rapids: Eerdmans, 1973), p. 1305.
50. H.C. Leupold, *Exposition of Ecclesiastes* (Grand Rapids: Baker Book House, 1981), p. 211.
51. *Reasoning from the Scriptures*, p. 169.
52. *Ibid.*, p. 377.
53. H.C. Leupold, *Exposition of Genesis*, vol. 2 (Grand Rapids: Baker Book House, 1968), p. 924.
54. *Reasoning from the Scriptures*, p. 174.
55. *Ibid.*, pp. 174-75.
56. *Ibid.*, p. 175.
57. *Ibid.*
58. Reed, pp. 63-64.
59. *Reasoning from the Scriptures*, p. 287.
60. *Ibid.*, p. 288.
61. Robert M. Bowman, *Understanding Jehovah's Witnesses* (Grand Rapids: Baker Book House, 1991), pp. 99-100.
62. *Ibid.*
63. Bowman, *Understanding Jehovah's Witnesses*, p. 101.
64. Bodine, p. 42.
65. Hoekema, p. 353.
66. Bowman, *Understanding Jehovah's Witnesses*, pp. 104-08.
67. *Ibid.*, p. 108.
68. *Reasoning from the Scriptures*, p. 171.
69. *Ibid*, emphasis in original.
70. *Man's Salvation Out of World Distress At Hand!* (Brooklyn: Watchtower Bible and Tract Society, 1975), p. 274.
71. Arndt and Gingrich, p. 441.
72. J.H. Moulton and William Milligan, *The Vocabulary of the Greek New Testament* (Grand Rapids: Eerdmans, 1976), p. 352.
73. J.H. Thayer, *A Greek-English Lexicon of the New Testament* (Grand Rapids: Zondervan Publishing House, 1963), p. 353.
74. Gerhard Kittel, *Theological Dictionary of the New Testament* (Grand Rapids: Eerdmans, 1964), III:816.
75. Alan Gomes, "Evangelicals and the Annihilation of Hell," Part One, *Christian Research Journal*, Spring 1991, p. 17.
76. John Gerstner; cited in Gomes, p. 18.
77. Gomes, p. 18.
78. William G.T. Shedd; cited in Gomes, p. 18.
79. Alan Gomes, "Evangelicals and the Annihilation of Hell," Part Two, *Christian Research Journal*, Summer 1991, p. 11.
80. Gomes, I:18.
81. *Reasoning from the Scriptures*, pp. 171-72.
82. Moulton and Milligan, p. 445; cf. Leon Morris, *The First and Second Epistles to the Thessalonians* (Grand Rapids: Eerdmans, 1959), pp. 153-54.
83. Robert L. Thomas, "2 Thessalonians," *The Expositor's Bible Commentary*, ed. Frank E. Gaebelein (Grand Rapids: Zondervan, 1978), p. 313.
84. *The Wycliffe Bible Commentary*, eds. Charles F. Pfeiffer and Everett F. Harrison (Chicago: Moody Press, 1974), p. 1362.
85. Gomes, I:18.
86. *Reasoning from the Scriptures*, p. 172.
87. *Ibid.*, p. 173.
88. Thayer, p. 96.
89. Arndt and Gingrich, p. 134.
90. Gomes, II:11.
91. R.C.H. Lenski, *Revelation* (Minneapolis: Augsburg, 1961), p. 438.
92. Gomes, II:18, insert added.
93. *The Bible Knowledge Commentary*, New Testament, eds. John F. Walvoord and Roy B. Zuck (Wheaton, IL: Victor Books, 1983), p. 964.
94. Gomes, I:19.

Chapter 13—Prophecy and the Watchtower Society: A History of Failures

1. *The Watchtower*, 1 October 1982, p. 27.
2. *The Watchtower*, 1 October 1964, p. 601.
3. *The Watchtower*, 1 April 1972, p. 197.
4. *The Watchtower*, 1 March 1965, p. 151.
5. *Light*, vol. 2 (Brooklyn: Watchtower Bible and Tract Society, 1930), p. 47.
6. *Prophecy* (Brooklyn: Watchtower Bible and Tract Society, 1929), p. 22.
7. *Paradise Restored to Mankind—By Theocracy* (Brooklyn: Watchtower Bible and Tract Society, 1972), pp. 353-54.
8. *1980 Yearbook of Jehovah's Witnesses* (Brooklyn: Watchtower Bible and Tract Society, 1980), pp. 30-31.
9. *1975 Yearbook of Jehovah's Witnesses* (Brooklyn: Watchtower Bible and Tract Society, 1975), p. 245.
10. *The Watchtower*, 15 March 1986, p. 19.
11. *The Watchtower*, 15 May 1976, p. 297.
12. *Studies in the Scriptures*; cited in Ruth A. Tucker, *Another Gospel* (Grand Rapids: Zondervan Publishing House, 1989), p. 124, emphasis in original.
13. Tucker, p. 124.
14. *The Watchtower*, 15 May 1925, p. 148.
15. *The Watchtower*, 15 November 1928, p. 344.
16. David Reed, *How to Rescue Your Loved One from the Watch Tower* (Grand Rapids: Baker Book House, 1989), p. 47.
17. *Ibid.*
18. *Studies in the Scriptures*, vol. 4 (Brooklyn: Watchtower Bible and Tract Society, 1897), p. 621.
19. *Creation* (Brooklyn: Watchtower Bible and Tract Society, 1927), p. 289.
20. *Prophecy*, p. 65.
21. *The Watchtower*, 1 March 1922, p. 67.
22. *The Truth Shall Make You Free* (Brooklyn: Watchtower Bible and Tract Society, 1943), p. 300.
23. *"Let God Be True"* (Brooklyn: Watchtower Bible and Tract Society, 1952), p. 250.
24. *Man's Salvation Out of World Distress At Hand!* (Brooklyn: Watchtower Bible and Tract Society, 1975), p. 288.
25. *Studies in the Scriptures*, vol. 2 (Brooklyn: Watchtower Bible and Tract Society, 1888), pp. 98-99.
26. *Ibid.*, emphasis added.
27. *Studies in the Scriptures*, vol. 3 (Brooklyn: Watchtower Bible and Tract Society, 1891), p. 126.
28. *Studies in the Scriptures*, vol. 3 (Brooklyn: Watchtower Bible and Tract Society, 1913), p. 228, emphasis added.
29. *Ibid.*
30. *Light*, vol. 1 (Brooklyn: Watchtower Bible and Tract Society, 1930), p. 194.
31. *Salvation* (Brooklyn: Watchtower Bible and Tract Society, 1939), p. 311.
32. *The New World* (Brooklyn: Watchtower Bible and Tract Society, 1942), p. 104.
33. *Millions Now Living Will Never Die* (Brooklyn: Watchtower Bible and Tract Society, 1920), pp. 88-90.
34. *The Watchtower*, 15 October 1917, p. 6157.
35. *The Watchtower*, 1 April 1923, p. 106.
36. *The Watchtower*, 15 July 1924, p. 211.
37. *1975 Yearbook* (Brooklyn: Watchtower Bible and Tract Society, 1975), p. 146.
38. *Awake!*, 8 October 1966, p. 19.
39. *The Watchtower*, 15 July 1894, p. 1675.
40. *Our Kingdom Ministry*, March 1968, p. 4, insert added.
41. *Our Kingdom Ministry*, June 1969, p. 3.
42. *Our Kingdom Ministry*, May 1974, p. 3.
43. *The Watchtower*, 15 October 1974, p. 635.
44. *The Watchtower*, 15 July 1976, p. 441.
45. Leonard and Marjorie Chretien, *Witnesses of Jehovah* (Eugene, OR: Harvest House Publishers, 1988), p. 58.
46. William J. Schnell; cited in Ankerberg and Weldon, p. 37.
47. *Reasoning from the Scriptures* (Brooklyn: Watchtower Bible and Tract Society, 1989), p. 134.
48. Robert M. Bowman, *Understanding Jehovah's Witnesses* (Grand Rapids: Baker Book House, 1991), p. 54.
49. *The Watchtower*, 15 May 1930, p. 154.
50. *Reasoning from the Scriptures*, p. 341; cf. David Reed, *Jehovah's Witnesses Answered Verse by Verse* (Grand Rapids: Baker Book House, 1992), p. 53.
51. *The Greatest Man Who Ever Lived* (Brooklyn: Watchtower Bible and Tract Society, 1991), Section 111.
52. *Reasoning from the Scriptures*, p. 234.
53. *The Greatest Man Who Ever Lived* (Brooklyn: Watchtower Bible and Tract Society, 1991), Section 111.
54. *Man's Salvation Out of World Distress At Hand!*, p. 23.
55. *"Let God Be True,"* p. 141.
56. William F. Arndt and F. Wilbur Gingrich, *A Greek-English Lexicon of the New Testament and Other Early Christian Literature* (Chicago: The University of Chicago Press, 1957), p. 635.
57. *Vine's Expository Dictionary of Biblical Words*, eds. W.E. Vine, Merrill F. Unger, and William White (Nashville: Thomas Nelson Publishers, 1985), p. 111.
58. J.H. Thayer, *A Greek-English Lexicon of the New Testament* (Grand Rapids: Zondervan Publishing House, 1963), p. 490 (emphasis added).

59. Stanley D. Toussaint, *Behold the King: A Study of Matthew* (Portland, OR: Multnomah Press, 1980), p. 269.
60. Robert H. Gundry, *Matthew* (Grand Rapids: Zondervan Publishing House, 1982), p. 476, emphasis added.
61. *The New International Dictionary of New Testament Theology*, ed. Colin Brown, vol. 2 (Grand Rapids: Zondervan Publishing House, 1979), p. 45.
62. *Vine's Expository Dictionary of Biblical Words*, p. 32.
63. Walter Martin and Norman Klann, *Jehovah of the Watchtower* (Minneapolis: Bethany House Publishers, 1974), pp. 72-73.
64. Jerry and Marian Bodine, *Witnessing to the Witnesses* (Irvine, CA: n.p., n.d.), p. 55.
65. *Reasoning from the Scriptures*, p. 342.
66. See *The Expositor's Bible Commentary*, ed. Frank E. Gaebelein, "Acts" (Grand Rapids: Zondervan Publishing House), p. 258.
67. F.F. Bruce, *The Book of Acts* (Grand Rapids: Eerdmans, 1986), p. 41, inserts added, emphasis added.
68. *Ibid.*, p. 41.
69. *Reasoning from the Scriptures*, p. 343.
70. *Ibid.*
71. *"Let God Be True,"* p. 198.
72. John F. Walvoord, *Revelation* (Chicago: Moody Press, 1980), p. 39.
73. Arndt and Gingrich, p. 581, emphasis in original.
74. Thayer, p. 451, insert added.
75. *Vine's Expository Dictionary of Biblical Words*, p. 556.
76. *Awake!*, 8 October 1968, p. 13.
77. *The Watchtower*, 1 October 1978, p. 31.
78. Reed, *Jehovah's Witnesses Answered Verse by Verse*, p. 57.
79. *The Watchtower*, 15 October 1980, p. 31.
80. *The Watchtower*, 15 May 1984, p. 5.
81. *The Watchtower*, 1 May 1985, p. 4.
82. *Awake!*, 8 April 1988, p. 14.
83. *Reasoning from the Scriptures*, p. 239.
84. Norman Geisler and Thomas Howe, *When Critics Ask* (Wheaton, IL: Victor Books, 1992), p. 359, emphasis added.
85. *Ibid.*, pp. 358-59.
86. *Reasoning from the Scriptures*, p. 134.
87. *Zion's Watch Tower*, February 1881, p. 3.
88. Jerry and Marian Bodine, *Witnessing to the Witnesses*, prepublication manuscript of the 2nd edition (Irvine: n.p., 1993).
89. *Reasoning from the Scriptures*, pp. 136-37.
90. *The Watchtower*, 15 February 1981, p. 19.
91. Bowman, p. 53.
92. Norman L. Geisler, *A General Introduction to the Bible* (Chicago: Moody Press, 1986), p. 57.
93. Bowman, p. 53.
94. Bruce, p. 38.
95. *Ibid.*
96. Bowman, p. 54.
97. *Ibid.*
98. See *The Wycliffe Bible Commentary*, eds. Charles F. Pfeiffer and Everett F. Harrison (Chicago: Moody Press, 1974), pp. 848-49.
99. Walter C. Kaiser, *More Hard Sayings of the Old Testament* (Downers Grove, IL: InterVarsity Press, 1992), p. 257.
100. Bowman, p. 54.101. Bowman, p. 54.

Chapter 14—Controversial Issues: Blood Transfusions, Birthdays, and Wearing Crosses

1. David Reed, *How to Rescue Your Loved One from the Watch Tower* (Grand Rapids: Baker Book House, 1989), p. 20; *Jehovah's Witnesses Answered Verse by Verse* (Grand Rapids: Baker Book House, 1992), pp. 12, 22.
2. Reed, *Jehovah's Witnesses Answered Verse by Verse*, p. 22.
3. *Reasoning from the Scriptures* (Brooklyn: Watchtower Bible and Tract Society, 1989), p. 75.
4. *Aid to Bible Understanding* (Brooklyn: Watchtower Bible and Tract Society, 1971), p. 243.
5. *Reasoning from the Scriptures*, p. 75.
6. *Ibid.*, p. 76.
7. *Jehovah's Witnesses and the Question of Blood* (Brooklyn: Watchtower Bible and Tract Society, 1977), pp. 18-19.
8. *Blood, Medicine, and the Law of God* (Brooklyn: Watchtower Bible and Tract Society, 1961), p. 55.
9. *Man's Salvation Out of World Distress At Hand!* (Brooklyn: Watchtower Bible and Tract Society, 1975), p. 10.
10. Reed, *Jehovah's Witnesses Answered Verse by Verse*, p. 22.
11. *Reasoning from the Scriptures*, p. 73.
12. *Ibid.*
13. Leonard and Marjorie Chretien, *Witnesses of Jehovah* (Eugene, OR: Harvest House Publishers, 1988), p. 14.

426

14. See Reed, *Jehovah's Witnesses Answered Verse by Verse*, p. 89.
15. *The Golden Age*, 4 February 1931, p. 293.
16. Reed, *How to Rescue Your Loved One from the Watch Tower*, p. 104.
17. *Awake!*, 22 August 1965, p. 20.
18. See Reed, *How to Rescue Your Loved One from the Watch Tower*, pp. 104-06.
19. *The Watchtower*, 15 November 1967, pp. 702-04.
20. *Awake!*, 8 June 1968, p. 21.
21. *The Watchtower*, 15 March 1980, p. 31.
22. Reed, *How to Rescue Your Loved One from the Watch Tower*, p. 106.
23. H.C. Leupold, *Exposition of Genesis*, vol. 1 (Grand Rapids: Baker Book House, 1968), p. 331.
24. James W. Sire, *Scripture Twisting: 20 Ways the Cults Misread the Bible* (Downers Grove, IL: InterVarsity Press, 1980), p. 86, emphasis added.
25. Walter Martin and Norman Klann, *Jehovah of the Watchtower* (Minneapolis: Bethany House Publishers, 1974), p. 97, emphasis added.
26. Norman Geisler and Thomas Howe, *When Critics Ask* (Wheaton, IL: Victor Books, 1992), p. 434.
27. *Ibid*, emphasis added.
28. Erich and Jean Grieshaber, *Redi-Answers on Jehovah's Witnesses Doctrine* (Tyler, TX: n.p., 1979), p. 4.
29. Martin and Klann, p. 95, emphasis in original.
30. *Aid to Bible Understanding*, p. 244, emphasis added.
31. *The New Treasury of Scripture Knowledge*, ed. Jerome H. Smith (Nashville: Thomas Nelson Publishers, 1992), p. 131.
32. Reed, *Jehovah's Witnesses Answered Verse by Verse*, p. 30.
33. Reed, *How to Rescue Your Loved One from the Watch Tower*, pp. 105-06.
34. Martin and Klann, p. 96.
35. *Reasoning from the Scriptures*, p. 70.
36. Geisler and Howe, p. 434.
37. Sire, p. 86.
38. Martin and Klann, p. 97, emphasis added.
39. M'Clintock and Strong, *Cyclopedia*; cited in *Aid to Bible Understanding*, p. 245.
40. *Reasoning from the Scriptures*, p. 71.
41. Sire, p. 86.
42. Grieshaber, p. 4.
43. These questions are derived from Edmond Charles Gruss, *Apostles of Denial* (Phillipsburg, NJ: Presbyterian & Reformed, 1983), p. 188.
44. *Ibid*.
45. George Eldon Ladd, "Acts," in *The Wycliffe Bible Commentary*, eds. Charles F. Pfeiffer and Everett F. Harrison (Chicago: Moody Press, 1974), p. 1152.
46. Reed, *Jehovah's Witnesses Answered Verse by Verse*, pp. 11, 25.
47. *Ibid.*, p. 25.
48. *Reasoning from the Scriptures*, pp. 68-69.
49. E.M. Blaiklock, *Zondervan Pictorial Encyclopedia of the Bible*, ed. Merrill C. Tenney, vol. 1 (Grand Rapids: Zondervan Publishing House, 1978), p. 616.
50. Reed, *Jehovah's Witnesses Answered Verse by Verse*, p. 25.
51. See *Evangelical Commentary on the Bible*, ed. Walter A. Elwell (Grand Rapids: Baker Book House, 1989), p. 342; Albert Barnes, "Job," *Barnes Notes on the Old and New Testaments* (Grand Rapids: Baker Book House, 1977), p. 95; cf. Reed, *Jehovah's Witnesses Answered Verse by Verse*, p. 26.
52. Adam Clarke, *The Bethany Parallel Commentary—Old Testament* (Minneapolis, MN: Bethany House, 1980), p. 870.
53. Reed, *Jehovah's Witnesses Answered Verse by Verse*, p. 13.
54. David Reed, *Index of Watchtower Errors* (Grand Rapids: Baker Book House, 1990), p. 73.
55. *Creation* (Brooklyn: Watchtower Bible and Tract Society, 1927), pp. 161, 265, 336.
56. *The Watchtower*, 1 January 1891, p. 1277.
57. *1975 Yearbook of Jehovah's Witnesses* (Brooklyn: Watchtower Bible and Tract Society, 1975), p. 148.
58. *Awake!*, 8 November 1972, p. 28.
59. *The Watchtower*, 15 August 1987, p. 29.
60. *The Imperial Bible Dictionary*, I:376; cited in *Reasoning from the Scriptures*, p. 89.
61. *Reasoning from the Scriptures*, p. 92.
62. Robert M. Bowman, *Understanding Jehovah's Witnesses* (Grand Rapids: Baker Book House, 1991), p. 143.
63. *Ibid.*, p. 144.
64. See *The New Treasury of Scripture Knowledge*, p. 1224.
65. Grieshaber, p. 8.
66. *"Let God Be True"* (Brooklyn: Watchtower Bible and Tract Society, 1952), p. 148.
67. *Reasoning from the Scriptures*, p. 92.
68. *Ibid*.
69. F.W. Grosheide, *1 Corinthians*, New International Bible Commentary (Grand Rapids: Eerdmans, 1980), p. 230.
70. *"Let God Be True,"* p. 146, insert added.

71. Geisler and Howe, p. 84.
72. *Evangelical Commentary on the Bible*, p. 54.

Chapter 15—Witnessing to the Jehovah's Witnesses

1. Walter Martin, "The *Do's* and *Don'ts* of Witnessing to Cultists," *Christian Research Newsletter*, January-February 1992, p. 4.
2. *Ibid.*, emphasis in original.
3. *Ibid.*, emphasis in original.
4. *Ibid.*
5. *Ibid.*
6. *Ibid.*
7. David Reed, *Jehovah's Witnesses Answered Verse by Verse* (Grand Rapids: Baker Book House, 1992), pp. 115-16.
8. Martin, p. 4.
9. *Ibid.*
10. *Ibid.*

Bibliography

1. Critiques on the Jehovah's Witnesses

Ankerberg, John and Weldon, John. *The Facts on Jehovah's Witnesses*. Eugene OR: Harvest House Publishers, 1988.

Bodine, Jerry and Marian. *Witnessing to the Witnesses*. Irvine, CA: n.p., n.d.

Bowman, Robert M. *Jehovah's Witnesses, Jesus Christ, and the Gospel of John*. Grand Rapids: Baker Book House, 1989.

——————. *Understanding Jehovah's Witnesses*. Grand Rapids: Baker Book House, 1991.

——————. *Why You Should Believe in the Trinity*. Grand Rapids: Baker Book House, 1989.

Chretien, Leonard and Marjorie. *Witnesses of Jehovah*. Eugene, OR: Harvest House Publishers, 1988.

Countess, Robert H. *The Jehovah's Witnesses' New Testament*. Phillipsburg, NJ: Presbyterian and Reformed Publishing Co., 1982.

Expositor's Bible Commentary. Ed. Frank E. Gaebelein. Grand Rapids: Zondervan Publishing House, 1978.

Franz, Raymond. *Crisis of Conscience*. Atlanta: Commentary Press, 1984.

Grieshaber, Erich and Jean. *Exposé of Jehovah's Witnesses*. Tyler, TX: Jean Books, 1982.

——————. *Redi-Answers on Jehovah's Witnesses Doctrine*. Tyler, TX: n.p., 1979.

Gruss, Edmond. *We Left Jehovah's Witnesses*. Nutley, NJ: Presbyterian and Reformed, 1974.

Hoekema, Anthony A. *The Four Major Cults*. Grand Rapids: Eerdmans, 1978.

MacGregor, Lorri. *Coping with the Cults*. Eugene, OR: Harvest House Publishers, 1992.

——————. *What You Need to Know About Jehovah's Witnesses*. Eugene, OR: Harvest House Publishers, 1992.

Magnani, Duane. *The Watchtower Files*. Minneapolis: Bethany House Publishers, 1985.

Martin, Walter and Klann, Norman. *Jehovah of the Watchtower*. Minneapolis: Bethany House Publishers, 1974.

Martin, Walter. *The Kingdom of the Cults*. Minneapolis, MN: Bethany House Publishers, 1982.

Reed, David. *How to Rescue Your Loved One from the Watch Tower*. Grand Rapids: Baker Book House, 1989.

——————. *Index of Watchtower Errors*. Grand Rapids: Baker Book House, 1990.

——————. *Jehovah's Witnesses Answered Verse by Verse*. Grand Rapids: Baker Book House, 1992.

Sire, James W. *Scripture Twisting: 20 Ways the Cults Misread the Bible*. Downers Grove, IL: InterVarsity Press, 1980.

Thomas, F.W. *Masters of Deception*. Grand Rapids: Baker Book House, 1983.

Tucker, Ruth. *Another Gospel*. Grand Rapids: Zondervan Publishing House, 1989.

Weathers, Paul G. "Answering the Arguments of Jehovah's Witnesses Against the Trinity." *Contend for the Faith*. Ed. Eric Pement. Chicago: EMNR, 1992.

2. Primary Watchtower Publications

Aid to Bible Understanding. Brooklyn: Watchtower Bible and Tract Society, 1971.

Blood, Medicine and the Law of God. Brooklyn: Watchtower Bible and Tract Society, 1961.

Creation. Brooklyn: Watchtower Bible and Tract Society, 1927.

God's Kingdom of a Thousand Years Has Approached. Brooklyn: Watchtower Bible and Tract Society, 1973.

The Greatest Man Who Ever Lived. Brooklyn: Watchtower Bible and Tract Society, 1991.

The Harp of God. Brooklyn: Watchtower Bible and Tract Society, 1921.

Holy Spirit—The Force Behind the Coming New Order! Brooklyn: Watchtower Bible and Tract Society, 1976.

Is This Life All There Is? Brooklyn: Watchtower Bible and Tract Society, 1974.

"The Kingdom Is At Hand." Brooklyn: Watchtower Bible and Tract Society, 1944.

"Let God Be True." Brooklyn: Watchtower Bible and Tract Society, 1946.

"Let Your Name Be Sanctified." Brooklyn: Watchtower Bible and Tract Society, 1961.

Life Everlasting—In Freedom of the Sons of God. Brooklyn: Watchtower Bible and Tract Society, 1966.

Light, vols. 1-2. Brooklyn: Watchtower Bible and Tract Society, 1930.

"Make Sure of All Things." Brooklyn: Watchtower Bible and Tract Society, 1953.

Man's Salvation Out of World Distress At Hand! Brooklyn: Watchtower Bible and Tract Society, 1975.

Millions Now Living Will Never Die. Brooklyn: Watchtower Bible and Tract Society, 1920.

New World Translation. Brooklyn: Watchtower Bible and Tract Society, 1981.

1975 Yearbook of Jehovah's Witnesses. Brooklyn: Watchtower Bible and Tract Society, 1975.

Paradise Restored to Mankind—by Theocracy. Brooklyn: Watchtower Bible and Tract Society, 1972.

Prophecy. Brooklyn: Watchtower Bible and Tract Society, 1929.

Qualified to Be Ministers. Brooklyn: Watchtower Bible and Tract Society, 1955.

Reasoning from the Scriptures. Brooklyn: Watchtower Bible and Tract Society, 1989.

Reconciliation. Brooklyn: Watchtower Bible and Tract Society, 1928.

Should You Believe in the Trinity? Brooklyn: Watchtower Bible and Tract Society, 1989.

Studies in the Scriptures, vols. 1-7. Brooklyn: Watchtower Bible and Tract Society, 1886-1917.

Theocratic Aid to Kingdom Publishers. Brooklyn: Watchtower Bible and Tract Society, 1945.

"Things in Which It Is Impossible for God to Lie." Brooklyn: Watchtower Bible and Tract Society, 1965.

The Truth That Leads to Eternal Life. Brooklyn: Watchtower Bible and Tract Society, 1968.

You Can Live Forever in Paradise on Earth. Brooklyn: Watchtower Bible and Tract Society, 1982.

"Your Will Be Done on Earth." Brooklyn: Watchtower Bible and Tract Society, 1958.

3. Books on Jesus Christ

Ankerberg, John; Weldon, John; and Kaiser, Walter C. *The Case for Jesus the Messiah*. Chattanooga, TN: The John Ankerberg Evangelistic Association, 1989.

Buell, Jon A. and Hyder, O. Quentin. *Jesus: God Ghost or Guru?* Grand Rapids: Zondervan Publishing House, 1978.

Erickson, Millard J. *The Word Became Flesh: A Contemporary Incarnational Christology*. Grand Rapids: Baker Book House, 1991.

Geisler, Norman. *To Understand the Bible Look for Jesus*. Grand Rapids: Baker Book House, 1979.

Gromacki, Robert G. *The Virgin Birth: Doctrine of Deity*. Grand Rapids: Baker Book House, 1984.

Machen, J. Gresham. *The Virgin Birth of Christ*. New York: Harper, 1930.

McDowell, Josh and Larson, Bart. *Jesus: A Biblical Defense of His Deity*. San Bernardino, CA: Here's Life Publishers Inc., 1983.

Pentecost, J. Dwight. *The Words and Works of Jesus Christ*. Grand Rapids: Zondervan Publishing House, 1982.

Reymond, Robert L. *Jesus Divine Messiah: The New Testament Witness*. Phillipsburg, NJ: Presbyterian and Reformed Publishing Co., 1990

_____. *Jesus Divine Messiah: The Old Testament Witness*. Scotland, Great Britain: Christian Focus Publications, 1990.

Rhodes, Ron. *Christ Before the Manger: The Life and Times of the Preincarnate Christ*. Grand Rapids: Baker Book House, 1992.

Shephard, J.W. *The Christ of the Gospels*. Grand Rapids: Wm. B. Eerdmans Publishing Co., 1975.

Walvoord, John F. *Jesus Christ Our Lord*. Chicago: Moody Press, 1980.

Warfield, Benjamin B. *The Lord of Glory*. Grand Rapids: Baker Book House, 1974.

_____. *The Person and Work of Christ*. Philadelphia: Presbyterian and Reformed Publishing Co., 1950.

Wells, David F. *The Person of Christ*. Westchester, IL: Crossway Books, 1984.

4. Books on General Theology

Basic Christian Doctrines, ed. Carl F. Henry. Grand Rapids: Baker Book House, 1983.

Berkhof, Louis. *Manual of Christian Doctrine*. Grand Rapids: Wm. B. Eerdmans Publishing Co., 1983.

_____. *Systematic Theology*. Grand Rapids: Wm. B. Eerdmans Publishing Co., 1982.

Buswell, James Oliver. *A Systematic Theology of the Christian Religion*. Grand Rapids: Zondervan Publishing House, 1979.

Calvin, John. *Institutes of the Christian Religion*. Ed. John T. McNeill, Trans. Ford Lewis Battles. Philadelphia: The Westminster Press, 1960.

Chafer, Lewis Sperry. *Systematic Theology*. Wheaton: Victor Books, 1988.

Enns, Paul. *The Moody Handbook of Theology*. Chicago: Moody Press, 1989.

Erickson, Millard J. *Christian Theology*. Unabridged one-volume edition. Grand Rapids: Baker Book House, 1987.

Hodge, Charles. *Systematic Theology*. Abridged edition. Ed. Edward N. Gross. Grand Rapids: Baker Book House, 1988.

Lightner, Robert P. *Evangelical Theology*. Grand Rapids: Baker Book House, 1986.

_____. *The God of the Bible*. Grand Rapids: Baker Book House, 1978.

_____. *The Saviour and the Scriptures*. Grand Rapids: Baker Book House, 1966.

Packer, J.I. *Knowing God*. Downers Grove, IL: InterVarsity Press, 1979.

Ryrie, Charles C. *Basic Theology*. Wheaton, IL: Victor Books, 1986.

_____. *The Holy Spirit*. Chicago: Moody Press, 1965.

Thiessen, Henry Clarence. *Lectures in Systematic Theology*. Grand Rapids: Wm. B. Eerdmans Publishing Co., 1981.

Vos, Geerhardus. *Biblical Theology: Old and New Testaments*. Grand Rapids: Wm. B. Eerdmans Publishing Co., 1985.

Walvoord, John F. *The Holy Spirit*. Grand Rapids: Zondervan Publishing House, 1958.

Warfield, Benjamin B. *Biblical and Theological Studies*. Phillipsburg, NJ: Presbyterian and Reformed Publishing Co., 1968.

5. Commentaries

Barnes, Albert. *Barnes Notes on the Old and New Testaments*. Grand Rapids: Baker Book House, 1977.

Bible Knowledge Commentary, Old Testament. Eds. John F. Walvoord and Roy B. Zuck. Wheaton, IL: Victor Books, 1985.

Bruce, F.F. *The Book of Acts*. Grand Rapids: Wm. B. Eerdmans Publishing Co., 1986.

_____. *The Epistle to the Hebrews*. Grand Rapids: Wm. B. Eerdmans Publishing Co., 1979.

_____. *The Gospel of John*. Grand Rapids: Wm. B. Eerdmans Publishing Co., 1984.

Cole, R. Alan. *Exodus: An Introduction and Commentary*. Downers Grove, IL: InterVarsity Press, 1973.

Eadie, John. *A Commentary on the Greek Text of the Epistle of Paul to the Colossians*. Grand Rapids: Baker Book House, 1979.

English, E. Schuyler. *Studies in the Epistle to the Hebrews*. Neptune, NJ: Loizeaux Brothers, 1976.

Evangelical Commentary on the Bible. Ed. Walter A. Elwell. Grand Rapids: Baker Book House, 1989.

Expositor's Bible Commentary. Ed. Frank E. Gaebelein. Grand Rapids: Zondervan Publishing House, 1978.

Gaebelein, Arno C. *The Gospel of Matthew*. Neptune, NJ: Loizeaux Brothers, 1977.

Hendriksen, William. *Exposition of the Gospel According to John*. Grand Rapids: Baker Book House, 1976.

Henry, Matthew. *Commentary on the Whole Bible*. Grand Rapids: Zondervan Publishing House, 1974.

International Bible Commentary. Ed. F.F. Bruce. Grand Rapids: Zondervan Publishing House, 1979.

Jamieson, Robert; Fausset, A.R.; and Brown, David. *A Commentary—Critical Experimental and Practical—on the Old and New Testaments*. Grand Rapids: Wm. B. Eerdmans Publishing Co., 1973.

Keil, C.F. and Delitzsch, Franz. *Biblical Commentary on the Old Testament*. Grand Rapids: Wm. B. Eerdmans Publishing Co., 1954.

Kidner, Derek. *Genesis: An Introduction and Commentary*. Downers Grove, IL: InterVarsity Press, 1967.

Lenski, R.C.H. *1 Corinthians*. Minneapolis, MN: Augsburg Publishing House, 1961.

_____. *First Peter*. Minneapolis, MN: Augsburg Publishing House, 1961.

_____. *Hebrews*. Minneapolis, MN: Augsburg Publishing House, 1961.

_____. *The Interpretation of St. John's Gospel*. Minneapolis, MN: Augsburg Publishing House, 1961.

Leupold, H.C. *Exposition of Genesis*. Vol. 1. Grand Rapids: Baker Book House, 1968.

Lightfoot, J.B. *St. Paul's Epistles to the Colossians and to Philemon*. Grand Rapids: Zondervan Publishing House, 1979.

MacArthur, John. *Hebrews*. Chicago: Moody Press, 1983.

_____. *The Superiority of Christ*. Chicago: Moody Press, 1986.

Morris, Leon. *The First Epistle of Paul to the Corinthians*, Tyndale New Testament Commentaries. Grand Rapids: Wm. B. Eerdmans Publishing Co., 1976.

_____. *The Gospel According to John*. Grand Rapids: Wm. B. Eerdmans Publishing Co., 1971.

_____. *The Gospel According to St. Luke*. Grand Rapids: Wm. B. Eerdmans Publishing Co., 1983.

Moule, H. C. G. *Studies in Colossians & Philemon*. Grand Rapids: Kregel Publications, 1977.

Newell, William R. *Hebrews: Verse By Verse*. Chicago: Moody Press, 1947.

Pink, Arthur W. *Exposition of the Gospel of John*. Swengel, PA: Bible Truth Depot, 1945.

Robertson, A.T. *Word Pictures*. Nashville: Broadman Press, 1930.

Shedd, William G.T. *Romans*. New York: Scribner, 1879.

Toussaint, Stanley D. *Behold the King: A Study of Matthew*. Portland, OR: Multnomah Press, 1980.

Vincent, Marvin R. *Word Studies in the New Testament*. Grand Rapids: Wm. B. Eerdmans Publishing Co., 1975.

Walvoord, John F. *Daniel: The Key to Prophetic Revelation*. Chicago: Moody Press, 1981.

——————. *Revelation*. Chicago: Moody Press, 1980.

——————. *The Revelation of Jesus Christ*. Chicago: Moody Press, 1980.

Westcott, Brooke Foss. *The Epistle to the Hebrews*. Grand Rapids: Wm. B. Eerdmans Publishing Co., 1974.

Wuest, Kenneth S. *Wuest's Word Studies*. Grand Rapids: Wm. B. Eerdmans Publishing Co., 1953.

Wycliffe Bible Commentary. Eds. Charles F. Pfeiffer and Everett F. Harrison. Chicago: Moody Press, 1974.

5. Reference Works

Archer, Gleason. *Encyclopedia of Bible Difficulties*. Grand Rapids: Zondervan Publishing House, 1982.

Arndt, William and Gingrich, Wilbur. *A Greek-English Lexicon of the New Testament and Other Early Christian Literature*. Chicago: The University of Chicago Press, 1957.

Brown, Francis; Driver, S.R.; and Briggs, Charles A. *A Hebrew and English Lexicon of the Old Testament*. Oxford: Clarendon Press, 1980.

Draper's Book of Quotations for the Christian World. Grand Rapids: Baker Book House, 1992.

Geisler, Norman and Howe, Thomas. *When Critics Ask*. Wheaton, IL: Victor Books, 1992.

New Bible Dictionary. Ed. J.D. Douglas. Wheaton, IL: Tyndale House Publishers, 1982.

New International Dictionary of New Testament Theology. Ed. Colin Brown. Grand Rapids: Zondervan Publishing House, 1979.

New Treasury of Scripture Knowledge. Ed. Jerome H. Smith. Nashville: Thomas Nelson Publishers, 1992.

Thayer, J.H. *A Greek-English Lexicon of the New Testament*. Grand Rapids: Zondervan Publishing House, 1963.

Theological Wordbook of the Old Testament. Ed. R. Laird Harris, vol. 2. Chicago: Moody Press, 1981.

Vine's Expository Dictionary of Biblical Words. Eds. W.E. Vine, Merrill F. Unger, and William White. Nashville: Thomas Nelson Publishers, 1985.

Zodhiates, Spiros. *The Complete Word Study Dictionary*. Chattanooga, TN: AMG Publishers, 1992.

Zondervan Pictorial Encyclopedia of the Bible. Ed. Merrill C. Tenney. Grand Rapids: Zondervan Publishing House, 1978.

Subject Index

435

436

Scripture Index

Other Books by
Ron Rhodes

Reasoning from the Scriptures with the Mormons

Their arguments are convincing, their teachings seem indisputable, and they stand on what they believe is firm. Cult experts Ron Rhodes and Marian Bodine help you understand the main points of Mormonism and discover where it falls short of God's truth. Learn to effectively communicate to the Mormons that their gospel does not match up with the truth of the Bible.

Reasoning from the Scriptures with the Masons

Many people are unaware of the far-reaching impact the Masonic Lodge has today. Ron Rhodes provides accurate information on the structure and beliefs of Masonry, then carefully contrasts its practices with Scripture.

Angels Among Us

Angels are very much involved in our lives today—of that we can be certain. But when it comes to angels, how can we tell what is real and what isn't? How can we separate truth from fiction? *Angels Among Us* provides solid, biblically based answers to these pressing questions by taking us on a fascinating—and highly inspirational—tour of God's Word. Discover who angels are, what they are like, what they do...and most exciting of all, the ministry they have in your life right now.

Miracles Around Us

A fascination with miracles and the supernatural permeates our society today. In this enlightening book, Ron Rhodes lays a biblical foundation for miracles, exploring the wonders performed by Old Testament prophets, Jesus, and the disciples. Stripping away the myth and mysticism from many modern teachings about miracles, Ron reveals what God's Word says about the purpose of true miracles as well as satanic signs and wonders.

Dear Reader:

We would appreciate hearing from you regarding this Harvest House nonfiction book. It will enable us to continue to give you the best in Christian publishing.

1. What most influenced you to purchase *Reasoning from the Scriptures with the Jehovah's Witnesses*?
   - ☐ Author
   - ☐ Subject matter
   - ☐ Backcover copy
   - ☐ Recommendations
   - ☐ Cover/Title
   - ☐ _____

2. Where did you purchase this book?
   - ☐ Christian bookstore
   - ☐ General bookstore
   - ☐ Department store
   - ☐ Grocery store
   - ☐ Other

3. Your overall rating of this book:
   - ☐ Excellent   ☐ Very good   ☐ Good   ☐ Fair   ☐ Poor

4. How likely would you be to purchase other books by this author?
   - ☐ Very likely
   - ☐ Somewhat likely
   - ☐ Not very likely
   - ☐ Not at all

5. What types of books most interest you?
   (check all that apply)
   - ☐ Women's Books
   - ☐ Marriage Books
   - ☐ Current Issues
   - ☐ Christian Living
   - ☐ Bible Studies
   - ☐ Fiction
   - ☐ Biographies
   - ☐ Children's Books
   - ☐ Youth Books
   - ☐ Other _____

6. Please check the box next to your age group.
   - ☐ Under 18
   - ☐ 18-24
   - ☐ 25-34
   - ☐ 35-44
   - ☐ 45-54
   - ☐ 55 and over

Mail to: Editorial Director
Harvest House Publishers
1075 Arrowsmith
Eugene, OR 97402

Name _____

Address _____

City _____ State _____ Zip _____

**Thank you for helping us to help you
in future publications!**